NEW YORK

The Virago Woman's Travel Guides

Series Editor: Ros Belford

New York
Paris
Rome

forthcoming:

Amsterdam
Barcelona
London
San Francisco

VIRAGO WOMAN'S GUIDE TO

NEW YORK

JOSIE BARNARD

Published by VIRAGO PRESS Limited March 1993
20–23 Mandela Street, Camden Town, London NW1 0HQ

Printed in Great Britain by Cox & Wyman Ltd, Reading, Berkshire

CONTENTS

ACKNOWLEDGEMENTS

This book is dedicated to John Barnard, Hermione Lee, Stephen Masterson, and Clio Barnard.

Thanks to Jeanine Moss at the New York Convention and Visitors Bureau, Ken White at British Airways, Debra Aspin at Virgin Atlantic, Betsy Boyd at the I Love New York offices of the New York State Division of Tourism, Robin Day at Eagle Creek, and John Bennett at Osprey.

Thanks for hospitality to Liz Wood and Catharine Stimpson, Diane Lewis, Eleanor Goldsmith and John; thanks for information and practical assistance to Victoria Bridges, Alexis and Amy Beth Danzig, Ruth Grimberg, Jane and Kenneth MacDonald, Rebecca Mead and Susan Schulman. Thanks for everything to Fenton Bailey, Maria and Randy, Jewelle Gomez, Tod Lippy and Pamela, Sandy Markman, Jan and Richard Marshall, Mark Marvel, Ruby Rich, Lincoln Rose, Tracy Quan, Jocelyn Taylor and Janice Zwingli; also to Rachel Brownstein, Shelley Clarke, Sam Clayton, Ellen Gold, Zena Parkins, Merri Pearsall, Jon Porter, Lola Preiss, Gwen Roginsky, Bernie Stone, Jean Strouse and Mike and Luna Wind; and in England to Pascal Cariss, Lindsay Cooper, Julie Gallagher, Sand Helsel, Kate Hibbert, Gareth Jones, Moira Sweeney, Eileen Taylor and Val Wilmer.

Disclaimer

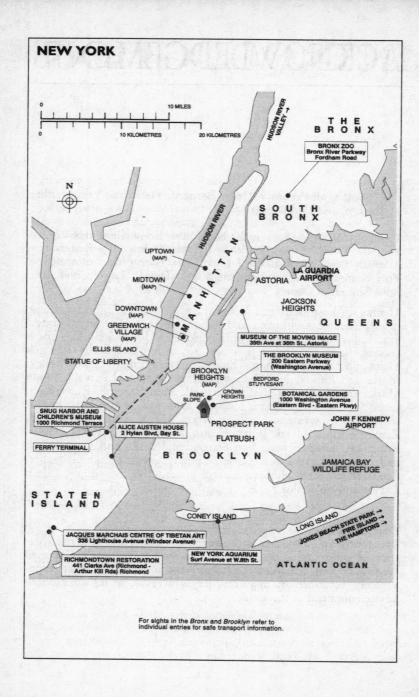

NEW YORK

0   10 MILES

0   10 KILOMETRES   20 KILOMETRES

N

THE BRONX

HUDSON RIVER VALLEY

BRONX ZOO
Bronx River Parkway
Fordham Road

SOUTH BRONX

HUDSON RIVER

MANHATTAN

UPTOWN
(MAP)

MIDTOWN
(MAP)

DOWNTOWN
(MAP)

GREENWICH
VILLAGE
(MAP)

ELLIS ISLAND

STATUE OF LIBERTY

LA GUARDIA
AIRPORT

ASTORIA

JACKSON
HEIGHTS

QUEENS

MUSEUM OF THE MOVING IMAGE
35th Ave at 36th St., Astoria

THE BROOKLYN MUSEUM
200 Eastern Parkway
(Washington Avenue)

BROOKLYN
HEIGHTS
(MAP)

BEDFORD
STUYVESANT

PARK
SLOPE

CROWN
HEIGHTS

BOTANICAL GARDENS
1000 Washington Avenue
(Eastern Blvd - Eastern Pkwy)

PROSPECT PARK

FLATBUSH

**JOHN F KENNEDY
AIRPORT**

**SNUG HARBOR AND
CHILDREN'S MUSEUM**
1000 Richmond Terrace

ALICE AUSTEN HOUSE
2 Hylan Blvd, Bay St.

FERRY TERMINAL

BROOKLYN

**JAMAICA BAY
WILDLIFE REFUGE**

**STATEN
ISLAND**

CONEY ISLAND

LONG ISLAND

JONES BEACH STATE PARK →
FIRE ISLAND →
THE HAMPTONS →

JACQUES MARCHAIS CENTRE OF TIBETAN ART
338 Lighthouse Avenue (Windsor Avenue)

RICHMONDTOWN RESTORATION
441 Clarke Ave (Richmond -
Arthur Kill Rds) Richmond

NEW YORK AQUARIUM
Surf Avenue at W.8th St.

ATLANTIC OCEAN

For sights in the *Bronx* and *Brooklyn* refer to
individual entries for safe transport information.

INTRODUCTION

New York wants **YOU!**, which is a big change for the city that's prided itself on scorning visitors. You've got the 1980s Depression to thank. Prime Manhattan office space emptied, so did the City's coffers, and someone at Gracie Mansion, the mayor's office, clicked: hey, tourist trade is valuable *income* – it must be courted! The mayor gave the tourist bureau a budget to hire an international PR firm; he ordered clean-ups in notoriously unsafe areas such as neon-billboarded Times Square; and he launched a 'Safe Streets Safe City' programme which has so far involved increasing the number of cops on the beat by 290% in less than 12 months and trumpeting from the skyscraper tops reports of *decreases* in crime. For example, from 1990 to 1991 instances of subway felonies, aggravated assault and rape all fell by between 3 and 10%. In a list of America's 52 most crime-ridden cities, New York ranks only 30th, way below Boston and Washington.

Restaurateurs, cabbies, hoteliers and club promoters have all felt the pinch and will at least tone down the fabled New York rudeness (if they don't, just be rude back – it's the quickest way to get what you want, and won't offend because it's construed only as directness). There's even talk of an economy upturn, and in a sense the economic facts of the matter are irrelevant, because New Yorkers are bored with the quiet life that followed the heady cocaine–champagne-filled eighties and they're determined to get good times rolling again. Clubs host special theme nights, restaurants do *prix fixe* bargains, and bars sell 'cognitive enhancement' Think Smart vitamin cocktails to keep New Yorkers grooving till dawn.

But with these accommodating changes, there are negatives. The 1980s Depression aggravated yet further New York's poverty, which draws Third World comparisons. Health care is unaffordable and state benefit is unavailable for so many that you'll become inured to repeated images of homeless people huddled in cardboard boxes and countless beggars – some singing for dimes, others speeding down subway carriages on makeshift skateboards because they have no legs.

Meanwhile, as ever, the rich are getting richer. New York is a city of extremes, and you can judge your area by the garbage cans, which are sunk tastefully out of sight under pavements near plush

Upper East Side apartments, at the end of functional conveyor belts in Midtown's business district, and dented and chained together in the Lower East Side, the red-brick tenement area that has been first stop for new immigrants throughout history. New York will always be a melting-pot of hopefuls seeking fame, fortune or a better life. The Hispanic community is vast now (many ads on the subway trains are only in Spanish). Within a decade Koreans who came seeking political freedom and better education for their children have set up enough grocers (at least 2,400) for the stores to earn a generic term, 'Koreans'. According to the city's Taxi and Limousine Commission, the most recent big influx comes from the Indian Subcontinent (43% of new cab drivers, the traditional first job for immigrants, are from India, Pakistan or Bangladesh). And there's a steady flow of beautiful college graduates serving drinks in trendy bars to survive while they brown-nose at model agencies and recording studios.

New York was dubbed the 'Big Apple' by jazz musicians but, less romantically, the 'Big Onion' by hobos in the 1930s because, they said, it thrived on dirt and made your eyes water if you got too close. It's associated with violence and crack shoot-outs, with Woody Allen films and Ivana Trump divorce dramas. For various reasons, including the activity of PONY and the City Department of Lesbian and Gay Affairs, you're likely to hear a surprising amount about sex (see p.25). You may stumble across an unusual community church, a peaceful atrium or not once see daylight through a whirl of bars and night life. But one thing is certain: shake off preconceptions, open yourself to new possibilites and you'll have a trip that might be mad, bad or wonderful, possibly all three, but you won't forget New York.

PRACTICALITIES

WHEN TO GO

Spring and autumn are the best times to visit New York. From late September to early November skies are generally bright, the yellow and red fall colours are spectacular and temperatures are in the comfortable 50s and 60s Fahrenheit. **Summer** is so hot and sticky that New Yorkers leave if they can during July and August, when temperatures hit the 90s. **Winter** is bright with only scattered snowfalls but very cold (often well below freezing in January and February). Take a raincoat for **spring**, which is balmy with frequent but brief showers, and any time of year pack **layers of clothing**. In summer overefficient air-conditioning makes buildings ice-cold; in winter the heating is on full blast.

It's very important if you're travelling alone that you can be independent and in control when you are carrying luggage, since single women struggling with awkward suitcases are easy prey. Invest in one of the following: strap-on wheels; a suitcase with built-in wheels; or – best of all – a bag that transforms from rucksack to shoulder bag to hand luggage to suit the situation. Karrimor, Lowe and Eagle Creek are three of the best Travel Pack manufacturers, and of these American Eagle Creek makes the smartest (expect to pay around £100).

New York has business seasons rather than tourist seasons. In autumn and spring particularly, the city hosts national conventions, and hotels can be fully booked months in advance. The best times for cheap packages are weekends, July and August and just after Christmas.

Getting there

There's an **air war** going on, which is good news for travellers in general, because prices stay down, and for women in particular,

FESTIVALS

Some of New York's liveliest festivals are the sporadic **neighbourhood block fairs**, when children can bob for apples, laugh at clowns and munch home-made fudge cakes. You'll find them advertised in the *Village Voice* and local shops. It's always worth checking for new fairs and festivals with the New York Convention and Visitors Bureau (see p.11), where you can also confirm this year's dates for these events:

January For a spectacle of firecrackers and dancing dragons go to the **Chinese New Year** in Chinatown around Mott Street, first full moon after 19 January, but be warned – it gets busy, so watch your purse.

March The **St Patrick's Day Parade** down Fifth Avenue is a robust, boozy, sentimental occasion for New York's Irish community, and for all-round family entertainment you can't beat the **Ringling Bros and Barnum and Bailey Circus** at Madison Square Gardens.

April On Easter Sunday Fifth Avenue around St Patrick's Cathedral fills with families posing for home videos in amazingly elaborate hand-crafted Easter costumes for the **Easter Parade**.

May This month it's **Mother's Day**, which is on the Sunday before the 15th of May in the States, and a very big deal – even exclusive executive restaurants open their doors to children with Mother's Day special offers. Eating is a national hobby, so for many the **Ninth Avenue International Food Festival** between 37th and 57th Streets is the eat-yourself-silly highlight of the year. To see the East Village at its most resplendent, with stunning Ukrainian costumes and folk-dancing, go to the **Ukrainian Festival** on East 7th Street between Second and Third Avenues. For an introduction to Lower East Side revelry and community spirit, don't miss the **Loisada Street Fair**, which is traditionally on the last weekend in May.

June Look out for the *free* **Metropolitan Opera** concerts in parks throughout the City, and for jazz go to the `Summerpier' concerts at South Street Seaport on Friday and Saturday nights. People fly from all over the world for **Gay Pride March**, which goes south from Columbus Circle to Greenwich Village on the last Sunday in June. On the second Tuesday in June from 6 to 9 p.m., as part of the Museum Festival, every art gallery on Museum Mile is free, and there's performance art on every block.

July You can't escape the fireworks and popping corks on July the 4th **Independence Day Celebrations** (Macy's fireworks are best viewed from the East River or high rooftops). You're spoilt for cultural choice: check out **Shakespeare in the Park** at Central Park's Delacorte Theatre and **Mostly Mozart Festival** concerts at Avery Fisher Hall.

September The ten-day **Feast of San Gennaro**, the patron Saint of Naples, shows shrinking Little Italy at its vibrant best, when Mulberry Street bursts with street stalls and, on the last night, a grand procession. Catch the best and the worst new films at the **New York Film Festival** at Lincoln Center's Alice Tully Hall.

October After St Patrick's Day, the biggest drunken binge occasion is the **Columbus Day Parade** in the middle of the month down Fifth Avenue. The highlight of the **Halloween** chase on 31 October is its Washington Square finale.

November The **Big Apple Circus** in a small tent at Lincoln Center is not cheap, but it's a must for women with children. Sports fans – go to the **Virginia Slims Women's Tennis Championships** at Madison Square Gardens. Joggers and sadomasochists alike will enjoy the **New York City Marathon** – the edges of the route, from Verrazano-Narrows Bridge to Central Park/67th Street, are lined with mechanical foot-massagers and scarlet, dripping cardiac cases. **Macy's Thanksgiving**

Day Parade down Broadway on the last Thursday of the month rates top favourite with thousands of New Yorkers . . . if you can stand the crowds and rumbling floats, you'll love it too. 'The Magnificent Christmas Spectacular' featuring the Rockettes at Radio City Hall is one of those tourist traps that are worth falling into, especially for women with children. .

December This month 5th Avenue stores unveil extravagant **window displays** (Barney's especially are famous), the **Rockefeller Center Christmas tree** is lit, and on **New Year's Eve** revellers gather at Times Square.

because their needs come to the fore in the battle to win and keep custom. Two main opponents in the fray are **Virgin Atlantic** and **British Airways**. Virgin was recently awarded 'Best Business Class' by the *Business Traveller Magazine*. Virgin boasts 15% more legroom in Upper Class than other airlines, and it shows businesswomen on the ads while British Airways has a boys'-club reputation which it's desperate to shake off. Consequently, on BA Club Class you now get Body Shop handcream in your travel pouch, and almost any request will be honoured, from asking the receptionist at the airport club lounge to post your mail to having BA staff carry your luggage through Customs. For **mothers**, Virgin Economy beats BA, as staff are specially briefed to be child-friendly and the children get a free Fun Pack featuring games, puzzles, colouring books and stories. American Airlines is close behind, with a FlightFacts sheet featuring advice on travelling with children and, once on board, complimentary Infant Amenity Kits containing a feeding spoon, bib, storybook, two nappies, changing sheets and scented disposable bags. All three airlines' business classes offer the usual complimentary champagne, so you might base your final decision on the food – will it be American Airlines for its best Business Class food award, or the Gleneagles Hotel menu on British Airways Club Class, or the Cranks vegetarian selection on all Virgin tickets? Unless you already have a favourite airline, you should phone around to find the best current offers – or get a local independent travel agent to do the legwork for you.

For cheap flight offers, look at the ads in the travel sections of the Sunday papers, in London's *Evening Standard* and in *Time Out* magazine.

Flying time to New York is seven or eight hours going and only six or seven back, thanks to prevailing winds. **Outward** journeys tend to leave first thing to arrive in New York in the evening, and most **return** journeys are overnight, which makes for uncomfortable sleeping but helps to overcome jet lag – if you take a day flight home, your body clock stays in New York time much longer. Flights to New York are plentiful and frequent, but if you do have trouble getting one and you've been asking for JFK airport, try asking for Newark airport, which is just as convenient for Manhattan but less used. Most flights leave from Gatwick, but **British Airways serves Glasgow and Manchester** and **Aer Lingus serves Dublin.**

Fares vary depending on the season and time of week you're travelling, but the best airline for cheap offers is Virgin, whose medley of offers includes Late Savers and Economy in addition to the usual Apex. **Standard** fares are pretty much the same on all airlines: midweek low season (autumn) they cost from £400 to £500; in the high season (Christmas and Easter) they rise to over £600. Pay £30–£50 more at weekends and around £100 less if you get an **Apex** ticket, which must be booked 21 days in advance. Standbys are few and far between, but Virgin **Late Savers** can go down to £279.

AIRLINES AND AGENCIES
Airlines
American Airlines, 23–59 Staines Road, Trinity Square, Hounslow, Middlesex TW3 3HE, tel. 081 572 5555;
British Airways, 421 Oxford Street, London W1, tel. 081 897 4000;
North West Airlines, 8–9 Berkeley Street, London W1, tel. 0345 747800;
United Airlines, 193 Piccadilly, London W1, tel. 0800 888555;
Virgin Atlantic, Sussex House, High Street, Crawley, West Sussex RH10 1BZ, tel. 0293 38222.

Low-Cost and Independent Flight Agents
Campus Travel, main branch of national network is 52 Grosvenor Gardens, London SW1, tel. 071 730 8111;
STA Travel, 117 Euston Road, London NW1 2SX, tel. 071 937 9971, also 25 Queens Road, Bristol BS8 1QE, tel. 0272 294399; 75 Deansgate, Manchester M3, tel. 061 834 0668;
Supersonic, 13 Villiers Street, London WC2 6ND, tel. 071 839 6856.

Specialist US Flight Agents
Globespan, PO Box 149, Glasgow G2 3EJ, tel. 041 332 6600 or 0293 541541;
Jetsave, Sussex House, London Road, East Grinstead, West Sussex RH19 1LD, tel. 0342 3131911;
North American Travel Club, 38 Hurstpierpoint, West Sussex BN6 9RG, tel. 0273 8350595.

Courier Firms
Inflight Polo Express, 208 Epsom Square, London Heathrow Airport, Hounslow, Middlesex, TW6 2BL, tel. 081 759 5383;
TNT Skypack, 346 Fulham Road, London SW10 9UH, tel. 071 351 0300.

Prices for **children** are generally 60–75% of the full fare if they're between two and twelve years old, and 10% of the full fare if the child is under two. Most airlines offer cardboard beds, but it's better to get to the airport early and request a seat below the movie screen, where there is space to construct a makeshift bed with blankets; or, when you're checking in, ask if they can leave the seat next to you free.

Business fares are generally around £1,000, the assumption being that your company pays.

For **unofficially discounted tickets** and **special offers**, a travel agent will be able to give you an up-to-date overview. If you're a student, go to a travel agent specialising in low-cost flights and you might get a return for £200. The specialist agents can sniff out charter flights cut to £300–£400.

If none of these is cheap enough for you, try a **courier flight**, which will probably require you to carry a package, limit you to one- or two-week stays and allow hand luggage only, but might get you a Club Class for £150–£200.

Last, consider **package deals** if you just want a weekend in New York. You should be able to get three nights in a mid-range midtown hotel and the flight for around £390. The huge number of operators offering package deals to New York include Osprey, Broughton Market, Edinburgh EH3 6NU; **Poundstretcher**, Atlantic House, Hazelwick Avenue, Three Bridges, Crawley, West Sussex RH10 1NP; **Thomson**, Greater London House, Hampstead Road, London NW1 7SD; and **Virgin Holidays**, Sussex House, High Street, Crawley, West Sussex RH10 1BZ (tel. 0293 775511).

Regulations

To get into the States for 90 days or less you will need a full passport and a non-refundable return plane ticket. If these conditions are satisfied, British citizens do not need a visa but will be handed a pink immigration form on the plane which must be completed and given to one of the Immigration Control officers on arrival. Be prepared to prove that you have enough money (at least $150 to spend per week) and a place to stay (if not a hotel reservation, then the address of a friend).

Regulations do change, so it is always worth phoning the US Embassy to double-check.

The **duty-free** allowance on the way in (if you are over twenty-one) is 200 cigarettes or 50 cigars plus 1 US quart of alcohol. Coming back to Britain, you are allowed the same amount of nicotine with two litres of table wine plus one litre of spirits or two more litres of wine.

If you want to stay longer than originally planned, you should go to the **US Immigration and Naturalization Service** at 26 Federal Plaza, New York (tel. 206 6500) and apply for an Issuance or Extension of Permit to Re-Enter the USA. Your interviewer will

PRACTICALITIES

want to know why you didn't anticipate a longer visit in the first place. You could say that your money hasn't run out, or that you have a friend or (preferably) a close relative coming to visit you. Remember – you must convince them that you are not trying to stay because you want to work illegally. Take along a respectable US citizen for added credibility.

Work permits should be obtained before you leave for the States from a US Embassy or consulate. The type you get will depend on why you want to go and how long you intend to stay. Permits are easiest to get if you have relatives there already (parents/children over twenty-one), or if you have a letter confirming employment from a US company. Promises of work from individuals are valid but less convincing. The authorities look especially kindly on posts involving, for example, academic institutions and computers. Otherwise, work permits are extremely difficult to get. It has – literally – become a lottery (tickets are sold annually and the lucky winners are interviewed on TV). It used to be possible simply to invent a social security number and get work illegally at bars and restaurants. The authorities have clamped down. Employers face fines of up to $10,000. They now insist on seeing work permits. The building trade still hires casual labour – for women, painting and decorating work is probably the best option. If you do stay on, medical care should be a prime consideration because it is phenomenally expensive. The law requires all *bona fide* employers to take out health insurance for their employees, but check the small print of your contract. If you are working illegally you should pay out for your own insurance scheme. It will be cheaper in the long run.

An E111 (get a form from the post office) entitles you only to basic medical care. It does not cover contraception. Basic consultancy fees are $50–$75. You'd be well advised to get a fully comprehensive insurance policy (which will include loss/theft of luggage). These don't, unfortunately, come cheap. Thomas Cook's is the cheapest at £43.80 for 17 days. Buy them from a travel agent or an insurance broker.

Money

US currency is dollars: note denominations are $1, $5, $10, $20, $50, and $100. $1 is made up of 100 cent coins (1c), also known as pennies. 5c is a nickel, 10c is a dime, and 25c is a quarter. All these coins and bills feature the heads of significant historical male figures (Washington, Lincoln, Grant, Franklin), but you might occasionally be given in your change a half-dollar coin with the head of nineteenth century feminist Susan B. Anthony on it.

If you can, get hold of some quarters and dollar bills before you go. You'll need quarters in the airport for the luggage trolleys and dollar bills for tipping. While in New York keep at least a dollar's worth of quarters for phones, cigarette machines, etc. Because all the bills are the same size and colour, it's also worth keeping your big ones separate from your little ones or you might find you've handed over $20 for a $4 cab ride and told the driver to keep the change.

Traveller's cheques ('travelers checks' in the States) are a good way to take your money, but not if they are Thomas Cook and/or in English pounds: both are looked upon with suspicion in most New York banks. Ideally, buy **American Express** traveller's cheques and buy them in **dollars**. American Express traveller's cheques are available in Britain from the TSB, Lloyds, the Royal Bank of Scotland and American Express offices at a cost of 1% of the amount ordered. The exchange rate will probably be around 1.6 or 1.8 dollars to the pound and to the Australian dollar. Once in New York, *always* check the commission rates before you change money – they can be anything from disadvantageous to disastrous, but are not always bad in hotels.

Known-brand traveller's cheques in dollars can also be used in shops and changed for cash at most 24-hour Korean green-grocers/delis.

Life is hard without a credit card. If you don't have a Visa, Access, Diners Club or American Express card you should try to get one. They will buy you almost anything anywhere, and they establish your creditworthiness. Hotels and car rental firms will insist on seeing one for security. Visa and Access can also be used to withdraw cash over the counter at banks that feature stickers bearing the relevant logo. They can be used in cash dispensers – see below for addresses or look for your logo by the dispenser – but you risk having your card eaten (a Visa employee said off the record that she wouldn't trust her card in an American cash dispenser). Credit cards have two other advantages: they sidestep any commission; you don't have to pay till you get home.

Try to make sure you have enough US currency to survive a couple of days when you arrive in New York, because it can be hard to find a place to change money. It is *not* the norm for banks to change money/traveller's cheques. Most branches of Citibank and Chemical Bank will. All branches of Chemical Bank will exchange English pounds for dollars. All major hotels will change cheques. Hotels are less likely than banks to be sniffy if you haven't got American Express, and their hours are longer – often 24 hours. All airports have exchange offices.

Banking hours are usually Mon–Fri 9 a.m.–3/3.30 p.m.

EXCHANGE OFFICES

All the following open outside banking hours:

American Express Travel Service (no commission if you're changing Am Ex traveller's cheques in dollars)
1 World Trade Center (in lobby of Building One near airline counters), 8 a.m.–5.45 p.m. 7 days a week, tel. 775 0370.
770 Broadway (on 9th St near 4th Ave), 9 a.m–5 p.m Mon–Fri, tel. 598 5000.
Macy's Herald Square, Mon and Thurs 9.45 a.m.–7.45 p.m., Tues, Wed and Fri 9.45 a.m.–6.15 p.m., tel. 695 8075.
New York Hilton, 1335 6th Avenue, 8 a.m.–7 p.m. 7 days a week, tel. 664 7798.
150 East 42nd Street, Mon–Fri 8.30 a.m.–5.30 p.m., tel. 687 3700.
374 Park Avenue (at 53rd St), Mon–Fri 9 a.m.–5 p.m., tel. 421 8240, $1.00 per transaction.
Bloomingdales (at 59th St and Lexington Ave), Mon–Sat 10 a.m.–6 p.m., tel. 705 3171.
822 Lexington Avenue (at 63rd St), Mon–Fri 10 a.m.–6 p.m., Sat 10 a.m.–4 p.m., tel. 758 6510.

Deak International
1 Herald Center (at 34th St and 6th Ave), Mon–Fri 9.30 a.m.–4.30 p.m., tel. 736 9790, $3.50 fee per transaction up to $350 then 1% (applies to all locations).
41 East 42nd Street, Mon–Fri 9 a.m.–5 p.m., Sat 10 a.m.–3 p.m.
630 5th Avenue (bet. 50th and 51st Sts), Mon–Fri 9 a.m.–5 p.m., Sat 10 a.m.–3 p.m.

Chequepoint USA
551 Madison Avenue (at 55th St), Mon–Fri 8 a.m.–6 p.m., Sat and Sun 10 a.m.–6 p.m., tel. 980 6443, 4c per dollar fee per transaction.

Freeport Currencies
132 West 45th Street and 49 West 57th Street, Mon–Fri 9 a.m.–6 p.m., Sat 10 a.m.–3 p.m., tel. 221 2000, $2 fee per transaction.

Harold Reuter and Co, Inc.
Pan Am Building, 200 Park Avenue, Room 332, Mon–Fri 8 a.m.–5 p.m., tel. 661 0826, no fees.

AUTOMATIC CASH DISPENSERS
Locations of dispensers that will accept Mastercard and Visa 24 hours include:
Grand Central Terminal on 42nd Street at Park Avenue;
100 World Trade Center;
11 West 51st Street at Rockefeller Center;
14th Street and 6th Avenue;
and *59 West 86th St* at Columbus Ave near Natural History Museum.

American Express branches listed above have Am Ex cash dispensers. Also: *JFK airport* near the American Ticketing and American Airlines desk, terminal B.]

Cost of Living

Note that accommodation in New York is very expensive – stay with friends and you'll reduce your costs substantially.

A BUDGET DAY = $50

Night in a hostel, $20 or in a cheap hotel, $35.
Bagel/coffee breakfast under $1; $4 diner sandwich for lunch.
Dinner in a cheap restaurant, $10.
A couple of drinks in a basic bar, $3.

AN AVERAGE DAY = $150

Room with bath, $90.
Breakfast in a café, $5.
Day's public transport (3 subway/bus journeys and one cab), $12.
Lunch in a café, $10.
Dinner in a mid-priced restaurant, $25.
Drinks in a pleasant café or bar, $15.

AN EXPENSIVE DAY = $450

Room in a 4* hotel, $250.
Breakfast in a hotel or an upmarket café, $10.
Day's public transport (2 subway/bus journeys, 2 cabs), $20.
Dinner in an upmarket restaurant, $100–$200 and more.
Drinks in a classy café or bar, $30.

ENTERTAINMENT

Art galleries/museums average $6.
Clubs start at $5 but average $10.
Entertainment, including theatre and concerts, starts at $5 for alternative events and can go up to over $100 for exclusive Broadway and opera tickets.

Information

You can get free maps of New York, booklets and a glossy magazine, *The Big Apple Guide,* from the United States Travel and Tourist Information in the UK at 2 Cinammon Row, Plantation Wharf, York Place, London SW11 3TW, tel. 071 978 5233.

Once you're in New York, go to the **New York Convention and Visitors Bureau,** which is the Moorish white block at 2 Columbus Circle (Mon–Fri 9 a.m.–6 p.m., Sat and Sun 10 a.m.–6 p.m., tel. 397 8222). They have basic maps of the city as well as bus and subway maps and leaflets. Alternatively, visit the **I Love New York** offices, New York State Department of Economic Development (Tourist Division), 51st floor, 1515 Broadway (tel. 827 6250); they will provide you with some of the same information plus information on the rest of New York State.

The **Grand Central Station** information booth (42nd St at Park Ave) also has basic maps of the city.

It's crucial to get a good map – preferably before you arrive in New York, or at the beginning of your stay. In London go to **Stanfords** (12–14 Long acre, London WC2) or **Daunts** (83 Marylebone High Street, London W1) travel bookshops. The **H.M. Gousha** comprehensive street map of New York City and the five boroughs for £2.50 is rather big for use on the streets (study it in your hotel *before* you set off for your destination) but it gives you all the detail and information you'll need. If you can afford it, supplement your comprehensive map once you're in New York with a pocket-sized laminated map that is easier to use inconspicuously on the street. In some areas it's wise not to look like a tourist.

Go to any big bookshop or the **Complete Traveller** bookshop (199 Madison Ave) for Gousha and **Rand McNally** comprehensive maps of the city and the five boroughs for $1.95. Innumerable fancy laminated maps that are easy to use inconspicuously on the street include the **Gousha 'Fastmap'** ($4.95). If you want a gift or souvenir map, get the laminated 3-D-style **Unique Media** map for $16.61 to stick on your wall.

Ask for **bus/subway maps** at any subway station because trains and buses are often rerouted, and this ensures that you will have the most up-to-date map.

The Press

For news coverage read *The New York Times* (40c), a quality national, every day. Give it a long breakfast . . . the Sunday edition is huge. Buy *The New York Times* in London before you go at one of the newsagents on Old Compton Street or at the Leicester Square Tower Records shop.

For City gossip and incredible tabloid headlines read the *Daily News* (40c) and *New York Post* (40c). The *Wall Street Journal* (75c) is a national financial paper which is also good on general news and the arts. *USA Today* (50c) is a dull colour spread that doesn't get much beyond news round-ups.

For its features and arts coverage, everyone buys the weekly *Village Voice* ($1.00 weekly). You have to wade through ads, but once you've mastered it (spend a morning early in your trip poring in a coffee shop) you'll find everything on film, off-Broadway theatre, dance, clubs and music (rock, jazz and classical). You can buy the *Village Voice* before you go in London at one of the newsagents on Old Compton Street or at the Leicester Square Tower Records shop.

The glossy *New Yorker* magazine ($1.75 weekly) has long been perceived as stodgy in content and format and useful only for its arts listings, but it is currently being spruced up.

New York magazine ($1.95 monthly) also has listings but is of more interest for its in-depth special reports – on health care, for example, or where to go for Christmas gifts.

The coolest magazine, particularly for clubs and the trend-scene, is currently *The Paper* ($2.50 monthly).

Founded by the late Andy Warhol, glossy *Interview* magazine ($2.95 monthly) is mainly, as the title suggests, gossipy interviews.

QW ($2 monthly) recently replaced *Outweek* as the city's lesbian and gay magazine (if *QW* is defunct too, ask for its successor). It has good news, features, classifieds and a 'selective' (i.e. nice and

short) arts and events listings. Since many of the best nightclubs are
lesbian or gay, *QW* listings are a good source for anyone. The magazine is widely available (most street newsstands will have it).

Ms. (pronounced mizz, not mzz) magazine ($5.50 bimonthly), originally founded by Gloria Steinem, has been relaunched – without any advertising revenue (hence the cost). The ads, it was felt, exploited women's bodies so were incompatible with editorial policy. It has news and health features and a large books section.

Rome ($5) is a photocopied high-trend underground magazine published by glitterati know-them-all George Wayne. Clubbers adore it but Claudia Schiffer sued him for printing paparazzi shots of her nude, so the future is shaky and since Wayne delivers to newsagents by hand, it's luck of the draw if you get hold of one. You just have to ask around.

Also look in the freestanding newspaper containers on street corners for free weekly newspapers. The *New York Press* and Uptown's *New York Perspectives* both have local news and good entertainments listings. Many neighbourhoods, including Greenwich and the East Village, have their own newspapers, which you can pick up in shops and bars.

Look out in lesbian bars for the free tri-State monthly newspaper *Sappho's Isle*, which includes current health-care and restaurant information and in-depth interviews.

Women's and lesbian information

For lesbian and women's events go early in your trip to **Judith's Room** or **A Different Light**, and to the **Lesbian and Gay Community Services Centre**.

At the Lesbian and Gay Community Services Centre on 208 West 13th Street (bet. 7th and 8th Aves, tel. 620 7310), look at the noticeboard and pick up the bimonthly flyer called 'Centre Happenings'. This lists events (readings, dances, lesbian movie nights) and meetings that take place at the Centre. Nearly one hundred different groups, ranging from the Butch/Femme Society to Moonfire Women's Spirituality Circle and Siren's Motorcycle Club, use the Centre as their downtown base.

Phone the Lesbian Switchboard (Mon–Fri 6 p.m.–10 p.m., based at Community Centre, tel. 741 2610). This is *the* place to get absolutely up-to-the-minute information on everything from clubs and events to accommodation. They'll even give basic counselling, or try and put you on to organisations that can help.

At the women's bookshop Judith's Room (see p.328), as well as books, you'll find 'zines' such as *Fabulous Babes and Hot Rods* and *Pussy Grazer* (edited by Annie Thing and Glenda Orgasm). These are generally photocopied and hand-stapled and priced around $3. They feature poems, comic strips, collages – they are for entertainment rather than information. The bookshop also has a space given over to flyers (including up-to-the-minute club details) and helpful counter staff.

A Different Light bookshop on 548 Hudson Street (tel. 989 4850) has gay and lesbian publications as well as many of the same zines and club and event flyers. Again, strike up conversation with the employees.

You can also pick up current flyers at the lesbian and gay bars (see p.285).

For research and general interest, visit the world's oldest and largest lesbian archive, the Lesbian Herstory Archives, which is in the process of rehousing in the Park Slope neighbourhood of Brooklyn. Write to PO Box 1258, New York, NY 10116, phone 718 768 DYKE or phone the old number, 212 874 7232, which will have a recorded message. Co-founder Deborah Edel, who is also an educational psychologist, says the archives have information on all aspects of lesbian culture and history from past to present, from the printed word to oral history to videos, slides and photos. The emphasis is on inclusivity: any lesbian may donate any three personal items and become part of the Archive's Special Collection.

Communications

Post In general post offices are open Mon–Fri 9 a.m.–6 p.m. and Sat 9 a.m.–1 p.m. Some close earlier on Saturdays. The James A. Farley Central Post Office on Eighth Avenue and 33rd Street is open 24 hours 7 days a week, but be careful at night because it's in a district that can be dodgy. A centrally located post office that usually has small queues is at 446 Madison Avenue between 37th and 38th Streets. Call 212 967 8585 for zip-code information and other post office locations.

To receive something poste restante, have it addressed to the General Post Office, 421 Eighth Avenue, NY 10001. The phrase 'c/o General Delivery' should be used after the name of the addressee. To collect letters you'll need two forms of ID (passport, credit card, driving licence). Mail will be kept for 30 days before being returned to sender.

You can buy stamps from shops, supermarkets and post offices. It's cheaper to send aerograms than letters, but cheaper still is 40 cents for a postcard. Air mail takes around six days to get to Europe. If you post it at a larger post office it seems to get there quicker than if you use a blue mailbox or the chute system in hotels.

The post office has strict, complicated rules on parcels. Read the instructions at the front of the Yellow Pages and buy the post office's regulation packaging. Expect staff to be impatient and brusque if you haven't done exactly as the instructions say.

Telephones The code for England is 011 44 and you should omit the first '0' of the number when dialling. If you're calling international from a pay-phone, go through the operator and it will cost you $5.70. The operator will tell you how much to put in for the first three minutes, then either cut in to ask you for more coins or phone back afterwards to charge the extra. If you don't pay, the person you called will be charged. If you're calling from a hotel, check the charges, as they can be outrageous. A local call, which is free from a domestic phone and 25c in a pay-phone, can cost over $1 in a hotel. International calls could bankrupt you.

Local calls from pay-phones cost at least a quarter with 10c and 5c top-ups. Telephone 411 for Directory Assistance in Manhattan and the Bronx and 718 555 1212 for Brooklyn, Queens and Staten Island. In a 10-figure number the first three digits are the area code: for example 212 for Manhattan. If you are calling from within Manhattan, omit 212. If you are calling Queens, Brooklyn, or Staten Island dial a '1' before the area code. The Bronx recently became 718.

There are a lot of public pay phones, and they generally work.

Media

Television

American television is hypnotic, some say dangerous. Certainly, if you have children in a hotel, be warned: they can easily tune into porn channels, and some of the film and hard-porn channels are pay-per-view – that is, you get a big bill at the end of your stay. All TVs in New York get at least 8 broadcast TV channels, and up to 60 cable channels are available by subscription – hotel TVs usually have all of them, and individuals like to have most. The American way to find out what's on TV is to flick mindlessly from channel to channel. Alternatively, you can buy the weekly *TV Guide* for 89 cents. The *New York Times* has daily listings and a TV pull-out on Sundays.

Broadcast TV There has been a general rise in the numbers of look-don't-touch titillating sex programmes, most notably **Studs** (11.30 p.m. weekdays, Channel 7), in which three babes date two guys and then, through a series of on-air comments such as 'One munch of my maraschino and he went limp', the women decide which man is the better stud. Shows like these are only just surpassed in popularity by Games Shows, including **Jeopardy** (7 p.m. weekdays, Channels 7 and 8), in which the compere shouts an answer and the contestant has to say what the question would have been. There are innumerable chat shows which fall broadly into two categories: late-night ones with lean, mean male hosts like **David**

Letterman (12.30 a.m. weekdays, Channel 4), whose reputations depend on a steady stream of lewd innuendoes; and early-evening confessionals hosted by women-with-social-consciences, most famously **Oprah Winfrey**, who invites Drunk Drivers Who Have Killed to tell their tales on live TV and arranges surprise reunions with The Person Who Took My Virginity. These chat shows are considered by TV producers to be 'for women', as are the many Lycra and techno-music **work-out shows**. The two best news programmes are CBS News (6.30 p.m. weekdays, Channel 2) and ABC News (6.30 p.m. weekdays, Channel 8). You'll find most serious programmes on the **Public Broadcast** Channels, 13, 31 and PBS, which buy in European programmes with familiar hosts including Jonathan Miller, and on Channel 13 you'll find **Sesame Street**, for which Brooklyn-born animation producer Edith Zornow was honoured with a Sesame Street animation retrospective at the Whitney Museum in 1979 and at the Museum of Modern Art in 1989.

The daunting number of different channels all have numbingly frequent **commercial breaks** – there's even one between the end of most programmes and the credits. Some ads are surprisingly frank – for example, for vaginal yeast infection creams; and because health care is mainly private in America, many ads recommend specific health-care expenditures, for example: 'A mammogram can be your breast friend'. Advertising revenue is supplemented by **corporate sponsorship**, so text flashes up on programme credits to inform you that 'this was brought to you by' a bifocals or heartburn tablet company.

Cable TV Cable TV facilitates Public Access TV, which is still the subject of raging debate. A condition of franchise for cable companies in New York City is that they make 'public access' channels available for airing programmes made by members of the public. Supporters of cable TV say public access is about freedom of speech and of choice. Ionnis Mookis, director of the public access programme **Deep Dish TV**, says: 'One of the first things that Reagan tried to do when he came into office was get rid of public access. We see ourselves as part of the need for an alternative voice for the communities.' Critics point to the porn programmes, including **Voyeur Vision**, in which lingerie-clad hostess Lynn acts out telephoned sex requests; and the vintage **Robin Byrd Show**, which is a stripper-and-sex talk show (times vary, but Robin Byrd is on most nights at around 10 p.m. and 1 a.m. on Channel 35). Both shows are funded by the long commercial breaks, which feature lurid ads for phonelines including 'Chicks with Dicks' and 'Geisha to Go'.

The wide variety of single-subject cable channels include several for **sport** (SC is one), several for credit-card **home shopping** (including HBO), **Black Entertainment** (BET), **pop music** (MTV), **news**

(CNN) and **Playboy at Night** (PLA). New York's two main cable companies are Paragon and Manhattan Cable. Both have public access channels but different policies: families tend to prefer Paragon because it won't show hard-core porn; trendies prefer Manhattan Cable because it has the Robin Byrd Show and Voyeur Vision – with-it women arrange drunken hen nights round the public access porn shows. The few women's programmes, including **Women's Issues** (Channel 16) and **Woman of the Week** (Channel 17), are basically talk shows aimed at housewives. Lesbians and gays are served by **Out in the 90s** (Channel 16). The pay-per-view channel **Spectravision** shows several current films and some soft-porn ($7.95 for each screening).

A new cable venture that might horrify mothers but will delight children is **interactive family games shows**. The International Family Entertainment (the FAM channel) will have one up and running by early 1993 using 1-900 interactive telephone technology, which bodes badly for your phone bills.

Radio Most New Yorkers dismiss AM radio stations completely and use only FM for the legendary **Howard Stern** on **WXRK** (92.3 FM for four hours every morning). Stern, says artist Barbara Kruger, 'is vintage blurting asshole . . . And since those of us who tune into his morning radio show are treated to myriad descriptions of his cellulite-ridden buttocks, I'd like to think of his assholism in both the physical and intellectual sense.'

Shows for women and lesbians on **WBAI Radio** (99.5 FM) include: **The Gay Show** and **Outlook**; **This Way Out**; and the serious current affairs **Women's Magazine**.

Tune to **WKCR** (98.9 FM) for an acclaimed jazz station; **WBGO** (88.3 FM) plays a good mixture of jazz, Afropop and gospel; **WNYC** (93.9 FM) is one of the best classical stations; and twiddle with the dial for innumerable local stations which set up and close down fast. Lastly, if you're homesick, tune into **BBC World Service** on the 49 metre short-wave band.

You'll find radio highlights in the *New York Times* and a selective listings sponsored by TDK in the *Village Voice*.

Newspapers There's been a widespread attempt by metropolitan newspapers nationwide to woo back women readers. Papers including the Cleveland *Plain Dealer* and the *Chicago Tribune* have recently started sections with unambiguous names like 'WomenWise' and 'Womannews' because, according to a survey by Simmons Market Research Bureau, 60% of women read a newspaper on a typical day in 1991 compared to 67% in 1981. As well as making up 52% of the population, research shows that women are more likely to make families' buying decisions than men. Yet New York papers aren't keen to set aside pages specifically for women. Why? They fear that by covering traditional 'women's subjects' like food and shopping they will offend career-minded women – of which there are many in New York – and that by presenting topics like childcare and job discrimination as women's subjects they will be seen as unfairly segregating the news. The end result is a plethora of compromise sections, at which the *New York Times* (see p.12) excels: on Wednesdays see the 'Living' section for articles on health and food; Thursdays look in the 'Home' section for domestic decor trends and a heavy child psychology 'Parent and Child' column; and Sunday's 'Style' has fashion, Egos and Ids gossip strips and tiny His and Hers columns alternate weeks . . . 'Hers' is renowned as a facetious monologue that tackles traumas such as how to mend a broken nail.

British and European Publications

It's easy to get hold of British and European newspapers, and they're usually no more than a day old. See p.343 for locations that have a wide selection of stock.

Language

You may have trouble communicating in New York. New-York-speak is fast and blunt. Most New Yorkers are intolerant of Queen's English pronunciation and long-winded sentences. Say 'toona' for 'tuna' and 'wodder' for 'water'. Don't politely ask a telephone receptionist 'I wonder if you could put me through to . . .' – demand to speak to 'X'. Prepare too for misunderstandings arising from usage, not just accent. If New Yorkers are 'pissed', for example, they are angry, not drunk. And if you call someone 'a wanker', New Yorkers take it not as a generic insult but as a precise description of their private activities. You should also be aware, if you aren't already, that Political Correctness is a much hotter topic in the States than it is in England. PC has entered an enormous number of areas of American life, from campus politics to art gallery and museum policies to activism on behalf of the 'differently abled', and because PC affects the daily usage of language, it is also the subject of satire and ridicule. It is often difficult to tell what is jokey and what is serious, so if in doubt, don't laugh. 'Time-challenged' as a PC description of children began as a skit, but many use the phrase seriously now.

New York is a city of immigrants, and English is fast becoming the second language, Spanish the first. Many ads on the subway are in Spanish, and there are Spanish-speaking TV and radio stations. In parts of Chinatown English is never spoken; in Little Odessa a grasp of Russian is helpful; and you could well find your cab driver speaks only Hindi.

A selection of useful phrases, pronunciations and commonly used slang:

B & T Crowd:	Bridge and Tunnel people, or those commuting to Manhattan.
Big Bang for your Buck:	Good value for money.
CEO:	Chief Executive Officer – i.e. top dog in giant corporation.
Coffee Regular:	Coffee with milk no sugar.
Crack:	A smokeable, addictive derivative of cocaine.
Cut to the Chase:	Get to the point.
Cute:	When used to describe a person this means attractive and engaging; when used about an object it means dinky.
Enjoy!:	Command used by restaurant staff after they've served you food.
Erb:	Herb.
Gross:	Revolting.
Have a Happy!:	Used by New Yorkers in place of 'Have a Nice Day!'
In Your Face:	An in-your-face conversation is heated, involved, angry.
Jappie:	A young, rich, beautiful Jewish Princess.
Make a Rez:	To make a lunch/dinner reservation.
Mommie Track:	What you fall into when you sacrifice your career to have children – the prevalent conviction among New York businesswomen is that you can't have both.
Pissed:	Angry.
Preppie:	Before yuppies there were preppies, who went to Ivy League Universities and wore round glasses and cricket sweaters.
Schlep:	If you schlep around you're being lazy, and if something's a schlep it's a bore.
Schmear:	To have a schmear in your bagel is to have a small amount of cream cheese filling.
Seltzer:	Generic term for non-flavoured fizzy drinks.
Slice:	Piece of pizza.
Soda:	Generic term for flavoured fizzy drinks.
Stand on Line:	To queue up.
Steel Works:	Syringes used for injecting drugs.
Sucking Face:	French kissing.
Swiss Cheese Press Release:	Template press release with holes to fill in.
TNA:	Tits 'n' Ass, used to describe types of videos/movies.
Turn a Dollar:	Make a profit.
Turtle Skin:	Thick-skinned.
WASP:	White Anglo-Saxon Protestant.
Yo!:	Hey, you!
Yuppie:	Young Urban Professional.
Zoned:	Phased, worn out.

In 1991, Human Rights Commissioner Dennis DeLeon upheld the sex-bias complaints filed by 124 female police officers in 1974 and so accelerated the drive by the Police Department to recruit women and ethnic minorities. The percentage of women officers in the New York force is currently about the same as in England – around 10% – but in New York women are breaking into previously male-dominated areas more quickly, including the aviation, harbour control, and bomb squad divisions, and the highest-ranking woman officer in 1992 was Inspector Julia Thompson. After Inspector, only Chief Inspector is higher and there are only five Chief Inspectors in New York State's force.

Crime rates in New York are *not* the highest in the country. As far as *per capita* crime rates go Boston, Dallas and Washington are more dangerous. Murders and rapes obviously make the headlines – 2,154 and 2,892 respectively were reported in New York in 1991 – but it's the basics you have to watch out for. Bag- and purse-snatching is big business. Don't waste time worrying, but take sensible precautions. Crime Prevention Police Officer Merri Pearsall advises against knapsacks because the backs can easily be slashed with razor blades and the chosen items removed; she says bum-bags – called 'fanny-pouches' in the States – rate well because they can be hidden under your clothes; she suggests handbags be held in the crook of your arm or hung over your shoulder under your coat but *never* across your body, as the purse-snatcher may then pull you down and thus cause injuries as they try to take the bag. Merri Pearsall recommends that you never keep anything in your bag that you'd fight for, for example objects of sentimental value; you should hand over your bag immediately, especially if a weapon is involved; and don't make yourself a target by wearing expensive jewellery on the subway. Many people keep a separate wad of 'mugger's money', but Merri Pearsall recommends that if you are asked for your money you should give your attacker everything – if your attacker discovers you've kept money back, he/she could become violent. Pickpockets often involve work in pairs: one causes a distraction by squirting ketchup on you then making a great fuss about cleaning it off while their colleague takes your purse.

If something is lost or stolen, report it to the police immediately. This is important for insurance purposes (companies will want a police statement as proof), in case someone does return it, and so that the police can monitor trends. Yours may be one of a number of purse snatches at a particular street corner, which the police will then patrol more heavily. Phone **374 5000** to find out the nearest precinct.

If you are the victim of a 'sex crime', call Emergency on **911**. You don't have to go to a police precinct – the police will come to you. You can ask for a woman officer, who will go to hospital with you if necessary. Alternatively, ask a cab driver to take you to the nearest precinct – they shouldn't charge and if they do, the police should pay when you get there. Whatever you do, don't stand around looking lost or you'll invite more trouble. If you decide not to report the crime to the police but need counselling and/or medical referrals, call 212 267 7273. The New York Task Force Against Sexual Harassment on 212 274 3210 can also refer you to appropriate counselling and medical agencies. See p.35 for Rape Hotline numbers.

Laws on smoking are strict. You are not allowed to smoke in taxis, buses, or subways, banks, hotel lobbies, sports stadiums or public rest rooms. You cannot drink if you are under twenty-one. American women (and men) are licensed to keep guns at home, but are rarely granted 'carrying permits'. Many women carry a gun illegally in their handbag for self-defence, but crime prevention specialists strongly advise against this. The weapon can be wrenched away by the aggressor and used against you. It is illegal to carry mace in New York State, and although you could carry a can of hairspray to spray in your attacker's eyes, these are not recommended either. First, you may have to fumble to get them; secondly, the wind or air conditioning can blow the mace/spray back in your own eyes.

Health and Sex

It's *vital* that you go to New York armed with a comprehensive health insurance policy – private health-care costs in the States are crippling, and the fast-diminishing emergency services are overrun.

If you have a **minor illness**, go to one of the many drugstores (see p.326). Otherwise, it's unusual but possible to have a doctor come to you (see directory p.33). Or you can go to a doctor – see directory, or look in the Yellow Pages under 'Clinics' or 'Physicians and Surgeons', or call the British Consulate on 212 752 0202 for their selected list of names. Alternatively, you can go to a hospital casualty department (see directory). If it's your child who's ill, all the above applies, but you should ask for a paediatrician at hospitals and clinics. If you are insured, keep all your receipts for the insurance company and check the small print to see how much you are covered for; if you are not insured, go to Bellevue Casualty (see directory), which will treat regardless of ability to pay, but expect to wait as long as 12 hours.

You can get a variety of tampons, many perfumed, in any chemist's, but most cheaply from Duane Read (see shop section). As for contraception, condoms are available in all drugstores. So too are vaginal sponges, but these are not widely accepted as reliable. To protect against the AIDS virus during oral sex with a woman, use Dental Dam, which is available in the Dental Hygiene section of any drugstore, or as a second best, clingfilm, but avoid the microwavable brands as these are porous. If you're on the Pill, *make sure* you've brought sufficient supplies with you, otherwise you'll have to have a full examination before any clinic will authorise a represcription. Prices vary wildly, but the Women's Care Clinic – one of the cheapest – will charge $90 for the exam. If you suspect you're pregnant, wait till you get home for a doctor's test if you can. Private clinics are exorbitant, and although Planned Parenthood, America's Brook Advisory Centre equivalent, is cheaper than most clinics, no Manhattan branches will accept payments on a sliding scale according to your income. If you're a student you could try the Bronx and Brooklyn Planned Parenthood branches for discounted prescriptions and treatment, but expect very long, depressing waits and impatient, overworked staff. An abortion at Planned Parenthood costs between $275 and $650 according to how many weeks pregnant you are. They need at least two days' notice. The Women's Care Clinic charge $325 for test and abortion, although the test is free if your period's more than two weeks late.

FAMILY PLANNING

Planned Parenthood of New York City (the Margaret Sanger Clinic, 3rd Floor, 380 Second Avenue, NY 10010); ring 212 274 7200 for information on your nearest Planned Parenthood branch, on birth control, pregnancy testing, abortion, treatment of sexually transmitted diseases and counselling and testing for the AIDS virus; phone the Woman's Health Line on 212 230 1111 for free or low-cost referrals (depending on ability to pay) to hospitals and clinics in all five boroughs for all aspects of family planning, including the morning-after pill and check-ups for venereal diseases. Go to the Women's Care Clinic (235 East 67th Street, Suite 204, tel. 734 5700) for gynaecology, obstetrics and infertility; or go to the oldest lesbian clinic, the St Mark's Women's Health Collective (9 Second Avenue, NY 10003, tel. 228 7482 for the clinic or 675 1778 for the collective) for 'low-cost health care in a safe, confidential, supportive and relaxed atmosphere', including a wide range of care from AIDS testing and breast exams to massage and 'alternative' medicine.

The abortion laws in New York are amongst the country's most liberal: there's no age limit and no parental consent is necessary as long as the abortion is performed by a licensed physician within the first 24 weeks.

Abortion: a brief history

The years 1850 to 1880 saw abortion become a major political issue in America for the first time. In 1873 the Comstock Law banned all mailed material deemed obscene by the United States postal agent, Anthony Comstock, and that included any drug, medicine, or article for abortion or contraceptive purposes. In New York State alone, Anthony Comstock destroyed fifty tons of 'obscene' books. Comstock felt vindicated when Madame Restell, perhaps Victorian America's most famous abortionist, committed suicide, and he later forced birth control advocate Margaret Sanger (see p.138) to flee to England to avoid arrest. Men like Comstock joined forces with the newly formed American Medical Association and, with the co-operation of the Roman Catholic Church and many of the Protestant clergy, pushed through in 1881 a severe New York State anti-abortion law that made 'the giving or prescription of a poison or noxious drug or the use of mechanical means to cause an abortion in a pregnant woman' a felony. For nearly a century, women resorted to back-street abortions. In 1964 alone ten thousand women suffering severe complications from criminal abortions were admitted to New York public hospitals, and many died.

Public opinion began to shift after a widely used drug, thalidomide, caused thousands of babies to be born deformed and Sherry Finkbine, a woman in Arizona who had taken the drug, demanded a legal abortion. In 1970 New York was one of four States to legalise abortion, but Texas – like most – did not, and in that year Norma McCorvey (known as Jane Roe to protect her privacy) challenged the constitutionality of the anti-abortion law as a violation of the right to liberty guaranteed in the Fourteenth Amendment. She won her case in 1973, but since then various cases have undermined Roe v. Wade – most notably the 1989 Webster v. Reproductive Health Services case, which left Missouri women free to have an abortion, but only if no public funds or services were used. In a 1992 Pennsylvania case, the Supreme Court upheld the Roe v. Wade landmark ruling, but at the same time gave its blessing to Pennsylvania State laws further restricting abortion.

Meanwhile, women pressured by cost still resort to back-street abortions, and even where abortion laws are lenient they can have trouble finding doctors who are trained and willing to perform abortions: only 12% of hospital residency programmes require obstetrics–gynaecology specialists to learn first-trimester abortion procedures; and even though 84% of obstetricians and gynaecologists favour abortion rights, fewer than one-third perform the operation because clinic work pays badly and because systematic pro-life harassment includes death threats.

New York's comparatively lenient laws look set to stay, so if other States continue to jump on the anti-abortion bandwagon, more women will be forced to travel from America's heartland to the East Coast in order to have abortions.

AIDS and Women

Anyone coming to New York *must* use condoms and must *not* share needles. A representative of New York's AIDS Institute states baldly that New York is the epicentre of what is now an epidemic in the Western world, that in New York State women are the fastest-growing HIV positive group and that the highest concentration of HIV positive women is in New York City. Of the AIDS cases in the under-twenty-fives in New York State in 1990, 25% were women.

The largest numbers of women testing HIV positive are black. 'We think condoms are not being used and a lot of men are hiding their HIV status,' said Lorna McBarnette, executive deputy commissioner in the State Health Department, who is instituting a $75,000 education campaign that targets the black community (you'll see ads on the subway). Yvonne Graham, executive director of the Caribbean Women's Health Project, estimates that 50–60% of people in black immigrant communities believe that AIDS is a form of genocide. Many dedicated black health workers and Church leaders refuse to disavow fears that AZT, the drug used to combat the disease, is a plot to poison blacks; that campaigns urging use of condoms, the best way to prevent sexual transmission, are a scheme to reduce the number of black babies; and that distributing clean needles to slow down transmission among addicts is a plot to encourage drug abuse in their community.

AIDS is also spreading within the lesbian community, partly because education campaigns have concentrated on how the disease is transmitted between men or in heterosexual sex, and partly because less is generally known about the manifestation of AIDS in women. Sadomasochistic sexual practices and unprotected oral sex between lesbians can be high-risk activities. HIV positive women don't get Karposi's Sarcoma, the easily recognisable purple blotches; they commonly die of cervical cancer resulting from human papilloma virus (HPV). Sexual contact woman-to-man results in transmission in 60–70% of cases, and it is not clear how much transmission is prevented by condoms or the diaphragm. Garance Franke-Ruta, who has worked on ACT-UP's Treatment and Data Committees, writes: 'HPV is transmitted by skin-to-skin contact, not just sexual secretions. While it is often sexually transmitted, HPV has also been found in female virgins, including one whose only risk factor for HPV infection was sharing underwear with someone who had it.'

You can have a free, anonymous AIDS test while you are in New York, but there's at least a two-week wait between the test and the results, and your status as a visitor if you plan a long stay could be prejudiced if you test positive. Regulations have relaxed, but visitors with HIV will be allowed only an extended visitor's passport, and even that will be awarded only if you succeed in assuring the authorities that you will not be passing on HIV or using social welfare.

To find out about test sites, telephone the New York State AIDS hotline on 1 800 541 AIDS or the New York City AIDS hotline on 718 485 8111. Support groups to contact include Persons With AIDS (PWA) on 1 800 828 3280 or 532 0568; and Gay Men's Health Crisis (GHMC) on 807 6664. If these organisations have folded, contact the AIDS Institute on 613 2494 and someone will refer you to another support group.

Sex in New York

Sex is a big issue in New York for the following reasons.

Sex is Politics   New York City has the largest lesbian and gay population in the country (1 million of its 9 million inhabitants) and under Mayor Dinkins administration it became the first city in the country to boast a city government Department for Lesbian and Gay Affairs. The Department meets every six weeks with the Commissioner of Police to suggest 'sensitising' staff from the start by appointing openly lesbian and gay instructors to train new recruits. The Department opens discussions with school boards on how to combat homophobia, pushes for harsher penalties on bias-related incidents, and celebrates lesbians' contributions to the community over breakfasts at Gracie Mansion, but the Department's most important role is to advise the mayor.

The department may or may not last, but one thing's for sure: now the needs of one of New York's largest communities have been recognised by City government, it will be hard for any mayor to backtrack.

Sex is Business   New York is a convention city, and where there's business conventions there's pornography and prostitution to accommodate male clients. Hotel TVs have soft- and hard-core porn channels. 'A man checking into a hotel who wishes to find a prostitute', writes Priscilla Alexander in her book *Sex Work*, 'has only to ask the bell captain for "referrals"' and he will be sent a "masseuse"'.

Hotel security staff screen prostitutes. This involves taking any woman who looks suspicious (inelegantly dressed and often black) to the basement, where she's photographed, warned not to come back to the hotel and told that her photograph will be circulated to other hotels in the area. She may even be abused and relieved of her illegal earnings. Determined to eliminate such violations, Prostitutes of New York (PONY) organised in the mid 1970s to fight for the legalisation of prostitution. PONY members are currently trying to raise a legal defence fund. If they can hire a staff lawyer they'll be able to adopt relevant lawsuits with the hope of pushing a precedent through the courts (feminist groups used the Roe v. Wade case like this effectively to legalise abortion). PONY also distributes condoms on the streets, offers safe-sex counselling (how to keep your client happy by rolling the condom on with your mouth), refers women to doctors and to shops for equipment, and serves as a forum for women in the sex industry to meet each other.

PONY members find gay men supportive but consider lesbians prudes and organisations like NOW obstructive. They say mainstream sex has got kinkier over the past ten years, with more Mr Averages indulging in a bit of s/m, probably as a result of porn's increased accessibility (just switch on a cable TV channel). They say well-established outcall prostitutes have been only marginally affected by the recession (they might not buy a new Mercedes this year); the middle price range has been worse affected (junior executives cut down on visits to massage parlours); and street girls have got more custom (salary cuts cause blue-collar workers to downgrade from a parlour to a back car seat). PONY has been getting more calls recently as a result of economic bad times (throughout history women with debts and no job have turned to prostitution for 'easy' money), and because attitudes are changing. 'Nice' middle-class girls will dabble in sex work as anything from a lark to a political statement about freedom.

Sex is Sexy Incredibly seedy go-go bars, such as the Baby Doll Lounge (see p.288), attract the 'in' crowd. Public Access TV's **Voyeur Vision** and **Robin Byrd** have won a cult following. The hosts of both shows wear classic sex-shop naughty lingerie outfits and boast guests like Sandra Bernhard and Madonna. Robin Byrd applies the standard talk-show format entirely to sex; **Voyeur Vision** invites viewers to phone in so that Kim can act out their fantasies on screen.

'Sex sells' has long been a favourite advertisers' by-line – the difference in New York is that not much of the market is into 'straight' sex. Look out for the Levi's Silver Tab jeans ad: it caused a furore. At last, claimed the gay community, advertisers are specifically targeting gay men who make up such a large percentage of Manhattan's buying population. The ad in question featured a muscle-bound honcho with a shaved chest. There aren't many copies of it left, as gay men pinched them from bus stops to adorn bedroom walls. Even the *New York Times* has commented on the homoerotic subtexts of many ads, from Anne Klein suits and Calvin Klein underwear to Johnny Walker whisky. It's not that stereotypes of beautiful women don't feature in ads, it's just that when they do they're often squeezed in with the copy giving the gorgeous hunk centre stage, or they appear in embraces with other women.

Advertising executives deny that the tendency is intentional. *QW* magazine claims that's because the numerous gays and lesbians in the corporations don't want to be 'outed'.

IN ANSWER TO THE NEW LIBERALISM

Feminist and novelist Andrea Dworkin, who has alienated many other feminists with her strong advocacy of censorship (see p.32), wrote a letter to the *New York Times* recently 'as a woman determined to destroy the pornography industry' in response to liberals who, 'in defending pornography as if it were speech,' she argued, 'defend the new slavers'.

'I am 45 years old now,' she wrote, and described how she was sexually assaulted three times before she was nineteen years old.

I have since discovered that what happened to me is common: homeless, poor, still sexually traumatized, I learned to trade sex for money. I spent a lot of years out on the streets and other streets in hard cities . . . I know about the lives of women in pornography because I lived the life. So have many feminists who fight pornography. Freedom looks different when you are the one it is being practiced on . . .

I would do virtually anything to get women out of prostitution and pornography, which is mass-produced, technologized prostitution. With pornography, a woman can still be sold after the beatings, the rapes, the pain, the humiliation have killed her . . .

The only fiction in pornography is the smile on the woman's face.

Sexual Harassment

Sexual harassment of the wolf-whistling-on-the-streets variety is rare in New York. No-nonsense, powerful businesswomen have been yelling back their objections since the 1970s, and so many men in the City are gay that a huge proportion of the male population simply won't be interested in you.

There are currently three main types of sexual harassment in the news that have caused women's organisations and lesbian and gay organisations to fight for tougher related laws: sexual harassment at work, mainly by male bosses against women, the incidence of which rose nationally by 70% between 1981 and 1989; harassment on the basis of sexual orientation, such as the 1989 case in which Ann Hopkins was denied a partnership in Price Waterhouse because she was 'too masculine': and 'date rape', which hit the media headlines with the precedent-setting Mike Tyson case – his defence was typical: he maintained that she said 'no' but meant 'maybe'.

On the streets you're most likely to get harassed for money by beggars and panhandlers, who can get angry if you refuse. New Yorkers' trick is to meet the harasser's gaze briefly and coolly but not stare, thereby establishing themselves as confident and not-to-be-messed-with but not encouraging further attentions. If you want to sit alone in Central Park, take a book with you and position yourself where there are lots of people – for example on a bench near a children's playground. In restaurants and bars, Downtown especially, you're unlikely to have any trouble because staff and customers are inured to the sight of women alone.

In mid-to-upmarket hotels, if you look a little scruffy there's an outside chance that porters might mistake you for a prostitute (see p.25), in which case they'll try to hurry you somewhere out of the way – feel free to get angry, but *don't* feel embarrassed or belittled. Occasionally bellboys or bar staff might get fresh. A jovial refusal is jovially accepted. If you jovially accept, bear in mind that a surprisingly high number of young American men are complacent about AIDS – in New York, *insist* on condoms.

Women and Feminism

New York has a huge number of women's support groups, political organisations and pressure groups – use NOW, the National Organisation of Women, as a resource centre to find more than the ones listed here. NOW gives referral over the phone, or will let you go into their offices to look through their library of books and files. A great many organisations meet at the Gay and Lesbian Community Centre. Go there for listings information.

ACT UP
135 W. 29th Street, tel. 564 2437.
Within Act Up there is a women's group which is campaigning over women and health, particularly ethnic minorities. Join meetings every Monday night at Cooper Union – phone first for details.

BARNARD CENTRE FOR RESEARCH ON WOMEN
101 Barnard Hall, 3009 Broadway, NY 10027, tel. 854 2067. The Barnard Centre does a series of programmes that include bringing speakers and films to campus, and it has a resource collection that is over twenty years old and subscribed to by over 100 feminist journals from around the world.

LESBIAN AND GAY COMMUNITY CENTRE
208 W 13th Street (bet. 7th and 8th Aves), NY 10011, tel. 620 7310.
A major information and events centre. Seven lesbian and gay organisations as well as the Lesbian Switchboard, are headquartered at the Centre, and more than 250 groups rent the space for meetings, social events and cultural programmes.

NATIONAL ABORTION RIGHTS ACTION LEAGUE (NARAL)
2 W 64th Street, NY 10023, tel. 724 5770.
You won't get practical assistance from this grass-roots political organisation, but you could find out if they need help with campaigns which include working to elect pro-choice candidates to the City Council and the State Senate.

NEW YORK CITY COMMISSION ON THE STATUS OF WOMEN

52 Chambers Street, Suite 207, NY 10007, tel. 788 2738.
Write ahead for a publication called *Women's Organisations, a New York City Directory* for $7.95 including mailing.

NOW

15 W 18th Street (bet. 5th and 6th Aves), tel. 807 0721. NOW has 30,000 members nationwide, so it has some political clout – it can raise funds for and campaign for party nominees. It is also a resource centre for any woman – you can get addresses for political action or support groups from them and they have a list of health-care agencies. All women are welcome to offer their services as volunteers, and to attend the open general meetings on the third Thursday of every month.

QUEER NATION

At the Gay and Lesbian Community Centre, tel. 978 8720.
This, the most successful lesbian and gay 'multicultural direct action' group in America dedicated to fighting homophobia and queer invisibility, was responsible for the 'outing' posters. You can go to the meetings, which are held every Thursday at the Community Centre at 7.30 p.m.

WOMEN'S ACTION COALITION (WAC)

tel. 967 7711 ext. 9226.
Members of WAC, including Laurie Anderson, Cindy Sherman, Karen Finley and Barbara Kruger, meet on Wednesday nights and conspire to outlaw misogyny through in-your-face public campaigns involving posters and leaflets that give facts such as: 'A woman will die of breast cancer every 12 minutes'; '75% of women who are raped know their attacker. What is it about the word no that you don't understand?'; and '36 billion owed in child support'. WAC has drawn from the tactics of the Guerrilla Girls and the organisational expertise of ACT UP.

Within corporate industry and the media there are a number of groups pressuring for equal rights. On the whole they are conservatively reformist rather than political. They include **Women in Communications** for journalism (tel. 212/532 3669); **Advertising Women of New York** (tel. 212/593 1950); and the **National Association of Female Executives** (NAFE) (tel. 212/645 0770).

Feminism: a brief history

In the history of American suffrage and feminism, New York has been a centre of debate and radical thinking rather than activism, which has inevitably focused on Washington, the seat of national government.

The first key date is 1848, when the Seneca Falls Convention took place in New York State. The Seneca Falls suffragists, most notably Elizabeth Cady Stanton and Susan B. Anthony (see p.92), used the Declaration of Independence as their model. 'All men and women are created equal,' they said, and so demanded the individual self-determination that was central to the Declaration. They wanted the vote.

The fight was not won, however, until, seven decades later, Woodrow Wilson told the lawmakers on Capitol Hill in 1918 that woman suffrage was 'vital to winning the war'. Within two years the Constitution's Nineteenth Amendment had been passed, but victory caused turmoil within the women's movement. It could no longer fight for suffrage, so what next? 'Feminism' developed in the form of warring factions. Some groups revelled in rebellion, including the members of a Greenwich Village group called 'Heterodoxy' who simply declared their right to 'not be orthodox' in their opinions or actions (which involved free love and lesbianism; see p.95). The only group to emerge with a clear manifesto was the National Woman's Party (NWP), which proposed an Equal Rights Amendment to the Constitution (ERA) in 1923 that read: 'Men and women shall have equal rights throughout the United States and every place subject to its jurisdiction' (ERA's demand was evident in the 1848 Seneca Falls declaration, and has yet to be instituted). The biggest change on a personal level was the increased number of women who sought and found employment. But by 1929 America was sunk in Depression and reaction gripped the country: women in jobs were urged to leave them (as they were again after World War II).

In 1938, 80% of the American people strongly opposed married women working, but war changed everything. By 1943 over 60% of Americans approved of women working, and Betty Friedan (see p.103) was groping towards the conclusion that American culture destroyed the minds and emotions of (mainly white middle-class) women, thereby preventing them from developing an identity of their own. In 1963 she published her ideas as *The Feminine Mystique* and generated a debate that put feminism on the public agenda. Friedan founded the National Organization of Women (NOW, see p.29) and Gloria Steinem founded Ms. magazine (see p.127). In 1973 the Supreme Court ruled in the Roe v. Wade case (see p.23) that women could decide, in consultation with their physician, to terminate their pregnancy, and that no State could intervene. The ruling seemed a powerful affirmation that women had the freedom to control their own bodies, but it came at the end of what turned out to be a brief heyday.

A force called 'Middle America', or the 'New Right', emerged and declared that feminism was evil. By the mid 1970s Republican Phyllis Schlafly's anti-ERA coalition had convinced both men and women nationwide that feminists wanted to make men and women the same, that they wanted to destroy cherished ideals such as God and the family in favour of rampant homosexuality. Roe v. Wade was challenged, and by the 1980s feminism was again divided into warring factions.

Radical feminists harangued socialist feminists; lesbian feminists and feminists of colour split off, saying their needs had not been addressed. In 1982 New York's Barnard College annual feminist conference debated the politics of sadomasochism and the practice of butch/femme roles (defenders of 'femme' included Lesbian Herstory Archives founder Joan Nestle; see p.14). Other women, most prominently Andrea Dworkin and Catharine MacKinnon, identified pornography as key to women's oppression and drafted a law (not instituted) that would allow women who have been injured by pornography to sue those who make and distribute it for violating their civil rights.

The 1990s have brought change on all fronts. 'Libertarian' or 'Sex Positive' feminists are decrying 1980s feminists, including Dworkin and Adrienne Rich, for portraying lesbians as sexless. Sex Positive feminists show porn at New York clubs (see p.296) and swap tips at the Lesbian Sex Conference on how to get more pleasure out of sex. Prostitutes of New York (PONY, see p.25) have organised to get prostitution legalised. Meanwhile, the word 'feminism' is acceptable again, thanks largely to Susan Faludi's book *Backlash*, which has been compared to *The Feminine Mystique* for its sudden social impact. In *Backlash: The Undeclared War Against American Women*, Faludi exposes 'The Big Lie' that feminism's battle is won with 500-odd pages of alarming statistics showing, amongst other things, that women are still worse paid than men and barred from top jobs. *Time* magazine summarised:

In the '80s this backlash surfaced in the Reagan White House, the courts, Hollywood, and, above all, the mass media, whose collective message went something like this: Feminism is your worst enemy. All this freedom is making you miserable, unmarriageable, infertile, unstable. Go home, bake a cake, quit pounding on the doors of public life and all your troubles will go away.

In 1991 *Backlash* hit No. 1 on the *New York Times* Bestseller lists, as did Gloria Steinem's *Revolution from Within*. Steinem's book which tells you how to 'empower yourself', has been dismissed by some critics as squishy New Age thumb-sucking, but it struck a chord with the nation – crowds for Steinem's book-signings outnumbered those for Oliver North's.

A NEW YORK DEBATE

Kate Millett: In her 1970 book *Sexual Politics*, early radical feminist Kate Millett argues that behavioural differences between women and men are not inherent, but socially constructed:

The heavy musculature of the male, a secondary sexual characteristic common among mammals, is biological in origin but is also culturally encouraged through breeding, diet and exercise. Yet it is hardly an adequate category on which to base political relations *within civilization*. Male supremacy, like other political creeds, does not finally reside in physical strength but in the acceptance of a value system which is not biological.

Anne Koedt: In 1973, Koedt – author of the 1968 article 'The Myth of the Vaginal Orgasm' – shared rising anger over the idea that feminists were presuming to judge one another's sex lives:

If you are a feminist who is not sleeping with a woman you may risk hearing any of the following accusations: 'You're oppressing me if you don't sleep with women'; or 'You don't love women if you don't sleep with them.' I have even seen a woman's argument about an entirely different aspect of feminism be dismissed by some lesbians because she was not having sexual relations with women... There is an outrageous thing going on here strictly in terms of pressuring women about their personal lives.

Andrea Dworkin: Dworkin's 1974 'Renouncing Sexual Equality' speech to a NOW conference said that all relations of dominance stemmed from men's sexual relations with women:

There is no *freedom* or *justice* or even common sense, in developing a male sexual sensibility – a sexual sensibility that is aggressive, competitive, objectifying, quantity oriented... I think that men will have to give up their precious erections and begin to make love as women do together. I am saying that men will have to renounce their phallocentric personalities, and the privileges and powers given to them at birth as a consequence of their anatomy, that they will have to excise everything in them that they now value as distinctly 'male'. (See p.27 for Dworkin's views on pornography.)

Audre Lorde: Audre Lorde, the late African-American writer, wrote in 1980:

Differences expose all women to various forms and degrees of patriarchal oppression, some of which we share and some of which we do not. For instance, surely you know that for non-white women in this country, there is an 80% fatality rate from breast cancer; three times the number of unnecessary eventurations, hysterectomies and sterilizations as for white women; three times as many chances of being raped, murdered or assaulted as exist for white women.

Adrienne Rich: In 1985 the Feminist Anti-Censorship Task Force (FACT) formulated a brief that said in support of pornography: 'Women need the freedom and the socially recognized space to appropriate for themselves the robustness of what traditionally has been male language.' The poet Adrienne Rich, who was one of the first radical feminists to say that women's biology was *not* inherently oppressive, signed the FACT brief, but attached a qualifying statement:

I brought no automatic assent to the FACT brief, and there are parts of it with which I quarrel. I think it underrepresents the actual toll taken on women's lives by the *actions* associated with sexual slavery, while claiming that actions, not images, are the problem... I am less sure than Dworkin and MacKinnon that this is a time when further powers of suppression should be turned over to the State.

AIDS
To find out about test sites and support groups see p.25.

AIRLINES
Air Canada, 1166 Sixth Avenue (tel. 1 800 776 3000); Aer Lingus, 122 East 42nd Street (tel. 212 557 1110); American Airlines, 405 Lexington Avenue (tel. 212 455 6385); British Airways, 530 Fifth Avenue (tel. 1 800 247 9297); Continental Airlines, 560 Lexington Avenue (tel. 212 735 1922); Virgin Atlantic, 96 Morton Street (tel. 212 242 1330).

AIRPORTS
John F. Kennedy Airport, tel. 1 718 656 4520; La Guardia Airport, tel. 1 718 476 5000; Newark Airport, tel. 1 201 961 2000.

AMBULANCE
Tel. 911.

BABYSITTING
See p.337.

BUS/SUBWAY INFORMATION
Tel. 718 3300 1234.

CAR BREAKDOWN/SERVICING
Express Auto Repairs, 276 Seventh Avenue (at 26th St), tel. 212 242 5982. For 24-hour gas (petrol) stations go to Hess, Tenth Avenue (at 45th St), tel. 212 245 6594 or Mobil, 577 First Avenue (at 33rd St), tel. 212 725 9479.

CAR HIRE
See p.343.

CASUALTY DEPARTMENTS
24-hour casualties include Bellevue Hospital, First Avenue at East 29th Street, tel. 212 561 4141; St Vincent's Hospital, 153W, 11th Street, tel. 212 790 7000; New York Hospital, 525 East 68th Street, tel. 212 746 5050; Mount Sinai Hospital, 1 Gustave Levy Place, tel. 212 241 7171.

CHEMIST (24-HOUR)
Kaufman Pharmacy, 557 Lexington Avenue (at 50th St), tel. 212 755 2266; orders will be delivered free within a ten-mile radius of COD by taxi.

CRECHES AND PLAYGROUPS
It's very hard to find crèches or playgroups unless you're prepared to pay hefty annual fees – see p.337 for babysitters, whom you can employ for whole days.

DENTAL CARE
Tel. 212 679 3966 before 8 p.m. and 212 679 4172 after 8 p.m. for a recorded list of the names, addresses and telephone numbers of four dentists, all members of the First District Dental Society.

DOCTOR, HOUSE CALLS
Doctors on Call has 40–60 doctors available to make house calls 24 hours a day: $95 per hotel call, $70 for a private house; tel. 718 238 2100.

DOCTOR'S WALK-IN
All physicians are board-certified specialists on the staff of the Beth Israel Medical Centre, tel. 212 683 1010.

DRY CLEANERS
All except the cheapest hotels offer dry-cleaning services. Otherwise, you'll find plenty in the Yellow Pages, and one that's open on Sundays for collection or delivery – although it is not same-day service – is Mr Dry Clean, 92 Eighth Avenue (near 14th St), tel. 212 627 5980.

PRACTICALITIES

EMBASSIES AND CONSULATES
Australia, 630 Fifth Avenue (tel. 212 245 4000); Canada, 1251 6th Avenue (tel. 212 768 2400); United Kingdom, 845 Third Avenue (tel. 212 745 0202); New Zealand, 1 United Nations Plaza (tel. 212 826 1960).

EMERGENCY
Call the 24-hour hotline of the Victims' Services Department at the Travellers' Aid Society (2 Lafayette Street, NY 10007) on 577 7700 with all emergencies from muggings to rape. If you're stranded in New York after a mugging without money, passport or accommodation, call the tourists' crisis intervention unit, the Travellers' Aid Service, on 944 0013.

FAMILY PLANNING
See p.22.

FEMINIST ORGANISATIONS
See p.28.

FINDING A FLAT
Look in the ad sections of the *Village Voice*, *The New York Times*, *New York Magazine* and other publications, and on noticeboards (as above).

FINDING A JOB
For casual work, look on the noticeboard just inside the doorway of the *Voice* office at 842 Broadway (near Union Square) and also the numerous noticeboards around the Columbia University campus and in the Loeb Student Centre of New York University on Washington Square. Also look in papers and magazines (as below).

HELPLINES
Alcoholics Anonymous (tel. 212 683 3900); Crime Victims Hotline (tel. 212 577 7777); Drugs Anonymous (tel. 212 874 0700); Missing Persons Bureau (tel. 212 374 6913); Restaurant Hotline (tel. 212 838 7030); Suicide Helpline (tel. 212 532 2400); Time and Temperature (tel. 212 976 1616); Traffic Report (tel. 212 374 6930); Weather (tel. 212 976 1212).

LAUNDERETTES
Hotels have laundry services, or you can go to a launderette (called laundromat). You'll find plenty in the Yellow Pages because New Yorkers simply don't have washing machines. The YMCAs have coin-ops.

LEFT LUGGAGE
Grand Central Station (42nd St and Park Ave) has a luggage department (open Mon–Fri 7 a.m.–8 p.m., Sat and Sun 10 a.m.–6 p.m.; charges $1 an item, $2 a rucksack, $3 for a bike); Port Authority Bus Terminal (41st St and 8th Ave) does too (daily 7 a.m.–12 p.m.; charges 80c per item, $1,60 for a backpack).

LEGAL HELP
For a $25 consultancy fee, the New York City Bar Association (tel. 382 6625) will give you the names of three good attorneys.

LESBIAN ORGANISATIONS
See p.13.

LIBRARIES
The New York Library on Fifth Avenue (see p.116) has a vast selection of books available to anyone, but only for reference, not to take home. There are many branch libraries (get addresses from Central Library) whose lending services you can use if you can prove residence.

LOST PROPERTY

Belongings lost on buses or on the subway: MTA Lost Property Division, 370 Jay Street, Brooklyn (tel. 718 625 6200). Anything lost in a cab: Taxi and Limousine Commission Lost Property Information Department, 211 West 41st Street (tel. 212 869 4513).

POLICE

Tel. 911 emergency or 212 374 6700 for general information, including your nearest precinct.

RAPE HOTLINE

Tel. 212 267 7273.

SWIMMING POOLS AND SPORTS CENTRES

See p.314.

TIPPING

Restaurants and taxi drivers, 15%–20%; hotel bellhops, $1 per 1–2 bags absolute minimum; hotel doorman, $1 per taxi. Tipping is not just a courtesy – it is the recipient's wages. Europeans are known for being stingy. If you confirm their prejudices you will receive anything from the cold shoulder to a barrage of abuse. In restaurants and taxis you either tip or get a hard time; in hotels and at airports/stations insist on carrying your own bags if you don't want to tip.

TOILETS

Public toilets in Manhattan are few and far between. If you are in a hotel, restaurant, gallery or museum, make use of the rest rooms. If you are caught short, have a coffee in a café to make yourself a patron or just ignore the 'Rest Rooms for Patrons Only' sign and stride boldly in. Hotels are good places to go (again, stride purposefully), especially the Waldorf-Astoria – the Ladies' Rest Room there is renowned for its sheer luxury.
Official public toilets include:
Olympic Tower Atrium (connects 51st St and 52nd St, east of 5th Ave; open daily 7 a.m.–midnight);
Citicorp Center (153 E 53rd St, lower level; open Mon–Fri 7 a.m.–8.30 p.m., Sat and Sun 8 a.m.–8.30 p.m.);
Park Avenue Plaza (55 E 52nd St; open 8 a.m.–10 p.m. daily);
Sculpture Court at the Whitney Museum of American Art at Philip Morris (Park Ave at 42nd St; open Mon–Sat 7.30 a.m.–9.30 p.m., Sun 11 a.m.–7 p.m.);
IBM Garden Plaza (590 Madison Ave near 57th St, lower level; open Mon–Sat 8 a.m.–10 p.m.);
Trump Tower (725 5th Ave near 57th St, downstairs near the café; open Mon–Sat 8 a.m.–10 p.m.);
GE Building (30 Rockefeller Plaza, concourse level; open 8 a.m.–7 p.m.);
City University Graduate Center (bet. 33 W 42nd St and 34 W 43rd St, in the covered walkway; open daily 8 a.m.–10.30 p.m., Sat 9 a.m.–5 p.m.);
New York Public Library (bet. 5th Ave and 42nd St, ground and third floors; open Mon–Wed 10 a.m.–9 p.m., Thurs–Sat 10 a.m.–6 p.m.).

TRAIN INFORMATION

Grand Central Terminal, bet. 42nd St and Park Ave (tel. 212 340 2588); Amtrak (tel. 212 582 6875); Pennsylvania Station, 31st–33rd Sts and 7th–8th Aves (tel. 212 582 6875); New Jersey Transit (tel. 201 460 8444); Long Island Railroad (tel. 718 217 5477); Port Authority Bus Terminal, bet. 41st St and 8th Ave (tel. 212 564 8484); George Washington Bridge Bus Terminal, bet. W 17th St and Broadway (tel. 212 564 1114); Greyhound Bus Office (tel. 212 635 0800).

SOME CURRENT 'INS'

Transport Motorised scooters for commuters; Harley Davidsons for clubbers; and racing bikes for everyone (watch out – night-time cyclists with no lights speed down streets on the wrong side).

Drink Watery overpriced bottled beers.

Cigarettes Camel Wides at trendy bars; all brands of European cigarettes for everyone, and Silk Cut in particular for sailors.

Health Body-sculpting your arms for clubbers; and for executive men and women, jogging with your child tied into a luridly coloured three-wheeler pushchair that's triangular-shaped for extra speed.

Dress Goatee beards and lots of boxer-short showing for trendy boys; pristine Doc Marten boots or top designer suits, both with immaculate make-up, for trendy girls; dressage ponytails for media men; Nike trainers with bobby socks for Midtown businesswomen, and for upscale businesswomen, a white streak in lightly permed brown hair.

Pets Jack Russells are in, pointers are avant-garde, and Dalmatians are passé pooches for monied women on Madison Avenue.

CRUCIAL!

You *must* get travel insurance for the States – emergency health-care costs are exorbitant.

Take American Express traveller's cheques in US dollars or you'll have trouble changing your money.

Take plastic – credit cards buy you almost anything, and are necessary as deposits or proof of ID in, for example, hotels and car-hire firms.

ARRIVAL AND GETTING AROUND

Arrival

New York has three airports. Most international flights go to the largest, John F. Kennedy. **Newark**, which has one international and two domestic terminals, is a smaller, nicer airport, and although it's a little further from Manhattan than JFK it's more convenient for Downtown. La Guardia is for domestic flights only.

When your plane lands it is best not to trust anyone unless they are an **airport official** with badge and uniform to prove it, a **bus driver** working for one of the companies named below, or a **medallion cab driver** whose cab will be yellow with a beacon on top (as seen in innumerable New York films). Ripping tourists off has turned into organised crime – individuals and pairs travel to airports as they would to an office job. There are a few obvious but frequently successful **scams** to watch out for: if someone offers to help you with your bags, they'll probably run off with them; gypsy cabs offer cheap lifts and charge the earth.

Getting into Manhattan All three airports have several legitimate **Consolidated Ground Transportation Centres** where uniformed employees will help you find the service that best suits your needs. Options include cabs, limos and helicopters, but **bus** is generally the cheapest and easiest. Buses will stop at large hotels for a good-value two-dollar surcharge. All buses to Manhattan stop at Grand Central Train Station and Port Authority Bus Terminal, where you catch the bus back to the airports at the end of your stay. Of the two arrival/departure points, Grand Central is preferable: it's less seedy and more convenient for most hotels. It is possible to go from JFK to Manhattan and back by subway, but unless you're with someone who knows the route well, use this option only as a last resort. If you do go by subway, make absolutely sure that your luggage is easy to carry, and that you get on an express train, which skips the bleaker local stations.

FROM JFK

The **Carey Airport Express Coach Bus** (tel. 718 632 0506) runs every 30 minutes JFK–Manhattan from 6 a.m. to midnight. The Carey takes between 35 and 75 minutes and costs $11 one way. Medallion **Cabs** are metered and will come to around $30. **New York Helicopter** (tel. 800 645 3494) operates frequent 10-minute flights to and from the East 34th Street Heliport for $65 before tax (lower shared fares available). For the last-resort **express bus–subway** journey (tel. 718 330 1234), you'll need $1.25 for the subway token and steely nerves. Take the free shuttle bus (every 10 minutes or every 30 after midnight) from JFK to Howard Beach Station, where you get on the A subway line for Manhattan.

FROM NEWARK

Olympia Trails Airport Express Bus (tel. 212 964 6233) runs every 20 minutes from Newark to several stops in Manhattan, the best of which are the World Trade Center in Manhattan's Financial District, and Grand Central. A single fare is $7 and the journey time is about 35 minutes. Medallion **Cabs** will cost you $40 plus toll for bridges. No helicopter or direct bus/subway link.

LA GUARDIA

Carey Airport Express Coach Bus (tel. 718 632 0506) runs every 20–30 minutes to Grand Central (6 a.m.–1 a.m.) and Port Authority (7.30 a.m.–10 p.m.) with a journey time of 30–40 minutes at a cost of $8.50, or $10 if you want to be dropped at a hotel. A medallion cab will cost about $20.

When You Arrive in Manhattan Be cautious of strangers, just as you were at the airport. As in any major city, be careful at the bus and train stations, Port Authority and Grand Central terminal. Of the two, Port Authority is considered dodgier; it is therefore well policed. Both are fine as long as you avoid quiet areas (i.e. the rest rooms) and look purposeful. Both attract pickpockets and homeless people, who in New York include drug addicts and patients from mental hospitals who have been discharged too early. At all times, as in any major city's points of entry, keep an eye on your bags.

Orientation

New York City is made up of four outer boroughs – Brooklyn, Staten Island, Queens and the Bronx – and the central island of Manhattan, where you'll probably spend most of your time.

Manhattan Island is 13 miles long and 2 miles wide. Its streets are arranged in a grid pattern. The cross-town street numbers increase as you go north. Avenues run the length of the island, and their numbers increase as you go from east to west. Manhattan divides into three main sections: Uptown is above 59th Street; Downtown is below 14th Street; and Midtown is between the two. These sections then divide into neighbourhoods; for example, Greenwich Village and the Lower East Side are both Downtown. Walking distances are described in terms of the number of blocks.

New York's most dangerous neighbourhoods are mainly contained and identifiable, and therefore easy for the visitor to avoid. Don't go to Harlem unless you're with a tour (see p.199), don't go to the South Bronx or certain parts of Brooklyn, most notably Bedford Stuyvesant, Crown Heights and East New York. As a general rule, avoid the far eastern and western sides of Manhattan Island. Don't go to Manhattan's Avenues C or D. Go to the Lower East Side only by cab after dark. And remember that the Financial District and Midtown can be unnervingly quiet, although not necessarily dangerous, after business hours.

Getting Around

The fastest way to get up and downtown is by **subway**. Master two routes early on. Go **by foot** for short trips. It will take you about fifteen minutes to walk ten north–south blocks (a bit more during morning, lunchtime and early-evening rush hours). The **buses** are slow, but many women feel safer travelling by bus than by subway. **Taxis** are the fastest and safest way to travel at night.

By Foot   In theory, the grid system makes orientation straightforward; in practice the symmetrical sameness of blocks and streets can be confusing. Don't ever let it be obvious that you are a lost stranger, for example by looking at maps. Tests in prisons showed that muggers and thieves will pick on those who look unsure of themselves and vulnerable, not on people who stride out with purpose and confidence. Don't walk *too* fast, though, or you'll appear scared. If in doubt, walk on until you come to a shop, where you can go in and look at your map or ask the shopkeeper – or, if you see one, ask a police officer. Alternatively, ask a nice-looking New York. New Yorkers will be helpful and voluble if you ask them directions, but bear in mind that they may not be accurate. Rather than admit that they don't know, they will guess, so it's always worth asking someone else as a fail-safe.

THINGS TO DO

For orientation: go round the island on the **Circle Line Ferry** (p.47), go up the **Empire State** (p.112) or up the **World Trade Center** (p.69), and cross the **Brooklyn Bridge** (p.81).

For social history: take the ferry to the **Ellis Island Museum of Immigration** (p.53), go to the **Old Merchant's House** (p.96), visit the **Museum of the American Indian** (p.65), take a day trip to the **Richmondstown Restoration**, and take a bus up 5th Avenue to the **Museo del Barrio** (p.206).

For art and artefacts: the biggest museum is the magnificent **Metropolitan Museum of Art** (p.165), the wackiest is the **Guggenheim** (p.173); two of the nicest are the **Frick** (p.163) and the **Pierpont Morgan Library** (p.114), and for modern art go to **MoMA** (p.151).

For architecture: you can't miss the Art Deco spire of the **Chrysler Building** (p.125); take a look at the understated **Seagram Building** (p.130) and spend some time at the **Cathedral of St John the Divine** (p.189).

For atmosphere: eat dim sum in **Chinatown** (pp.76 and 260), drink mid-morning coffee in arty **SoHo** (see p.71); go to **Orchard Street Market** midday Sunday (p.86), spend evenings in cheap **East Village** restaurants (p.283) or **Greenwich Village** bars and jazz clubs (pp.284 and 300).

For children: visit the **Museum of Natural History** (p.188), then **Central Park** (p.180) or the **Manhattan Children's Museum** (p.188); devote a day to the **Staten Island Children's Museum** (p.221), get nautical at the **South Street Seaport** (p.67), and make time for a trip to Coney Island's **New York Aquarium** (p.212).]

If you are hopelessly lost or in a panic, telephone **718 330 1234** – give them your location and destination, and they will tell you the most direct route by bus or subway.

Subway The 704-mile New York subway system is famous for being dirty and dangerous. But it is now being cleaned up, and it's an efficient way to travel.

At street level, look for a globe with an 'S' on – this marks the subway entrance. You must know whether you are going uptown or downtown, as entrances give access only to trains going one way. Study the map by the ticket booth, as there are no maps on the platform. You will need a token to get through the barrier. Buy your tokens at the booth, where notes of more than $20 are not accepted. Have your money ready beforehand, so you don't have to

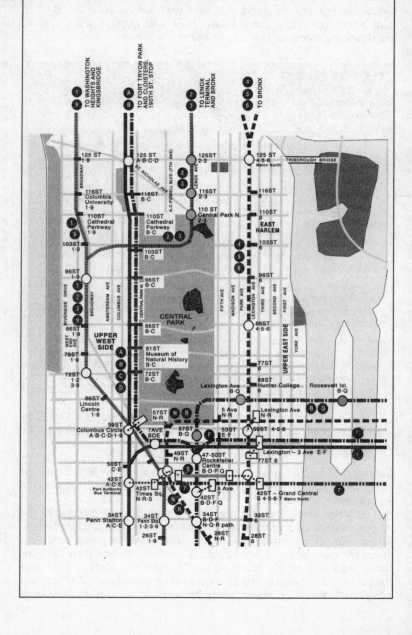

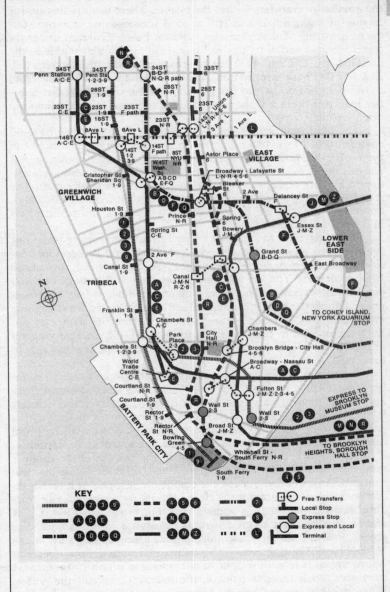

fumble. A **single fare** is $1.25, regardless of distance you travel or the number of transfers within the system. There is no reduction for buying in bulk, but this is still a good idea because it avoids frequent queueing. Tokens are also valid on buses. Children under six travel free; six and older pay full fare. Half fares are available to the disabled (tel. 212 240 4131 for information) and senior citizens (tel. 212 577 0819 for information). Up-to-date maps are available from most operator booths and from Grand Central concourse. Get one – our map was correct at the time of going to press, but train lines are often rerouted.

The **platforms** are generally colourless and bleak (they have no ads). In some of the older downtown stations there are cracked but pretty tile friezes, inappropriately of rural scenes. Busking has recently been made legal in stations, and all performers are auditioned by City representatives, so the quality is generally high. The stainless-steel-sheathed trains are mostly graffiti-free. At least once on every journey you'll be approached by beggars and panhandlers in the train carriages.

In the daytime the subway is used by a wide variety of people (businessmen and women, shoppers, students) and is therefore considered safe. At night take cabs, or see below for information. Almost all New Yorkers use the subway, but with provisos. If you are wearing expensive jewellery, hide it or remove it (slip necklaces under jumpers and turn earrings round). Be aware of what is going on around you, but don't stare. Remember that the names of stations correspond to their overground location – if you find yourself in the 100s by accident, for example, you are in Harlem and should turn back.

Trains run 24 hours a day. Trains are known by letters or numbers (the 'E' line, or the '1', '2' or '3'). They are labelled on the front and at the side of carriages by the doors. Express trains (clearly labelled 'Express') can be useful (they stop at only a quarter of the stops) but they can be a nuisance if you hop on one unwittingly and rattle past your stop at high speed. Local trains stop at all stations.

Few women feel comfortable using the subway after about 8 p.m. If you do decide to use it after hours, take the following precautions. At street level, check the colour of the globe. If it is red, do not go down as the entrance is closed (homeless people may be bedding down there or drug addicts injecting their next fix). If it is amber, it is best not to go down, as the station is unmanned. The green globe means go – use this station. Once inside, stay in the 'After Hours Waiting Area'. This is marked with yellow lines and yellow signs. It is within sight of the operator booth or monitored by videos, so if there is trouble, the operator can call the police. When the train arrives, use the central carriages. You can tell which one the guard will be in by looking for the black and white/yellow striped boards that he uses to line up the train correctly with the platform.

Bus Buses are wonderful for women on tight budgets because most routes are safe to use at night. Drivers have a telephone so they can call for help if necessary, and because workers on night shifts get to know each other on the bus route home, the after-hours atmosphere on buses is comradely. Buses are also great for the disabled and for women burdened with pushchairs, since nearly all are 'kneeling buses' (look for the writing on the door), which means that the bus driver can make the whole bus tip hydraulically until the step is level with the pavement.

During working hours traffic is heavy and it can be faster to walk than to catch a bus. Most bus routes follow the grid pattern, so go uptown–downtown or crosstown. Bus stops are marked by yellow kerbstones, by signs on posts indicating bus times, and sometimes by a blue sign with a bus picture on it. Buses have their destination and number displayed on the front. There are three kinds of buses: **regular**, which arrive every five or ten minutes (15–20 at night) and stop every two or three blocks; **limited stop**, which travel the same routes less frequently and stop only every ten or fifteen blocks; and **express** buses, which may stop only at their final destination. You must either have $1.25 in exact change or use a subway token, which also costs $1.25 and can be bought in subway stations (see above). Children under six go free (as in the subways). When you get on you can ask for 'a transfer' and you'll get a slip of paper which allows you to change buses at an intersecting route within an hour. Pick up maps from Grand Central, NYCVB or a subway station, as above.

Taxis Taxi travel in New York is cheap compared to most big cities, but the cabbies are notorious for erratic driving and for not knowing their way around. Make sure you can tell them the cross-streets of your destination, and if they don't speak English, don't feel embarrassed about pointing out your destination on a map. Use only yellow **medallion cabs**, which you'll see everywhere and are easy to hail. Avoid **gypsy cabs** – they'll rip you off.

If the yellow light on top is lit, the cab's free; if the two small sidelights are lit, the cab's on call and won't stop. You can fit four people into a medallion cab. You're charged for the ride, not per person. The cost is $1.50 for the first fifth of a mile, then 25 cents for each fifth of a mile thereafter and 20 cents for each minute not in motion, with a 50 cents surcharge after 8 p.m. Drivers expect 15% tips, or you can just round up the fare. Many will refuse to go to Harlem and the Outer Boroughs – you'll just have to keep hailing till you find someone amenable.

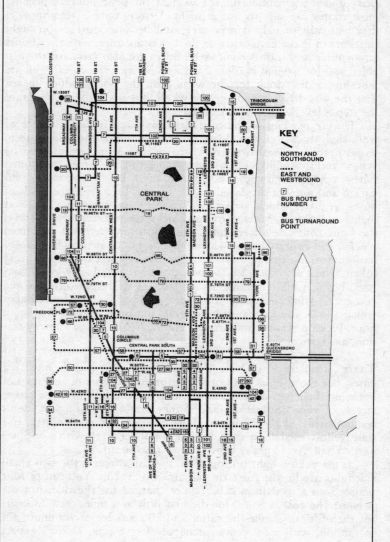

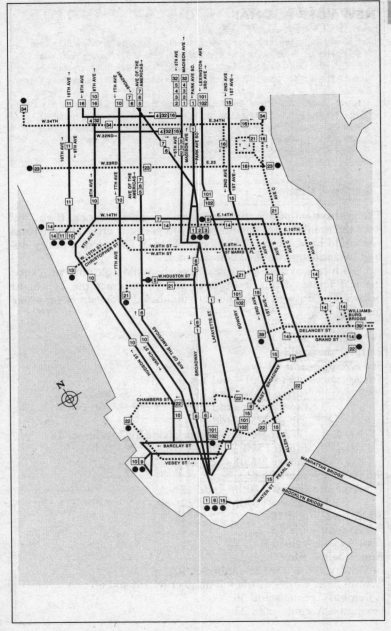

PRACTICALITIES

Address Finder

The grid system means that streets and avenues are long. If you just have the number of a building and you guess its cross-street wrong, you could have several long blocks' walk or end up in a dodgy district by accident. Use the address finder.

To locate avenue addresses, take the building's number, cancel the last figure, divide it by two, add or subtract the key figure below. The answer is the nearest numbered cross-street (approximately).

1st Avenue – add 3
2nd Avenue – add 3
3rd Avenue – add 10
5th Avenue – (up to 200) – add 13
              (up to 400) – add 16
              (up to 600) – add 18
              (up to 775) – add 20
              (775 to 1286) – do not divide by 2, subtract 18
              (up to 1500) – add 45
              (above 2000) – add 24
6th Avenue – subtract 12
7th Avenue – (below 110th) – add 12
              (above 110th) – add 20
8th Avenue – add 10
9th Avenue – add 13
10th Avenue – add 14
Amsterdam – add 60
Broadway above 23rd St – subtract 30
Central Park West – divide full number by 10, add 60
Columbus Avenue – add 60
Lexington Avenue – add 22

Madison Avenue – add 26
Park Avenue – add 35
Riverside Drive – divide full number by 10, add 72
West End Avenue – add 60

To find an address on numbered cross-streets, remember: numbers increase east or west from 5th Avenue, which runs north–south.

Tours

If you just want to orientate yourself in New York, there's no better way than to go up the Empire State or the World Trade Center for bird's-eye views, but if you want to combine orientation with entertainment and information, take a tour. Ask NYCVB (see p.11) for mainstream tours, look in *New York* magazine under 'Other Events' for more esoteric tours, or try one below. Most walking tours are weekends only.

Water

THE CIRCLE LINE FERRY
This is the best way to get a sense of Manhattan as an island. A lively commentary keeps you company for three hours while the boat chugs past some of Manhattan's best and worst, including the Statue of Liberty, Gracie Mansion, the Bronx and Fort Tyron Park. Evening Harbor Lights cruises do the same at sunset. *Pier 83, 12th Ave (at 42nd St). tel. 563 3200; $16 for adults, children under 12 $8.*

Air

ISLAND HELICOPTER SIGHTSEEING
You need money and a strong stomach for this one. The helicopters are victim to unpredictable air currents caused by Manhattan's skyscrapers, but if you can handle the swooping and jiggling, the views are spectacular and the experience is unforgettable. *Tours leave from East 34th St Heliport at East River. Fares $40–$90 depending on the tour. Tel. 718 895 1626 for information.*

Land

GRAY LINE BUS TOUR
If you want to do the Empire State, the Statue of Liberty, the Metropolitan Museum of Art and more all in one day but don't want to bother with public transport, take a Gray Line Bus tour. Gray Line also organises day trips to Atlantic City. *254 W 54th St, tel. 212 397 2620. Prices start at around $20.*

HANSOM CARRIAGE RENTALS
Take a romantic trot round Manhattan in a horse-drawn hansom. *59th St (at 5th Ave), tel. 212 246 0520. $34 for the first 20 minutes then $10 each additional 15 minutes.*

Walking Tours

BIG ONION TOURS

Seth Kamil and Ed O'Donnell's excellent walking tours concentrate on New York's immigrant history. They aim to have tours on free Blacks and women's history up and running by 1993. *Tours average $10, but mention Virago and get a discount. Tel. 662 5512 or 663 8440 or find them through the 92nd St Y (see below).*

HISTORYTOURS WITH JOYCE GOLD

Joyce Gold is a self-styled local historian who does occasional tours that might take in Ladies Mile or Dutch New York. *Tours cost around $10, tel. 242 5762.*

LOWER EAST SIDE TENEMENT MUSEUM

The museum's tours of the Lower East Side, Chinatown and Little Italy are led by academics who are expert at extracting information that entertains and informs. *97 Orchard St (bet. Delancey and Broome Sts), tel. 431 0233. Tours cost around $12.*

NEW YORK CITY DEPARTMENT OF PARKS AND RECREATION

Urban rangers will take you on free educational walks all over the city. *Go to the Dairy in Central Park or tel. 212 860 1353.*

92ND ST Y

This does the most varied and rich range of tours. See the Meat Market, famous disaster sights, or spots that inspired books. Known artists and writers often lead the tours. *Will do customised tours for large groups. Usually costs $8–$10. 1395 Lexington Ave, tel. 415 5599.*

Beyond Central Manhattan

BRONX COUNTY HISTORICAL SOCIETY

If you're determined to see more of the Bronx than the view from the Express bus to the Zoo (see p.226), *don't go alone* but contact the Bronx County Historical Society for details of their occasional tours. *Write to 3309 Bainbridge Ave, Bronx or tel. 718 881 8900.*

BROOKLYN HISTORICAL SOCIETY

If you're nervous about Brooklyn, organised tours are a great way to see it, and if you're expecting burnt-out tenements you'll be surprised. The Brooklyn Historical Society will show you genteel Brooklyn Heights, relaxed Park Slope and more. Gray Line do bus tours of Brooklyn (see above). *128 Pierrepont St, Brooklyn, tel. 718 624 0890. Cost around $8.*

HARLEM SPIRITUALS

Don't go to Harlem alone – take one of these wonderful tours for conventional sights as well as a soul food lunch and a Gospel service. See p.199.

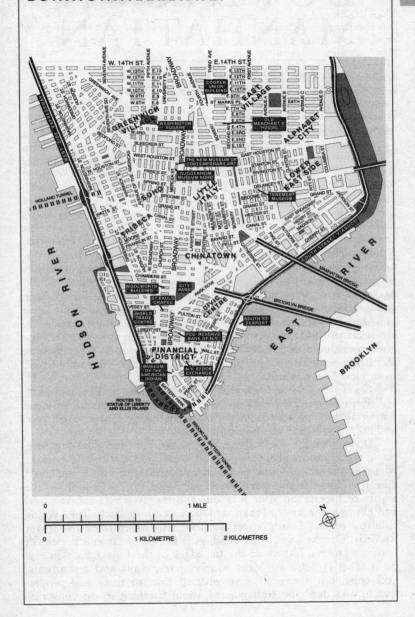

W. 14TH ST. — E.14TH ST.

SEVENTH AVENUE · GREENWICH AVE · FIFTH AVENUE · UNIVERSITY PL · BROADWAY · THIRD AVE · FIRST AVENUE

W.13TH — E.13
W.12TH — E.12
W.11TH — E.11
W.10TH — E.10
W.9TH — E.9
W.8TH — E.8

COOPER
UNION
BUILDING

E.13TH
E.12TH
E.11TH
E.10TH
E.9TH

ST MARKS PL
E.7TH
E.6TH
E.5TH

EAST
VILLAGE

AVENUE A · AVENUE B · AVENUE C · AVENUE D

GREENWICH
VILLAGE

W.3RD

BLEECKER ST.

WASHINGTON
SQUARE

OLD
MERCHANT'S
HOUSE

E.4TH
E.3RD
E.2ND
E.1ST

ALPHABET
CITY

BEDFORD ST.

WEST HOUSTON ST.

BOWERY · SECOND AVE

EAST HOUSTON ST.

LOWER
EAST
SIDE

PRINCE ST.

THE NEW MUSEUM OF
CONTEMPORARY ART

SPRING ST.

GUGGENHEIM
MUSEUM SOHO

PRINCE ST.
SPRING ST.

STANTON ST.
RIVINGTON ST.

COLUMBIA ST.

SOHO

BROOME ST.

DELANCEY ST.

BROOME ST

TENEMENT
MUSEUM

GRAND ST.

LITTLE
ITALY

GRAND ST.
HESTER ST.

EAST BROADWAY

HENRY ST.
MADISON ST.

HUDSON ST.

TRIBECA

WATTS ST.

MOORE ST.
FRANKLIN ST.

CANAL ST.

LAFAYETTE STREET · CENTRE ST · MOTT ST · ELIZABETH ST

CANAL ST.

BAYARD ST.

PELL ST.

CHERRY ST.

SOUTH STREET VIADUCT

HOLLAND TUNNEL

CHURCH ST · BROADWAY

CHAMBERS ST.

CHINATOWN

CATHERINE ST · PIKE ST

EAST
RIVER

HUDSON
RIVER

WOOLWORTH
BUILDING

ST PAULS
CHAPEL

CITY
PARK

PARK ROW

CIVIC
CENTRE

MANHATTAN BRIDGE

VESEY ST.

FULTON ST.

PEARL ST.

SOUTH ST.
SEAPORT.

BROOKLYN BRIDGE

WORLD
TRADE
CENTRE

LIBERTY ST.

FED. RESERVE
BANK OF N.Y.

WALL ST.

FINANCIAL
DISTRICT

MUSEUM
OF THE
AMERICAN
INDIAN

N.Y. STOCK
EXCHANGE

PEARL ST

BROOKLYN

BATTERY PARK

ROUTES TO
STATUE OF LIBERTY
AND ELLIS ISLAND

BROOKLYN BATTERY TUNNEL

0 — 1 MILE

0 — 1 KILOMETRE — 2 KILOMETRES

N

DOWNTOWN MANHATTAN

EVERYTHING BELOW 14TH ST.

Downtowners joke that if you go above 14th Street you get a nosebleed. You can do an alarming variety of things – shop for condoms and olive bread on cherry-tree-lined Bleecker Street; eat pierogis with club kids at 5 a.m. in Loisida's strip-lighted Kiev café; muse over genitals blown up in glorious Technicolor by Jeff Koons or Cindy Sherman at SoHo galleries; eat dim sum Sunday lunchtime in the heart of Chinatown and spend after hours drinking at a go-go bar with truckers; court at a TriBeCa restaurant that serves seafood sausages and champagne; or trawl a Greenwich Village dyke bar where the bouncer's called Freight Train – but whatever you do, make sure it's 'in'. And if you don't know what's 'in', don't worry. Just bluff. The stunning gold-lamé-outfitted NoHo maître d' with black-tape rectangles for eyebrows, the East Village college graduate with a green Mohican, and the dude with his Levis belted *under* his cute ass all have one thing in common: confidence. Do what you like, but do it with a steely look in your eye and, for good measure, a sneer about the B & T crowd, B & T being short for 'Bridge and Tunnel' people, i.e. those who day-trip to the island from New Jersey suburbs.

Good news for women with children: motherhood is definitely 'in'. Even busy restaurants will accommodate you. Single women? Eating alone is *de rigueur*. Take books, notes or a paper with you, and no one will give you a second glance.

Downtown is mainly about bar-, restaurant- and shop-hopping, but it's got good sights too. Top of everyone's list should be Ellis Island's Museum of Immigration. If you can't afford that, you could take the Staten Island ferry round trip, and for 50c you'll see the Statue of Liberty on your way out and the awesome soaring steel and glinting-windowed Financial District coming back. Take young children to the South Street Seaport and older ones to Tower Records. Orchard Street on Sundays is for glitzy tat and knock-off designer jackets, but avoid the far edges of the Lower East Side at night. For TriBeCa or Meat Market bars, clubs and restaurants, take cabs. But above all, give yourself time to relax and people-watch, and don't be embarrassed about listening in on conversations – New Yorkers expect it. The man with the handlebar moustache and leather cap telling his friend about the boy he hit *wants* you to hear too; you could muscle in on the East Village restaurant debate about NYU students having their essays read for Political Correctness; and you'll wince if you overhear plastic surgery stories on a NoHo barstool.

Finally, as New Yorkers will say to you incessantly: Enjoy!

The First American Women   Poor Princess Pocahontas died of pneumonia after being paraded as an exotic Indian at the seventeenth-century court of King James, and in doing so she won the dubious honour of a place in history as one of America's first women. Her non-royal North American sisters in hunting-and-gathering tribes were left out of history books but played active roles in their communities, including leaving their bark-hut homes with the men to trade with Europeans. In 1609 Henry Hudson's first mate recorded an incident in New York Harbour: 'There came eight and twentie Canoes full of men, women and children . . . They brought with them Oysters and Beanes, whereof we bought some.'

The Algonquin tribe, whose women were covered from head to toe with multicoloured tattoos simulating lavish jewellery, was most numerous at first on Manhattan Island. More powerful and longer-lasting were the Iroquois peoples, a confederation of five and later six previously warring tribes which, according to oral tradition, formed about 400 years ago, quite possibly in direct response to the potential threat of European colonisers. Iroquois women held considerable political and economic power. They owned the land and controlled food distribution; all property and titles passed through the female line; and although women could not themselves become 'sachems' (chiefs), they were responsible for hiring them – and firing them. One missionary wrote: 'They did not hesitate, when the occasion required, to "knock off the horns" as it was technically called, from the head of a chief and send him back to the ranks of the warriors.'

By the eighteenth century Iroquois women had abandoned the wrapround deerskin skirts that dangled with porcupine quills in favour of cotton tunics styled at the front like Anglo women's dresses and at the back like the court coats of Anglo male officials. But they still stuck firm to Iroquois culture when it came to division of labour. They wanted Europeans' advice on agriculture, and the Quaker missionaries caused much amusement by trying to teach the men. 'If a Man took hold of a Hoe to use it the Women would get down his gun by way of derision & would laugh & say such a warrior is a timid woman.'

A European Colony   Colonies couldn't grow without child-bearing women, so Niew Amsterdam was judged a *bona fide* colony only when the ratio of women to men was equal, but once there, women were powerless. The system of rights colonists brought with them denied women ownership of property, and no property meant no vote. While Native American women tilled and debated bare-breasted, colonial women were restricted by household duties, bonnets and floor-trailing dresses, and by pregnancies. Native American men had ritually prescribed periods of abstinence and Native American women averaged only four children; European women often had eight or twelve children in quick succession and often died in childbirth.

SOJOURNER TRUTH

Renowned religious mystic and abolitionist who won special awe from peers for travelling over 100 miles cross country in a lumber wagon and living to be 110, Sojourner Truth was born into slavery in New York around 1797. She escaped a year before emancipation was made mandatory in 1828 and became a public speaker with a national reputation. On 9 May 1867 in New York she addressed a hallfull of white women, who had gathered as the First Annual Meeting of the American Equal Rights Association, at a time when 'colored men [had] the right to vote' and women did not. Here is some of her speech, a rare social document that should be read slowly:

'I come from another field – the country of the slave . . . I want it root and branch destroyed . . . There is a great stir about colored men getting their rights, but not a word about the colored women; and if colored men get their rights and not colored women theirs, you see the colored men will be masters over the women, and it will be as bad as it was before . . . White women are a great deal smarter, and know more than colored women, while colored women do not know scarcely anything. They go out washing, which is about as high as a colored woman gets, and their men go about idle, strutting up and down; and when the women come home, they ask for their money and take it all, and then scold because there is no food . . .

'I am above eighty years old; it is about time for me to be going. I have been forty years a slave and forty years free . . . I have done a great deal of work; as much as a man, but did not get so much pay. I used to work in the field and bind grain, keeping up with the cradler; but men doing no more got twice as much pay . . . We do as much, we eat as much, we want as much. I suppose I am about the only colored woman who goes about speaking for the rights of colored women. I want to keep the thing stirring, now that the ice is cracked . . . It is a good consolation to know that when we have got this battle once fought we shall not be coming to you any more. You have been having our rights for so long, that you think, like a slave-holder, that you own us. I know that it is hard for one who has held the reins for so long to give up; it cuts like a knife. It will feel all the better when it closes up again.'

Sojourner Truth ended her address by saying that she had heard a lot of talking since she came, but no singing, so she sang: 'In heaven we shall rest from all our labors; first do all we have to do here . . . I do not mean to stop till I get there, and meet you there too.'

Life in the infant colony, which was contained below what is now Wall Street (see p.59), was precarious, because the Dutch and the English governments were in conflict and using Niew Amsterdam as the rod to beat each other. Predominant architecture changed with governments. In 1625 about 1,000 colonists were in 120 houses built Dutch-style: thin, in brick or wood, with tiled roofs and Dutch gables, served by a windmill and a ditch (now Broad Street). Four decades later the British ruled, the Dutch ditch was filled in, and soon the area was covered with three- and four-storeyed square red-brick Georgian houses such as the Fraunces Tavern (see p.67). Inhabitants must have been almost relieved that the streets at least remained constant: always muddy and roamed by pigs.

Slavery   In 1619 the first shipload of African slaves arrived, and slave markets were set up on Wall Street. Colonists prodded and poked the men and women lined up on a platform. Then there was shouting and gavel-banging, and sales to the highest bidder. A good male slave was strong; a good female was strong and pretty. Later, abolitionists accused masters of breeding slaves like cattle. Women called it rape; masters called it 'strong encouragement' and said the high birth rates among slave women were evidence of high levels of nutrition and good treatment. Husbands and wives, children and parents were split up. Sojourner Truth shared the fate of many slaves in having two daughters and a son sold away from her, but she broke rank by becoming a political orator (see box) – an especially remarkable feat, since as slave and woman she got no formal education.

THE STATUE OF LIBERTY AND ELLIS ISLAND

Circle Line ferries to the Immigration Museum at Ellis Island and the Statue of Liberty leave from Battery Park every half-hour between 9.15 a.m. and 3.30 p.m. (the last ferry will not allow you to see both the statue and the museum). Buy round-trip tickets at Castle Clinton in Battery Park, Manhattan, price $6 for a round trip, $3 for children aged 3–17. Tel. 212 264 8711 or 212 269 5755 for timetable information. Arrive early on a weekday morning if you want to avoid the queues, which can be an hour or more long. Allow at least two hours for the museum and the same for the statue, where there are further queues at the base.

The Statue of Liberty endorses products in advertising campaigns, represents a city and a nation in countless postcards, and symbolises freedom. For some 12 million immigrants arriving at the turn of the century squashed in ships' holds, she was the first glimpse of America. Today 1,500,000 visitors a year climb up inside the 151-ft-high hollow verdigrised copper monument, and the immigrants' arrival is celebrated in a morbidly fascinating museum on nearby Ellis Island.

The queues for the ferry that will take you to the museum and the statue start at the quay beyond Castle Clinton. Sweaty T-shirted Circle Line Ferry employees corral you into lines behind ropes, where you'll be entertained by buskers, who might include an old man sawing with a violin bow at a rusty saw, and hassled by salesmen touting glittered 'I love New York' sweatshirts – canny shoppers should pull the neck elastic to see if it will wash well or go baggy.

The Statue of Liberty

Entrance fee included in Circle Line ferry ticket (see above).

A whole host of people throughout history have been moved by the statue. Nineteenth-century anarchist 'Red Emma' Goldman found that she began to weep when she saw it at dawn in 1886: 'Ah, there she was, the symbol of hope, freedom, opportunity!' Today, camera-snapping tourists and American schoolchildren go to see her out of a bored sense of duty. They're more likely to weep tears of anger at the prices of coffee and pretzels on the boat than wilt at the sight of Liberty.

Construction   The Statue of Liberty was a gift from the French. America had to supply only the base. The logic went like this: since the American Revolution had been inspired by exported French philosophies, the centenary of Independence should be commemorated by a French monument. In France funds were raised by public subscription and a young Alsatian sculptor, Frédéric-Auguste Bartholdi, was commissioned. In 1874 he set to work, starting with a 4-ft-high clay model. On and off for five years his wife posed patiently in his studio, but although the finished product had her body, the face was without a doubt his mother's. In *Monuments and Maidens*, Marina Warner describes Bartholdi's widow mother as grim and overbearing, suggesting that this shows in the finished Statue of Liberty: the mouth is sour and the eyes, with their jutting brows and too-perfect irises, are sinister. While other nineteenth-century female representations of high ideals had swelling breasts and fecund bellies, Bartholdi's was so thoroughly covered in stiff drapes as to be almost androgynous. The hands are mannish, the breasts diminutive, and the styled hair looks like a helmet.

In 1884 the statue was shipped to the States in 214 different crates, but despite threats that it would have to be sent back, America failed to come up with the base. Not until the newspaper magnate Joseph Pulitzer promised to print the names of all donors, whatever the size of their contribution, in the New York *World* was sufficient money forthcoming. After more hitches, which included finding that reassembly left a gap between some of the copper plates (this was adjusted by putting extra struts under Liberty's right armpit), the statue was finally unveiled on 28 October 1886.

Although Bartholdi had chosen a woman to represent 'liberty', women were not allowed to attend the ceremony. While President Grover Cleveland and national and international dignitaries lounged around Liberty's base listening to speeches and toasting one another, a dinghy-full of angry suffragettes rowed out. Their shaking fists were ignored and their shouts were drowned out when foghorns bellowed and 21-gun salutes sounded from nearby batteries as the cover was ripped off the 151-ft-high copper statue. Men tossed their hats in the air, Liberty's torch was lit, and the suffragettes could do nothing but row home again. They were not free to vote for another three decades.

THE POEM ON THE BASE

In 1883 Emma Lazarus felt compelled, in the face of immigrations caused by pogroms in tsarist Russia, to write the poem that was later engraved on the pedestal of the statue. It helped to raise funds:

Here at our sea-washed, sunset gates shall stand
A mighty woman with a torch, whose flame
Is the imprisoned lightning, and her name
Mother of Exiles. From her beacon-hand
Glows world-wide welcome; her mild eyes command
The air-bridged harbour that twin cities frame.
'Keep ancient lands, your storied pomp!' cries she
With silent lips. 'Give me your tired, your poor,
Your huddled masses yearning to breathe free,
The wretched refuse to your teeming shore.
Send these, the homeless, tempest-tost to me,
I lift my lamp beside the golden door.'

The Visit At first, as you stare across the water clutching the ferry railings, Liberty looks as if she's floating stiffly in midair. Only when you've chugged closer is it possible to make out clearly the grey wedding-cake-shaped base, which merges with the trees and earth of the island. As you approach you might consider the intended meanings of Miss Liberty's stance and accessories. The little lumps at her feet are the broken shackles of tyranny she has just trampled with a slightly bent leg; the seven points in her crown signify liberty radiating to the seven continents and the seven seas; and the tablet in her left hand represents the 1776 Declaration of Independence.

When you land, walk along the path, stand at the base and look up. The mother of exiles may not be a work of great artistic merit, but she is *big*. It is impossible to get from any reproduction the sense of how very big she feels when you get there. She weighs in at 225 tons; her right hand raises the symbolic torch 305 ft above sea level; her upstretched arm alone is 42 feet long, and each of her eyes is 2½ feet wide. Prepare for hard work and adverse conditions if you decide to climb to the top.

At the entrance one board warns: 'Two hours from this point', another states that vision from the crown is restricted, and yet another instructs that if you are suffering ill-health, particularly a heart condition, you should not go up at all. From ground to crown is the equivalent of 22 storeys. You can take a lift up the plinth, which cuts down the journey, but there are still 168 steps to go, up two spiral staircases, one inside the other, each wide enough for only one person at a time. It can be hot and claustrophobic. People have died here.

The views of Liberty Park and the Manhattan skyline are more spectacular from the walkway at the top of the plinth than from the crown. Up top it's like being in the bow of a ship, with a projecting curve of small square portholes – small and cloudy and surrounded by metal and rivets – where visitors have to jostle for a limited view.

It is perhaps best not to consider while you are inside that the copper skin is only 2.5 millimetres thick. The wind can shake the structure.

Unfortunately, what goes up must come down. It's a tiring trip. Be sure to save some of your energies for the museum on Ellis Island.

Ellis Island Immigration Museum

Entrance fee included in Circle Line ferry ticket (see above).

Ellis Island was opened as an immigration station on 1 January 1892 to control the quality of new immigrants. If they were judged insane, carriers of contagious diseases, or incapable of supporting themselves while contributing through hard work to the American economy, immigrants were sent back. Many rejects tried in desperation to swim from the island to Manhattan.

Unless you could afford first- or second-class tickets, the transcontinental boat journeys to the New World were hellish. The cheapest option, travelling 'steerage', meant being crammed into the bottom of a steamship for weeks or maybe months, depending on the weather. Conditions were dirty, dark, airless, and if passengers ran out of food, then that was tough. Many died in transit. The lucky few travelling first and second class were questioned at their leisure on the boat and taken direct to Manhattan, while an estimated 16,000,000 immigrants entered the States through Ellis Island before it closed as an immigration station in 1924.

Ellis Island continued to serve through the 1930s as a detention centre for immigrants whose status in America was questioned, and between 1941 and 1954 it was a deportation centre for enemy aliens. It had a brief life as a Coast Guard Station, then in 1954 it closed completely. Photographs show that it was a ghost town until 1984, when a $16,000,000 renovation programme began.

In 1990 a museum opened to 'tell the story of immigration at Ellis Island'. That story is often grim. Although America was known as 'The Land of Promise', Ellis Island was known as 'The Isle of Tears'. After being fumigated, immigrants were subjected to humiliating tests and often separated from their loved ones before finding that Manhattan offered mainly exploitation and tenements. The image conjured up of day-to-day life on Ellis Island is bizarre. A whole staff of tired and overworked doctors, nurses and inspectors lived permanently on the island, removed from the rest of the world, surrounded by water. Steamships might arrive at any time of the day or night, and the island would suddenly be swarming with immigrants – old and young, scared and hysterical. In 1907, the peak year, an average of 3,300 immigrants landed each day. Today, a large proportion of the visitors are American tourists because almost half of all living Americans can trace their roots to an ancestor who came through the Island, and for many a trip to the museum is an emotional retracing of steps.

The Visit   The museum building is a cluster of many-windowed squares and oblongs with four bulbous towers on the main central section. It has been restored to look as it did on completion in 1898. The Circle Line ferry moors at the lawn-flanked path that leads to the main entrance. You walk into what was once the Baggage Room, a large and echoey pillared hall where old suitcases and carpet bags are stacked up in the middle as if awaiting collection. The information desk on the left is where you can rent Audio Tours and collect tickets for the introductory film, which is narrated by Gene Hackman and shows in the ground-floor theatre. The ground floor also houses the gift shop and the fast-food restaurant. If it's sunny, you can eat outside on picnic tables that command views of Manhattan's Financial District on one side and Miss Liberty on the other.

Upstairs, the **Registry Room** is a depressing 17,000-ft space with iron-laced windows that give it the feel of a huge cage. This is where immigrants were channelled into lines by metal railings to register, and then later dined canteen-style from tin bowls.

The **east wing** of the second floor houses the Peak Immigration Years exhibition. Amongst the steamship company posters and outsize black-and-white photos of hollow-eyed steerage passengers, there's a glass case showing pairs of Czech, Chinese and Austrian infants' shoes and telephone stands where you can listen to recordings of immigrants recounting their arrival – for example: 'I will never forget the joy I felt when I saw the tall buildings of New York and the Statue of Liberty after so many dark days on board that crowded ship. There was the symbol of all my dreams – freedom to start out in a new life. Then came Ellis Island. When I landed the noise and commotion were unbelievable. There were so many languages being spoken. The shouting and pushing guards calling out the big numbers on the tags attached to our coats created more noise and confusion. Surely, I felt, the noise surrounding the Tower of Babel could not have been worse.' An old Italian story is printed on the wall: 'Well, I came to America because I heard the streets were paved with gold. When I got here, I found out three things: first, the streets weren't paved with gold; second, they weren't paved at all; and third, I was expected to pave them.'

The **west wing** is a mixture of pristine partitions and gloomy corridors clad in white fissured tiles where the exhibition 'Through America's Gate' illustrates how Ellis Island processed the immigrants. Bent rusty forks and bits of graffitied wall are in Perspex case, and in the Immigrant Aid Societies Room there are displays of Bibles, prayer books and Americanisation tracts brought by representatives of private and social welfare groups – including the Daughters of the American Revolution and the Red Cross – who came to help immigrants adjust to life in America. These lady reformers also brought clothing and money and helped to reclaim lost baggage.

The Mental Testing section contains examples of what look like wooden children's games. They are special tests which were devised to diagnose mental impairment. They were favoured because they did not have to be explained through an interpreter. The cube test, for example, simply required the immigrant to tap a series of cubes in the exact order shown by the doctor. Pauline Notkoff, a Polish Jew who arrived in 1917, recalls: 'They asked us questions. "How much is two and one? How much is two and two?" But the next young girl, also from our city, went and they asked her, "How do you wash stairs, from the top or from the bottom?" She says, "I don't go to America to wash stairs." '

Upstairs on the **third floor** in the 'Silent Voices' section you can see eerie photographs of the building after it was closed down in 1954. Next door, 'Treasures from Home' displays some of the items – religious icons, crockery, dolls – that immigrants brought with them to create a feeling of home in an unfamiliar land. Last stop is the 'Ellis Island Chronicles', which gives a 300-year overview of the island's history. Here visitors who have been totally absorbed in the recorded audio tour, mouthing and gesticulating in silent response to the information being fed into their ears, finally remove the Walkman headphones.

FINANCIAL DISTRICT

Book ahead to see piled slabs of gold behind bars at the Federal Reserve Bank; give children hours of fascination at South Street Seaport museum and boats, then on weekday evenings watch South Street bars turn into slick bankers' pick-up joints; as night draws in, slide up the World Trade Center for the twinkling view of Manhattan and a romantic cocktail.

The mess of tiny winding streets in the mile below Chambers Street has low crooked pre-Revolutionary buildings next to sheer soaring skyscrapers in front of ships' masts and rigging. You know you're near a working fish market because of pungent odours, and you know you're in a business district because pinstripe-suited men have their shoes shined outside Trinity Church and street stalls sell racks of ties, socks, and bumper bags of nuts or sweets as desk-drawer nibbles. Women are still largely excluded from the top echelons of finance, but they're evident on the pavement. Look down and you'll see scattered cards for 'Wall Street's Hottest Topless Bar', featuring Chessie Moore and Candy Cummings.

Low rents have lured finance houses off Wall Street, and fashion has forced beautiful bright sparks into altruism. Banking went out with the 1980s; 'my work for charity' is the dinner-party conversation of the 1990s. As a result, the Financial District is easier to visit. Even in the pouring rain you'll get a cab. Go midday midweek, unless there's a special evening jazz event or boat cruise at the Seaport, and if you wonder how the fraught brokers churning in and out of the New York Stock Exchange spend their leisure time, here's the answer.

Gun Clubs   Golf is passé. The Downtown Rifle and Pistol Club is the place to be seen and let off steam. Senior doctors from several City hospitals like to come here to blast a clipful of Colt .45 bullets into a torso-shaped target. 'The first night I came here,' said one client, Ms Roxy Rifken, 'I had the best night's sleep I've had for months.' Some use it for dating. The club's owner, Michael Zirmo – also a gun dealer – explains: 'The profile of one of our members would be late twenties to early thirties with an income in excess of $100,000. Even if they're not single, they can still meet themselves a honey.'

WALL STREET AND AROUND

Wall Street has been swelled to such mythic proportions that the words can conjure pictures of tickertape reeling out of windows and swarms of cocaine-sniffing champagne-quaffing whizzkids. The real thing is at first an anticlimax. Buildings are 20, not 60 storeys high; two lanes of traffic can barely squeeze through. Wall Street could be mistaken for a side street.

Originally the wood plank wall to the city – built by Dutch Governor Peter Stuyvesant in 1653 to keep Indians out and used by his citizens to prop up their homes or burn in their hearths – Wall Street has, since the middle of the last century, been the financial hub of America, some say the world – and it's had two devastating crashes.

Nightmares on Wall Street   Perhaps the first fiscal crisis came in 1665, when Dutchman Frederick Philipse hoarded barrels of wampum. 'Quahog', bits of Long Island clam shells, was the legal tender or 'wampum' of the colony, and by creating an artificial shortage Philipse ensured that everyone had to buy it from him – at inflated prices. By the middle of the nineteenth century Wall Street was a flourishing financial centre. Coffee shippers and railroad magnates like Jay Gould, Cornelius Vanderbilt and J. Pierpont Morgan needed places to stash their fortunes, so they expanded into banking. In 1893 Senator Orville H. Platt declared: 'We are the most advanced and powerful people on the earth,' showing the same hubris that caused cigar-puffing stockbrokers and bankers in the heady swirling twenties to build, as Alastair Cook described it, 'a mountain of credit on a molehill of actual money'. The tiniest element of doubt could shake the foundations. The DOW Jones Index (the average price taken from a representative selection of stocks) dipped a little – and suddenly everyone was selling. On 23 October 1929 a record 12.9 million shares changed hands. It was mayhem. The superintendent said the brokers on the Stock Exchange floor 'roared like a lot of lions and tigers. They hollered and screamed, they clawed at one another's collars.' On 'Black Tuesday' 650,000 shares in US Steel, the most respectable of 'securities', were dumped on the market in the first three minutes, and collapse was total. The Great Depression began. One popular song, 'Button Up Your Overcoat', went: 'Steer clear of frozen ponds (ooh! ooh!); Peroxide blondes (ooh! ooh!); Stocks and bonds (ooh! ooh!); You'll get a pain, ruin your bankroll.'

Then the same thing happened again. The 1980s saw economic boom. During the Reagan presidency Wall Street added more than 100,000 new jobs to New York's employment roll, and in 1987 the market crashed. One in every five floors of downtown office space became empty.

Today rents remain high for buildings that have tiny elevators and outdated wiring systems. Power failures regularly destroy business. With liberating computer and telecommunications technology, why stay in a squashed bit of island where taxes and crime rates are high? The money men are drifting out of Manhattan's Financial District, some uptown and many to Connecticut. Terms from the Depression have been adopted again, for example 'panhandlers' for the beggars who sell nominal services (like holding a bank door open) or useless objects (broken wind-up toys). Local workers count pennies and go to fast-food pushcarts on Wall Street – restaurants entice with cut-price meals.

MURIEL SIEBERT

In 1967 Muriel Siebert, the daughter of a Cleveland dentist, became New York's 'First Woman of Finance'. She has since won a host of other accolades (first woman to chair the Boy Scouts in 1985; second woman on the London Stock Exchange floor in 1968), but it was her 1967 first that rocked the Establishment. The New York Times reported: 'bubbly and ebullient and fortyish, . . . [Siebert] stands ready to become the first woman member in the 175 year history of the New York Stock Exchange.' It was far from easy. Men mocked her. Before considering her membership the Stock Exchange imposed a new condition: a letter from her bank promising a loan of $300,000 of the near-record $445,000 seat price (a 'seat' is simply the right to buy and sell on the floor). Banks would not lend the money until the Stock Exchange had agreed to admit her. She overcame the double-bind, but not men's prejudice. Her personal fight for equality continued. She helped to found 'Women's Forum' to counter the old boy network (the organisation currently has 225 eminent New York businesswomen members and branches worldwide). In the 1970s Siebert took five years out as a government Superintendent of Banking, and took drastic measures to halt the steep climb of interest rates. She insisted on mergers (which are still regarded with suspicion), she forced one Bank president to cut his salary by $100,000, and then she wryly pointed out to victims that the initials SOB stand not only for 'Superintendent of Banking' but also for 'Son of a Bitch'.

Today in lectures, on talk shows and panels Muriel Siebert still feels that it is necessary to state: 'The men at the top of industry and government should be more willing to risk sharing leadership with women and minority members who are not merely clones of their white male buddies . . . The real risk lies in continuing to do things the way they've always been done.'

Since the New York Stock Exchange went co-ed, progress has been slow. Of the 1,366 seats available, only 40 women have a seat, and most do not own their seat but represent a company. In her airy Madison Avenue office, Muriel Siebert's concentration flits between the fluctuating DOW Jones on the green flickering screen, and her yapping dog on the floor. 'Feisty little thing, isn't he?' she says as the dog shreds a bit of cloth before scampering into the portable box labelled 'Dog Taxi'. She reflects with regret and pride that Siebert & Co. is still the only member firm on her street, or even in New York, that is run by a woman.

Blonde and petite, much as the New York Times described her in the 1960s, Muriel Siebert believes a healthy body keeps a healthy mind. She likes to play tennis at the River Club Tennis House.

26 Wall St (at Nassau St). Open Mon–Fri 9 a.m.–5 p.m. Free.

A Doric temple-style marble box containing a scattering of George Washington memorabilia, this small museum is rather dull, but it stands on the site of New York's first City Hall – which was key to America's fight for independence.

Insurrection   Built in 1699, the first City Hall was English, and a stake was placed out front. Minor offenders were tied to it and publicly flogged. The Hall was also a courthouse and a debtors' prison. The British authorities were, to say the least, wary of dissident voices in this still infant colony. In 1733, John Peter Zenger started the New York *Weekly Journal*. He used it to attack the Governor, and was put in prison for a year. After a high-profile trial at the courthouse, Zenger's acquittal symbolised the beginning of a free press in New York, 50 years before the same was achieved in England.

On 7 October 1765 the 'Stamp Act Congress' met to object to the British Parliament's Stamp Act, which required citizens to attach big blue stamps to items purchased as proof that the tax had been paid. The stamps could cost anything from twopence to £10, and were for necessities and luxuries (newspapers, marriage licences, playing cards). The British were trying to raise money to pay for the cost of maintaining a British army in the colonies. The Congress wrote a 'Declaration of Rights and Grievances', affirming the principle that Americans had the same rights and liberties as Englishmen in England, and could not be taxed without their consent. This signalled the beginning of the fight for independence. The building was reconstructed as a Federal – i.e. American – hall. On 30 April 1789 George Washington of Virginia stood on the second-floor balcony wearing a brown cloth suit featuring silver buttons decorated with spread eagles. He took the oath of office and became the first President of the United States. The present 1842 building was the US Customs House, then after 1862 the home to various government offices, and in 1955 it was designated a National Monument.

New York Stock Exchange

20 Broad St (at Wall St), 3rd floor. Visitors' Gallery open Mon–Fri 9.15 a.m.–4 p.m. Free.

On this 1903 façade Roman deities symbolising commerce romp along a triangular pediment supported by Corinthian columns with a pomposity Pop artist Claes Oldenberg mocked by proposing a corset for the entrance of the Stock Exchange. If he'd had his way, brokers would enter between cut-off thighs below a reinforced elastic stomach panel.

Today you don't enter through pantyhose or Greek columns. You follow an arrow to the 'Visitors' Entrance', which is a glass-and-metal side door.

Security is tight. Prepare to be escorted by a peak-capped guard and have your bags X-rayed before you're let into the small exhibition space. An introductory film helps you make sense of the flashing numbers and scurrying figures you'll see below on the Stock Exchange floor when you squash into the glass-walled visitors' gallery. You won't hear much about the 1929 or 1987 financial crashes in the recorded commentary. The tourist brochures advertise NYSE as 'the Best Regulated Market in the World'. There is a gift shop selling pencils, sweatshirts and NYSE umbrellas.

Chase Manhattan Bank Building

1 Chase Manhattan Plaza (bet. Liberty and Nassau Sts).

Designed by Skidmore, Owings and Merrill, this 1967 glass-and-aluminium box soars in bleak isolation to an awesome 813 ft. Neither its architecture nor its plaza, which has a fountain spurting in the summer, will keep you long, but the corporation inside has significance in America's banking history.

Mr Chase of the title was Salamon P. Chase (1808–73), who is celebrated as the father of the modern banking system because he saw that the hotchpotch of little banks would hold his country back from greatness. As Lincoln's Secretary of the Treasury Chase drafted an 1863 Bill that established for the first time a unified national currency and the present Federal banking system.

Louise Nevelson Plaza

Bounded by Maiden Lane, William and Liberty Sts.

This small sunken triangle features seven spiky brown Louise Nevelson sculptures, eight black stone benches and some limp trees. It is popular with drunks, who lie for warmth in winter over the holes that billow steam from the subway, and at lunchtimes the odd office person comes with sandwiches. Despite its aim – to brighten up a corporate area – Louise Nevelson Plaza is dull or even depressing.

LOUISE NEVELSON

Born in Kiev in 1899, Louise Nevelson arrived in New York with her parents at the age of six. She studied comparative religion and philosophy. After working in Munich with painter Hans Hofmann, she became Diego Rivera's assistant in Mexico City from 1932 to 1938. By the 1950s she was making sculptures out of everyday objects — balustrades, table legs, driftwood formed into cupboards or shelves and screens painted in black, white or gold. The works in the Plaza are examples of her later experiments with metal and glass.

Federal Reserve Bank of New York

Tours of the vaults must be booked at least a week in advance. Write to Public Information Department, Federal Reserve Bank, 33 Liberty Street, NY 10045, or tel. 212 720 6130. Tours 10.30 and 11.30 a.m. and 1.30 and 2.30 p.m. Mon–Fri, closed bank holidays.

Sixty-five per cent of the guards are expert marksmen; the entire building can be shut down in less than 30 seconds; even an unpaid parking ticket disqualifies prospective employees. This is the bankers' bank: it stabilises their separately erratic activities. Its huge iron-gated Ohio sandstone 1924 façade was modelled on the fancy fifteenth-century Italian Renaissance palaces that housed the very wealthiest Florentine banking and merchant families.

The tour takes you to the basement vaults, where you're shown one of the magnesium shoes men have to wear to protect their feet while moving the gold blocks that are actual representations of the balance of trade as it shifts between nations. Upstairs dirty money and counterfeit notes are weeded out of circulation by automated checking machines in glassed-off booths. 'What keeps the workers who feed money in honest?' asks the guide after telling you that the lifespan of the $1 bill is about 18 months and all bills rejected by the machine as counterfeit are sent to the Secret Service. The Reserve Banks operate what is known as 'a buddy system'. If any money goes missing, everyone in the booth is held responsible.

Trinity Church

Broadway (at Wall St).

The inside of Trinity Church is most interesting on a winter week-day lunchtime when its pews are lined with picnicking businessmen and women. They balance their sandwiches under their macs on their knees and flick newspapers guiltily as you pass. Some pews seem empty from a distance, but a bird's-eye view reveals a snoring drunk or hobo. In summer everyone migrates to the shaded, grassy cemetery where Alexander Hamilton, William Bradford and Robert Fulton are buried, Hamilton beneath a small pyramid. Graves of the famous are marked with placards where gravestone inscriptions have worn away.

Built in 1847 by Richard Upjohn with bronze doors by Richard Morris Hunt, the square-towered, bobbly-spired 280-ft building is currently ensconced in scaffolding while restorers strip away layers of coal dust and pollutants to reveal rosy sandstone.

ON YOUR WAY TO SOUTH STREET

Bowling Green

Broadway (at Battery Place).

It's said that on this site Peter Minuit, the first Dutch Governor, bought Manhattan for 60 guilders, the equivalent of $25, from a group of Indians. It was a good deal for the Indians: they didn't own the island in the first place.

In the eighteenth century English colonial gentlemen trimmed it down to a neat oval piece of grass they could play bowls on. No bowls today, but the iron fence around the edge is the original. Only the crowns from the tops of the spikes are missing. They were melted down for cannonballs during the Revolution.

This is another lunching spot for office employees.

George Gustav Heye Center of the National Museum of the American Indian

Between State St and Whitehall St (at Battery Place), tel. 283 2420. Open Tues–Sat 10 a.m.–5 p.m. and Sun 1 p.m.–5 p.m., closed Mon. $3 adults, $2 students and senior citizens, under-7s free. Phone ahead in case the museum has been delayed in its 1993 move from the original 3753 Broadway at 155th St location.

Housed in the landmark US Customs House building, this museum was founded by W. Richard West Jr, a member of the Cheyenne-Arapaho tribe, to 'change forever the way people view Native peoples of this hemisphere'. It boasts 'the finest collection of American Indian artifacts in the world' and it's a *living* museum, which means that American Indians continue to influence and contribute to exhibitions. The museum represents native peoples from all over the Americas and the West Indies. Highlights of the exhibits from tribes of the eastern woodlands and the northern plateau regions include

Iroquois silver jewellery and beadwork, wampum (shell) belts, the feather bonnet worn by Crazy Horse, moosehair embroidery and 'Van Cortlandt Suit', one of the oldest existing deerskin garments made by the Native Americans of New York.

Shrine of Saint Elizabeth Bayley Seton Rectory

7–8 State St (at Water St).

This was once the house of Elizabeth Ann Seton, America's first-born saint; it is now a working chapel founded by the Catholic Daughters of America. You have to look quite hard in the brick-work of this restored eighteenth-century Georgian house to find the plaque to Mother Seton, who lived here with her husband in 1801 before moving to Maryland, where she founded a religious community.

ELIZABETH ANN SETON

Elizabeth Ann Seton was canonised in 1975 for rather Thatcherite reasons. The Pope stressed that Seton's 'extraordinary contributions' as wife, mother and widow should be examples to future generations of American women. He almost forgot to mention her claimed miracles: cures of a case of leukaemia and severe meningitis.

Eliza was born in New York in 1774. After her mother died three years later she was raised by her Episcopalian doctor father, who was famous worldwide for discovering the cure for croup. Dr Bayley was worried by the new spirit of independence in America's youth, noted Eliza's biographer, the Reverend White, in 1852; he went on, with obvious approval: 'Convinced that a "brilliant character is not always a solid character," [Dr Bayley] diligently impressed upon the minds of those under his charge the necessity of self-restraint, reflection and curtailment of pleasure.'

Eliza lapped it up. Soon a fervent frequenter of the Protestant Episcopal Church, she possessed every facility (good looks and charm) 'for mingling in the amuse-ments and dissipation of the world'. But at eighteen, petite and vivacious Eliza was diligently avoiding such frivolities as men and parties. She noted in her diary: 'There is a certain temper I am sometimes subject to, it is not sullenness or absolute discontent, 'tis a kind of melancholy' which, she concluded, she liked 'bet-ter than those effusions of cheerfulness, that hilarity of spirits, which a good night's rest and fine morning often inspire'.

At twenty she agreed to marry William Magee Seton, a rich, witty merchant. They started a family. Eliza imparted to her offspring the knowledge and fear of God, believing that 'the rod and the reproof give wisdom, but the child that is left to his own will bringeth his mother to shame.' She went on errands of mercy to help the poor.

In the summer of 1794, Eliza had written to a friend: 'We are not always to have what we like best in this world, thank Heaven!' By 1800 she had got more than she bargained for. Magee Seton ran into financial trouble. In 1801 her beloved father died. In 1803 her delicate husband's health deteriorated. Mr and Mrs Seton deposited four of their children with relatives and took the youngest with them on a round-the-world voyage, in the hope that sea air would aid Magee's recovery. He contracted yellow fever on board and died. He was interred in Florence, where Eliza had her first real brush with Catholicism: ritual, wax tapers, heavenly music, gold, damask and Indian tapestry. She loved it. On her return to Protestant America, she converted: 'At last God is mine and I am his.' On 9 June 1808, the model mother packed her sons off to college and took her three daughters to Baltimore, where she founded an Order based on the rule of Vincent de Paul, devoted to helping the poor. Today, it is one of the largest and most influential orders in America. Eliza died a nun in 1821.

Fraunces Tavern

54 Pearl St (at Broad St). Open 10 a.m.–4 p.m., Sun noon to 5 p.m.; closed Sat and major holidays. Museum has free admission Mon–Fri 10 a.m. to noon; other times contribution suggested.

This is primarily a bar and restaurant with a small museum attached. The colonial menu and faux historic surroundings attract bankers entertaining foreign clients for lunch. The museum upstairs attracts hardly anyone, but the scant period artefacts, which include rather nice wallpaper depicting scenes from the Revolution, are worth a brief look.

A handsome red-brick 1719 house that became a tavern under Samuel Fraunces in 1762, here Washington spent his last ten days before being sworn in as President of the new country in 1789.

SOUTH STREET SEAPORT

This 11-block historic district only narrowly missed demolition in the 1960s thanks to a group of concerned citizens led by architect-critic Ada Louise Huxtable, who warned in her book, *Classic New York*, that New York's waterfront heritage was at stake. Through the eighteenth and nineteenth centuries this thriving port area was crucial to New York's and America's economy, but the counting-houses, ships' chandlers and warehouses were left to rot when shipping moved to deepwater piers in the Hudson. Now the South Street Seaport comprises Museum Block, The Fulton Market Building and Pier 17.

Bounded by Fulton, Front, Beekman and Water Sts. Open daily 10 a.m.–5 p.m. and 4 July–Labor Day till 6 p.m. Entry to area free; all-inclusive admission to exhibits $6, $5 senior citizens and students, and $3 under-12s. Tel. 212 669 9400 for information.

This is an 'open museum', which means that everything, from cobbled streets to shops and ships as well as a scattering of museums and galleries, is an exhibit. A culture–commerce mix has been encouraged ever since J.B. Hightower, the museum's president in the 1970s, said: 'The fact is that shopping is now the chief cultural activity in the United States.' Curators hope that twee stores – such as Captain Hooks, Laura Ashley and Body Shop – will lure punters into educating museum spaces. Go first to the **Visitors' Centre** at 14 Fulton St to pick up information leaflets and buy tickets.

The long list of Museum Sites includes the **Children's Centre**, which has hands-on marine theme exhibits (check out weekend and after-school workshops, when parents can leave children). At **Bowne and Company Stationers** you can operate a nineteenth-century printing press. See sailors' bunks and a film on **The Peking**, a barque which carried guano between South America and Europe at the beginning of the century, and is now one of the small fleet of historic vessels on Piers 15 and 16. For an extra $12 (or $11 for senior citizens, $10 for students and $6 for children aged 2–12) board the replica nineteenth-century paddlewheeler **Andrew Fletcher** or steamboat **De Witt Clinton** for a sightseeing **Seaport Line Harbor Cruise** (tel. 212 233 4800 for information about special cruises, which include some with disc jockeys, 'Fireworks Music' and 'Holiday Cocktail').

Finally, go beyond the little hexagonal green huts selling postcards to the end of the wood plank Pier 16 that stretches 400 ft into the Hudson, just to feel the sea breeze in your hair before burrowing back into Manhattan.

Fulton Fishmarket

Fulton St (at Water St). The market operates between midnight and 8 a.m. Catch the end at 8 a.m. or take a tour for $10 on the first and third Thursday of every month at 6 a.m. (reservations necessary – tel. 212 669 9416).

This is the most workaday part of the district. Turn up early and you'll see men in rubber gloves tossing red snappers from ice-packed polystyrene boxes into old brass scales in front of fading red-brick warehouses with peeling painted fronts reading 'oysters and clams', 'fresh salt and smoked fish'. What you won't see is the racketeering.

The nation's largest fish market, with annual business of more than $1 billion, has since the 1930s been victim to labour rackets, extortion and loan-sharking by the Genovese and Bonanno organised-crime families. Fish buyers pay unlicensed loaders hefty parking fees – or get clubbed with dock hooks and have their trucks wrecked. One North Carolina seafood supplier stopped doing business at the market because a wholesaler pulled out a gun when the supplier came to collect a bill. The City is currently being begged to fill the law enforcement vacuum.

Pier 17 Pavilion

Off South St (at Fulton St).

Pier 17 is basically a shopping mall – a clean, safe stretch of shops and eateries set apart only by a riverside promenade and views of ships for atmosphere. American high-school kids devour pizzas and buckets of soda.

OVER TO THE WORLD TRADE

Enter World Trade Center Plaza and you'll see rows of fold-out rickety chess and backgammon tables. Year in, year out the Plaza hosts a gang of chess-master hustlers, and on Tuesdays and Thursdays the city's Greenmarket, when farmers in wellies and caps sell maple syrup and Catskills Bulich mushrooms.

World Trade Center

Church St (bet. Liberty and Vesey Sts).

Come up for the view – touted as one of the best in the world – which costs $3.50 from the 107th-floor observation deck (9.30 a.m.–9.30 p.m. daily), or the price of a drink from the Windows of the World bar at the top of 1WTC. If you choose the observation deck, which is best at the end of the day when crowds are smaller, go to the open-air rooftop if it's not closed due to bad weather. Even the planes are below you. As you clutch your stomach, consider the gap between the towers. Philippe Petit once walked a tightrope between them.

What's it for? The instantly recognisable 110-storey steel-and-glass twin towers are part of the five-building 1966 World Trade

Center (designed by Minoru Yamasaki and Associates and Emery Roth and Sons), which has been called a 'United Nations of Commerce'. International business services including freight forwarders, Custom House brokers, federal, state and overseas development agencies occupy office space here. There's a hotel for business travellers, and the 50,000 people who work in the complex are serviced by a labyrinthine 8 acres of concourse-level shops, which can be alienating and confusing. Throughout the day crowds of impatient, elbowing Center employees heave down the slippery passages, which are eerily empty at night.

Battery Park City

West St (bet. Liberty and Vesey Sts).

A million cubic yards of earth and rock was dug out for the World Trade Center's foundations and then dumped in the Hudson, expanding Manhattan Island by 92 acres of landfill. Battery Park City was built on top. Battery Park was begun in 1979 by Cooper, Eckstut Associates as a complex of office blocks and luxury apartments with 10% of housing set aside for low-income groups, but as the City went into recession the 10%-for-poor-people idea was scrapped. Instead the City has promised to invest just under half of the $1 billion it hopes to receive in profits into philanthropic housing schemes. It is still not complete, and given the current Depression, profit seems unlikely.

Much of Battery Park is still a building site, and much is 'No Entry' private residential. You could, however, take a walk along the 1.2-mile-long Esplanade, which is dotted with Victorian-style cast-iron benches and olde worlde lampposts, and has a great view of the New Jersey shore.

Finish off at the Winter Garden, a glass dome filled with 45-ft palm trees and shops, and a good if pricey restaurant, Le Pactole, for Sunday brunch.

TRIBECA

Standing on the corner of Greenwich and Harrison Streets, wind whistles under corrugated metal awnings, a wary jogger passes, Debra Winger scurries across cobbles into a bar that has no name: you're in the heart of TriBeCa (the Triangle Below Canal). It's dull during the day. Come at night, by cab, for groovy bars and swish restaurants (see p.256).

TriBeCa housed light industry until recently (a lot of egg and cheese depots). In the 1980s real-estate sharks saw a new SoHo, but they inflated prices before yuppies had moved in – and then recession bit. Now only earners in the league of MTV's CEO (Chief

Executive Officer) can afford those luxury lofts behind bleak warehouse doors. TriBeCa has been left rather in limbo. It has a school, and the Greenwich Street red-brick multistorey with a medical centre at the bottom is middle-income housing. A handful of brave gallery owners have opened, and the former Martinson Coffee warehouse houses Robert De Niro's restaurant and film production centre (tenants include Steven Spielberg, Martin Scorsese and Brian dePalma). But there are few shops – a natural food supermarket, a run-down glass-cutter's, a couple of delis – so TriBeCa, while feeling safe, lacks the appeal of streetlife. For women with children, though, it's worth a trip for Washington Market Park, which is clean, safe and great fun for youngsters, and for Just Kidding, 22 Harrison St, between Staple St and Hudson St, a shop which makes cotton hand-printed clothes in the basement and has a children's play area in the back.

SoHo
'SoHo' stands for 'South of Houston' (pronounced Howston).

Two 'very SoHo' hang-outs are on Prince Street, and both serve coffee. Absorb SoHo either perched on one of Jerry's restaurant's zebra-skin bar stools (see p.258) or beneath the palms and whirring fans of Dean and Delucca café (see p.257), and at the same time draw up a shop and art gallery hit list.

Weekdays midday, Agnès B-suited gallery-owners behind Ray Bans take swift arrugula salad lunches; elaborately coiffured staff of *the* coolest designer clothes stores clatter to work in stack heels and expensively antiqued leather jackets; the few artists who held on to industrial loft spaces stumble out on to metal steps for breakfast, grumbling about the grinding diggers and workmen busy recobbling the streets. Yes, *recobbling* the streets, to make it quaint, for at weekends SoHo swarms with tourists, including suburban day-trippers (the B & T crowd) buying up art for their Hamptons mansions. The shop and gallery opening hours say it all: generally not open till noon, closed Mondays, open Sundays till 7 or 8 p.m. Many of the shops are indistinguishable from galleries. One imports nouveaux French velvet furniture, another specialises in Wurlitzers, a shoe shop has more chandeliers and sponged Greek pillars than shoes, and Enchanted Forest – a children's shop – is in the City's *Gallery Guide*.

Use the *Gallery Guide* listings (free from any gallery) to help decide which shows you want to see, and read *Art Forum*, *October*, and the *Village Voice* for current reviews and listings. Despite the recession, new galleries are opening all the time. Below are some examples of what you might find.

SoHo Gallery Trail A handful of streets in tiny SoHo are the nerve centre of the international art market. The strip called the

Broadway Gallery Buildings (594 to 560 Broadway) is typical. Number 560 alone houses 15 galleries. Peer at the plaques outside, slide up in the elevator and step into immaculate, airy gallery spaces where the reminders of industrial origins – pipes bursting through floorboards to lace ornate tin ceilings – are painted out white. Through wide windows look for Chinese sweatshops next to primal-scream workshops in neighbouring lofts. As for the art shows, you might be required to participate. Maybe you'll have to don galoshes to enter a dark water- and incense-filled tent, or perhaps you'll find that the prim 'docent' (gallery guide) who is gradually subverting her talk is both exhibit and artist, Andrea Fraser. And you're likely to see graphic sexual images.

If the **Max Protech Gallery** (560 Broadway) is showing **Marilyn Minter**, a sign at the door will warn that her work is explicit. Minter, who keeps a 'five-foot-high' stack of porn in her studio as source material, aims to make 'sex-positive imagery' to help women 'own their own sexual representation'.

Cindy Sherman makes no comments, but her gallery, **Metro Pictures** (150 Greene St), may also have a warning at the door. Best known for 'film stills' in which she poses as heroine in imagined 1950s or 1960s B-movies, Sherman has recently been photographing oversized medical-supply companies' plastic and rubber body parts (most prominently, genitals) in luridly lighted sexually explicit poses.

The **Paula Cooper Gallery** (155 Wooster) stable includes lesbian and AIDS activist **Zoe Leonard**, and **Pat Hearn** at 39 Wooster has **Julie Scher**, who makes lesbian s/m installations.

Mary Boone at 417 W Broadway has been well established since the 1970s, when she 'discovered' Barbara Kruger, who is best known for her blown-up, severely cropped photographs of women with a short accompanying text: 'I shop therefore I am', or 'Your gaze hits the side of my face'. Boone and Illeana Sonnabend, who runs a gallery practically opposite, are often criticised for being aggressive self-seekers interested only in big money and fame with no policy for promoting women artists. **Sonnabend** *(420 W Broadway)* is associated with the mid-eighties 'Neo-Geo' movement, and in particular with artist Jeff Koons. Koons's recent work has been kitsch, much-bigger-than-life-size Technicolor photos of himself and his wife, the Italian porn-queen-turned-politician Cicciolina, having sex. He is praised by some for pulling the rug from under the art world; others say his stance of amorality becomes immorality by default. Sonnabend is Leo Castelli's wife. Castelli, 'Mr Pop', whose gallery is in the same building as Sonnabend's, is associated with the rise of artists including Andy Warhol, Jasper Johns and Robert Rauschenberg. Research has shown that in 30 years of dealing, only two women artists have passed through Castelli's hands. The research was done by a group called the Guerrilla Girls.

The Guerrilla Girls Since the 1970s the Guerrilla Girls have been pasting up posters all over SoHo which graphically and statistically document sexism and racism in New York galleries. One listed 'The Advantages of Being a Woman Artist'. These include: 'Working without the pressures of success . . . Having an escape from the art world in your 4 free-lance jobs . . . Knowing your career might pick up after you're eighty . . . Not having to choke on those big cigars or paint in Italian suits . . . Being included in revised versions of art history . . . Not having to undergo the embarrassment of being called a genius.' The Guerrilla Girls are anonymous, but it is said that most women artists working in New York today are or have been involved. Look out for their activities.

Cast-Iron Buildings As you walk round SoHo, take time every so often to knock on a wall. If it looks like stone but rings like metal, you've found a cast-iron building.

The Cast-Iron Building, an architectural phenomenon that is unique to New York and thought by many to be America's only contribution to nineteenth-century architecture, was perfect for factories – quick and easy. They sprung up all over SoHo. Prefabricated sheets of moulded iron were mass-produced and fitted together on site, rather like Airfix kits. Once painted they required little upkeep. Floors were supported by iron beams instead of massive, space-consuming walls. And the fun part was that developers could do almost any architectural style. The Italian Renaissance, the French Second Empire and Ancient Greece were favourites. Mad mixtures of fluted columns, pilasters, elaborate cornices and balustrades decorated factory fronts. The cast-iron façades often imitate stone so successfully that they can be easy to miss. On the more decrepit specimens, rust and flaking paint are a giveaway. The **Haughwout Building** (at 488 Broadway) is a classic example. It's built to look like a Venetian palace – the pattern of arches flanked by columns is repeated 92 times down the length of the building, which is run-down and houses a Fabrics Mill outlet.

In the nineteenth century SoHo was known as Hell's Hundred Acres because flammable materials and machinery sparks in warehouses so often combined to cause devastating fires. By the 1960s light industry had moved out and artists took over the cheap loft space. Developers soon sniffed big bucks, but the City stepped in and named SoHo a protected National Historic District in 1973.

Most of the buildings between Canal and Grand Streets and most of the buildings between Grand and Broome Streets on the West Side have façades in cast iron built between 1869 and 1895.

Guggenheim Museum SoHo

575 Broadway (at Prince St), tel. 423 3500 or 423 3600. Open Sun, Mon and Wed 11 a.m.–6 p.m.; Thurs–Sat 11 a.m.–10 p.m.; closed Tues. Adm. $5; $3 senior citizens and students; under-12s free.

The 1992 6-storey SoHo Guggenheim branch, founded to show a mixture of newly commissioned shows and exhibitions from the Guggenheim permanent collection, is housed in a classic 1881 Landmark Cast-Iron building. Its four grey floorboarded gallery spaces are punctuated by cast-iron pillars. The Mercer Street entrance leads directly into the museum space – it's the Broadway entrance that's special: go through the glossy museum store to a blackened raw steel bridge, flanked with stainless steel cables, that crosses to the galleries above the cellar that holds the Club QI tea-room, which is accessible by a triangular stairway down a frosted-mirror wall.

Museum of Holography

11 Mercer St (bet. Canal and Grand Sts). Open daily 11 a.m.–6 p.m, tel. 212 925 0581. Admission $3, under-12s free.

The gift shop is more exciting than the exhibition space, which has teetering chipboard partitions and a peeling tile floor. The museum was founded in 1976 to explore holography – that is: 3-D images recorded by laser light – as a science. *Holo* means whole and *gram* means message. The generally small exhibits are installed at national height level. Tall people have to stoop; small people must jump or stand on tiptoe. If you are interested in holography, it's a must; otherwise, skip it.

The New Museum of Contemporary Art

583 Broadway (bet. Prince and Houston Sts). Open Wed, Thurs and Sun noon to 6 p.m.; Fri and Sat noon to 8 p.m.; Mon and Tues closed. Suggested admission $3.50 or $2.50 artists/students/senior citizens. Members and children under 12 free.

Founded by Marcia Tucker in 1977, the museum aims to give struggling living artists leg-ups into the art Establishment. It is proud to have introduced, through its regularly changing exhibitions, now famous (and infamous) figures including Keith Haring. The museum also commissions 'window projects'. Jeff Koons did one in 1980, and in 1991 passers-by saw a collaboration called 'Love for Sale;

Free Condoms Inside' by Gran Fury and PONY (Prostitutes of New York).

LITTLE ITALY

If you think Little Italy's going to be full of machine-gun-toting gangsters in spats and opera stars leaping on café chairs to sing impromptu arias, prepare to be disappointed. As soon as the 1870s influx of labourers and peasants from Southern Italy and Sicily who clustered around Mulberry and Elizabeth Streets had made enough money in the construction trade, they moved to suburban Queens. Today on Mulberry around Grand Street you can buy 'Hug me, I'm 1/2 Italian' t-shirts or gaudy plaster Madonnas in the Little Italy gift shop, you can pay over the odds for a coffee laced with anisette, but you'll have to fight through busloads of camera-laden tourists, and you'll see mostly Chinese sweatshops through the windows of the 6-storey red-brick blocks zigzagged with fire escapes, for Little Italy is fast being swallowed up by Chinatown. Even the legendary Italian Mafia, is reportedly dying out, and the real power is said to lie with Vietnamese gangs, which are known as 'Triads' and have names like 'the Green Dragons'. Women have little place in this underground world of racketeering and extortion. The mid 1980s to 1990s FBI crackdown put Italian Mafia trials in the headlines and nearly all the 'capos', or 'captains', behind bars. Although it seems unlikely that wives, daughters and mistresses know nothing, they were rarely required to give evidence in court. They appear in mourning at funerals, and – since compassion is a required virtue of any aspiring Mafia member – they are apparently often given consolation money by the man who bereaved them.

You'll find the last remains of Little Italy on Mulberry Street around Grand Street. The best time to visit is during a festival (see p.4), when nights twinkle with fairy lights, life-size cutouts of the Virgin Mary are paraded down Mulberry Street, and the air fills with smells of fried pastries. Otherwise you can only laze with a coffee in a café or look at the outside of the Banca Stabile.

The Banca Stabile

189 Grand St (SW corner Mulberry St).

This was established in 1885 as a family bank. It has been kept as it was: tin ceilings, terrazzo floors, oscillating electric fans, bare-bulb incandescent fixtures. The son of the last owner maintains the relic while conducting a real-estate business from the offices.

CHINATOWN

Come to Chinatown for the atmosphere and to eat. On the main thoroughfares, Pell, Mott and Bayard Streets, shop windows display high-collared brocade dresses, jade figurines, swinging racks of whole red wind-dried ducks and tanks where bearded fish swim. Liquor stores sell cordials medicated with snakeskin and tiger bone; wooden boxes stacked up on the pavement contain Chinese cabbage, blanched beansprouts and fibrous brown lily roots; the telephone booths have pagoda roofs; and the street signs are in Chinese characters. It is also one of the few areas in Manhattan where people cluster round shops and street corners instead of marching purposefully from A to B. Street stalls hawk cut-price seasonal fruit and two crouched old women, one hunchbacked, both wearing hairbands and Chinese slippers, do card readings from a stall's cast-off vegetable boxes.

The Chinese New Year is held on the first full moon after the 19th of January: dragons dance down the street and firecrackers chase evil spirits away. Whatever the season, it's worth coming for an evening meal or dim sum, the long lunch – traditionally on a Sunday – in which baskets of steamed pastry parcels and fish balls pile up on the table as the day drifts into evening. The restaurants are used by the Chinese community and are consequently authentic, clean and reasonably priced. Choose one from the restaurants section, or simply walk into any that takes your fancy. There are few tourist traps.

From Gold Fields to Chinatown   In the 1850s Chinese immigrants who had planned to make their fortunes building the intercontinental railroad and digging in the California gold fields ran out of jobs. Many travelled east to New York, intending to stay only long enough to earn their passage home. Few managed. By the 1880s the Italians had been eased out of the Pell/Mott Street area and a 10,000-strong, initially almost entirely male and always insular Chinese community had been established, which preserved the religious and cultural customs of old China. Mixed marriages and American citizenship were frowned upon, and rival underground societies called 'tongs' formed. The six major tongs served many legal functions to their members, but they were better known for gambling raids, opium smuggling, white slavery rings, and for their bloody feuds: the Tong Wars. The tong violence prompted the City to bar further Chinese settlers in 1882 with the Chinese Exclusion Act.

Around the early 1900s, New Yorkers dared not enter Chinatown, until in 1913 the *Brooklyn Daily Eagle* commissioned bohemian journalist Djuna Barnes to explode the myth. She wrote of her preconceptions – crooked streets 'lit with blood-red lanterns'; 'heavy curtained rooms where half-dead little bundles of yellow bone and skin sucked the pipe' – and she described her disappointment. Instead of chop suey, she was served American food.

It was only in 1965 that the immigration laws were relaxed and Chinese could flood in legally again. Mainly women came this time, providing a large, unskilled and exploitable workforce. The midtown garment industry was flagging and entrepreneurs seized the opportunity to set up vast sweatshops. There are more than three hundred. Workers are responsible for breakages of needles; their employers collect 'tax' from their below-minimum wages and pocket it; women doing piecework are paid 17c per inner seam on suits that are sold for hundreds of dollars at Saks on Fifth Avenue.

'There is no Chinatown', declared Djuna Barnes in a 1913 article. She must have missed it. Today journalists fight to get to the *real* Chinatown and report excitedly on New York-born women in their nineties who have not once in their lives spoken American or set foot outside Chinatown. There are still flophouses where men rent a dormitory bed for a dollar a night and keep millions stashed in a shoebox ready for the day they return rich to their homeland. The devout arrange for their remains to be sent back: first buried in America (complete with identification tag in casket), the decayed corpse is dug up ten years later, removed to a zinc-lined box two feet by one, and shipped to China for reburial at a fraction of the freight cost.

Things to Seek Out The 1977 **Wall of Respect** mural at the Bowery–Hester Street junction, painted for the Working People of Chinatown, has a fire-breathing dragon intertwined with a gambler, a sweatshop machinist, a man with a wok and a youth smashing a window. In Chatham Square there's a branch of the **Manhattan Savings Bank** built to resemble a Chinese temple, and **Confucius Plaza** is named for the great Chinese philosopher. A darker chapter of Chinese history is remembered at the bend in Doyers Street, which is known as the **Bloody Angle**. It was here that opium dealers would lure their competitors and ambush them beyond the blind turn. In the 1900s Doyers Street was the site of a vicious battle between the henchmen of the Hip Sing Tong, led by the gambler Mock Duck, and the On Leong Tong, captained by Tom Lee, for control of a lucrative gambling racket.

Finally, a word of warning if you've a mind to shop in Chinatown: store-keepers may speak only Chinese. One tourist thought she was buying a turtle as a pet for her daughter. She was in a food shop. Before she could object, the shopkeeper had chopped the turtle's head off, wrapped the body in newspaper and popped it in her basket.

CIVIC CENTER AND BROOKLYN BRIDGE

Except for the kitsch Woolworth's building, the Brooklyn Bridge and Century 21 discount designer store (see p.323), there's little to lure you into the Civic Center, which is a workaday bird-shit-splattered area in which pompous pollution-chewed neo-classical piles sit between dull skyscrapers in choked streets lined with cigar-tobacco booths and cheap electronic goods stores. Don't, however, miss a walk at sunset across the raised central boardwalk of the Brooklyn Suspension Bridge when the skylines of Manhattan glow red through the filigree of cables. On your way across you should watch out for speed-freak cyclists and marathon runners and could end your day sipping cocktails in the bar of the barge River Café (see p.281).

The area is of general interest as the present seat of local government, and it is infamous as the nineteenth-century stamping ground of Tammany Hall's 'Tweed Ring'.

Foundations of Local Government – 'Bossism' Throughout the 1860s and 1870s City Hall and nearby Tammany Hall (once on the corner of Frankfort Street and Park Row) formed the base for power-freak 'Boss' Tweed and his greedy cohorts, known together as the 'Tweed Ring'.

Tammany, which was founded in 1789, started as a social organisation. New immigrants played an essential part in its development as a political machine. The City had a number of practical needs – sewers, street lighting, police, roads, prisons – and citizens looked to politicians to sort them out. America, a relatively new country, was still experimenting with solutions. 'Bossism' was one of the earliest.

Each City ward had its own boss, who gained votes by foul means more often than fair. Boss George Plunkitt explained his strategy at the beginning of this century: 'I know every man, woman, and child in the Fifteenth District . . . and I reach them by approachin' the right side. For instance, here's how I gather in the young men . . . [a] young feller gains a reputation as a baseball player in a vacant lot. I bring him into our baseball club. That fixes him. You'll find him workin' for my ticket at the polls next election day . . . I rope them all in by givin' them opportunities to show themselves off. I don't trouble them with political arguments. I just study human nature and act accordin'.'

Bosses looked after the interests of the immigrants especially carefully. By hurrying through their citizenship, bosses secured a large number of votes. Plunkitt said: 'The poor are the most grateful people in the world, and, let me tell you, they have more friends in their neighbourhoods than the rich have in theirs.' When fires broke out in slums, the Bosses were first on the scene, weeping and offering condolences. Meanwhile, Tammany Hall was accepting payoffs from landlords to wink at precisely the breaches in regulations that encouraged fires in the first place. Women did badly out of the Bosses – many of them worked in the factories which had such appalling conditions – but then women could not vote. They were no use to the Bosses.

Many of the immigrants were Irish, and many Irish came to prominent positions in the Tweed ring. 'The Irish was born to rule', said Plunkitt.

Plunkitt was a canny operator, but he never gained infamy equal to that of the super-Boss, William Marcy Tweed, who began his rise to power in 1848 and compounded his reputation for corruption with acts that included pocketing $10 million of the $14 million it cost to build 'Tweed' Courthouse (40 Center St at Foley St). One carpenter was paid $360,747 for a month's work, and a plasterer received nearly $3,000,000 for less than a year's work. In all, Marcy Tweed's dirty dealings cost the city around $100 million, and that's a conservative estimate.

Boss Tweed came a cropper after 1873 attacks by cartoonist Thomas Nast in *Harper's Weekly* and died in his own prison three years later. Corruption, however, did not die with him. Mayor Ed Koch (elected 1978) was almost respected for reputedly dubious carry-ons in the Tammany tradition, and his successor, Mayor David Dinkins (elected 1989) – the city's first black mayor – fell foul of New York citizens for refusing to pander to the media. Dinkins has answered to the needs of the black, Hispanic, and lesbian and gay community both by offering employment and by forming sympathetic policies (see p.25 on the Department for Lesbian and Gay Affairs). More and more the people's mayor, he can sometimes be spotted sipping coffee in Ellen's greasy Café and Bakeshop (see p.255).

The Civic Buildings

In summer, City Park (Murray St bet. Broadway and Park Row) is a hive of activity, a foot-tapping jazz quartet playing next to a man calling himself the first black rap ventriloquist next to a hunched-up woman selling knock-off perfume to a grateful lunchtime or coffee-break Civic Center crowd. In winter, however, the park is a gloomy spread of browning grass and trees that look rather the worse for pollution, white-dappled and thin-leaved, a far cry from when it was the City's common ground and covered with apple trees. The two most accessible buildings are **City Hall** and the **County Courthouse**. The 1812 stodgy mini-Château (Murray St between Broadway and Park Row) is the city's third City Hall. The Dutch had theirs in a tavern on Pearl Street, the English built a grander one on the present site of the Federal Hall National Memorial (see p.62), and today's was built for about half a million dollars with a light-filled, wrought-iron-balconied **Rotunda** inside (open Mon–Fri 10 a.m.–4 p.m.) that has been used for receiving kings, poets and astronauts. When enough staff are available, it is possible – but not riveting – to visit the **Governor's Room,** which houses a small portrait gallery and a museum which has George Washington's writing desk. The New York County Courthouse (52 Chambers St [bet. Broadway and Center Sts]) is a hexagon-shaped lump with a Corinthian colonnade that has Roosevelt-commissioned WPA murals inside (open Mon–Fri 9 a.m.–5 p.m.) illustrating the history of justice (these have been sealed off for cleaning, but are due to reopen soon).

The Woolworth Building

233 Broadway (bet. Barclay St and Park Place).

This intricately detailed 800-ft Gothic extravaganza was made to house Mr. Woolworth's humble five-and-dime store. Woolworth, once a farm boy, showed uncanny foresight. His 1913 tower, designed by Cass Gilbert, was built at a time of boom and economic hubris, yet his store could have been custom-made for the 1929 Crash and ensuing Great Depression. Household basics on Woolworth's shelves cost either 5c or 10c, and there was strictly no credit.

F.W. Woolworth paid the entire thirteen and a half million dollars for its construction *in cash* on its completion. President Wilson declared it officially open from Washington, where he pressed a button that lit up 80,000 lights on the building's exterior. Today 'Foot Locker' and 'Mrs Field's Cookies' shops adorn the base.

Inside, the 3-storey-high lobby has the echo and quiet of a cathedral. Mosaics glitter on the vaulted ceiling, and under the supporting crossbeams on the Barclay Street side there are gargoyle-style bas-relief caricatures of Woolworth counting nickels and dimes and Gilbert showing off a model of the building.

St Paul's Chapel

Broadway (bet. Church and Fulton Sts). Come for free concerts of classical and church music (Mon–Thurs at 12.10 p.m.) or for services (weekdays 1.05 p.m.; Sun 8 a.m.).

This is Manhattan's only remaining pre-Revolutionary church. It was built on the site of a wheatfield in 1776 by Thomas McBean, who based his design on the monument his teacher James Gibb built: London's St Paul's.

The pastel insides of St Paul's are lit by Waterford crystal chandeliers. Above the cream and gold pulpit the feathers of the Prince of Wales remind you that this was the 'Established' – i.e. English – Church before the Revolution. Washington worshipped here, and you'll find his pew in the north aisle.

Outside, the chapel, made of native New York stone, stands in a leafy, pleasant cemetery.

Burying has always been good business, but not long after the chapel was ready to receive coffins, the yellow fever and cholera epidemics provided even more employment. Women were buried quietly, but their husbands' corpses got star treatment. Men licensed by the City to act as Inviters to Funerals marched in pairs from house to house, extolling the virtues of the deceased. The sombrely dressed Inviters had black streamers attached to their stovepipe hats. One rang a bell; the other bashed the pavement with a black pole. They were later the masters of ceremonies at the services. They handed the twelve pall-bearers' spoons, featuring carvings of the apostles, that were so badly cast and bent they were called monkey spoons. The women – wives, daughters and aunts who sobbed into lacey handkerchiefs a tactful few paces behind the male mourners – were given a mourning brooch or ring, which had a compartment containing strands of the deceased's hair. If he was a bald dead man, then the women got hairs from his nearest male relative instead. None of this came free. The trinkets were selling items; the payment was part of the Inviters' fee.

Brooklyn Bridge

The pedestrian walkway can be reached by crossing Park Row from City Hall Park, or from the Brooklyn Bridge–City Hall subway station. Get to the Brooklyn side from the High St–Brooklyn Bridge subway station.

Today the Brooklyn Bridge is thought humdrum by the commuters striding along the pedestrian lane or whizzing down the cyclists' lane on motorised scooters and swerving rollerblades, but the official nineteenth-century opening was momentous, as the bridge came to signify the beginning of the Industrial Revolution, and with industrialisation came increased opportunities for women. Lower-class women took up factory jobs and domestic employment (see box); upper- and middle-class women embarked on Temperance and Moral Reform work (see p.141), while Mrs Washington A. Roebling benefited directly from the construction of the Brooklyn Bridge, which she had to oversee and so became the envy of her peers because as reward she was invited to royal European Courts, occasions for which she wore a House of Worth dress that is now at the Brooklyn Museum (see p.213).

Construction Built between 1869 and 1883 and now more than a century old, the Brooklyn Bridge was a milestone in civil engineering. For twenty years it was the longest suspension bridge in the world (6,775 ft) and it was the first to use steel cables, which are spun in an intricate web and swoop between two vast Gothic-arched stone pillars.

DOMESTIC EMPLOYMENT

'Domestic Employment' meant 'servant'. The work involved long hours, low pay and often humiliating treatment at the hands of precocious mistresses. By 1920 labour-saving appliances were common fixtures in middle-class homes, but not in 1901 when Inez Godman, who earned $2.75 a week, recorded her days. She rose at 6 a.m. to begin work. In the sitting-room she had to wipe every slat of the Venetian blinds. Then there was the bread to check (her mistress had become 'weary of baker's stuff'), and the halls, stairs and vestibules to clean: 'It was heavy work, for the halls were carpeted with moquette, but I sat on the stairs as I swept them with a whisk broom, thus saving my feet.' By midday she had already worked seven hours. After donning cap and apron to serve the lunch and doing more cleaning, Inez on one occasion passed her mistress, who 'sat with a flushed face still sewing'. Inez offered to help and finished the skirt in half an hour before doing more chores, including ironing, and starting the dinner. 'Dinner was a complex meal, and coming at night when I was tired was always something of a worry. To have those different courses ready at just the right moment, to be sure that nothing burned or curdled while I was waiting on the table, to think quickly and act calmly; all this meant weariness.' Most often, domestic employees complained of physical fatigue and collapsing into bed at night, too tired even to undress properly. One wrote: 'If one of the twelve labours of Hercules had been to solve the servant girl problem, he never would have had the reputation he has.'

Disasters haunted the project, which was proposed by German-born John Augustus Roebling in 1855 but not commissioned for another fourteen years. Then, while he was taking measurements at the Brooklyn pier, his foot was crushed by a stone. His leg was amputated, gangrene set in and he died three weeks later, before construction had even begun. His son, Washington Roebling, took over. Washington went with workers in 'caissons' (diving bells) underwater to supervise construction of the foundations. The underwater air pressure burst several workers' eardrums and gave others, including Washington Roebling, the dreaded 'caisson disease', more commonly known as 'the bends'. This was when his wife became involved. Roebling was partially paralysed, so he could only direct from a room overlooking the site, and it was Mrs Washington Roebling who issued the orders.

Less than a week after the official opening, a day when 150,000 walked over the bridge, a woman fell on the stairway. Her screams

set off panic. Twelve people were killed and countless injured. The
bridge has always been a favourite spot for suicide attempts, but by
1983 it had shaken off its gloomy past and was lovingly decorated
with a sign saying 'Happy Birthday Brooklyn Bridge', and a fire-
work display went off from a ship.

LOWER EAST SIDE

Here's a relaxing, entertaining and informative way to spend your
Sunday: first go to the delightfully dilapidated Jewish café 'Yonah
Schimmel' (see p.268) for a glass of borscht (chilled beetroot broth)
or clabbered milk (liquid yoghurt) while you read the *New York
Times*; then go to Orchard Street market and rummage through
glitzy bric-a-brac and wind-up plastic robots to see if you can find a
knock-off Ralph Lauren or Charles Jourdan outfit; finally, go to the
Tenement Museum and take one of their excellent historic walking
tours of the Lower East Side.

During the week especially, you may find the area's two subway stations (both on Second Avenue) a bit grim, but they are generally considered safe. Alone or with friends, however, you'd be
unwise to venture north of Houston into Avenues C and D, an area
known as 'Loisida' to its largely Puerto Rican inhabitants and
Crack City to others. In 1983 the police mounted a buy-and-bust
campaign (one officer buys drugs, the other busts) called 'Operation
Pressure Point'. They didn't manage to eject all the drug barons, but
at least they seriously curbed their activities. Even so, at night take
cabs.

A lazy weekend walk in the neighbourhood – preferably either
in pairs or with a Tenement Museum tour if you're new to the area
– will take you past a sometimes bewildering mix of shops at the
base of 8- and 12-storey red-brick tenement buildings next to graffitied, wired-off school playgrounds. Whether it's pickles or avant-
garde hats, you'll notice that stores selling the same things tend to
localise. Get polyester shirts and ties on Allen Street, underwear and
hosiery and sheets and linen on Grand Street (which is also known
as 'Wedding Street'), and on both get electronic goods that won't
work in America without considerable tampering, because their
voltage is for use in Israel. Ludlow between Houston and Stanton
Streets harbours several bar-restaurants (Max Fish and Ludlow St
Café, see p.283) that are hip precisely because they're in a roughish
area, and Stanton has been dubbed the New Fashion Stanton Street
Strip for the handful of eccentric innovative clothes shops, including
Amy and Mary's **The Dress** (103 Stanton St, tel. 473 0237). One
street down on Rivington and you can have an entirely different
experience again by touring and tasting at the only still-operating
winery in the city, **Schapiro's House of Kosher and Sacramental
Wines** (126 Rivington St at Suffolk, tel. 674 4404 to make an

appointment during the week or drop by on Sunday between 11 a.m. and 5 p.m.).

Going north, on the gentrified side of Loisida (also known as Alphabet City see p.89), you can look at the sometime performance venue **The Gas Station** (Ave B [at E 2nd St], tel. 228 4587), which, with its gaudy cyberpunk-decorated wire fences, seems typical New York; or you could go to poetry readings at the **Nuyorican Poet's Café** (see p.306). But don't just go wandering into bars. It's possible that you'd be not the only woman but the only non-Puerto Rican, and although you'd be treated perfectly civilly, everything would go quiet and you would be stared at.

Calcutta, USA In the nineteenth century, the Lower East Side was a notoriously dirty, overcrowded tenement area where a great many immigrants started their lives in the States. Dickens said that its slums made Calcutta look like paradise. Illegal immigrants still flood in. It is said that living conditions are worse now than they were 100 years ago. Lower East Side rents are the highest in New York. Newspapers report individuals paying as much as $4,500 a month to live squashed with ten other people in one room of a tiny cold-water flat. The same money could get them an Upper West Side apartment with a park view.

At the turn of the century there were an average of 60 people per acre living in New York. In the Lower East Side there were 700 per acre, making it the most crowded place in the world, second only to Bombay. Tenements were erected quickly and cheaply, designed to cram in as many immigrants as possible. To attract particular communities, real-estate agents would incorporate appropriate features, such as a Star of David in the brickwork for the Jews. Basic amenities were at best poor, often non-existent. Outdoor toilets could be reached only by passing through several other tenement blocks, water pressure was low and so water was scarce when demand was highest, in the mornings and evenings. It is known that the crime rate was high, but exact figures are not available, because the area was not policed.

Why did immigrants put up with such conditions? They spoke little English; they found security in numbers and comfort in their compatriots; they had fled appalling economic conditions or religious persecution, so they were grateful for whatever new freedom they had.

Many male immigrants chose 'Pushcarting' to earn their living. Pushcarting, which involved pushing a cart loaded with wares for sale (usually food) around the streets, required little investment and it allowed the owners, if they were religious, to work their own hours. Ultimately, the pushcarter's ambition was to set up his own store front. But competition was tough, particularly for the richer pushcarters who had horses. Opponents would poison each other's pushcart horses to put them out of business.

Pushcarting thrived around Orchard Street. During the 1830s disputes between merchants, pedlars and the City blew up into the Pushcart Wars. For immigrants, peddling was a means of survival, but storekeepers and the City considered the pushcarts a nuisance. The pushcarters proved resilient. You'll still see pushcarts all over Manhattan, now flash chrome and run on electricity but nevertheless pushcarts, selling hot dogs, pretzels, donuts and coffee. The man in the hat wielding the tongs will often speak no English.

While fathers and brothers were out with the pushcart, the women had to work too. At the turn of the century Allen Street was the red-light district. Young immigrant women known as The Handkerchief Girls would saunter along holding handkerchiefs. If they met a man's eye, they would drop the handkerchief. The man picked it up, and they were in business. Italian prostitutes tended to walk one side of Allen Street, and Jewish prostitutes on the other.

Precise figures are not available, but it's probable that more women were in garment factories than on the game. It's a matter of opinion which was the better option. Garment working earned less money.

The Garment Industry Starts on the Lower East Side
By the end of the nineteenth century, women who had been doing piecework by candlelight in their tenement dwellings had been corralled into sweatshops (so-called because, whatever the weather, a stove was kept stoked constantly to heat the water to press completed items). Sweatshops sprang up all over the Lower East Side, often above stores and many on Orchard Street. Later the work was done in small factories, some lurking on the Lower East Side's far edges, including the Triangle Shirtwaist Factory on Washington Place, which in 1911 was the scene of one of New York's most awful industrial tragedies.

The eight-storey wooden building had no sprinkler system; the doors to the fire escapes were locked to stop workers nipping out for a quick break. When fire broke out, five hundred employees were trapped behind locked doors. Some smashed windows and jumped to their death; others burned or asphyxiated inside. The fire claimed the lives of 146 women. A newspaper reporter looked at charred bodies on the street and noted that some of these women had gone on strike only months before to demand decent wages, more sanitary working conditions, and safety precautions (see p.92).

Pauline Newman worked at the Triangle factory before she became the organiser for the International Ladies Garment Workers' Union (ILGWU). Before her death in 1986 she described her time as a garment worker. She said that of course there were child labour laws, 'but no one bothered to enforce them. The employers were always tipped off if there was going to be an inspection. "Quick," they'd say, "into the boxes!" And we children would climb into the big boxes the finished shirts were stored in. Then some shirts were piled on top of us, and when the inspector came – no children. The factory always got an okay from the inspector, and I suppose someone at City Hall got a little something too . . . The employers had a sign in the elevator that said: "If you don't come in on Sunday, don't come in on Monday." You were expected to work every day if they needed you and the pay was the same whether you worked extra or not . . . Only now, I'm a little discouraged sometimes when I see the workers spending their free hours watching television – trash. We fought so hard for those hours and they waste them. We used to read Tolstoy, Dickens, Shelley, by candlelight, and they watch the "Hollywood Squares". Well, they're free to do what they want. That's what we fought for.'

By the middle of the twentieth century the garment factories had moved north-west and unionised – the ILGWU has a closed shop – so those intent on exploiting illegal immigrants in sweatshops have returned to the Lower East Side. Allen and Eldridge Streets house sweatshops. There have been spontaneous strikes for safety conditions (demands are as basic as for windows that open). There is currently a TB and measles epidemic.

Orchard Street Market

Start at Houston end of Orchard St.

Orchard Street shops always have bargains, but on Sundays the street is closed to traffic and becomes a seething indoor and outdoor bazaar of discount dresses, coats, shoes, linens, fabrics and accessories piled on tables and hanging from fire escapes that captures the Lower East Side at its vibrant best. Yelling storekeepers will haggle down to the last cent. Take cash with you, because not all the stores will accept credit cards, and see p.20 for pickpocket precautions.

The Tenement Museum

97 Orchard St (bet. Delancey and Broome Sts), tel. 431 0233. Gallery hours: Mon–Fri, 11 a.m.–4 p.m., closed Sat; Sun 10 a.m.–4 p.m. Suggested donation $2. Walking tours $12 adults, $10 students and senior citizens (they would be tiring for young children). Call for information, and to reserve a walking tour place.

The door into the museum is easy to miss – it's above street level, up a short flight of thin stone steps.

The museum site was erected fast in 1893 to house as many immigrants as possible. In 1929 a law was passed that every apartment must have a toilet and a window, but the owners of this building decided not to waste the money and closed the residential section down, leaving only the store fronts open.

The museum's ground floor is two rooms of exhibition space which often show Arnold Eagle's 1930s tenement photographs. There is also a regularly scheduled 'open mike' format in which the public are invited to share their memories and immigrant family history with other participants.

By 1993 the upstairs will be a re-creation of tenements and apartments dedicated to the six major ethnic groups in the area, one apartment each (in historical chronology of when they arrived): Afro-American, Irish, German, Italian, East European/Jewish, Chinese. Original furniture and knick-knacks abandoned by the tenants who were turfed out in the 1930s will form the core of the exhibition, and actors will help to re-create daily life. Visitors will be able to interact. This museum has friendly and informative exhibitions. Highly recommended.

The Ritualarium

At 313 E Broadway (near Grand St), which is a little further East than most people choose to go, there is a mikvah, which is a ritual bath for Orthodox Jewish women. Women go to the baths to prepare for marriage, and then return on a monthly basis. According to the Scriptures, the water must be pure, so rainwater is collected in cisterns. Tours are given by appointment. Call Mrs Bormiko on 212 674 5318 for information.

WOMEN AND JUDAISM

Of the three main kinds of Judaism in late-nineteenth century American immigrant Jewish communities, it was Reform and Secular Judaism that allowed women most freedom.

The Eastern European Jews who arrived after 1880 practised Orthodox Judaism, in which the segregation and subordination of women was the rule, with daily prayers requiring men to thank God 'that I am not a woman'. Reform Judaism, which was introduced by German Jews who arrived between 1840 and 1880, allowed desegregation of the sexes during worship in the temples, and through 'sisterhood' organisations it allowed women to engage in administrative activities for charitable and social services – although feminists later argued that these Sisterhoods still tied women to domestic duties and therefore continued to marginalise them. More liberal again was Secular Judaism, which accepted Jewish identity but practised it through culture rather than temples – for example in literature and theatre. Its acceptance of equality between the sexes made Secular Judaism

DOWNTOWN MANHATTAN

attractive to Orthodox and Reform Jewish women, who then often became involved in socialism through the radical political arm of the movement. Esther Luria, born in 1877 in Warsaw, was one of the first generation of immigrant radical Secular Jewish intellectuals. In 1912 she escaped from Siberia, where she had been sent for Marxist activism, and came to New York City as a socialist journalist advocating political activism for women in magazines including the International Ladies Garment Workers' Union Yiddish weekly, *Glaykhhayt* (*Equality*).

By 1920, the Jewish community was well enough established in the States to have class conflicts and a number of journals, including a Yiddish–English version of the *Ladies' Home Journal* called *Der yidisher froyen zhurnal*, which was published in New York between May 1922 and October 1923 for a first-generation immigrant middle-class audience. The *froyen zhurnal* printed sentimental poetry, articles about marriage, childcare and mother–daughter generational conflicts. At the turn of the century, Jews' isolation in a new country had still been a prime concern, but by the 1930s elders were worried that second-generation Jews had assimilated too well, and had lost the faith. Education was crucial. Almost all religious schools were boys-only, yet it was thought that boys were less susceptible to the perils of assimilation than girls. So by the late 1930s some schools for girls were up and running in New York, and Orthodox schools began to break the rules by accepting female students. And it was often women, who at this time made up one-third of the teaching force, who pioneered new philosophies for Jewish education. Fannie R. Neumann of the Brooklyn Jewish Center developed a teaching method she hoped would offer Jewish children a 'cultural synthesis' and create 'a new type of Jew – steeped in Jewish culture, yet thoroughly at home in . . . [the] American milieu, disciplined yet free, adjusted to the machine age but saved from its serfdom by a critical eye and a sentient heart'.

Real power in Jewish institutions, however, remained with the men. In the 1970s Jewish feminists began to fight for changes they considered fundamental to equality, including the right for a woman to be ordained, which they won, and today Jewish feminists have turned to a reinterpretation of the Bible to legitimise sexual equality in Judaism. Rabbi Laura Geller points to the first chapter of Genesis, which reads: 'in the image of God created He them, male and female', and she says: 'Just as God is the father, God is also the mother.'

EAST VILLAGE

The East Village comes alive at night. It seems as if all the City's cheapest restaurants are crammed on and around St Mark's Place next to the sleaziest pre-club bars, with hairdressers and Goth shops buzzing till midnight. Street traders sell porn; grimy clothes and stolen bikes strewn around Cooper Square's pavements are an unofficial flea market; walking fashion statements range from felt hats with Ray Bans and tinsel to Heidi plaits plus fisherman's jumpers and cropped sweatpants; with great effort and mirth, tipsy revellers revolve the giant cube in the junction above Cooper Union.

Some uptowners say parts aren't safe. Certainly, on a winter's day the East Village can look grim and bare – its grey blocks, zigzagged with fire escapes, repeat and repeat down windswept streets that are often empty of traffic – but the most threatening presence is the bike-revving gang of Hell's Angels from 3rd Street. You should be careful, though, in Alphabet City.

The first two avenues (A and B) of Alphabet City have to some extent been yuppified. Property was bought and eateries were set up just before the recession hit in the late 1980s. Alphabet City apartments are now white elephants, but the life that sprang up as a result remains enticing. In the summer, bars and restaurants spill out on to the pavements and the air is filled with clinking glasses, music and laughter. Take tales of gun violence with a pinch of salt. New Yorkers love packaging their city as a war zone – but don't go carelessly beyond Avenue B, and if you feel unsure, especially after dark, use cabs.

The East Village has gone in–out–in–out of fashion through the ages. The affluent Astors liked it in the 1830s; bohemians exiled by soaring Greenwich Village rents took cheap light industry loft space in the 1920s; by the 1950s it was crawling with Beat poets; and now it has an in-between status. Once entirely experimental venues, such as La Mama theatre company (see p.303), have become mainly mainstream – uptown media moguls clamour to have La Mama's founder Ellen Stewart at their glitzy dinners.

There is still a vibrant artistic community. Women stream excitedly into a WOW Café performance (see p.305); rock fans discover new talents at the Space at Chase (see p.299). In May the Ukrainian Festival (7th St bet. 2nd and 3rd Aves) brings out merchants, priests, wheat, beer, decorated eggs and general merriment. And if you don't fancy culture or streetlife, you can always go for a steam at the 10th St Baths (Wednesday night is women's night – see p.315).

JOYCE JOHNSON

Women had little place in the Beat movement, other than as a stream of groupies who might, if they were very privileged, briefly become girlfriends. Joyce Johnson is the best-known groupie-girlfriend, because she wrote about her stormy association with Jack Kerouac in her memoirs, *Minor Characters*.

Joyce Johnson was a well-heeled Upper West Side girl who went to Barnard College, Columbia University, in 1951. She first read the words 'Beat Generation' in 1952 when her father came back on a Sunday with the papers and coffee cake. She went into publishing and had her first novel bought when she was twenty-one, though her main pursuit was not writing but getting 'in' with the 'in' crowds. She hung out round the shabby block between 4th Avenue and the Bowery on 10th Street because it housed painters Franz Kline and Willem de Kooning. The lumberjack-shirted Beat poets conducted readings and took drugs at Ginsberg's East 7th Street house. Johnson got herself invited and went to bed with Jack Kerouac.

druggy author of cult novel *On the Road*. For years Kerouac traipsed carelessly in and out of her life, rucksack on back, always returning to New York more for his bowl of wheaties by the kitchen window than for Joyce Johnson. Their haphazard relationship ended in 1959: 'We split up on a street corner . . . "You do what you wanna do,"' he said. She said, 'You're nothing but a bag of wind.' He said, 'Unrequited love's a bore.' She last saw him tottering drunkenly down a Manhattan street with an adoring blonde acolyte on his arm.

Joyce Johnson has found new acclaim as a writer in the 1990s, but she will probably always be best known as the woman who spent time with Jack Kerouac.

St Mark's-in-the-Bowery

2nd Ave (at E 10th St).

You can't miss St Mark's because it lies at an angle to the grid system, and it has greenery at its base – not much, but it's definitely live grass behind the surrounding iron railings. St Mark's is, however, an unattractive building: a triangular-roofed dun-coloured square box built in 1799 (the clumsy steeple was stuck on top in 1829) on the site of Peter Stuyvesant's chapel. Stuyvesant (1592–1672), the first Dutch Governor, was by reputation a stern and forbidding man who always wore black and became known as 'peg-leg Pete' for the stick of wood that replaced a limb he'd lost at war in the Caribbean. He was buried beneath his chapel, later rebuilt by a relative as St Mark's and now a designated historic and architectural landmark.

St Mark's was nearly destroyed by fire in 1978. The local community mounted a vigorous campaign to raise funds and, with architect Herman Hassinger overseeing the work, the building was restored. St Mark's flourishes, not so much as a religious institution – although it does offer church services – but as a venue for poetry readings, modern dance performances, and neighbourhood meetings. In the 1950s the Beats gave readings here.

Go inside and you'll find that it's even less like a church. After the 1978 fire the interior was gutted and done out in sleek white with modern stained-glass windows. If you're not here for a performance, sound engineers and electricians will doubtless be setting up for one. Information on events and services can be found in the narthex.

Cooper Union Foundation Building

7 E 7th St (bet. 3rd and 4th Aves). Go to the Great Hall for one of the Cooper Union 'Forum' lectures. Forum is the nation's oldest free public lecture series. The subject is usually public affairs, but there are also programmes in philosophy, poetry and fiction, photography and film. Tel. 212 353 4195/6 for information.

On the triangle of grass in front of this big old gloomy brownstone there's a statue of Peter Cooper, the man best known for inventing steel beams and jello. His statue is positioned so that you feel minuscule beneath his feet and trouser hems, his hooked nose and protruding lower lip far, far above you.

Victorian philanthropist Peter Cooper believed that learning should be 'as free as water and air', and put his money where his mouth was in 1859 by founding the Cooper Union Foundation for the Advancement of Science and Art. Born in 1791 to working-class parents, Cooper had only one year of formal education, and – even though he became a millionaire who manufactured the first steam engine to run in the United States ('Tom Thumb') and worked with Samuel Morse on the telegraph – the fact that he could not read or write was a constant source of shame. He established an education institute for the 'boys and girls of this City, who had no better opportunity than I'. It was the first co-educational college, the first open to all races and creeds, and the first to offer free adult education courses, many at night, to accommodate people who work in the daytime. It still provides free education for all on a non-sectarian basis. It is hard to stress how uncommon this is in America. During the day, the atmosphere is busy. Students and professors go in and out of lectures on engineering and architecture in classrooms made pristine by the 1974 renovation.

Making It   Cooper, a man with a big beard but no moustache and long receding hair, was an inventor and innovator, and so were many of his friends. This inevitably affected the construction of the building, which was designed by Frederick A. Peterson. Peterson used a grid of the T-shaped rails produced in Cooper's iron works to transmit loads to the walls. Cooper Union is the oldest extant building in the States to be supported by steel beams, which of course were manufactured by Cooper. The use of an elevator was another breakthrough (Cooper was so ahead of his time that he had the shaft built before the first elevator had been finished). Cooper Union also had a primitive air-conditioning system. Fresh air was pumped from the basement through vents under each of the 2,000 seats in the Great Hall auditorium. This plethora of energising oxygen no doubt facilitated the often revolutionary ideas that came out of the historic Great Hall.

Organising in the Great Hall

Here in 1860 Abraham Lincoln gave the famous 'Right Makes

Might' speech. The US branch of the Red Cross was first organised in the school's Great Hall, and it was here that Susan B. Anthony catalysed the women's suffrage movement. A thin woman who scraped her hair back in a bun and favoured severe dress, Anthony was not a great orator, but she had a friend who was (see box), and she had contacts. She gathered female benevolent organisations together in the hall so she and Elizabeth Cady Stanton could tell them they should be fighting for the right to vote, not for bans on alcohol and prostitution.

The Shirtwaisters On 23 November 1909 – three years after Anthony's death – thousands of women shirtwaist makers met in the Great Hall to discuss wages, which were often as little as $3.50 a week, and working conditions (women had to pay for their own needles, and for electricity). The meeting was orderly until suddenly a young Russian woman stood and announced that she had heard enough speeches: 'I am one who thinks and feels the things they describe. I too have worked and suffered. I am tired of talking. I move that we go on general strike.' Her motion received thunderous applause. By the next night over 25,000 garment workers had walked out on their employers and the 'Uprising of the Twenty Thousand' had begun. It was a long haul – there was police brutality on the picket lines – but women's organisations contributed funds and the strikers were determined. Although employers refused to recognise a closed shop, most instituted a fifty-two-hour week, limited the use of overtime, and took steps to spread work out over the slack season. The International Ladies Garment Workers' Union grew from a small organisation of a few hundred before the strike to a mass union of over 100,000 afterwards.

TWO SUFFRAGISTS

Susan B. Anthony and Elizabeth Cady Stanton defied the convention that said they should stay home and be good wives and mothers (Anthony didn't marry at all). Their aims in life were unabashedly political.

Susan B. Anthony was born in 1820 into a Quaker family which was hit in 1837 by economic disaster: her father lost his cotton mill. Susan and her sisters went out to teach. Susan became passionately attached to the idea of self-support and personal independence for women. By 1850 she had joined the Temperance movement but had been angered by the male leaders' sentimental and patronising approach to their women workers. In 1851 Amelia Bloomer introduced her to Elizabeth Cady Stanton.

Born into high society in 1815, Stanton always had great confidence. She was brilliant and learned, and she was also sensuous, defending her vast weight (175 pounds in 1860 and over 240 when she was an old woman), her frequent naps, and the sexuality of all women when none of these things was considered respectable. She kept her hair in fat sausage curls on top of her head and draped a shawl over her shoulders.

Anthony knew the network of female benevolent organisations. Stanton realised that women were using issues like temperance to protest against their vulnerability to and dependence on irresponsible and abusive men. Stanton believed that this spirit could be turned in a feminist direction. Stanton and Anthony lectured and organised as a team.

In later life, the focus of the two women split. Stanton insisted that suffragists fight for emancipation *and* social reform, but it was Anthony's belief that no other issue must be allowed to intrude on the question of political equality for women that came to predominate for the next generation of suffragists. Stanton died in 1902; Anthony in 1906. After the vote was won, the history books remembered Anthony, whose head was put on the half-dollar coin.

Colonnade Row

428–434 Lafayette St (at E 4th St).

Colonnade Row is one of the few reminders that this was once a desirable area, and it's very run-down indeed. The 1833 Corinthian façade is graffitied, and washing is often strung between the columns of the houses that were home to Warren Delano (F.D.R.'s grandfather) and John Jacob Astor. Astor, a tycoon who made some of his money in the beaver fur trade, was so fat he had to be tossed up and down in a blanket for exercise.

Tompkins Square

E 7th–10th Sts (Aves A and B).

You're getting into Alphabet City now. This ugly, wired 16-acre space was originally meant to extend all the way east to the river. It was to be a market with a canal cut through the middle which would give easy access to Long Island farmers. Instead it became a parade ground in the 1830s. In 1874 it was the site of America's first labour demonstration, when a carpenters' union clashed with club-wielding police. The park became notorious during the 1970s hippy days of flower-power, when it served as the grounds for love-ins. In the 1980s it was the site of violent confrontation over real-estate speculation and efforts to enforce a night-time curfew. Today it is neither especially dangerous nor particularly inviting.

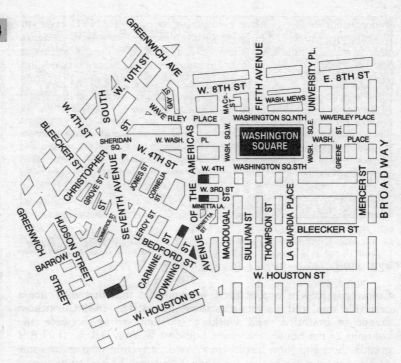

GREENWICH VILLAGE

When New Yorkers talk about a 'villagey feel', remember – it's relative. Sure, the buildings here are lower and older than elsewhere, but what village has a condom shop on the main street and a host of dyke bars (see pp.329/284).

In the daytime go to the shops, do the Old Merchant's House for history (Sundays only), and spend as much time as you can chilling out, either on a Washington Square Park bench or in a European-style café over a Viennese coffee and a canolli.

At night, Greenwich Village is about jazz, drinking, and checking out the gay pick-up scene. Get winked at by a kool saxophonist in a smoky jazz club, slug back Wild Turkey at a journalists' bar to the strains of Art Pepper, or go to the meat market area for clubs (gay and straight) and a meal at Florents (see p.264), where glitterati slum it and trendies on a budget splash out.

But be prepared to get lost. Once you've mastered Manhattan's grid system, Greenwich Village can seem like a maze, for its thin winding streets originally followed babbling brooks and cowpaths. Enjoy the chaos. Pass mosaiced lampposts at Broadway and a novice rollerblading student clambering steps to an NYU class on Washington Square. Grapple with collectors for AIDS benefits under a vast billboard advertising the Ultimate in Gay Vacations at the 6th Avenue–Bleecker Street junction while a raucous wedding party teeters across led by a redheaded bride in shades, platforms and a precarious cleavage. Make way for the shuffling old couple who have just found a pigeon nesting in the fire escape behind the tiny flat over the drugstore they've lived in for fifty years. Browse in fancy delis where Hollywood dropouts like Nicaragua activist Susan Sarandon go for faccio and balsamic vinegar. Gaze in awe at the perfect buttocks of the bobbing blonde uptown girls who have popped down to the Village for a work-out and a gossip. On Christopher Street, which still throngs with guys who look as if they sing for Village People, pay homage to the 1969 Stonewall riots, when gay men surrounded the Stonewall bar to stop police expelling its occupants and thus marked the beginning of the Gay Rights movement (the annual Gay Pride march, held on the last Sunday in June, still ends in Greenwich Village). Over by the river there's New York's only women's bookshop, Judith's Room (see p.328).

Apart from the Merchant's House and Washington Square Park, the 'sights' of Greenwich Village need imagination. The buildings are of interest not architecturally but for the lives, loves and dramas that went on inside them.

GREENWICH VILLAGE AND THE NEW WOMAN

By 1881 New York State had made abortion illegal for the first time in America's history. This marked the demise of the the 'bourgeois matron' (Victorian women of Susan B. Anthony's generation (see p.92), who avoided motherhood, separated sex from reproduction and asserted their own will), and heralded a new social phenomenon: The New Woman. The New Woman of the 1920s and 1930s smoked and read Oscar Wilde, wore men's suits and short hair, and moved to bohemian Greenwich Village. They included journalist Djuna Barnes (see p.103) and anarchist Emma Goldman (see p.101), who saw sexual autonomy not as freedom from marital oppression but as the right to sexual experimentation. Edna St Vincent Millay wrote the famous 'First Fig' poem: 'My candle burns at both ends; It will not last the night; But oh, my foes, and oh, my friends – It gives a lovely light!' The British sexologist Havelock Ellis labelled New Women deviants, saying they were 'Mannish Lesbians', perverted for their 'unnatural gender apeing'.

Greenwich Village thrived as a centre of artistic innovation, personal experimentation and political agitation until the end of World War I. Socialism was fashionable, and so was draft resistance. But soon tales of 'free love' and rumoured supplies of Prohibition liquor attracted tourists. Rich women came looking for artist lovers; rich men installed their mistresses in lofty apartments. Political reaction gripped the country. Women like Emma Goldman and Djuna Barnes fled, political and sexual exiles.

Jane Jacobs Saved the Village Greenwich Village was a quiet suburb until cholera and yellow fever in the 1790s and a fire in 1835 drove thousands of city-dwellers north of Wall Street. Nineteenth-century high society, including Henry James and Edith Wharton (see p.102), enjoyed grand Washington Square town houses – before moving to Fifth Avenue. By the late 1950s Greenwich Village was a mixture of new and old that some considered a bit of a mess. A few arty lofts remained from its 1920s bohemian heyday, Lower East Side immigrants were filtering in through housing projects, seedy stores opened under the three- and four-storey pastel-coloured brick houses. New York's foremost city planner, Robert Moses, called it a slum and said it must be levelled to accommodate high-rise blocks. 'Mr Moses conceded that some new housing might be "ugly, regimented, institutional, identical, conformed, faceless,"' reported the *New York Times* in January 1961. 'But he suggested that such housing could be surrounded by parks.' Jane Jacobs, a resident of Greenwich Village and author of a heated attack on town planning, *The Death and Life of Great American Cities*, began a three-year campaign – which she won – to have the Village designated a national historic district. It has since been largely unchanged.

Old Merchant's House

29 E 4th St, tel. 212 777 1089. Open Sun 1–4 p.m. (closed August); admission $2; senior citizens and students $1; under-12s free; groups Mon–Thurs by appointment.

Victorian spinster Gertrude Tredwell devoted the last impoverished years of her life to maintaining the family home 'exactly as Papa would have wanted it' – which included keeping children's potties and ladies' packets of pins – and so preserved for posterity what Ada Louise Huxtable, architecture critic of the *New York Times*, described as a 'unique social, esthetic and historical document'. The three-storey red-brick Greek Revival building was bought by a well-to-do retired merchant of marine hardware, Seabury Tredwell, in 1835, and stayed with the family for nearly a century. Gertrude Tredwell, the youngest of eight children, died in 1933 in the same majestic canopied double bed she had been born in 93 years earlier.

The Old Merchant's House museum operates a system called 'self-guided tours', which means you go round at your own pace and ask the guide in each room questions. You'll get sometimes conflicting but always riveting information, and plenty of it.

Enter through the basement, where in the kitchen curlicued servants' bells dangle above a tin cupboard called the Pie Safe, which has spikes on the door to keep flies and children out. One flight up, the back parlour has the mirrors Seabury's wife and daughters checked their hats in, and the floor-level mirrors they checked their petticoats in. The front parlour has on the pianoforte fine examples of face-sized screens the ladies held up to stop the fire melting their heavy wax make-up in the presence of courting gentlemen callers.

Look out for special spring and summer tours (around $6), some of which involve champagne in the garden, where the privy is currently being excavated in the hope that it will throw more anthropological light on life during the Victorian age.

Washington Square

Washington Square's park isn't much in itself – about half a football pitch's worth of flagstone and concrete with a bit of tired grass – but go on a sunny day and it's teeming. At weekends it houses fairs and flea markets. During the week whistle-blowing kids with goatee beards and turned-round baseball caps do BMX stunts, groups of cross-legged teenage punks sip soda pop, octogenarian widows while away afternoons chatting about interfaith seders, lunatics rant to crowds from soapboxes, students lean on bollards conversing between classes, hustlers invite you to play 3 Card Monte (an offer you'd be wise to refuse, or you come away substantially poorer), and on the East Side locals bring Dalmatians and terriers to yap together in the fenced-off Dog Run.

The square is dominated by a rather gloomy, dirty 1889 McKim, Mead and White freestanding arch (built to commemorate George Washington's inauguration) which has 110 steps inside. In 1916 artist Marcel Duchamp forced open the door and ran to the top of the arch to declare the Village the separate city of New Bohemia. It is said that during World War II a man lived inside secretly for seven months. He gave himself away when he hung his washing out to dry.

The Past Once a marsh, the square was a popular site for duels and public hangings before it became a military parade ground. In 1828 it was claimed as a public park. In 1831, 28 Greek Revival houses were built in a row on the North of the square as homes for New York's high society. Henry James set his novel *Washington Square* (pub. 1881) at No. 18, the 'solid, honourable dwelling' that was his grandmother's house. Edith Wharton (see p.102), who lived for a time at No. 1 Washington Square, was one of America's first women to abandon the horse-drawn carriage in favour of a 'motorcar', which she insisted on driving herself. Society ladies must have been horrified to see one of their members roaring round in goggles, scarf fluttering behind with wild abandon in the wind.

In 1916 Djuna Barnes described the odd appeal of Washington

Square in a *Parson's Magazine* article: 'Satin and motorcars on this side, squalor and push carts on that . . . On benches in the Square men and women resting; limbs wide-flung, arms pendent, listless; round the fountains and on the corners children, dark-eyed Italian children shrieking now with Yankee-cockney accent, a moment later whispering to their deep-bosomed mothers in the Tuscan of Dante.' In Willa Cather's 1920 story 'Coming Aphrodite!' Washington Square residents are all aspiring artists and singers who pass silk-factory girls and pigeons on their way to lunch in basement oyster houses that have no handles on the coffee cups at a time when Puccini was new.

By the 1950s the Square was in a sorry state. The City transit authority was using the arch as a turnaround point for buses, and City planner Robert Moses proposed a downtown expressway that would require spaghetti ramps to come from the heart of Washington Square. Jane Jacobs headed the Greenwich Village Association that prevented him, and now the Square is unofficial campus for New York University (NYU), with 15,000 full-time students the country's largest private university, whose film school spawned Martin Scorsese and Susan-*Desperately Seeking Susan*-Siedelman.

NYU (New York University)

A number of the NYU buildings on Washington Square are open to the public and worth going into briefly.

The grand neo-classical **Main Building** has that institutional bleach smell, and it has the **Grey Art Gallery** (use Washington Place entrance). This white one-room gallery, which opened in 1975, has changing exhibitions that are free (open Tues and Thurs 10 a.m.–6.30 p.m., Wed 10 a.m.–8.30 p.m., Fri 10 a.m. – 5 p.m. and Sat 1 p.m.–5 p.m.; closed holidays).

The mock Roman **Judson Memorial Baptist Church** (55 Washington Square South bet. Thompson and Sullivan Sts) is a yellow-brick box shape with a neat triangle roof that has rows of bricked-up arched windows along the sides and a high square bell tower sprouting to the west. When it was built in 1892 by McKim, Mead and White it served as common ground for the rich who lived in the mansions on the north and the poor in the tenements on the south of the Square. The Duncan Dunbar Memorial Fountain at the north-west corner of the church spurted cold water for public use. One immigrant woman said in 1900: 'When my child was sick, and I that poor I couldn't buy ice, and the child cried for a cooling drink, didn't I go in the middle of the night and draw water just as cool and fresh as it was in the middle of the day? I wouldn't have known what to do without it.' The church has always had a full social programme, serving sometimes as a health centre and at others as a venue for modern dance. Pick up leaflets in the church for details of performances and services. Otherwise, sadly, there is no longer good reason to go inside, as the once magnificent celebrated stained-glass windows by John La Farge are in an appalling state of decay. Two of the thirteen have been put in storage until funds can be raised to repair them. They were so damaged that a rainstorm would have destroyed them.

The **Hagop Kevorkian Center for Near Eastern Studies** (entrance on Sullivan Street) is, in stark contrast to the rest of the square, modern. Designed by Philip Johnson and Richard Foster in 1972, it is a small corner building. Go in its beautiful entrance hall, which is a reconstruction of a tiny Syrian courtyard. The elaborately tiled floor, mouldings, door panels and tinkling fountain were shipped over wholesale from a 1797 merchant's house in Damascus.

Provincetown Playhouse

133 MacDougal St (at W 4th St).

Resident Greenwich Village bohemian Djuna Barnes was a founder member of the Provincetown Players, a group which helped to change American theatre by offering the first real alternative to Broadway melodramas. The Playhouse, which still operates today, premiered works by Barnes herself, by Eugene O'Neill and by Edna St Vincent Millay.

Edna Wows New York Millay was an elfin twenty-five-year-old poet from Maine; her theatrical success was a classic casting-couch situation. She became a fully fledged member of the Players in 1917 only months after she arrived in New York because the influential critic and playwright Floyd Dell fell in love with her the moment she auditioned for the flighty part of Annabelle in his play *The Angel Intrudes*. Dell was only one of many. Millay won hearts and spurned them regularly. Literary critic Edmund Wilson said that falling in love was 'an inevitable consequence of knowing her'.

Liberal Club

Was at 137 MacDougal Street.

Upton Sinclair was a founder member of this now long gone bohemian club, which was considered a melting-pot of Village radicals but was mainly about throwing parties. It arranged drunken openings for exhibitions of Cubist paintings, and 'Pagan Routs' ran through the night. A piano player sang from a corner while figures whirled in silk and chiffon. People posed for portraits, met, fought, loved and passed out, and Feminist Alliance founder Henrietta Rodman padded about in sandalled feet. A high-school teacher who explained about sex to schoolgirls and agitated for saner, simpler dress, Henrietta Rodman wore a loose flowing gown that looked like a meal sack. Brown socks poked through the gaps in her sandals. She cropped her hair years before bobs were 'in'.

Downstairs in the basement was Polly's Restaurant, where the radicals lined their stomachs before revelling. Margaret Sanger (see p.138) came from her sex education lessons to discuss anarchy with Emma Goldman (see p.101); Mabel Dodge Luhan (see p.102), a self-declared 'unorthodox woman' who liked 'to do things and do them openly', recruited here ruthlessly for her 'Wednesday Evenings'; and Djuna Barnes wrote about it all:

> The Villager walks across the tiled floor of the café. From his shoulders hangs a long Mephistophelian cape; this he unclasps with long, white, convalescent hands. The cape slips back – ah, dear Lord, what have we done to receive so much beauty per flash! On his gaunt form is naught but a leopard skin, a little talcum, a string of beads, a garter of winking, seductive sapphires.

Jefferson Market Library

6th and Greenwich Aves.

Jefferson Market Library was supposedly modelled on Mad King Ludwig II of Bavaria's castle *Neuschwanstein*, so it's not surprising that it looks uncomfortable in Manhattan. The dark red-brick Victorian Gothic building – bristling with pinnacles, gables and turrets – crouches uneasily on its triangular patch of grass next to roaring Sixth Avenue. It was built in 1877 by Withers and Vaux as a District Courthouse, the clock tower once doubled as a fire lookout, and now the building is a busy local branch of the New York Public Library.

75 Bedford Street

This three-storeyed, three-windowed thirty-foot-deep 1873 house is, at nine and a half feet wide, the narrowest in the city. It was the last New York home of Edna St Vincent Millay.

Edna Settles Down   Edna met her husband Eugen Jan Boissevain at a party in 1923 when they acted the parts of two lovers in an impromptu play. Floyd Dell wrote: 'We were having the unusual privilege of seeing a man and a girl fall in love with each other violently and in public.' Eugen, then forty-three, was, according to his friend Max Eastman, a man who had 'the genius, the audacity, and the uncompromising determination to enjoy the adventure of life'. He also saw that, despite Edna's spirited performance, she was not well. He took her home and called a doctor. Three months later they married and she had major intestinal surgery. The same year they moved into 75´ Bedford Street where Boissevain, whom Edna's friends thought good for her because he was intelligent, romantic and fatherly, nursed her back to health. Boissevain controlled a large fleet of merchant vessels and a flourishing coffee-importing company, but he gave up work in the shipping business to help his wife. 'Anyone can buy and sell coffee,' he said, 'but anyone cannot write poetry.' He answered the telephone, dealt with stacks of mail, made sure she ate regular meals and got plenty of sleep. In 1923 she became the first woman ever to win the prestigious Pulitzer Prize for poetry. They decided they needed more fresh air than they got at No. 75´. In 1924 Boissevain gave his promised wedding present – a trip for them both round the world – and in 1925 they moved upstate to a farm surrounded by steepletop, a shrub that bears tall pointed flowers. She lived there with Boissevain and a large number of tamed wild birds till her death.

RED EMMA GOLDMAN

Still a teenager when her work at a St Petersburg glove factory brought her into contact with populist and nihilist ideas, Prussian born Emma Goldman (1869–1940) emigrated to the States with her half sister aged 16 and quickly gained notoriety as 'Red Emma', anarchist immigrant worker who colluded with her partner, Alexander Berkman, in a plot to assassinate the steel magnate Henry Frick during the Pittsburgh steel strike of 1892. The plot failed. After a stint in prison and a trip to Europe, from 1895 Red Emma lectured New Yorkers rigorously. While other women sought to modify the law, Goldman worked to replace it with anarchist principles of voluntary communism. She felt that society cramped 'human emotion and originality of thought' in order to create 'a patient slave, professional automation, taxpaying citizen, or righteous moralist'. Her talks included discussions of Shaw, Ibsen and Strindberg; she advocated breaking free of conventional marital restrictions; and with the outbreak of World War I she loudly opposed involuntary conscription. For the authorities, this was the last straw. Red Emma was sentenced in 1917 to five years penal servitude, and in 1919 she had her citizenship revoked and she was deported to Russia. Within 2 years she was disillusioned with the government and, unable to return to America, she travelled Europe, lecturing. The last years of her life are described variously as lonely and brave; Peggy Guggenheim's memoirs remember her as 'very vain... She was a Jewish cordon bleu and her gefilte fish was her *pièce de résistance*'; more recently Red Emma was resurrected as a feminist role-model: her pince-nez-clad face roamed New York again, on the t-shirts of women protesting in the 1970s.

MABEL DODGE LUHAN

Born in 1879 to a wealthy Buffalo family, Mabel was schooled in charm and groomed to marry, but she yearned for a life ennobled by Poetry and Beauty. Her quest took her through four husbands, and a Renaissance palace in Florence (which Gertrude Stein frequented), and left her trying to convince America that salvation lay in the way of the Pueblo Indians of Taos, New Mexico (she persuaded Georgia O'Keeffe to immortalise it with paint and D.H. Lawrence to celebrate it on paper). While in New York she was a leading symbol of the 'New Woman': sexually emancipated, self-determining, in control of her own destiny. She presided over perhaps the most famous salon in American history. From 1912 to 1915, her No. 23 Fifth Avenue house, which was draped in muslins, velvets, silks and damasks to dramatise her desire for a new cosmos, was filled every Wednesday evening with prominent writers and activists, among them Emma Goldman, Margaret Sanger, Max Eastman, A.A. Brill. Freud's latest theories were introduced; art, politics and society were discussed; and Mabel predicted that a brave new world would emerge from her gatherings to replace the anomie of twentieth-century life. But by 1916 she was an emotional wreck. She moved to New Mexico, where she finally died in 1962 of coronary thrombosis.

EDITH WHARTON

Seventeen-year old Edith spent her 'coming-out' party 'cowered beside my mother in speechless misery', but once 'out' she enjoyed the games and social manners of New York Society hugely, cheered an unhappy marriage by putting them into fiction, and so became one of America's greatest writers.

Born in New York in 1862, Edith Jones came of age just as 'the new game of lawn tennis, played on our lawn by young gentlemen in tail coats and young ladies in tight whale-bone dresses, began to supersede the hitherto fashionable archery', and when ladies filled all spare moments with the onerous labour of 'calling' in horse-drawn victorias to thank each other for the whirl of informal Sunday lunches, after-theatre suppers, gay polo and yachting parties. Edith didn't reject conventional notions of 'women's work' (arranging flowers and soothing men's tired brows), but she kept a critical eye. In one novel, Touchstone, a man describes a woman writer: 'One felt that if she had been prettier she would have had emotions instead of ideas.'

In 1885 she married Edward Wharton, a Boston socialite who liked to travel to Europe, where she met and befriended Henry James. Her first novel was not published till she was forty, but from then on she wrote prodigiously, pausing only during World War I to do war work, for which she was awarded the Cross of the Légion d'Honneur and the Order of Leopold. Meanwhile, she divorced and moved permanently to France, where she died at the age of seventy-five.

DJUNA BARNES

No one could understand why dashing white-skinned, red-haired Djuna Barnes, darling of bohemian Greenwich Village and later of the 1920s Parisian Modernist movement, stayed a recluse from the 1940s until her death in 1982. In a rare 1973 interview she recalled her heady youth to explain what she called her 'Trappist' period: 'It was all so very, very desperate . . . I used to be rather the life of the party. I was gay and silly and bright and all that sort of stuff and wasted a lot of time. I used to be invited by people who said, "Get Djuna for dinner. She's so amusing." So I stopped it.'

Born in an artists' colony north of New York in 1892, she had barely turned twenty by the time she was writing regular columns for the *Brooklyn Daily Eagle*, and in 1915 she published her first poems: *The Book of Repulsive Women*. She tried marriage, but left editor Courtenay Lemon in 1919 for Paris, where she arrived with letters of introduction to Ezra Pound and James Joyce and in 1921 began a ten-year relationship with artist Thelma Wood. When this ended, Peggy Guggenheim put her up in her English home so that she could write *Nightwood*, which is now considered at least a minor masterpiece but was largely ignored on its 1936 publication. Peggy lured her back to New York by putting on a show of her paintings at the Guggenheim. Djuna found a small Greenwich Village apartment ('one room with appendages'), fell out with Peggy and ran out of money. Her neighbour, E.E. Cummings, would bring her chicken soup when she was ill, and every so often he would shout from his window: 'Are ya still alive, Djuna?' until she died six days after her ninetieth birthday.

MOTHER OF THE US FEMINIST MOVEMENT

Betty Friedan, who founded the National Organization of Women (see p.29) in 1966 'to take the actions needed to bring women into the mainstream of American society' (see p.108), was born Elizabeth Naomi Goldstein in 1921 in Illinois to an upper-middle-class family who ran a jewellery business, Goldstein's, that was known as 'the Tiffany's of Peoria'. She shone academically: 'I was that girl with all A's,' she said later, 'and I wanted boys worse than anything.' 1943 was a pivotal year. She got a boy, then won a prestigious scholarship which she turned down so as not to intimidate her lover; her father died; her asthma worsened; she dumped the boyfriend and moved to Waverly Place in Greenwich Village, where she took up political journalism. She exposed exploitation of women who filled men's places in factories riveting and making spark plugs during World War II, but she still yearned for the Doris Day-style respectability of married life. By 1947, still in her twenties, she had moved to the Upper West Side and wed Carl Friedan, a handsome young man from Boston. Betty threw herself into the conventional life of mother and homemaker, writing for popular magazines to help pay the bills. All this was fodder for her ground-breaking book *The Feminine Mystique* (1963), which analysed the dissatisfaction of the average American housewife and paved the way for the 1960s and 1970s American feminist movement. Her 1981 book *The Second Stage* brought her into disrepute with militant feminists for advocating that the sexes work together. Today Friedan writes about discrimination against the aged.

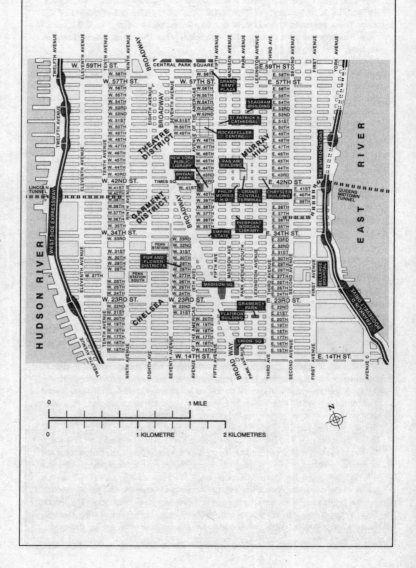

MIDTOWN
MANHATTAN

14TH TO 59TH STREETS

Cross the island via 42nd Street and you'll see some of the best and worst Midtown Manhattan has to offer, starting at Grand Central Station, which spurts commuters from its beaux-arts portals in the morning and then sucks them in again at dusk.

Businesswomen speed past in street uniform of white Nikes, bobby socks and pastel culotte suits. Businessmen stop to have their loafers polished, posing briefly with papers on tatty dentist's chairs that are upturned at night for use as the homeless shoe-shiners' shelters. If the pavement outside Grand Hyatt Hotel is swelling with security and bimbo baseball groupies, one of the country's star teams is staying. Going west you'll pass the black thrusting Philip Morris skyscraper and desperate smokers banned from offices sucking cigarettes in street doorways that double after dark as public toilets. Prepare yourself in sweltering summer for a sometimes overwhelming stench of urine, but in winter you'll be warmed by the sweet smell of frying candied nuts that billows from fleets of metal pushcarts. At Fifth Avenue, while you fight through shoppers, glance down at the Empire State before moving on to Times Square, which throbs with tourists and garish flashing neon signs advertising Coca-Cola, Samsung and Johnny Walker. Up Broadway the neon's flashing for musical spectaculars like *Cats* and *Guys and Dolls*, and down 8th Avenue the neon signs sell sex – massage parlours and topless dancing girls. The area around Port Authority bus station teems with seedy pimps, hollow-eyed prostitutes and drug addicts, and 'panhandlers', the beggars you'll be approached by everywhere but who seem particularly desperate here. Finally, you'll come to the river and the Circle Line boat tour of Manhattan, one of the few tourist traps that even time-toughened New Yorkers will happily be lured to.

The Circle Line and the Empire State are winners for women with children; the New York Public Library is perfect for a hassle-free Midtown break with a book; the Pierpont Morgan Library and Museum of Modern Art are two of the City's best museums; and the National Organization of Women offices in Chelsea offer a chance to get involved with grass-roots sexual politics campaigning.

Midtown Manhattan contains most of the hotels. The streets around Times Square and between West 23rd and West 14th Streets can be seedy after dark, so you may prefer to choose a hotel higher up the grid pattern. Unless you take a cab from the airport, you'll arrive at Grand Central Terminal or Port Authority. Port Authority especially should be approached with care during the day and extreme caution at night. For an extra $2 you can ask the bus driver to drop you at your hotel if it is a major one.

Lunchtimes are fine, but Midtown is not a particularly enjoyable area in which to eat or drink alone at night. Unless you're a well-dressed executive, the posher restaurants can treat single women with anything from contempt to hostility. With children, stick to diners, delis and pre-theatre suppers.

Apart from 42nd Street and Fifth Avenue, Midtown Manhattan does not merit casual wandering. Indeed, a large part of the West Side is best avoided. The various red-light districts make the streetlife colourful rather than safe.

Murray Hill on the east is respectable if dull, a mixture of sterile corporate tower and mansion blocks and staid residential brownstones, many run-down. When the commuters have gone home the area can be ominously quiet.

Down the middle, Fifth Avenue has some of the city's most expensive stores. Monied Upper East Side women on shopping sprees tangle briefly on the pavement with one-legged beggars and office girls.

Needlework to Suffrage   Until the mid nineteenth century the City was contained below Wall Street, Broadway was the highway out of town and the area was mainly farmland. Farmhouse parlours fostered what is referred to now as 'domestic feminism'.

Women were dissatisfied with the political status quo and used their needles to say so, stitching slogans into needlework cases and quilts. Slavery was a prime target in North America. 'May the points of our needles prick the slave owner's conscience,' declared Sarah Grimké, one of the first women to speak publicly against slavery.

As the nineteenth century progressed, the tradition of female reformers grew stronger. Groups formed to tackle intemperance and immorality found that much of their activity focused around Midtown, because with industrialisation factories and tenements mushroomed on the West Side. Working-class women and immigrants swarmed in through Grand Central Station, and many turned to prostitution for their livelihood. While upright Victorian women harassed working girls and brothel-owners, their two-faced husbands cavorted in boudoirs.

By the middle of the century Elizabeth Cady Stanton, one of a breed of respectable rebels later termed 'the bourgeois matron' (see p.92), was arguing that these Midtown reformists had to some extent missed the point. 'The prejudice against colour is no stronger than that against sex,' she said, and organised an 1848 convention in New York State's Seneca Falls to fight for women's right to vote, paving the way for New Women, including Margaret Sanger. Sanger said that sure, women needed the vote, but they needed birth control to gain real freedom, and she set up a Bureau on West 16th Street to research 'the Pill'.

World War II Brings Liberties and Lesbianism Industrialisation meant that brawn wasn't needed to work in factories, and women began to filter in – until the Depression, when they were advised to remember their place – home – and stay in it. The outbreak of war caused a number of dramatic changes. Scores of young women bade tearful farewells at steamy Grand Central, and a third of a million women left to join the forces themselves. National concern that a women's corps was 'the ideal breeding ground for lesbians' was wholly justified. General Eisenhower instructed WAC Sergeant Johnnie Phelps to ferret out the lesbians in her battalion and she replied that yessir, she would be happy to do this, but her name would head the list: 'You should also be aware that you are going to have to replace all the file clerks, the section heads, most of the commanders, and the motor pool.' General Eisenhower replied: 'Forget the order.'

The absence of men from the factories and the urgency of weapon manufacture during the war years took the women who had stayed back to work. Crackling black-and-white public information films told them to think of heavy industrial machines as no more complicated than washing machines. After the war similar campaigns told women to get back to the washing machines and leave the jobs for men. But women had tasted work, and they liked it.

Today you will see female staff pouring in and out of the advertising agencies and publishers around Lexington and Madison on the East Side. Advertising particularly has until recently been basically a boys' club. Tough 1980s economic times saw clients spending less, and agencies scrambling for innovative approaches. It's the big ideas that count, not who plays golf with whom, says one of a growing number of female advertising executives. The internationally renowned ad firm Ogilvy and Mather have Rochelle Lazarus in the prestigious position of president and chief operating officer at their New York office.

Image Midtown magazine publishers, ad agencies and plastic surgeons are all about image, which concerns New York women to a frightening degree. The exceptional forty-year-old woman on TV is the one who actually looks her age; clear-skinned teenagers beg doctors to prescribe the acne-clearing Retin-a because it also makes face skin tight as a drum; breasts, lips and thighs have all been moulded by the media's critical eye and the surgeon's knife, and the latest thing is 'body-sculpting' your arms. Girls in the ladies' rest rooms at cool clubs toss down their lipstick to twist and inspect their pectorals, which must be not too big and not too small, but just right – which requires hours of hard work in expensive gyms.

While feminist Betty Friedan was finishing *The Feminine Mystique* (see p.103), a New York copywriter from Arkansas, Helen Gurley Brown, was promoting *Sex and the Single Girl* (1962) with the message: flirt and show cleavage and you'll get places. As early as 1930, Helena Rubinstein (see p.111) had stated in *The Art of Feminine Beauty*: 'An abundance of fat is something repulsive.' Anorexia nervosa became a spreading disease, and the notion of 'slimming diets' was born. New York doctor Hy Tarnower was one of the first to gain fame and fortune by promising to vanish bulges. He had identified cholesterol as the key to helping his hard-arteried patients, and he photocopied an A4 list of eating do's and don'ts. The sheet was slipped to the *New York Times*, published, and the next day Tarnower was inundated with requests to write a diet book. 'This is silly as hell,' he reportedly said at first. 'How could you make a book out of a one-page diet?' But he did and hit the headlines with *The Scarsdale Medical Diet*, and then again in 1980 when his long-suffering girlfriend Jean Harris, dubbed the 'socialite headmistress' by the press, shot him four times with a .32 revolver.

Today the press gives the kind of space other countries reserve for royalty to the editors of rival magazines American *Vogue* and *Harper's Bazaar*, British Anna Wintour and Liz Tilberis. Indeed, Anna Wintour is known affectionately by the press as 'the Oracle' or 'Queen Mother Wintour'. Whole articles are dedicated to the length of her hemlines.

THE STREET SCENE

Tenth Avenue around the Javit Convention Center has a raunchy street scene, with explicitly dressed girls (10-inch heels and cleavages) and condoms all over the street.

Times Square is crazier and rougher than Tenth – women have to be desperate to go there.

14th Street around Ninth Avenue (the meat market area) is the favourite for fur-bikinied and spangle-dressed transvestite prostitutes.

The upscale street scene is Sixth Avenue in the 50s, around the Midtown hotels, where you won't be able to distinguish prostitutes from the area's milling business and tourist women.

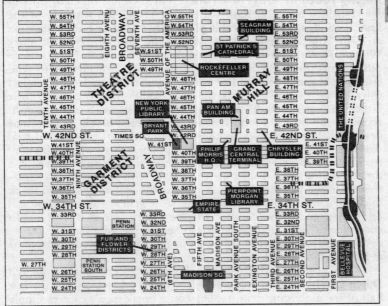

FIFTH AVENUE

Stretching from the Empire State to Trump Tower, this section of Fifth Avenue is a hotchpotch of banks, churches, tacky shops and nearly all of New York's very grandest department stores.

Shopping is a leisure activity for wealthy American women, and the Fifth Avenue stores cater for their comfort. Bergdorff's, Bendel's and Saks all have private rooms in which the latest designer items are modelled while one or two of their richest clients lean back in brocade armchairs sipping tea until they are ready to make their purchases. Women in fur coats speed out of revolving doors towards stretch limos with bag-laden red-faced chauffeurs scurrying behind.

For the less well-heeled, street traders supply fake Gucci watches or Chanel jewellery up and down the Avenue, displaying their wares in opened leather briefcases strapped around their necks. Andean pipe-players and fifteen-year-old hip-hop experts busk, as much for their own pleasure as for the dollar bills that float into their collection barrels. Women clutching cartons of coffee and bags of donuts stride to and from work in immaculate suits and grubby trainers.

Midtown is not blessed with lots of cafés you can slip into for their rest rooms, so it's worth remembering: the Public Library and Trump Tower both have free public toilets.

MIDTOWN MANHATTAN

Raging Feuds in 'Old New York'   Fifth Avenue officially opened for residence in 1837. Railroad tycoon Jay Gould was one of the first to decide it was a desirable place to live, and he built a mansion at 47th Street. The race was on. By the late nineteenth century William H. Vanderbilt had erected three mansions and was in serious competition with his sons, William and Cornelius, as to who could build the grandest. The young Vanderbilts settled on modest town house brownstones as the final solution to outdaring their father in construction, European-style gentlemen's clubs mushroomed, and by 1900 Fifth Avenue was chock-a-block, its mansions and town houses homes to the movers and shakers of industrial America – and to a soap opera of scrapping society wives who controlled New York's elite through a whirl of balls and dinners at a time when carriages rolled up and down Fifth Avenue and characters described in Edith Wharton novels had oysters and canvasback duck for dinner, when women wore jet jewellery for breakfast and refused to go to the country for the vague fear that they might encounter a bull, and when a mother might be ruined if others decided she had gone *too far* by serving melon before the consommé at her daughter's wedding breakfast.

'The beautiful Mrs Astor', who was descended from an old Dutch family, reigned supreme over New York society for the last half of the nineteenth century. She could break men's careers simply by not inviting them to a party, but she underestimated Mrs Vanderbilt's wiles when she judged her dreadful 'nouveau riche' and in 1883 failed to include her in her circle of 'old family' friends. Mrs Vanderbilt's son, William, was planning an eighteenth-century French costume ball. Strike Miss Astor's name from the guest list, said Mrs Vanderbilt, tapping her fan violently against her gloved hand, and of course Miss Astor – who had been practising her gavotte and mincing curtseys diligently in anticipation – threw a tantrum. Mrs Astor had to eat humble pie: she invited Mrs Vanderbilt to her home just in time for Miss Astor to receive an invitation.

But others resented Mrs Astor's powerful position and determined to wrest it from her – including Mrs William Waldorf Astor, her nephew's wife. Aunt Astor lived at 34th Street. In the 1890s the nephew sold his neighbouring 34th Street brownstone when he moved to Europe and, under strict and spiteful orders from his wife, had it turned into a hotel named the Waldorf. Mrs Astor was livid, but would not be defeated. She moved uptown and had her house turned into a hotel too – the Astoria.

Despite the family feud, the Waldorf and the Astoria worked together as friendly rivals. They even had connecting doors (on condition that Mrs Astor could close them at any time). Mrs Astor held her balls there. In 1892 she launched the term 'the 400' by sending out exactly 400 invitations. Her gallery–ballroom, she declared, could hold only that many guests comfortably. Exclusivity made her parties the social barometer of New York: Mrs Astor decided which 400 people in New York were worth knowing. They also gave her some control over who married whom, for the Waldorf-Astoria balls doubled as marriage marts. Mrs Astor thought it proper to introduce noble European stock. In just one year Consuela Vanderbilt had hitched up with the Duke of Marlborough and Pauline Whitney with the grandson of the Marquess of Anglesey.

After Mrs Astor's Inaugural Ball in 1896, Millionaires' Row moved with her uptown, and Fifth Avenue went downmarket. The Waldorf-Astoria nobly continued to host rooftop dances, but by the end of the 1920s the hotel too had moved uptown (see p.237). New York's elite women, however, regularly returned to Fifth Avenue for the healing hands of cosmetics diva Elizabeth Arden, known now as the woman who launched America's beauty industry.

Elizabeth Arden v. Helena Rubinstein Elizabeth Arden once declared to an interviewer: 'There's only one Elizabeth like me, and that's the queen.' Born Florence Nightingale Graham in 1878 in Canada, she first tried nursing, but 'I found I didn't really like looking at sick people' and instead wanted 'to keep people well, and young and beautiful'. So she transferred to dentistry and determined to make a beautifying skin cover-up cream at a time when 'nice' girls just sprinkled a little rice powder on their nose. Her father called her an ass, her cooking experimenting with ingredients like rotten eggs failed, so she decided to go to New York, which her appalled father said was full of 'Jews, Niggers, Chinks and opium dens'. 'It's no use, father. You can't stop me. But don't worry. Nothing is going to happen to me. I'm nearly 30 years old. If I haven't been wicked until now, I'm not likely to start at my age.'

It became clear while Florence worked for one Mrs Adair – practising the 'Ganesh' jaw-muscle-strapping treatment – that she had 'healing hands' and a head for marketing but no pharmaceutical nous, so in 1909 she joined forces with Elizabeth Hubbard. Adair catered only for 'gentlewomen of social standing'. Florence saw a wider appeal for Hubbard's 'Grecian Preparations', but split with Hubbard only a month after they had set up business at 509 Fifth Avenue. The words 'Mrs Elizabeth Hubbard' had already been written on the window in gold leaf, so to save money Florence kept 'Elizabeth', changed 'Hubbard' to 'Arden', renamed Hubbard's 'Grecian' Arden's 'Venetian', and brought in a milliner, Gladys, whose $45 hats sold like hot cakes. One employee said that working for Arden was like 'being caught in a revolving door'. She opened a branch in Washington and began running full-page ads in *Vogue*. But one bitterly cold January day in 1915, Mrs Titus, a.k.a.

Helena Rubinstein, arrived in New York. 'The first thing I noticed', Helena said later, 'was the whiteness of the women's faces and the oddly grayish colour of the lips . . . So I said to myself, here is not only a new country, but a huge market for my products.'

One of eight sisters born in the 1870s in Cracow, Poland, Rubinstein, like Arden, had gone into medicine, but found 'I grew dizzy at the first whiff of antiseptic'. She shipped creams a Polish doctor made for her mother out to Australia, then to Europe, where she studied at medical centres and introduced natural ingredients like grapes. To shake off the association of cosmetics with 'loose women', she used Somerset Maugham's words – 'The impact of beauty is to make you feel greater than you are, so that for a moment you seem to walk on air' – in reference to her products. By the time she came to New York, her reputation had preceded her. When she opened a salon on West 49th Street, most people called her 'Madame', but Arden called her 'that woman down the street'. They shared a love of hard work and fierce competition, they were both short, and for both business boomed, but Helena was dark and Semitic while Elizabeth was rosy-cheeked Anglo-Saxon. Arden's biographers Lewis and Woodworth noted: 'The racial prejudices of the day were subliminally stated in the locations of their respective establishments. Madame Rubinstein limited herself to cities in which Jews had always been accepted. Miss Arden was in many places that were not only anti-Semitic but boasted of their no Jews allowed policy.' Rubinstein could never appeal to the social elite. Arden explained: 'To be Catholic or Jewish isn't chic. Chic is Episcopalian.'

Between 1928 and 1929 gross trade generated by the beauty industry rose from $500,000,000 to $750,000,000, and Arden commented: 'The Depression seems to be good for our little business, dear. The more they chew their fingernails, wrinkle their brows and pull their hair, the more they need us.' Rubinstein remembers how she was assured by President Roosevelt that her war effort was 'to help keep up the morale of our women' with beautifying and confidence-boosting cosmetics, 'And you are doing it splendidly.' Even when Avon and Revlon outstripped Arden and Rubinstein products in sales, the two women's clashing personalities dominated the industry. Years later Rubinstein said: 'With her packaging and my products, we could've ruled the world.'

The Empire State

350 5th Ave (at 34th St). Entry $3.50, $1.75 for children. The Observatory is open 9.30 a.m. to midnight (tel. 736 6167). Consult the visibility notice before buying your ticket.

The Empire State is inextricably linked in the minds of millions with
King Kong, who clung to it in his desperate attempt to keep for ever
the kicking blonde film star he clutched in his hairy ape hand.
Today, Christmas, Easter and summer time a student, usually
female, puts on a gorilla suit for $7.50 an hour and prances round
the observation deck for families to take pictures.

Construction The Waldorf-Astoria Hotel was taken away as
16,000 tons of rubble in October 1929, and in less than two years
the Empire State had opened in its place. It was built at the height
of the Depression, which reduced the prices of labour and materials
and consequently construction costs which were, at $25,000,000,
considerably lower than original estimate. But bread queues and
despair were growing, and while the thrusting Empire State was a
symbol of hope to some, it was the 'Empty State' to many.

The designers, Shreve, Lamb and Harmon Associates, were told
that height was top priority. Its 102 stepped storeys and the spindly
TV antennae (203 ft) make it the third tallest building in the world.
Even today visitors worry that it might fall down. So far it has done
nothing more worrying than waver, and only one plane – a 1945
bomber – has crashed into it. Stunning when it is lit up in colours
appropriate for different occasions, including pink for Gay Pride
day, its observation deck – which offers panoramic views of
Manhattan, the Hudson and the neighbouring boroughs – is a good
first stop for orientation.

The Visit As you approach the Empire State, look up and you
won't be able to see further than the several yards of netting at first-
storey level. This was attached to catch the coins tourists took to
dropping when they learned that the impact of a dime dropped
from the top of the Empire State could kill someone.

Inside, the wood-panelled Art Deco lobby displays a series of
gaudy back-lighted paintings that depict, says the brochure, 'the
Seven Wonders of the Ancient World as well as the Eighth Wonder
of the Modern World', which is, of course, the Empire State. The
tickets are sold in a more prosaic room where the queue winding
through a maze of ropes and metal stands can be an hour or more
midweek peak season. Then there's more queueing for the two lifts
that take you to the 86th-floor gift shop and Observatory. Outside,
you are windswept immediately. The deck is encased in thick wire
that makes it so cage-like as to be rather disconcerting. If you
squash your face right against the fence, it no longer impedes your
vision, but then vertigo might replace claustrophobia. Try to
staunch both, as the vistas really are spectacular. Look south for the
Statue of Liberty, east for Brooklyn and to the north there's Central
Park, incongruously fluffy with its greenery – or reddery if its

autumn – sunk into a sea of skyscrapers. The only odd thing is that one of New York's most famous landmarks is not visible, because you are on it.

Pierpont Morgan Library

Short detour off 5th Ave to 29 E 36th St (bet. Park and Madison Aves). Open 10.30 a.m. (Sun 1 p.m.) to 5 p.m. (closed Mon and holidays). Suggested admission $5.00, $3.00 students, free for under-12s. There are free guided tours: 'Masterpieces of the Morgan Library' on Wed and Fri' and 'The History and Architecture of the Morgan Library' on Tues and Thurs, both at 2.30 p.m., meeting at the information desk.

One of the city's best museums, this was purpose-built as the library of a rich, superstitious nineteenth-century banker called Pierpont Morgan. A 1906 pink marble McKim beaux-arts masterpiece in miniature guarded by two crouching lionesses, it has some art and antique pots, but unlike his contemporaries – including Frick (see p.163) – Morgan's real interest lay in collecting manuscripts. He was also unusual in appointing a woman, imperious young Belle da Costa Greene, as his librarian and sometime buyer. Now public, the Library's vast archives include Renaissance Books of Hours, Aphra Behn's only surviving manuscript, a corrected typescript of Nobel Prize-winner Nadine Gordimer, and the finest Jane Austen holdings anywhere in the world.

The main **entrance** is closed to the public. You enter at the side.

The museum has recently been linked by a glassed-in garden court with a ski-slope roof to include the ground floor of the neighbouring brownstone, which was built by Morgan's son. The brownstone houses the museum shop, which sells books on books as well as the twee gifts more familiar to museum shops. The grey-tiled basement rest rooms are the newest and cleanest in the area.

You can visit three galleries displaying rotating selections from the archive before you come to the original McKim building. Here the marble-floored **Rotunda** is covered in murals that were designed to illustrate the Library's role as repository of the art and ideas from Antiquity to the Renaissance, but look more like scenes from lewd dramas. Half-naked women cavort around urns and acanthus foliage and act out scenes of bondage (Force chained by Wisdom), attempted homicide (Circe offers Odysseus poisoned drink) and adultery (Queen Guinevere kissing Lancelot).

The **East Room** is wall-to-wall books except for the area above the fireplace, where there's a worn tapestry depicting the Seven Deadly Sins, and the room has evidence of Morgan's superstitious streak. A committed member of the New York gentlemen's Zodiac

Club, Morgan had his 'lucky stars', Aries and Gemini, put in hexagons above the library doorway so that he would walk under them every day. One is his birth date, the other the date of his second marriage in 1865 to Frances Tracy. This may have been a stoic attempt to shake off the sad memory of his first wife, Amelia Sturgis, whom he married when she was twenty-four – knowing she had TB – just four months before her death. The sign Mimi died under, Aquarius, is a tactful distance away on the opposite wall.

In the midst of all this opulent superstition are display cases. The exhibitions vary but may include handwritten Bach and Wagner scores and curling printed ephemera from America's fight for independence, and they always include a fifteenth-century Gutenberg Bible, which was the first book to be printed from movable type. Gutenberg's invention of movable type was revolutionary because it ended the Church monopoly on written information. Previously, everything had been laboriously hand-scribed in Latin by clerics. With relatively cheap, quick and easy-to-use movable type came freedom of information.

The dark **West Room**, Morgan's study, has a wooden ceiling covered with coats of arms copied from a volume on Renaissance bookplates, and is dominated by a large dour portrait of himself.

Belle da Costa Greene (1883–1950)

Just twenty-two when Morgan's nephew Junius discovered her among the rare books at Princeton University, Belle Greene was immediately whisked back to New York and Morgan's library, where she later made history as the first woman library director in America. Initially Morgan's secretary, she soon became his personal aide and librarian and was sent in his place to haggle with rare-book dealers and auctioneers. In this mainly male world, Belle raised many eyebrows. Her beauty was often described as 'exotic', she was respected for her intelligence, and she was feared for what one friend called 'a certain imperious pungency of temperament'. She was free to the point of rudeness with her opinions – writing, for example, to Morgan's son: 'In regard to the Tennyson items which, personally I loathe, it is a question of perfecting your already very large and fine collection of imbecilities.' She was a canny negotiator, persuading Lord Amherst to sell seventeen books printed by Caxton the night before a 1908 public auction, and in 1911 she got more Caxton at a knockdown price by telling her competitor that if he bid the asked-for $50,000 she'd bid $100,000, thus scaring him out of the running and paying only $42,800. Belle was also well known for her long love affair with Bernard Berenson, which started in 1908. Berenson's biographer, Ernest Samuels, said their affair was the 'one romance in Berenson's life that would stand apart from all others in depth and intensity', and Berenson's wife called Belle Greene a 'most wild and woolly and EXTRAORDINARY young person'. She continued as director of the library until her retirement in 1948.

New York Public Library

5th Ave (bet. W 40th and 42nd Sts). Open 10 a.m. to 8.45 p.m. (5.45 p.m. Thurs, Fri, Sat); closed Sun and holidays. Free public toilets.

This place is revered by New Yorkers. Its collection is on the scale of the British Library's – one of the five largest in the world – but the New York Library is public. Anyone can order any book or rare document.

The vast expanse of Vermont marble steps in front is always busy, with an outdoor café and coffee drinkers in summer, and all year it's a favourite meeting-place for New Yorkers, whose joke about the classical lions, Patience and Fortitude, on either side of the entrance goes: 'reading between the lions'. As with so many New York institutions, the most important part women have played has been as 'benefactress'. Currently it is socialite Brooke Astor (see box), who campaigns vigorously to raise funds for the Library's upkeep, which is entirely appropriate. The Library was originally built to house the Astor Library, as well as the Lenox Library and the Tilden Trust.

This is a good place to sit quietly with a book if you're on your own with time to kill.

Inside the lobby, two grand marble staircases lead to the third-floor **Central Hall**. This is decorated with four arched 1940 murals in Socialist Realist style painted by Edward Laning under the WPA (Works Progress Administration) programme, a Roosevelt initiative to provide employment for artists and craftsmen and boost the economy after the Depression. They are supposed to depict 'The Story of the Recorded Word', and women play a sorry part. Only three feature. One high-up and small woman teaches her son to read, and in the eye-catching 'Moses with the Tablets of the Law', two coarse peasant women can only raise their hands pathetically in awe while decrepit bearded old Moses totters down Mount Sinai bearing the big stone tablets.

The murals aren't great art, but they're more entertaining than the paintings in the **Salamon Room** (off the Central Hall), which displays a stuffy portrait collection including five of Washington, a number of the library's benefactors and a couple of 'notorious beauties'.

On the other side of the Central Hall is the half-acre **Reading Room**. Here Betty Friedan (see p.103) spent three days a week researching *The Feminine Mystique* in the late 1950s before writing out her findings on legal pads in the dining-room of her home. It gets jam-packed. The readers – who come from all walks of life –

will hiss violently at newcomers to guard a friend's place. Incongruous amongst the wood panelling and brass light fittings is the huge digital number board, the only evidence that the Library has been computerised with highly sophisticated technology that gets books delivered minutes after request: the deli-ticket system combines with flashing numbers to call the next person for their books.

BROOKE ASTOR

Avenue Magazine has a society section which recently printed a photo of Brooke Astor as a girl with her 'beloved amah', a smiling Chinese woman, and this accompanying text: 'That's me in Peking. I was about eight years old. That was my *amah* – I called her amah, like nanny – and she would go walking with me. I adored her. She had these little tiny broken feet – you know, they bound the feet of baby Chinese girls – and she tottered around on them. I spoke to her in Chinese, of course. I knew Chinese. My father, who was a major in the army, said I could have anything I wanted if I asked for it in Chinese. So I had a pony, a donkey, three dogs, and a hedgehog. We lived in the embassy compound from the time I was seven until we left when I was eleven. I love China.'

Bryant Park

Between 40th and 42nd Sts (behind the Public Library).

This former no-go area has been reclaimed from drug pushers and transformed with an $8.9 million restoration into 4 acres of lawn surrounded by pastel flowers and gravel paths where office workers can now eat sandwiches. Rooftop floodlights have been installed to keep the park safe to walk past at night, and the public rest rooms are complete with baby-changing area. A rare and welcome piece of Midtown greenery.

Diamond Row

47th St (bet. 5th and 6th Aves).

Eighty per cent of America's diamond trade happens here – some of it in shops but most in booths the size of telephone kiosks, all with Fort Knox-style security systems. Federal Express mail vans jostle for unloading space and salesmen shout at you: 'Wanna buy a diamond?'

St Patrick's Cathedral

5th Ave (bet. 50th and 51st Sts).

St Patrick's is the seat of the Archbishop of New York, Cardinal O'Connor, one of the country's most powerful Catholics and a man who frequently clashes with the lesbian and gay community. New York *Newsday* accused him of championing 'suffocating bigotry and small-mindedness' at the 1992 St Patrick's Day parade, when he banned members of the Irish Lesbian and Gay Organisation from the march. 'Two! Four! Six! Eight! How do you know your kids are straight?' they booed from the sidelines.

Construction   When the spiky cathedral was finished in 1881, it was considered too far out of town. Now, of course, it is central, and Americans have always loved it because it is so terribly European. British architect James Renwick trawled France for design ideas and settled on Gothic. Pinnacles sprout up all round the outside, inside cross-ribbed Gothic arches rise 110 ft above the nave and there is a 26 ft-diameter rose window above the central portal. The glass of this window is a beautiful, intense blue, and is the only thing worth seeing. The cathedral has a cold, pompous atmosphere. It is somehow pleasing that it has been so dwarfed by the surrounding buildings, notably the Rockefeller Center opposite.

Villard Houses

451–455 Madison Ave (bet. 50th and 51st Sts).

This Italian Palazzo-style 1884 McKim, Mead and White carriage-yard is part of the sleek tower block Helmsley Palace Hotel, which was the jewel in 'Queen' Leona Helmsley's crown until she became prisoner No. 15113–054 in spring 1992 (see box) for tax evasion. The anti-Leona camp says the marriage of tower block and land-mark architecture is gauchely done, but the Villard Houses' lavish second-floor **Gold Room** has nevertheless become one of the City's top spots for the current version of 1980s power-breakfasts on yachts, power-teas. If you don formal dress and splash out on after-noon Earl Grey and bijoux plates of sandwiches in the Gold Room, you'll be among Chief Executives sealing multimillion-dollar deals with a dainty clink of fine bone china.

THE QUEEN OF MEAN

Barely before the prison door had shut on the woman loathed for saying 'Only little people pay taxes', Leona Helmsley was subject of a TV drama charting her ruthless rise from a penniless nobody in Brooklyn to the Queen of the Helmsley Palace and wife of one of the wealthiest men in America, Harry Helmsley. The nation revelled in her demise, and investigative reporters made their careers on it – most notably Ransdell Pearson of the *New York Post*, who wrote the proudly unauthorised *Queen of Mean* biography that boasted a list of 'revelations', including:

• Leona apparently pressured Harry Helmsley into marrying her by inventing a rival lover – complete with diamond ring and love letters proposing marriage.
• Leona's family members suspect that the 1973 stabbing in the Helmsley's Palm Beach Penthouse may actually have been done by Harry – not the female intruder in a 'World War II' gas mask that Leona reported to the police.
• Jay Panzirer, Leona's son, died during an extramarital tryst with a furniture sales-woman – despite the obituary that claims he died during a business meeting.
• Leona not only refused to pay for major items like TV sets and house renovation [but] also demanded freebies from her suppliers including toilet paper, cleaning supplies and toothbrushes.
• Leona used a computerised Scitex machine to take decades off her face and inches off her figure in photos of herself for her hotel's international advertising campaign.
• Her daily vituperative phone calls to son Jay probably hastened his death . . . When sister Sandra lay dying in the hospital for two weeks, Leona never even telephoned – and she did not attend Sandra's funeral.

Leona is currently serving four years in a Lexington prison for income tax fraud. Her hotel experience might qualify her to mop floors and launder bedsheets, said the warden.

Trump Tower

725 5th Ave (at 56th St), closed Sun. Plush free public toilets.

This highly reflective glass-sheathed skyscraper (built in 1983) contains condominiums including Donald Trump's own as well as boutiques and a six-storey atrium featuring an 80-ft waterfall that is cooling in summer and always relaxing to sit by for women with children, although the snooty porters put a damper on the atmosphere and the tower's real interest lies in its namesake, 'the Donald' as his ex-wife Bardot-lookalike Ivana calls Mr Trump.

IVANA TRUMPS THE DONALD

'The New York real-estate developer Donald Trump', wrote novelist Emily Prager recently, 'has come to personify all that was villainous in Ronald Reagan's Eighties: the idolatrous worship of money; the lust for superficiality; the narcissistic self-aggrandisement of the super-rich; the denigration, if not disappearance, of elegance, quality, soul and silence.' He razed prewar buildings, harassed and evicted tenants and erected 'Vegas-like battlements' as 'the vulgar domain of his fantasy monarchy', including Trump Tower. The man from New Jersey was never much liked, but his real downfall came in 1988 when he betrayed Ivana for one Miss Maples in public, causing Ivana to 'weep sincerely and pathetically with humiliation', wrote Prager. New York was outraged on Ivana's behalf and rejoiced when she resurfaced four years later, aged forty-three with a new man, Riccardo Mazzucchelli, a new nose courtesy of Michael Jackson's plastic surgeon, and a first novel, *For Love Alone*, which bears remarkable similarities to her own life – young Czech skis her way to freedom, starts a hotel business and marries a millionaire – but is not, she declares, autobiographical. She is endearingly open about the fact that it was 'co-crafted' by sometime scriptwriter for *Dallas* and *Dynasty* Camille Marchetta, whom Ivana calls 'My girl the Camille' and takes everywhere, 'so she can see things through my eyes'. And Ivana's view looks increasingly rosy, while Donald fades into oblivion. The divorce settlement left her a millionaire with assets in the Plaza Hotel plus ownership of a 100-room Manhattan triplex penthouse. She has posed for the cover of *Penthouse*, modelled for Thierry Mugler's Paris catwalk show, and has a cosmetics range in the pipeline – all just for the fun of it. 'I'm a very wealthy woman,' says Ivana, with satisfaction. 'I really don't need to work for the rest of my life.'

The Plaza Hotel

W 59th St (at 5th Ave).

This is a celebrity hotel. F. Scott Fitzgerald's wife Zelda apparently danced naked in the fountain out front; Solomon Guggenheim walled himself up in the state suite for years with a mini-gallery of priceless modern art; Frank Lloyd Wright used it as his New York headquarters; the Beatles stayed here; and since 1988 it has been run by Ivana Trump, who ordered a major renovation (which is not at all bad) and headhunted New York's top hotel personnel.

Built in 1907, the Plaza – a muck-grey block filled with little windows and crowned with two green triangles – is described as Edwardian and worth going to for the Neuchatel chocolate shop and breakfasts in the Palm Room.

BETTY AND THE OAK ROOM SIT-IN

The Oak Room at the Plaza Hotel became the target of *Betty Friedan* and the National Organization of Women (NOW), who planned a February 1969 sit-in to protest sixty-one years of the Oak Room barring women on weekdays from noon to three – a practice that allowed male executives to thrash out the really *big* deals in their female colleagues' absence, thus simultaneously humiliating women and reinforcing the glass ceiling they hit. The Oak Room was just one of many restaurants repeatedly to flout the five-year-old 1964 Supreme Court ruling that said no public facility could refuse service to anyone on the basis of their race or sex. The sit-in was well attended by the national media, but Friedan herself was one of the latest to arrive, embarrassed because she had a black eye which she'd got from her husband during an argument. She considers it one of the greatest ironies of her life that while leading the women of America on the path to liberation she couldn't free herself from a destructive marriage.

EAST 42ND STREET

A Broadway musical immortalised 42nd Street as naughty, bawdy, gaudy and sporty, a description which is not so apt today. 42nd Street is New York's major cross-town artery. The thundering traffic has taken its toll and large chunks of the road are usually cordoned off and undergoing major surgery. The most common kind of 'naughtiness' is probably white-collar crime (see box), and the nearest anything gets to 'gaudy' is the Woolworth's café (at the 170 42nd St branch), where greasy-haired waitresses in gaudy pinnies serve meatloaf and toast with jelly to secretaries on coffee break and to off-duty traffic wardens engrossed in well-thumbed paperback romances. Otherwise, East 42nd Street is a working display of 'cathedrals of commerce' in a range of styles and ages, including the 1929 **Chanin Building** (122 E 42nd St), which is decorated with a swirling William Morris-style bas-relief at third-floor level, and the ugly block-long 1955 **Mobil Building** (150 E 42nd St), which is covered in supposedly self-cleaning steel plates that are crisscross-patterned to encourage the wind to scour dirt off naturally. Women with children will welcome the cathedral of commerce that doubles as a summer haven: the 1967 **Ford Foundation** building's main feature is a heavenly atrium filled with ferns, lilies, flowering rose bushes, spider plants and 17 full-grown trees (321 E 42nd St, open working hours). Older children will also like the *Daily News* building lobby (220 E 42nd St), which resembles a tacky science-fiction set. The giant, gloomily lit rotating globe and the surrounding throbbing thermometers, blinking wind-speed indicators and swinging clock pendulums are meant to represent together the *Daily News* as a network of information spreading across the world. Most people now associate the newspaper with the Robert Maxwell pension fund scandal.

The Past 42nd Street was officially opened for residence in 1836 by the mayor, who hoped that the prospect of clean air would encourage people to move uptown. It did, but it was immigrants, not 'desirables', who flocked in. By 1860 42nd Street was a shantytown where children played in the dirt and sheep and goats held court.

Things changed only because of the railway. The railway ran down what is now Park Avenue, originally to a depot on 23rd Street, until rich Murray Hill residents complained vehemently of noise and air pollution, and locomotives were banned below 42nd Street. In 1871 the shantytowns were levelled for the new train depot that was to become Grand Central Terminal. Big businesses began to site themselves near the station – which became known as 'the gateway to the city' – and the area's prosperity was guaranteed. Its respectability was finally sealed in 1950, when the UN ousted the riverfront's breweries, slaughterhouses, glue factories, gas works and the hide-outs of gangs and criminals that went with them.

WOMEN AND CRIME

'A growing number of white-collar crimes are being committed by women today,' reports Working Woman magazine, 'and the crime of choice, says Peter Crusco, an assistant district attorney in Queens, N.Y., is embezzlement.' The number of women indicted for office-related crimes is up about 25% since 1985. Why? As women have entered the job market they've simply gained more access to money and opportunity to steal it, one argument goes. Another says women get frustrated by the glass ceiling that stops them reaching the very top, and wreak revenge through embezzlement. New York's Sandi Franklin fell into another trap: her business ran into debt in 1985, and rather than humiliate herself she issued bad cheques, ended up in prison and now works for the Fortune Society, a New York-based organisation that helps ex-offenders. Executive director of Fortune JoAnne Page hints that the instances of crime might not be rising so fast as businesses' willingness to prosecute women. Old-style patriarchal firms would simply let women go quietly, but an increase in celebrity cases, including hotelier Leona Helmsley's (see p.119), has inured courts and employers to the sight of repentant, tearful females. Sentences are harsh, and criminologists expect the trend of thwarted ambitious women turning to white-collar crime to continue climbing.

Grand Central Terminal

E 42nd St (at Park Ave). The Municipal Arts Society organises two free tours of Grand Central, one of the inside (every Wed at 12.30 from in front of the Chemical Bank in the concourse) and one of the outside (every Fri at 12.30 from in front of the Philip Morris Building). The station's public toilets are rather dismal – use the Grand Hyatt Hotel lobby rest rooms instead.

Who would think it of a station? Even if you're not catching a train, Grand Central is wonderful to visit. It's a triumph of urban planning, and people-watching from the Vanderbilt Avenue end café (see p.272) can keep you occupied through several cups of coffee, because the Grand Central Concourse the café overlooks is still 'the crossroads of a million private lives' described in a 1937 NBC Radio Broadcast. Various hazards on the concourse include getting bulldozed by a trainload of commuters, tripping over snoring vagrants, and losing your purse to a pickpocket.

Construction   One of the oddest things about Grand Central is that from the outside there's no evidence of trains or tracks at all. After the 1854 laws banning locomotives below 42nd Street, Cornelius 'Commodore' Vanderbilt was faced with laws in 1902 banning steam engines from New York altogether. If he was to stay in business, he had to move out or reroute trains underground. The last option had recently been made possible by electrification. Vanderbilt took it.

The building was designed by Whitney Warren and James A. Wetmore together with engineers Reed and Stem, who succeeded remarkably well in carrying out their brief, which was to integrate City and railroad. Directly below the busiest part of Park Avenue lie 33.7 miles of tracks and cavernous fan-shaped yards, and the station concourse is directly linked by escalators to the Grand Hyatt Hotel and the Pan Am building lobby.

When it opened in 1913, the terminal building must have been an awe-inspiring gateway to the City. Today, despite its size (it covers three blocks up to 45th Street), its florid beaux-arts structure is dwarfed by the surrounding skyscrapers, particularly by the slab of Pan Am building that soars up behind. However, lower your eyes and refocus, because Grand Central is still impressive.

The main southern façade is made up of three triumphal arches filled in with steel and glass. Spreading out above the central arch is a huge sculpture by Jules Coutan which features a 13-ft-diameter clock and an American eagle fraternising with three scantily clad lounging Roman deities.

The station has recently been made a National Historic Landmark and renovated, a process that involved scouring off thick layers of grime and installing an expensive and subtle lighting system. The exterior looks stunning when it's illuminated at night. The interior is at its best on a sunny day when light streams through the 60 ft × 33 ft arched windows. Enter by any of the street doors and an ingenious series of ramps and walkways will lead you into the main concourse, which – measuring 160 ft wide by 470 ft long and soaring to 150 ft at its apogee – is larger than the nave of Notre Dame de Paris. The floors are paved with opulent Tennessee marble and the ceiling, a plaster vault suspended from steel trusses, is speckled with 2,500 stars representing the constellations of the winter night sky.

As for the rest of the station, make sure to see the Oyster Bar, which, thanks to the echo of the vaultings covered with tiles made by Rafael Guastivino, is one of the loudest eating places in town (see p.273).

Underneath the Waldorf Hotel, at the bottom of a zigzagging iron staircase that seems bound for the centre of the earth, there's a secret offshoot of the Grand Central railroad complex. In the 1930s and 1940s Franklin Delano Roosevelt's private presidential train would pull into this underground barn. He would be whizzed in his wheelchair by a very private elevator up to his rooftop suite. Andy Warhol also used the space, but for a very different purpose: he threw a party. It was, according to someone who attended, Dantesque with lots of black, and very dingy lighting. Bands struck up on top of dead trains, and drinkers and revellers piled into the crumbling dining cars.

Philip Morris Headquarters

120 Park Ave (bet. 41st and 42nd Sts). Gallery talks in the lobby's Whitney Downtown take place on Mon, Wed and Fri at 12.30 p.m. The lobby is open to the public Mon–Sat 7.30 a.m.–9.30 p.m. and Sun 11 a.m.–7 p.m.: the gallery is open Mon–Sat 11 a.m.–6 p.m. Free.

Compared to the softly lit beaux-arts station, this cigarette company's HQ is really quite threatening. The 1983 Ulrich Franzen and Associates design has strips of granite shooting violently up a black reflecting-glass body. Clichéd it may be to describe Manhattan skyscrapers as phalluses, but if you glance at the Philip Morris and then down 42nd Street (notice the ejaculating Chrysler in particular), it is difficult to dismiss the connection.

The 42-ft-high Philip Morris lobby, however, is a welcome place with an enclosed garden, an espresso bar, a gift shop and the Whitney Downtown, a small exhibition space used by the Whitney Museum of Modern Art. The site is not prestigious, so the shows here are rarely thrilling – a room on the right has changing exhibitions of nineteenth- and twentieth-century American art – but because the museum runs a programme called Art Reach (reaching out to the community), if you're there on a weekday mid-morning or mid-afternoon the lobby is likely to be covered with children crouched earnestly over crayons and paper on the floor.

405 Lexington Ave (at 42nd St).

Designed by William Van Alen between 1928 and 1930, the Chrysler Building was the swansong of the twenties in New York. In its celebration of financial success, it captured perfectly the heady atmosphere of pre-Crash capitalism, but America went bankrupt the year before the Chrysler was finished. Rising to 850 ft, it was the tallest building in the world for only a few months before the Empire State outstripped it in 1931.

Everything about the Chrysler Building emphasises height. The windows are designed to mimic the elevator shafts at its core, zooming up the twenty-storey base, shooting through the 560-ft middle section and finally climaxing in a stainless steel sunburst motif with scalloped windows, surmounted by a spire. The light grey stone body is lavished with automobile motifs including, on the fourth setback, Chrysler radiator caps with wings linked by a frieze of abstracted car wheels.

While you're trying to get a good vantage point, be careful you don't step back a pace, and another, and again, until you're bang in the middle of the road, hopping to avoid maniac cab drivers and lorries.

The United Nations

E 45th St (at 1st Ave). 50-min tours leave every 15 mins Mon–Fri 9.15 a.m.–4.45 p.m., $5.50, students $3.50, under-5s not admitted. Tel. 212 963 7713. Free tickets to meetings of the various councils are available from the Information Desk in the lobby.

The UN was set up in 1945 as a postwar congress of peace, but since today the UN is having to dip into the peacekeeping fund to pay the electricity bills because 134 of the 159 member countries haven't coughed up their promised contributions, detractors are questioning the sincerity of those 134 debtors' commitment to peace. The worst culprit is America, with a debt of $407 million.

Construction Le Corbusier was consulted in the planning stages, and he hatched a grand plan to build a world parliament which would house the Secretariat and the UN's head, the Secretary-General (presently Boutros Boutros-Ghali), in a towering and appropriately majestic glass box. The UN took Le Corbusier's ideas but gave the commission to Harrison and Abramovitz. Le Corbusier returned to Europe empty-handed and bitter, only to have the knife twisted in 1950 when the finished product, so closely based on his own design, was universally panned by the critics. The slab Secretariat smacks of faceless bureaucracy, they said, and the curvaceous cantilevers inside of a seedy international hotel.

The visitor can be glad that at least one of Le Corbusier's original intentions survived: he wanted to liberate Manhattan from congestion, introducing light, space and greenery into the life of the metropolis. From wherever you're standing, the UN is striking for the way it spreads out. The main buildings are set out like sculptural objects on a platform, with plenty of breezy walkways and grassed areas in between.

LA BOCA GRANDE IN THE UN

Only months after the death of her husband Franklin D. Roosevelt, Eleanor Roosevelt was invited in 1945 by President Truman to become the only woman in the US delegation of the newly founded UN. She had her enemies, including journalist Westbrook Pegler, who dubbed her 'La Boca Grande' – or 'the Big Mouth' – and Cardinal Spellman who, infuriated by her support of birth control, publicly declared her an unfit mother. Eleanor's UN colleagues John Foster Dulles and Arthur Vandenberg expressed their negative confidence in her abilities by assigning her to 'humanitarian problems' in what was considered a backwater, Committee 3. Eleanor Roosevelt dedicated two years to drafting the Universal Declaration of Human Rights, and when it was presented to the General Assembly in 1948 she won a standing ovation. Her old foe Arthur Vandenberg said: 'I want to say that I take back everything I ever said about her . . . And believe me, it's been plenty.' Even Cardinal Spellman, years later, retracted his 'unfit mother' statement, speaking of 'great confusion and regrettable misunderstandings'.

Right at the start of Eleanor's work on the Universal Declaration of Human Rights, women from the Indian delegation fought the opening statement of Article 1, which read: 'All men are created equal'. The phrase was changed to 'all human beings', but it seems that the issue of women's equality died an early death at the UN. Today only two of the 159 nations' representatives are women; although there is a special programme for the advancement of women, based in Dominica, it meets rarely and has no clout; and as for an equal opportunities policy, by 1996 the UN hopes that 35% of their staff will be women, giving no breakdown of how many should be employed as secretaries, canteen staff and guides.

A Visit Approach the UN from 42nd Street and you'll pass the 159 member states' flags strung up like ostentatious party decorations. The daily tours, which are riveting PR exercises, start at the General Assembly Lobby (entrance near 1st Ave and 44th St), and if you don't do the tour you can visit only the basement shops and the grounds outside. Because the UN is partially open to the public, the tour is limited to parts of the General Assembly and Conference Buildings and the passage that links them. This corridor, first stop on the tour, can be distressing. The visual aids which fill the cabinets and line the walls are there to illustrate the devastating power of the nuclear bomb. With something like pride the tour guide will point out melted china, surreal wads of coins and a statue of St Agnes, who fell face-down at Nagasaki and is thus still serene viewed from the front, while her back is boiled concrete.

The whirlwind tour ends in the basement. Here you can buy burgers and fries in the UN coffee shop, corn dollies, flag pins and glasses engraved with the UN logo in the UN gift shop, or unique UN stamps in the post office.

PARK AVENUE

Park Avenue has perhaps *the* most important skyscraper of the last four decades – the Seagram Building – and it has a lot of big banks, so it's useful if you're changing money, but otherwise it's a rather sterile strip roaring with traffic where shrubs and flowers dotted about in the series of traffic islands only add to the 'total effect of chaotic architectural wilfulness overlaid on boredom' Jane Jacobs describes in *The Death and Life of American Cities*. It does, however, somehow typify New York. Standing outside the Seagram, maybe before going to its Four Seasons bar for a celebrity-spotting drink, look south from the middle of the Avenue for the best view of the Pan Am Building and for the almost unnerving sight of streams of cabs and limos – or just their tail-lights at night – apparently falling off the end of Park Avenue, where the road goes under the ornate Helmsley building before re-emerging beyond 42nd Street.

Women with children who need a rest surrounded by soothing waterfalls and a profusion of plants, remember the **Chemcourt** atrium protruding from the Chemical Bank building (between 47th and 48th Sts), which you can spot by the statue outside of a man hailing a cab. Everyone be thankful for the **Waldorf-Astoria Hotel** (between 49th and 50th Sts), which has some of the grandest ladies' rest rooms in town. And if you think you might like jazz vespers, check out **St Peter's** (see below).

Park Avenue is known for its banks, for its internationally respected advertising agencies, for housing most of the country's top plastic surgeons (see box), and it was in Park Avenue offices that Gloria Steinem co-founded America's first commercial feminist magazine, *Ms*.

Gloria Steinem and Ms. A bouncy blonde all-American teenager who was into double-dating with friends at high-school dances and stock-car races, Gloria Steinem was born in Ohio in 1934 at the height of the Depression to financially troubled parents who were anxious to divorce. Gloria immersed herself in *Gone With the Wind* at the Public Library and dreamed of becoming a Rockette at Radio City Hall, but instead she was taken to Washington by her sister for more schooling. Most young women in the 1950s studied art or literature, but Steinem majored in Government, travelled to India at the age of twenty-two and arrived in New York in 1958 determined to raise Americans' awareness of international issues through the media. Her first major signed article explored the birth-control Pill for *Esquire*, but the next year she took an assignment that nearly scuppered her chances of making it as a serious journalist: in 1963 she agreed to become a bunny girl to do an exposé of *Playboy* magazine clubs called 'A Bunny's Tale'. *Playboy* publisher Hugh Hefner – a man who had once rejected an article on the women's movement for being too 'well-balanced', saying 'these chicks are our natural enemies' – failed to sue Steinem but embarrassed her repeatedly for years to come by publishing pictures of her as a bunny girl 'amid ever more pornographic photos of other bunnies', said Steinem.

PLASTIC SURGERY

Snips and tucks to bagging eyes and sagging chins are considered not luxury or vanity but necessity in America, so smug plastic surgeons were filled with horror in November 1991 when the US Food and Drug Administration ruled that manufacturers must provide more proof that silicone implants are safe, or they will be banned.

Problems have been associated with silicone breast implants since they were invented in the 1960s by American plastic surgeon Thomas Cronin. Women complain of arthritis-like pains in joints and mouth ulcers; and forty-two-year-old Barbira Herzog described how her implants ruptured 'and silicone was all over the inside of my chest'. When this happens, the silicone degrades, bonds with bodily tissue and forms a known carcenogenic substance.

The 1991 Food and Drug Administration panel ruling gave the industry ten more years' trading before it finally has to clear up its act. Meanwhile, a surprising number of women are happy to risk silicone, saying they prefer quality of life to quantity. More than 2 million American women have had breast implants, 80% for cosmetic reasons. Women who have been scared off silicone haven't questioned surgery – they've merely turned to other products and methods, including saline breast implants, which have been known to burst on aeroplanes, and instead of collagen injections they have sections of inner thigh moved to make pouting upper lips.

Nevertheless, by 1965 she was making a full-time living as a writer, interviewing figures including Dorothy Parker, James Baldwin and Truman Capote for *New York* magazine. In 1968 she was sent to cover a meeting of a radical feminist group called the Redstockings; the topic: abortion, which was then illegal. Steinem was an immediate and vocal convert to the movement, but big magazines told her: 'We've done our feminist articles already.' She decided the feminist movement needed its own national magazine, which should be commercial and widely available, should cover job discrimination, sex roles and the need for women to work together, and should feed its profit into other feminist projects. The 230 Park Avenue offices were tiny, and voluntary staff worked to hair-raising schedules; but the 1971 first issue proved even more successful than its founders had hoped, and Steinem was suddenly famous nationwide as the leader of the women's movement. An *Esquire* article called her 'the intellectual's pin-up' and implied that she owed her success to shapely legs and a string of powerful boyfriends. Many feminists thought she should tone down her glamorous image – Steinem retorted that she wasn't about to 'put on combat boots or cut off my hair' – and Betty Friedan accused her of being too radical. Amongst other things, Friedan said that Steinem's open support of lesbians would alienate too many Americans and thus destroy feminism's mass appeal.

Today, some say that Steinem is populist and criticise her 1992 book *Revolution from Within,* which is about the importance of self-esteem and how to regain it. Steinem says she's never been happier. At over sixty she looks like forty, she says she's finally furnished her Upper East Side brownstone with more than boxes, saved money for the first time in her life, taken up exercise, and untangled her relationship with multimillionaire Mortimer Zuckerman. She is still a contributing editor to *Ms.* magazine, which, now completely free of advertising, celebrated its 21st birthday in 1993.

Pan Am Building

200 Park Ave (bet. 44th and 45th Sts).

The completion of the Pan Am building – designed by Walter Gropius of the Bauhaus school – in 1963 caused an uproar. Critics declared it an ugly failure: 'it hides the glorious Grand Central', they moaned; 'the helicopter pad on top is too noisy', they whined.

Gropius himself had caused quite a rumpus when, as a dashing young man in 1910, he stole German composer Mahler's beloved Alma, who declared Mahler impotent from overwork. Years later and long separated from Alma, he failed similarly to enamour the States with the Pan Am, which he had intended to make a grand statement about teamwork and anonymity through plainness of form. Many say he achieved only banality with the 59-storey cast-concrete octagonal tower, its shape supposedly a much-magnified version of a tiny bit of aeroplane wing. Until the World Trade Center was built, the Pan Am had, with 2,400,000 sq ft, the most office space of any building in the world. Now it's all that is left of a bankrupt airline.

St Bartholomew's Church

Between 50th and 51st Sts.

It is hard not to take comparisons of New York now with New York of the Great Depression years seriously when you are confronted in the narthex of this church with two rows of metal hospital beds, their single rough brown blankets rolled up at the end of bare mattresses. The church is open to the public only from 8 a.m. to 6 p.m. After hours on Tuesdays and Thursdays it's home to a handful of the city's vagrants, who are clothed and fed and given a decent night's sleep.

Architecturally, 'St Bart's', as it's called in the leaflets and handouts, is a patchwork. Its salmon-pink and grey limestone bulk topped with a multicoloured dome was built in 1919 by Bertram Goodhue and is considered Byzantine. The front portal, which features grand arches and sculpted bronze doors donated by the Vanderbilts, is dubbed Romanesque.

There is a garden at the side where street painters sell tearful clowns and landscapes 'after Turner'. This area is lively, in contrast to the inside of the church, which has a dead rather than celestial feel to it.

Seagram Building

375 Park Ave (bet. 52nd and 53rd Sts).

This is possibly the only building in New York that looks better in the rain. When wet, its street-level bronze pillars shine green, and raindrops merge with the splashing fountains on either side of the granite and marble plaza, which turns pink. This liquid enhancement is appropriate, for the building was commissioned by Phyllis Lambert as a 1957 'honest tribute' to her father's Seagram liquor business. Mr Bronfman got Seagram going with bootleg business during Prohibition, using gimmicks to oust competitors that included offering to throw the truck in for free with every truckload of liquor sold. It is still a family-owned business, and the Four Seasons restaurant inside is the city's only landmark restaurant. The building's lobby is notable for having been preserved, despite its corporate function, even to the point of having no newsstands or public pay-phones. But back outside, whatever the weather, above the pillars the 39-storey tower looks suspiciously like just another highrise of the reflecting-glass-box variety. And so it is, but it is considered an especially well-proportioned one. It is considered seminal.

In designing the Seagram, Mies van der Rohe and Philip Johnson rejected self-conscious 'artistic architecture'. Their building would be grand and honorific, but simple. They clothed it in elegant – and extremely expensive – materials, including bronze-tinted auburn glass, hoping to intimate a sublime industrial order. Critics applauded, and poor imitations sprang up everywhere. Johnson and Van der Rohe were inadvertently responsible for city centres the world over being made brutish in the 1960s and 1970s by slick, alienating glass-box office blocks.

370 Park Ave (bet. 52nd and 53rd Sts).

Built in 1918 by McKim, Mead and White, this is the building that caused Mies van der Rohe to put fountains in his plaza. He decided that the Seagram must complement the Racquets Club opposite in terms of nobility and Classical restraint. Visitors to both buildings walk between symmetrical rectangular pools flanked by ledges of marble. They then go under a portico and into a modest lobby. Well, men do. If a woman were to get as far as the lobby in the Racquets Club, there would be uproar: the club is gentlemen-only. Always has been, always will be, if its members have their way. It's only a matter of time before women petition to gain entry, but at the moment it seems that almost all New Yorkers hold it in awesome reverence as a New York institution.

Lever House

390 Park Ave (bet. 53rd and 54th Sts).

This blue and green glass upside-down 'T' on stilts was designed by Skidmore, Owings and Merrill, completed in 1952, and is considered inferior to the Seagram but still ground-breaking for achieving an illusion of weightlessness. The ground-floor pillars are in shadow, so it looks as if the mezzanine level is floating above the pavement, and a platform of trees and shrubs on top of the two-storey mezzanine level makes the 21-storey slab above it seem to shimmer in midair. Even so, Lever House really merits only a quick glance, perhaps on your way to the Museum of Modern Art (see p.151) or before going East a block to the Jazz Ministry, St Peter's Church.

St Peter's Church under Citicorp

E 54th St (at Lexington Ave).

St Peter's is the tiny angular lump of concrete stuffed between four colossal columns that support a precarious-looking, glinting 900-ft Citicorp tower block. The complex is especially spectacular when it's lit up at night, and the 45-degree roof billows steam from the cooling system. The odd 1977 design by Hugh Stubbins and Associates was the only way Citicorp could persuade St Peter's to sell its air rights. The deal was: the new church building had to look distinct visually, so that St Peter's wasn't associated with the corporate body, which is the HQ of a bank. Stubbins made the church hard to find and some say ridiculous from the outside, but inside it's stunning, entirely furnished in red oak. There are usually exhibitions in the narthex, most often photos of jazz performers, and if you want to hear the huge, very impressive organ in action, you could come for jazz vespers (tel. 935 2200).

STRESS MANAGEMENT

The 1980s were stressful in New York for everyone because of mergers and takeovers, but they were especially tough for women who were trying to juggle high-powered jobs and domestic responsibilities. When management realised that stress caused problems like ulcers, depression and back trouble, they suddenly became concerned for employees' wellbeing, because of medical costs. In America businesses are responsible for employees' health insurance, and the more often a person is ill, the higher the premiums. Stress was causing companies substantial losses through absenteeism and vast medical compensation outlays. Now, New York American Express employees can learn self-massage at their fitness centre, Manhattan's Gralla Publications offer 'Sleep Hygiene' seminars, and nurse–manager Penny Masson at Ogilvy and Mather says that because people handle stress in different ways, they offer yoga and massage. The Johnson and Johnson corporation, based in New Jersey, has been offering a programme of yoga, meditation and softball since 1979, and in the ten years from 1981 their medical costs rose 150% *less* than the national average. The number of companies introducing stress management programmes is rising fast.

HEALTH CARE

One reason so many of New York's beggars suffer such severe physical debilitations, including lost limbs, is because the country's health-care system has failed them.

America's National Health equivalent, Medicaid, has reached near-collapse under the Reagan and Bush administrations, and costs of private health care have soared beyond the reach of average earners. If individuals don't have insurance, they can't afford the care. It's a vicious circle. Prices often go up because doctors and retailers reason that insurance will cover it. Insurance companies say fraudulent claims by doctors, hospitals and patients cheat them out of about $60 billion a year, so they raise their premiums and then more small companies and individuals can't afford insurance. Medicaid should be there to help them, but Medicaid can afford to help only 40% of the poor (in 1980 the figure was 65%), and doctors will often simply refuse to treat Medicaid patients because of inadequate reimbursements and time-consuming bureaucratic tangle. One out of 9 American working families, a total of 37 million people, have no health insurance. In the decade after 1980, U S spending on health doubled to $733 billion a year, and over the next ten years – if it's not checked – spending is expected to rise to $1.6 trillion. A Bufferin tablet that should cost just a few cents costs a patient in a psychiatric hospital $3.75, just one day's intensive care for a crack baby costs $2,000, and the delivery of a baby by Caesarean section costs a phenomenal $7,500.

MURRAY HILL – UNION SQUARE TO BEEKMAN HILL

Unless you're staying in one of Murray Hill's many hotels, there's not much reason to visit the area, except for the once-weekly fruit and vegetable market at Union Square and perhaps for a drink in one of the city's most romantic bars, the Top of the Tower at the Beekman Hotel (see p.289). One place you won't want to visit is Bellevue Hospital over by the East River (E 26th St to E 30th Sts), because if you do it probably means your trip to New York has been ruined by a need for the Emergency Services. Bellevue, best known in medical circles for pioneering appendectomies and Caesarean sections, is special because its services are available to everyone regardless of ability to pay.

From Farms to Gangs   In the seventeenth century Murray Hill was farmland owned by the estate Dutch Governor General *Peter Stuyvesant* retired to when the British took over. The names of some of the original farms, including that of Murray Hill, were kept when the land around them became built up enough to be considered residential. 'Gramercy' was not the name of a farm. The word is a corruption of the Dutch for 'crooked little swamp' and the place was a marshy patch that a lawyer, Samuel Ruggles, drained and had laid out in 1831 as Gramercy Park. By offering residents private access to a London-style park he was able to lure the rich uptown.

By the turn of the century, however, the Gas House Gang ruled. Named for the grimy factories along the East River that made the gas that lit the city, the gang averaged 30 hold-ups a night – and that was just on 18th Street.

Today the area is largely a 'comfortable' mixture of publishers, hotels and town house residences that is uninteresting during the day and at night a little eerie but basically safe: hotel staff come and go between shifts; grumpy women from the East River middle-income projects walk scruffy dogs; and around Park and Lexington Avenues especially, there's a reassuring presence of hotel doormen on duty.

Emily Eaton Hepburn Breaks into Business   Emily Eaton Hepburn was largely responsible for transforming Beekman Hill from a danger zone of slaughterhouses and shantytowns into an area that is now not only 'respectable' but downright 'desirable'. A graduate of St Lawrence University, where she was a member of the Kappa Kappa Gamma sorority (see box), Emily had married president and chairman of the Chase National Bank A. Barton Hepburn, and was widowed in 1922. With time on her hands and corporate ambitions, she noted that New York at the time was teeming with fellow sorority women fresh from college who were seeking work but had nowhere to live. Men in similar circumstances could rely on the Fraternities to house them. If women were to do as well as men, they had to have the same facilities. Hepburn decided to build a massive equivalent to the male clubhouse, and at the same time prove that women could do 'big business'. She chose the place where real estate was cheap – the East River – for Pan Hellenic House (now the Beekman Tower Hotel), which would house resident and transient sorority members. It took her five years to raise the money through a mixture of hard work and social contacts: she sold ten shares in the project to her old friend Sara Delano Roosevelt over lunch at the Colony Club; she threw fund-raising balls at the Waldorf and the Plaza Hotels; and she sold stock to sorority women nationwide.

On 12 November 1927, Hepburn wielded a little gold spade and the building site was officially opened. She commissioned John Mead Howells to design the stepped red-brick Art Deco shell, which should have Greek letters denoting sororities carved into the façade, but Emily took an intense personal interest in the furnishings. Wall colour? She looked at the vegetable she'd just bought at a First Avenue market and said: 'Eggplant'. To save money she had the beds made shorter (to fit the average woman) and she refused to authorise carpets. This turned out to be wise.

Business was glorious for only a few months after the first cornerstone went in – then the 1929 Crash came. Hepburn was determined that her project would survive, so she turned the Pan Hellenic into the Beekman Hotel and opened it to men. Despite Hepburn's violent aversion to alcohol (she was also a Temperance Worker), after the lifting of Prohibition bars were installed in the hotel. Finally – and perhaps most significantly – Hepburn made the area accessible by persuading the authorities to provide a crosstown bus service, which still runs today. By the end of World War II the Beekman was showing a profit, the area was respectable, and Emily Hepburn had proved that women could do big business.

FRATERNITIES AND SORORITIES

'Fraternities' are old-established national Freemason-style organisations for a certain class of educated men. Each fraternity is named with a letter of the Greek alphabet. Fraternities still thrive today, with their sometimes fatal initiation ceremonies intact. 'Sororities', now more or less defunct, were the more sober female equivalent. To belong to a sorority a woman had to have certain moral standards. Like fraternities, they were basically about elitism, since members had to be nominated, then approved.

E 14th–E 17th Sts (Park Ave South – University Place).

A gathering point for political demonstrations in the 1920s, by the 1970s Union Square was full of dope-pushers, and in the 1980s the City's Parks Department cleaned it up. Undesirables were ousted and the Square was revamped in 1984. Today it is almost pleasant when the sun comes out and squirrels cavort in leafy trees. The best day to come is Saturday, when you can browse in the biggest of Manhattan's 25 Greenmarkets. Mud-spattered farmers from the farthest reaches of New York State arrive in clapped-out vans with fresh produce that ranges from plate-sized mushrooms and sugar-free pecan pie to barrels of black gluey molasses. Groaning wooden tables fill the Square. You might be jostling elbows with some of New York's top chefs, who, if they don't find their ingredients here, will have them flown in rather than buy elsewhere. Or you might be in line with 'low-income people' in the Women, Infants and Children (WIC) and Senior Citizens Nutrition programme who, under the 1988 New York State Farmers Market Coupon Program, are given coupons for fresh produce.

The Factory   Andy Warhol's Factory, now long gone, is the most famous practical example of New York's 1960s movement to fuse art, style and life. In Warhol's Union Square offices, friends (mostly male) would write poetry while they answered the phone, cut films and ate their lunch. In nearby cafés semi-celebrities posed, hoping Andy would make them international superstars by immortalising them in primary colours on canvas along with Jackie Kennedy, Liz Taylor, Marilyn Monroe and the Coke can.

> Here is an excerpt from **Valerie Solanis's 1967 SCUM manifesto**: 'Life in this society being, at best, an utter bore and no aspect of society being at all relevant to women, there remains to civic-minded, responsible, thrill-seeking females only to overthrow the government, eliminate the money system, institute complete automation, and destroy the male sex.
> 'Scum will kill all men who are not in the Men's Auxiliary of SCUM. Men in the Men's Auxiliary are those men who are working diligently to eliminate themselves.'

The Factory occupied the entire 6th floor of Union Square West between 1967 and 1974, during which time there was a lot of death and near-death. Andy's protégée Edie Sidgwick (see p.139) overdosed on sleeping pills in 1971, and a week later Warhol was shot by Valerie Solanis, a woman who had appeared briefly in one of his underground films and then joined SCUM, the Society for Cutting Up Men (see box). Women friends of Andy's – including Viva, who had appeared in his films, and Nico, who had featured in his pop group Velvet Underground – would call round to see him and ask how he was feeling. 'With my hands', he'd reply drily.

Gramercy Park

E 20th–E 21st Sts (Lexington Ave).

This elegant residential enclave has a decent hotel (see p.235), and it's interesting for some of the people who lived here in the past – including, at No. 19, Mrs Stuyvesant Fish. She succeeded Mrs Astor (see p.110) as leader of New York Society. Her innovations included reducing the time of a formal dinner from several hours to 50 minutes. Samuel J. Tilden, who broke up the corrupt local government 'Tweed Ring' and became Governor of New York himself, lived at No. 15. The combination of an angry Boss Tweed and the tinder-box union movement persuaded Tilden to install steel front doors and have a tunnel dug to 19th Street as a potential escape route.

Theodore Roosevelt's Birthplace

28 E 20th St (bet. Park Ave South and Broadway). Open Wed–Sun 9.00 a.m.–5 p.m. Admission $1.

This 1923 brownstone is a reconstruction of the 1854 house in which Theodore Roosevelt, 26th President of the United States, was born on 27 October 1858. The interior was designed to re-create the surroundings Theodore grew up in. It is of mild interest for what it reveals of life as a rich Victorian child.

The **dining-room** has horsehair chairs which, Theodore moaned, 'scratched the bare legs of the children when they sat on them'. He thought the cut-glass prisms of the chandelier in the elegant **parlor** had a 'peculiar magnificence', and upstairs the **nursery** is wallpapered with a village, castle and mill motif that Theodore's mother, Martha Bulloch Roosevelt, believed was good for young children's imagination. The piazza at the back housed the **gymnasium** Theodore's father built so that his sickly son could toughen himself up, saying: 'You have the mind but you haven't got the body. To do all you can with your mind, you must make your body match it.' From birth young Theodore's ailments had included severe asthma, but he rose to the challenge. By 1880 he was a robust cowboy in Dakota, he fought in the Spanish–American War, and he took up hunting. In the room that displays a lion he shot you'll also find the first teddy bear, a toy that was originally called 'Teddy's Bear' after Theodore refused to kill a helpless bear during a November 1902 Mississippi hunting trip.

Flatiron Building

175 5th Ave (bet. E 22nd and 23rd Sts).

This 286-ft brick and limestone upright Toblerone bar was New York's first true skyscraper. When it was built in 1902, it towered in glorious isolation, which apparently caused strange things to happen. Wind currents were diverted down its triangular sides and up women's skirts. So many men would gather to watch the spectacle of women beating down their petticoats that policemen had to be shipped in to scare voyeurs off.

Madison Square

E 23rd–E 26th Sts (bet. Madison and 5th Aves).

Now just another traffic-choked square, this once bordered the Madison Square Gardens sports stadium (see p.314), where a noteworthy turn-of-the-century murder took place.

The original Madison Square sports complex was designed by Stanford White of McKim, Mead and White fame – the team that built the glorious Grand Central, Central Library and General Post Office. Stanford White, licentious rake and womaniser, had an affair with a Broadway showgirl called Evelyn Nesbitt. The affair was such common knowledge that White felt no compunction, it is said, in modelling the garden's statue of a naked Diana on his mistress. This was the last straw for Evelyn's husband Harry Thaw, who one night burst into the garden's roof party, shoved drinkers and revellers aside and shot White through the head. Thaw spent the rest of his life in mental institutions. Nesbitt took to drugs and prostitution.

CHELSEA

Chelsea is best known for the Chelsea Hotel, where Warhol filmed Edie Sidgwick in *Chelsea Girls* and Sid Vicious allegedly stabbed his girlfriend Nancy Spungen to death. Today the main attractions are a scattering of clubs, bars and restaurants – including the Gothic Limelight (see p.294) and the 24-hour trendspot Empire Diner (see p.269) – and a Sunday stroll through the vibrant flower district past the Sixth Avenue Antique Market (see p.334) to Lola's for a rousing

Gospel brunch (see p.269). Otherwise, Chelsea is a mainly quiet residential sprawling architectural patchwork of flat-fronted 1950s and 1960s concrete blocks and pristine turn-of-the-century Federal town houses. One of the few parts with streetlife is Seventh and Eighth Avenue between 23rd and 29th Streets, which is a low-key red-light district. There are no peepshows, only working girls, so you might not even notice, but still – it's a bleak area you should steer clear of at night.

Working-Class Heyday   Chelsea never quite made it as a desirable address. In 1830 Clement Clarke Moore sold off the land he had inherited from his grandfather in lots. Any hopes that the area might flourish as a middle-class suburb were dashed in 1851, when the Hudson River Railroad opened on Eleventh Avenue, attracting breweries and slaughterhouses along with the shanties and tenements of their workers. The tone of the area was lowered, and life on the streets hotted up considerably.

By the turn of the century, Eighth Avenue had become *the* place to be seen for the working-class community. Attire was crucial, especially for newly arrived young immigrant women. By rejecting the clothes from home (dreary shawls and bonnets) they could at once establish their American identity and, if they were lucky, capture the heart of a nice young American man. Impoverished needlewomen and threadmill workers would scour fashionable magazines and sneak looks at Society ladies in stores, then throw together their own versions of chinchilla coats and willow-plumed straw hats from scraps, gluing and stitching at home by candlelight. For tips on bows and frills and applying cosmetics they looked to the prostitutes, whose haunt was two blocks East.

The stretch of Sixth Avenue from 24th to 30th Streets was worked by prostitutes from the Civil War until the 1920s, and known as Satan's Circus. Pimps prowled and prostitutes paraded outside the gaudy movie houses and dance halls. Tourists flocked to the Haymarket saloon on the corner of 30th Street and Sixth Avenue where the entertainment, known as the *grande soirée dansante*, was considered the most risqué in town. For an extra fee, patrons got a private demonstration of a new dance from Paris called the *cancan*.

17 West 16th Street

Margaret Sanger is a key figure in the history of birth control. This purple-painted brick house with bowed first-floor balcony and Greek Revival-pillared front doorway opened in 1923 to operate for fifty years as the headquarters of her Clinical Research Bureau.

A number of factors convinced Margaret Sanger (1879–1966) that sex and reproduction should be separated. One was her mother's death, which Sanger believed was directly linked to her father's voracious sexual appetite (he sired eleven children); another was a 1914 trip to England, where she met the British psychologist and sex expert Havelock Ellis. While Theodore Roosevelt was worrying about the high fertility rate of young immigrant women and exhorting women of the 'proper sort' to perform their maternal functions in the selfless fashion dictated by time and tradition, Margaret was in and out of prison for championing birth control and sex for pleasure. She could begin practical research only when she divorced William Sanger and married a wealthy oil man who was able to pay for the Birth Control Clinical Research Bureau on West 16th Street. Here Sanger pioneered the development of 'the Pill' in the early 1950s, a time when few scientists believed that an oral contraceptive was possible. The US Supreme Court took until 1965 to rule that married couples in America could use contraceptives, and by the end of the 1960s Sanger's Pill was widely available. Today the health clinics she pioneered have grown to a nationwide network called Planned Parenthood (see p.22), and Sanger's work is still attacked by pro-life activists.

The building on 17 West 16th Street is not wildly fascinating in itself, but if you do want a foray into Chelsea it's a decent starting point.

Hotel Chelsea

222 W 23rd St (bet. 7th and 8th Aves).

For many this is a place of pilgrimage. Devotees of various artistes and writers may want to stop and gaze at the decaying Edwardian 12-floor façade of floral balcony railings and ornate pillars, sliced by a vertical neon sign bearing the hotel's name.

When the Chelsea opened in the 1880s, 23rd Street was briefly the heart of the theatre district, and the hotel – which was then entirely residential – attracted a varied cast of down-on-their-luck geniuses and plain no-hopers. Sarah Bernhardt (see box) lived here for a while, so did Vladimir Nabokov. Dylan Thomas spent his last days at the Chelsea, Bob Dylan wrote songs about it, and here in the Swinging Sixties Edie Sidgwick ate breakfasts of roast beef and potato salad washed down with a cup of amphetamine-laced coffee in a studio apartment that was nearly destroyed by fire twice while she was in barbiturate-induced hazes.

Edie Sidgwick Described by Truman Capote as a 'charming, well born debutante from Boston', Edie was born to Francis Sidgwick, a wealthy member of the social register who in turn pampered and tyrannised her. She and two brothers spent time in psychiatric institutions as a result, and the brothers met suicidal deaths.

Petite and doe-eyed, Edie escaped to New York to live with her grandmother and get into film, and met Andy Warhol at a party. Mutual admiration was instant. Edie chopped off her glossy beehive and dyed the spiky remains silver, just like Andy's. They became so well-known as a lookalike couple that Roy Lichenstein and his wife went to a fancy-dress party as Andy and Edie. But Edie loved drugs more than film-making, and by the time *Chelsea Girls* was being filmed in the summer of 1966, not much over a year after they had first met, Andy had tired of her self-destructive streak and adopted new acolytes, Nico and Viva. Edie spent the rest of her short life in and out of hospital suffering cold turkey and nervous disorders until her death after a sleeping pill overdose in a hippy bikers' commune in California in 1971.

SARAH BERNHARDT

Paris-born Jew Sarah Bernhardt (1844–1923), who wanted to spend her life in a convent and shed tears of protest at being forced by her mother into the sinful atmosphere of the Odeon instead of the romantic Saint Sulpice, went on to become, some say, the greatest actress of her century. She also managed and directed her own plays, and continued to tour Europe and America even after she had her leg amputated above the knee in 1915.

Fur and Flower Districts

The blocks from 27th to 30th Sts between 6th and 7th Aves contain the Fur District and the Flower District.

THE FUR TRADE

In the seventeenth century, many of the wealthiest Manhattan colonists made their living from beaver hides. The burgeoning fur trade created a whole new mixed-race subculture. Travelling inland to hunt, English and Dutch men needed native Americans' help for immediate survival and for long-term trade. Indian women's ability to dress furs, build canoes, and travel in the wilderness made them invaluable. The mixture of dependency and isolation bred marriages, some merely for convenience – if a trader went back to Europe, his Native American wife was often merely passed on to his successor – but not all. William McNeil, ship captain for the Hudson's Bay company, mourned the loss of his wife Haida: 'The deceased has been a good and faithful partner for me for twenty years and we had twelve children together... [she] was a most kind mother to her children, and no Woman could have done her duty better, although an Indian.'

The Flower District is best at around 6.00 a.m., when retailers from all over the City haggle amidst a riot of colours and perfumes for stock to fill their florists' shops. It's quieter later, but exotic cut flowers and rampaging pot plants still spill out from shops on to the sidewalks. The Fur District, by contrast, has been hit hard by the recession and the anti-fur lobby. Not long ago, you'd have seen delivery boys with thousand-dollar silver fox fur capes slung casually over their arms. Now the words 'Sale-sale-sale' and 'Closing – everything must go' are splashed all over the heavily barred wholesale coat and hat shop front windows.

GARMENT DISTRICT

The Garment District is crucial to the New York economy. It accounts for one-fifth of the City's income by manufacturing three-quarters of the country's women's and children's clothing. The workshops, warehouses and showrooms are largely wholesale and therefore not of much interest to the casual observer. The streets can be colourful during working hours, when delivery boys push past with racks of clothes on handtrucks at dizzying speeds and roadside skips overflow with bright arrays of fabric remnants. But be careful.

The Garment Centre houses Penn Station, Port Authority Bus Terminal, Madison Square Gardens and the 24-hour General Post Office. Unless you need to go to these places for the purposes of travel, sport or urgent nocturnal package posting, the area is worth avoiding, especially after dark. The surrounding streets are filled with crack-heads and ranting lunatics. Ninth Avenue has shops selling cheap jewellery and 'adult books', and Eighth Avenue is home to 'adult entertainment' cinemas, all boasting that they're the best in New York and some having all-male shows with titles like 'Check My Fluids'. The area is well policed, but watch your step.

Enter the Moral Reformers The garment trade was originally based in the Lower East Side (see p.85). It began to move as early as the 1790s, when male wholesale merchants advertised for seamstresses to do piecework at home. Women responding to the ads were given cut pieces for pantaloons, cheap shirts and vests. These women possessed no specialised or highly valued skills, and they had no rights or job security. Clothes that took hours to make brought in only a few pennies; consequently seamstresses often turned for survival to prostitution. In those days they traded their wares in the western and southern reaches of the Garment District. Hell's Kitchen (the streets west of Eighth Avenue above 34th) and Satan's Circus (the district bounded by Fifth and Seventh Avenues and 23rd and 42nd Streets) became the targets of Female Moral Reformers and Temperance Workers. These reformers were 'respectable' women who found that if they wanted to object to society's wrongs and still remain respectable, they had to fight under the legitimising banner of religion.

One evening in May 1834, a small group of women met at the revivalistic Third Presbyterian Church to found the New York Female Moral Reform Society. The Society's goals were ambitious: to convert New York's prostitutes to evangelical Protestantism and close for ever the city's numerous brothels.

The executive committee appointed John MacDowall and two young male assistants to do their dirty work. MacDowall was instructed to descend systematically upon brothels, and pray and preach vigorously at the inmates. Early Sunday morning was a favourite time to catch women and customers unawares. The fearsome threesome would storm in reciting Bible passages and then root themselves in the hall to sing hymns and conduct services.

The Moral Reform Society, which declared itself 10,000 strong, went so far as to open the House of Reception, intended as a refuge for prostitutes seeking to reform. In March 1835 the executive committee reported fourteen women at the house. A year later, total admissions had reached thirty, only four of whom were considered saved. The building closed.

Temperance and moral reformers were by no means confined to New York, but they often ended up there. At the turn of the century a woman named Carry Nation was razing suspect establishments single-handedly in the Midwest, until John L. Sullivan, heavyweight boxing champion of the world, goaded her into tackling New York. He owned a saloon at the west end of 42nd Street. He declared that he would toss Carry into the gutter if she tried anything with his saloon. A week later she appeared, surrounded by newspaper reporters. Sullivan took one look at her face, which was burning with righteous indignation, and fled to the cellar.

The women managed to close some places down, but the male double standards which were at the root of the problem remained intact. Intemperance and debauchery flourished. Victorian values that were later dubbed the 'Cult of True Womanhood' continued to teach wives of the proper sort to despise base passion and covertly condoned husbands who wished to satisfy their lust elsewhere.

Prostitution and sweatshops have not gone completely, but they have largely moved (prostitution is further to the west and most of the garment sweatshops are back in the Lower East Side). The International Ladies Garment Workers' Union was founded and grew so strong that in 1962 it built Penn Station South, a 12-square-block complex of 2,820 middle-income apartments (W 23rd–29th Sts, 8th–9th Aves), to house its members.

The Garment District still has a humdrum image – its Fashion Institute of Technology (FIT) is scorned by Fifth Avenue's Parson's School of Design for churning out dull clothes technicians rather than designers – but it was on Seventh Avenue in the 1930s that Claire McCardell made her big designing breakthrough.

Claire McCardell   Picture the scene: 1938 on Seventh Avenue and a quiet, handsome thirty-three-year-old blonde, Claire McCardell, is working on a new outfit she calls the Monastic when a neighbouring dress manufacturer spots her plans ... 'Drop everything!' he shouts in deep distress to his dress designer. 'There's a girl up the street making a dress with no back, no front, no waistline, and my God, no *bustdarts*!' The Monastic was a runaway success, and McCardell gained fame as creator of 'the American Look'.

Born in 1905 in Maryland, McCardell had studied French haute couture at Parson's, but decided it was too formal and costly. She went into sportswear, and embarked on a personal mission. She was sick of travelling burdened with a steamer trunk, so she made outfits that did equally well for sport and soirées in order to reduce luggage to two suitcases. When World War II broke out she flourished under the financial and fabric restrictions that came with it. 'Claire could take five dollars' worth of common cotton calico,' said designer Norman Norell in 1943, 'and turn out a dress a smart woman could wear anywhere.' And she was jingoistic enough to earn a personal thank you from the President for her contributions to society. In *What Shall I Wear?* she wrote: 'We [designers] specialize in what satisfies us most deeply. For me it's America – it looks and feels like America. It's freedom, it's democracy, it's casualness, it's good health. Clothes can say all that.'

When she was fifty, *Time* magazine said she was still her own best model, but at fifty-eight she contracted cancer, and died the same year. The looks of designers like Calvin Klein and Donna Karan owe great debts to McCardell, whose fashion innovations, which are now taken for granted, included: double stitching (sometimes called top or blue-jean); visible use of rivets, grommets, and dime-sized brass snaps like those on a child's windcheater; the 1942 Diaper Bathing Suit, which replaced reinforced-bust-dominated fluorescent shiny costumes with draped halter necks and muted colours; and the 1942 Popover, which was a denim overdress made at the request of *Harper's Bazaar* to fit the requirements of wartime ladies whose servants had gone off to the defence plants, and first appeared in the November 1943 issue over the caption: 'I'm doing my own work'.

MIDTOWN MANHATTAN

W 33rd–W 31st Sts (bet. 8th and 9th Aves).

This is the Garment District's nearest approximation to a conventional sight, and its only McKim, Mead and White building. It is said that it was supposed to be shorter but that the Corinthian Greek-pillared façade had to be extended to fit the inscription on top – 'Neither snow nor rain nor heat nor gloom of night stays these couriers from the swift completion of their appointed rounds' – which refers to the building's 24-hour services. Inside, there's nothing like swift completion of anyone's rounds going on. The atmosphere is sleepy. Most of the old-fashioned windows are closed and only a handful of customers actually use the elegantly lit central stands. Go to the window marked 'All Services' for stamps.

THEATER DISTRICT

When the teenage Madonna fled her Italian Catholic background for international superstardom as singer, sex symbol and post-feminist role-model, she arrived in New York and told the cabbie to take her to 'where it's happening'. The taxi driver dumped her in Times Square.

Times Square is known worldwide as the heart of the Theater District and – now mistakenly – as one of the seediest places in New York, where young runaways less lucky or determined than Madonna end up on the game or drugs or both, pickpocketing awed tourists to fund their next fix. During the day it's safe but drab; at night it's spectacular. Six streets of traffic made up of screeching medallion cabs hooting at mammoth shiny tour buses and plodding horse-drawn carriages that cradle smooching couples converge under gaudy rippling yellow, red and emerald green neon billboards. Camera-laden German and Middle America tourists shuffle *en masse* out of *Miss Saigon* and *Les Misérables*, gawping between the electronic news tickertaping round the top of the Times Building and the centre islands' activities, which could be anything from buskers to fifteen Japanese dancers hamming it up for a pop video.

You'd still best be careful of Times Square in the small hours, and at all times beware of pickpockets (see p.20 for precautions), but be reassured: Times Square is target of two serious clean-up operations: one by the City, which has poured police in and closed three hotel-based drug HQs, and the other by the area's own businesses (including the peepshows), which have clubbed together to form the Times Square Business Improvement District (BID), a force of 41 men and women who patrol the area day and night. Confidence is running so high that a new upscale hotel, the Renaissance, has opened behind the Coca-Cola sign (see p.240).

Even if you're not coming for a Broadway show, it's worth just standing around awhile, or if the noise and flashing lights get too much, you could go to the Algonquin Hotel for a cocktail, or early for relaxing afternoon tea.

AN ARTIST'S SUBVERSION

The sky-high multicoloured assaults of Times Square impressed and horrified 1950 Ohio-born artist Jenny Holzer when she arrived in New York in 1977. The focus of her work that year at the Whitney Museum's Independent Study Programme switched from painting to language and resulted in her trademark 1977–9 'Truisms', or one-line 'mock-clichés', which Holzer intended to subvert the same public-space media she displayed them on. Opinions presented as factual information, like 'Money Creates Taste' and 'Private Property Created Crime', have appeared on posters, T-shirts, tractor caps, benches, and the 800-ft Spectacolor Board in Times Square.

Broadway . . . Known fondly as the Theater District's 'hardened artery', Broadway has long been a robust mixture of lugubrious and respectable. When the Metropolitan Opera House opened at 39th Street in 1883, the Floradora Girls were already luring hordes of men into the Casino Theater across the street. True, most of the seedier venues were soon bullied off the main Broadway strip when managers sniffed big bucks in melodramas, spectacle plays, comic operas, vaudevilles and burlesques. But by the 1930s Broadway was synonymous with the *Guys and Dolls* stories of sports journalist Damon Runyon in which bootleggers, gangsters, dreamers and dropouts thronged speakeasies, did time in the sneezer and often met death facing a Betsy. It was a man's world where women were broads, pancakes or tomatoes, but even before Mrs Libbie Runyan was in labour with Damon in 1880 in Kansas, Harriet Beecher Stowe had written the bestseller anti-slavery novel *Uncle Tom's Cabin*, which was adapted for stage and became *the* most popular play on Broadway through the last half of the nineteenth century.

. . . and Broadway's Women Women have most often made it on Broadway as actresses – Katharine Hepburn and Barbara Stanwyck, to name but two. Indeed, Broadway has been much criticised for excluding women as directors or writers unless they're white, middle-class and not interested in challenging the patriarchal status quo. Harriet Beecher Stowe, for example, is often dismissed as an apologist for a repressive social order who dished out weak-minded pap to nourish the prejudices of an ill-educated and under-employed female readership. There are exceptions. Black Harlem writer Zora Neale Hurston (see p.200) had a Broadway concert produced, and more recently Nzotake Shange won wide acclaim for her staged choreo-poem *Colored Girls*. Satirist Dorothy Parker (see p.147), who was white and middle- to upper-class but certainly not a weak-minded upholder of the status quo, had one play produced and was the subject of two, but it was Dorothy's friend Lillian Hellman who became perhaps Broadway's most famous woman writer.

Lillian Hellman   Playwright Lillian Hellman was confirmed a legend just eighteen months after her 1984 death when a play based on her life, *Lillian*, starring Zoe Caldwell, opened at the Ethel Barrymore Theatre.

Born in New Orleans in 1905, Lillian met Dashiell Hammett in Hollywood in 1930, and during their passionate thirty-year relationship she combined writing for Broadway and Hollywood with left-wing political activism and countless affairs. She was at the centre of the labour turmoil of the 1930s and the progressive movement in the 1940s, and a victim of the McCarthy witchhunts in the 1950s, and her lovers included two Broadway producers, a publishing giant, and an Undersecretary at the US Embassy called John Melby, who was knocked from power during the McCarthy era largely because of his liaison with branded communist Hellman. Described by Zoe Caldwell as 'difficult and intriguing', 'very, very bright' with 'an uncontrollable sense of anger', she insisted that her name be pronounced with only two syllables, 'Lill-yan', not the usual three, 'Lill-i-an.' At her Park Avenue apartment she would sometimes change three times before receiving friends, few of whom were women. Critic and director Robert Brustein remembers that 'she quarrelled with everyone, often over the most trivial issue – she broke with Bill Styron for an entire summer in a dispute over the proper way to cook a ham'. She was combative to the last, telling the nurse shortly before her death: 'If you don't give me a cigarette this minute, I'm going to start screaming.'

Algonquin Hotel

44th St (bet. 5th and 6th Aves).

Off Broadway towards Fifth Avenue, the Algonquin is an oasis of respectable gentility. It shows little sign of being affected by the recession: it does a roaring trade in pre- and post-theatre suppers; guests tend to remain loyal (one is in her late eighties); and the hotel's literary legacy will always be an attraction.

It was here at the turn of the century that Alexander Woollcott founded the literary circle known as The 'Round Table'. Robert Benchley and Robert Sherwood joined, but the member considered the leading light amongst a 1920s set of second- and third-raters was Dorothy Parker (born 1893). Poet, short-story writer and reviewer for the *New Yorker*, social satirist Parker put female comedy on the magazine scene. She was one of the most talked-about women of her day, rich and gifted, and she was a 'masochist', said one friend, 'whose passion for unhappiness knew no bounds'. Another described her as 'a Sappho who could combine a heartbreak with a wisecrack'.

Parker's work fell too quickly out of fashion, not because of its quality but for its decadent subject matter – her own elite social class – which was judged anything from irrelevant to outrageous after the Great Depression set in. Brendan Gill introduces *The Collected Dorothy Parker* by commenting on a final irony. Parker's stock in trade was 'the pleasingness of death', yet she lived to the ripe old age of seventy-three. Gill says the crotchety old woman in a Manhattan hotel with only her dog and the bottle for company committed 'an inexcusable social and aesthetic blunder: she was becoming the guest who is aware that he has outstayed his welcome and who yet makes no attempt to pack his things and go'.

The actual table at the Algonquin where Parker and her associates drank and quipped no longer exists. Hotel staff will point to where it once was: 'There . . . no, to your right, a little more . . . yes, there.' The round table under the chandelier is just one of many in a busy hotel restaurant that has recently been refurbished.

ROCKEFELLER CENTER AREA

There are three main reasons for coming here. One, the Museum of Modern Art. Two, the ice rink (winter only). And three, the Deco Rainbow Rooms, where an all-in dinner deal includes one of Manhattan's best romantic night-time views and a high-standard live Gershwin cabaret (see p.272).

Construction The Rockefeller Center is of note historically because it was built defiantly high after the Depression. J.D. Rockefeller, son of the oil magnate, had leased the land in 1928 when it was still notorious as a speakeasy belt, hoping to raise the tone of the area by building a new home for the Metropolitan Opera House. But the 1929 Crash rendered altruistic culture plans foolish, so he settled on a commercial centre instead and, with Wallace K. Harrison as main architect, completed the project in 1940.

Today The Rockefeller Center is set apart from Midtown Manhattan not by height, since it has been surrounded by skyscrapers, but by the otherworldly feel that results from its function as a city-within-a-city. The entire complex of office tower blocks is linked by a maze of wide underground passages lined with shops, cafés and boutiques. Once you've gone down the enticing sloped entryway at Fifth Avenue, you can have lunch and a haircut and do some clothes shopping and go for tea without once seeing daylight. The passages are echoey. Everyone is silent and swift, on their way to work or lunch. It is like being in a dated futuristic film set.

At street level you might notice that there are no lorries. Elsewhere, Manhattan streets groan with the weight of chunky chrome trucks that have fumes pumping out of pipes rising from the front bonnet, but not here. Under the Rockefeller pedestrian walkway, there is a cross-town lorryway, designed to alleviate Manhattan's congestion. It is used solely by heavy-goods vehicles, which means that above ground the traffic is mainly yellow cabs. All traffic is barred from the area, though, when the New York Hilton is hosting one of its regular high-security events, like a presidential address or a visit by a foreign dignitary. At such times there is a heavy but not unpleasant police presence. The police effort to be community-friendly involves posting a lot of women – look out for trousered women PC partnerships dragging great wooden barricades across the road or swinging batons with casual confidence.

Almost every building in the Rockefeller complex has something worth seeing, but it is a good idea to target only one or two and spend most time in MoMA. Children are really served only by the ice rink, although older children might enjoy MoMA – check out the film screenings.

ROCKEFELLER CENTER

The 22-acre commercial centre's 19 buildings are of varying degrees of interest. The **International Building**, for example, just scrapes into the worth-popping-into league with a cavernous lobby covered in thin copper leaf that would, if melted down, apparently sit easily in your hand and weigh about a pound (5th Ave bet. 50th and 51st Sts). If it's summer there's a cooling spot at the west wall of the 51-storey granite **McGraw-Hill Building**, where a massive arch is covered with water cascading into a pool below (49th St bet. 6th and 7th Aves). The shiny glass and aluminium 1960 **Time and Life Building** is of interest for the magazines published inside, including not only *Time* and *Life* but also *People*, *Money* and *Fortune*, as well as for pioneering a childcare policy (see box), and because Marilyn Monroe detonated the first charge of excavating dynamite (51st St bet. 6th and 7th Aves). Below are the Rockefeller buildings which warrant more than a passing nod.

CORPORATE CHILDCARE

The paucity of childcare facilities in the workplace has become a prime national issue – not because employers have suddenly got kind but because they realise they might get increased worker-efficiency if they have in-house child-minders. Sixty-three-year-old grandfather Richard B. Stolley, editorial director of Time Inc. Magazine Company, is also head of Child Care Action Campaign. The only male leader of any similar major organisation in the country, he freely confesses that for most of his life childcare was his ex-wife's problem: 'My awareness of childcare was, you picked up the babysitter, you took the babysitter home and sometimes you couldn't get a babysitter.' Now he's plotting to make childcare 'a national priority', and foremost weaponry in his arsenal is the fact that he's a man. 'It softens up other men, and they tend to listen.' Elinor Guggenheimer, who founded Child Care Action Campaign in 1983, explains that although she normally tries to promote women, 'we are never going to get a rational system for childcare services until men decide it is important.' Stolley uses his magazines to spread the message – 'Fortune has run a number of stories on childcare' – and he is building support for the still new Time Warner Children's Centre on the ground floor of the Time and Life Building. Time Inc. is so caring now that it will arrange for emergency childcare workers to be sent to employees' homes. Twenty-five years ago, the same company refused to hire a woman because 'you will get married, have babies and stay home'.

The Channel Gardens

5th Ave (bet. 49th and 50th Sts).

'Gardens' is too grand a word for a strip of concrete that features a couple of rectangular ponds and a spurt of greenery, but there are benches, so it's a nice place to flake out in the summer and pleasant to pass through in the winter. The shrubs and flowers are changed to match the season (Easter lilies on Good Friday, for example, and fir trees at Christmas). The promenade leads to the Lower Plaza. In the summer an expensive café spills out, and in winter the sunken plaza becomes a small ice rink. Stand and watch even if you don't fancy skating. Under a disproportionately large gold statue of Prometheus, bobble-hatted children hold hands and trip and giggle and wave to their parents, young lovers smooch and Jojo Starbuck – the rink's head pro – practises twirls, glides and hops in spangled, fringed outfits.

GE Building (formerly RCA)

30 Rockefeller Plaza. Lobby and free public rest rooms open normal working hours. Get tickets in the lobby for tours of the NBC TV studios upstairs. Tours leave hourly 9.30–4.30 Mon–Sat for $7.75. If you prefer to see a show as it's recorded, collect free tick-

ets at the mezzanine-level lobby or room 48. Pick your show carefully, as TV production is repetitive and can therefore be boring.

This is, at 70 storeys, the tallest building of the complex. Once a communications centre housing a radio and a broadcasting company, it's now owned by General Electrics. The lobby's two immense black and gold murals, by José Maria Sert, are impressive but faded – you have to squint to make out the square-shouldered industrious male figures.

Radio City Music Hall

50th St (at 6th Ave). One-hour-long backstage tours leave Mon–Sat 10.15 a.m.–4.45 p.m. and Sun 11.15 a.m.–4.45 p.m. from the lobby for $7.

This is a designated landmark, not for the outside but for the Art Deco inside which features a sweeping staircase and crystal chandeliers weighing two tons each. The stage, featuring a 50-ft turntable, is the shape of a scallop shell. It is so big (110-ft diameter) that on the opening night in December 1932 someone in the audience asked what those mice were doing down there, only to be told that they were not mice but horses.

Now, it seems, mostly American tourists come here to see the apparently world-famous Rockettes, a dance-troupe which was founded in the 1930s. If it's autumn you might be lucky enough to glimpse a couple of them on the pavement in minuscule fur-trimmed red outfits doing a TV promo for the Christmas spectacular with live camels and sheep. If you go on the official and very good backstage tour you'll get to meet a real live Rockette and ask her questions.

ON THE ROCKEFELLER OUTSKIRTS

The American Craft Museum

40 W 53rd St (bet. 5th and 6th Aves). Admission $3.50, students $1.50, free to under-12s and to everyone Tues 5–8 p.m. Open Wed–Sun 10 a.m.–5 p.m., Tues 10 a.m.–8 p.m.

The 1986 building's interior – a modern wood foyer with swirling staircase – is more interesting than many of its sparse exhibits, which are chosen by the American Crafts Council either from the small permanent collection which dates back to 1900 or from the work of the country's leading commercial craftsmen. And they are mostly craftsmen, rarely women, even though 'craft' was until recently considered a female domain.

11 W 53rd St (bet. 5th and 6th Aves). Open 11 a.m.–6 p.m. (9 p.m. on Thurs), closed Wed; $7, students $4, children under 16 accompanied by adult free, Thurs 5–9 p.m. pay what you wish (admission includes gallery talks and film screenings). July and August concerts (free) are held in the Sculpture Garden Fri and Sat evenings (go to Information Desk for details).

While John D. Junior was planning a commercial centre, his wife Abby Aldrich Rockefeller was busy executing a more radical plan. It all started in the winter of 1928–9 when she toured Egypt and, quite by chance, got chatting to a fellow contemporary art collector, Lillie P. Bliss, and an art teacher, Mrs Cornelius J. Sullivan. They decided, Abby's son Nelson later recalled, that Van Gogh's death in an institution for the destitute was simply dreadful. 'Mother's objective', wrote Nelson of her plans for a museum to show only modern art, 'was to reduce dramatically the time lag between the artist's creation and the public's appreciation of great works of art.' He concluded: 'It was the perfect combination. The three women among them had the resources, the tact, and the knowledge of contemporary art that the situation required. More to the point, they had the courage to advocate the cause of the modern movement in the face of widespread division, ignorance, and a dark suspicion that the whole business was some sort of Bolshevik plot.'

They raised support and funds at Society dinners and appointed as director Alfred Barr, who proposed further radicalism: that the museum should expand its definition of 'art' to include film and photography. It took ten years for the museum's committee to build up a permanent collection and commission Philip Goodwin and Edward Durell Stone to design the building, which finally opened to the public in 1939. At the time, the big modern flat front of the museum contrasted starkly with town houses. Today it merges so well with its new neighbours that it's easy to miss.

Look for colour rippling several feet above the pavement in the form of bright banners announcing the museum's name suspended above the revolving doors. Inside, the foyer is filled with light which pours through the 4-storey-high windows that overlook the Abby Aldrich Rockefeller Sculpture Garden, which is an ideal place for a woman alone to sit reading in summer.

The Collections   The ground floor consists of the café, a shop, the information desk – where you can pick up an indispensable floor plan – and the two video-film theatres. See p.309, or ask for a programme schedule at the information desk for details of frequent screenings from MoMA's magnificent archives. The relatively small fourth floor is devoted to architecture and design, but most visitors come for the painting and sculpture collections on the second and third floors. Only 30% of the museum's collection can be on show at any one time, so paintings mentioned below may not necessarily be on display, although something by the same artist will usually be in its place.

Step on the escalators at the ground floor, glide up the side of the windows, turn left and left again on the second floor and you're facing the museum's jade, violet and pale pink **Monet** triptych, **'Water Lilies'** (1920). The hypnotic wall-sized panels are in a specially adapted shrine-like room with padded benches – just the first example of the fine use of lights and seating that makes the museum a place you can enjoy for hours.

If you want to do the roughly chronological route, go back to the central hall and into the Post-Impressionist gallery. One of the most imposing works is in Gallery 5, **Pablo Picasso**'s 'Les **Demoiselles d'Avignon**' (1907), which for many signalled the beginning of Cubism. The painting's message is mixed. Five naked women pose like pin-up girls, enticing; their jagged edges and mask-like expressions – which range from lewd to hostile to contemptuous – threaten violence. This is a favourite stop-off point for tour guides, so you may find yourself tripping over cross-legged schoolchildren being asked to consider Picasso's representation of women: 'What do they remind you of? Yes. Broken bits of glass. Good, Miles.'

At Gallery 11, you start a whirl through international movements including German Expressionism, Fauvism, Futurism and Purism, with **Mondrian**'s black and primary-coloured Purist **'Broadway Boogie Woogie'** (1942–3) a high point in Gallery 13, and in Gallery 16 you'll find a 1932 work by the man who apparently once said: 'There are only two kinds of women – goddesses and doormats.' **Picasso**'s **'Girl Before a Mirror'** is disturbing. The main figure looks fecund, but her reflection is a skeletal insect with dislocated striped breasts and vacant hollowed eyes. She was modelled on his pregnant teenage mistress Marie-Thérèse Walter.

Pass into Surrealist and Dadaist rooms and you'll come to work by the man generally credited with first pulling the rug from under the art world's feet, **Marcel Duchamp**. Known as a 'ready-made', his **'Bicycle Wheel'** (1951 version of the 1913 original) is, as the title suggests, literally a bicycle wheel which has been stuck on a stool. It was designed to make people think: 'But that's just a rusty old bike wheel!'; and then to ask: 'Why should a place in a gallery mean an object is "art"?'

The last two galleries on this modern art marathon contain **Balthus** and strong hints of paedophilia. His portrait of a lustful **'André Derain'** has a meek, expectant girl with her top slipping off in the background. Round the corner is **Frida Kahlo**'s head-and-shoulders self-portrait, **'Fulang-Chang and Me'** (1937). Framed by bits of mirror, she is loosely but definitely tied with a mauve silk ribbon to the monkey. From under thick eyebrows her dark eyes challenge you to meet her steady gaze. Until the 1980s, when New York art historian Hayden Herrera published her biography *Frida*, Kahlo was known mainly as Diego Rivera's wife and Trotsky's lover. Now her work is considered one of Mexico's national treasures, and stars including Madonna collect her. As you leave gallery 22 turn round and look at the **Florine Stettheimer's 'Family Portrait II'** which, in contrast with Kahlo, seems so gossamer light-hearted as to be trite.

FLORINE STETTHEIMER

Florine Stettheimer, a New York Jew, was a West-Side Society woman in the 1920s. In 'Family Portrait II' she and her elegant flapper-girl sisters drape themselves around a pastel-shaded lacy salon that has a view of the Chrysler Building. Look closer. The characters are awkward and strained, the tendrils and huge flowers sprouting in the middle are unsettling, and the mother's role is unclear. She has a pack of cards, as if she is a fortune-teller. This looks like naive art, but Stettheimer was well aware of the most sophisticated art discourses (Marcel Duchamp was a close friend) and it is difficult to tell if she is criticising the artifices of her social set (titles of other paintings include 'Beauty Contest' and 'Sale at Bendels') or endorsing them wholeheartedly. She was full of contradictions (she was a snob and party-giver, and an ardent New Dealer). She also wrote poems, for example:

> Art is spelled with a capital A;
> And capital also backs it;
> Ignorance also makes it sway;
> The chief thing is to make it pay;
> In a quite dizzy way; Hurrah – Hurrah –

The **third floor** is dominated by Abstract Expressionism, or 'AbEx' as it's becoming known – a movement which emerged in New York after World War II and has since split critics. One camp says AbEx was 1950s Cold War propaganda – i.e. that the CIA and the Rockefellers funded artists like Jackson Pollock, Mark Rothko and Barnett Newman because their work was the very style of liberty – free and individualistic – as against Russia's conformist Socialist Realism. The opposition holds that AbEx was leftist subversion, pointing to accusations by McCarthyite Congressmen that the work was anarchist and communist. One thing's certain: the work is big and macho, and all the AbEx artists of note were male. The few women who struggled through are badly represented here. The Lee Krasner, an **'Untitled'** (1949) dark mesh of oil paint and Helen Frankenthaler's big dusky splodges **'Jacob's Ladder'** (1957) are considered poor examples of their works. Most visitors don't give them a first, let alone a second, glance. By contrast, two works by **Rothko**, **'Magenta, Black, Green on Orange'** (1949) and **'Red Brown and Black'** (1958), can absorb you indefinitely. There are – conveniently – benches in the middle of the room.

Coming to the end of this floor, you'll find Pop Art including **Lichenstein**'s blue **'Drowning Girl'** (1963), whose tearful think-bubble reads 'I don't care! I'd rather sink . . . than call Brad for help!', and on the ground nearby there's **Claes Oldenburg**'s giant squidgy plastic ice-cream cone, **'Floor Cone'** (1962). The last room contains contemporary art. The exhibitions here change regularly. **Kiki Smith**'s row of silver bottles filled with bodily fluids might be on display, or maybe **Vito Acconci**'s **'Adjustable Wall Bra'**, which is several feet in height and length and, because the cups are made of wire and concrete, has to be attached to the ceiling for extra support, leaving the straps to snake out of the exhibition space towards the visitor's feet.

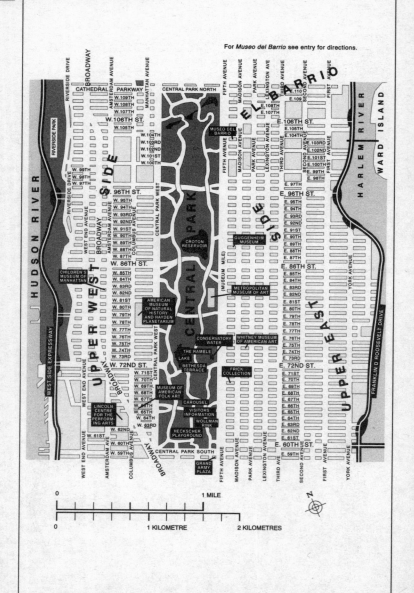

For *Museo del Barrio* see entry for directions.

For sights in *Harlem* see individual entry for safe transport information.

FORT TYRON PARK AND THE CLOISTERS MUSEUM

WASHINGTON HEIGHTS

WASHINGTON BRIDGE

ALEXANDER HAMILTON BRIDGE

RIVERSIDE DRIVE

LAUREL HILL TERR

BENNETT AVE
BROADWAY
FORT WASHINGTON AVE
WADSWORTH AVE
ST NICHOLAS AVE
AUDUBON AVENUE
AMSTERDAM AVENUE

W.181

191
190
189
188
187
186
185
184
183
182
181
180
179
178
177
176
175
174
173
172
171
170
169
168
167
166
165
164
163
162

MORRIS JUMEL MANSION

HARLEM RIVER

MACOMBS DAM BRIDGE

W.161
W.160
W.159
W.158
W.157
W.156
W.155TH ST.

154

145TH ST BRIDGE

HUDSON RIVER

RIVERSIDE PARK

RIVERSIDE DRIVE

BROADWAY
AMSTERDAM AVE
CONVENT AVE
ST NICHOLAS AVE
EDGECOMBE AVE
BRADHURST AVE
FREDERICK DOUGLASS BLVD

SUGAR HILL

HAMILTON GRANGE

W.153
W.152
W.151
W.150
W.149
W.148
W.147
W.146
W.145TH ST.

W.144
W.143
W.142
W.141
W.140
W.139
W.138TH ST.
W.137
W.136
W.135
W.134
W.133
W.132
W.131
W.130
W.129
W.128
W.127
W.126
W.125TH ST.

MADISON AVE BRIDGE

THIRD AVE BRIDGE

B R O N X

N

ABYSSINIAN BAPTIST CHURCH

SCHOMBURG CENTRE FOR BLACK CULTURE

HARLEM

POWELL JNR BLVD
FIFTH AVE
LENOX AVE
ADAM CLAYTON

STUDIO MUSEUM IN HARLEM

MARCUS GARVEY PARK

E.129
E.128
E.127
E.126
E.125TH ST.
E.124
E.123
E.122
E.121
E.120
E.119
E.118
E.117
E.116TH ST.
E.115
E.114
E.113

WILLIS AVE BRIDGE

TRIBOROUGH BRIDGE

HARLEM RIVER DRIVEWAY

BARNARD COLLEGE

COLUMBIA UNIVERSITY

RIVERSIDE DRIVE
BROADWAY
AMSTERDAM AVE
MORNINGSIDE AVE
MANHATTAN AVE
ST NICHOLAS AVE
NICHOLAS AVE
FREDERICK

MORNINGSIDE DR

W.124
W.123
W.122
W.121
W.120
W.119
W.118
W.117
W.116TH ST.
W.115
W.114
W.113
W.112
W.111
W.110TH ST.

MADISON AVE
PARK AVE
LEXINGTON AVE
THIRD AVE
SECOND AVE
FIRST AVE

FIFTH AVE

E L B A R R I O

E.116TH ST.
E.111
E.110TH ST.

CATH CH OF ST JOHN THE DIVINE

HENRY HUDSON PARKWAY

UPPER MANHATTAN

CENTRAL PARK SOUTH TO THE TOP OF MANHATTAN ISLAND

Upper Manhattan has something for everyone – including great galleries and elitist stores – but there are also places you'd be daft to go. Large parts of Harlem, particularly 'El Barrio', are notorious for club shoot-outs, and the area roughly from West 83rd Street to 102nd Street between West End and Columbus Avenue has lots of low-income housing projects that are unnerving, if not dangerous.

East of Central Park the streets are graced with elegant brownstones and turn-of-the-century mansions that house some of the richest women in the country and one of the biggest museums in the world, the Metropolitan Museum of Art. Soak up culture on Museum Mile, go broke at haute designer stores, into overdraft on lunch at Le Cirque, then later join Oxbridge-styled New York yuppies and celebrities like Mia Farrow at Upper East Side bars.

On the similar but in places more run-down Upper West Side, take your children to see dinosaurs at the Natural History Museum, spy dead rats and master stone-carvers at St John the Divine, and in the evening stay near the University for student haunts and down around 70th Street for a raucous day-glo urban-surfers crowd. At the high, wooded far end of the island, go to the eccentric medieval Cloisters, and for Harlem splash out on a rousing Harlem Spirituals Inc. tour. The Lincoln Center, the Park and Museum Mile are all within walking distance of the midtown hotel district, but for the rest you must master public transport or budget for taxis (note: some will refuse to go to Harlem – not because of the danger, but in case they don't get a ride back).

Women and Revolution By 4 July 1776 a revolutionary committee headed by Thomas Jefferson had declared that the King of Great Britain's 'absolute Tyranny' over the thirteen States of America must end. These radicals, also called patriots, faced not only British soldiers but fellow colonists still loyal to the King. War broke out, and much of it was fought on the land north of Central Park, including the 1776 Battle of Harlem Heights.

Women didn't fight, but they were active behind the scenes:

'At every house women and children making cartridges,' said an eyewitness of the 1774 battle at Lexington, 'running bullets, making wallets, baking biscuits, crying and bemoaning and at the same time animating their husbands and sons to fight for their liberties though not knowing whether they should ever see them again . . .'

Mary Ludwig Hays, a Republican, was a rare exception. She earned the nickname 'Pitcher Molly' for courageously carrying water to cannoneers at the height of battle. Her artillery sergeant husband was struck; she took his place. She went down in legend after a cannonball whizzed between her legs, tearing away her petticoat. She merely looked down to observe, 'with unconcern, that it was lucky it did not pass higher, for in that case it might have carried away something else; and so continued her occupation'.

Women ardently campaigned to raise money for patriot soldiers. One participant described their up-front policy with a grasp of basic grammar and spelling that belies the lack of education for women: 'Instead of waiting for the Donations being sent the ladys of each Ward go from dore to dore and collect them.' A loyalist, Mary Morris, wrote ruefully to her sister in June 1780: 'Of all absurdities, the ladies going about for money exceeded everything; they were so extremely importunate that people were obliged to give them something to get rid of them.' Many women felt that their activities were undervalued. Rachel Wells contributed funds by buying loan office certificates from the State of New Jersey during the Revolution. She left for Philadelphia and was refused interest payments on her return. She wrote a letter of complaint:

To the Honnorabell Congress I rachel do make this Complaint Who am a Widow far advanced in years & Dearly have occasion of ye Interst for that Cash I Lent the States . . . I have Don as much to Carrey on the Warr as maney that Sett now at ye healm of government . . . your asembly Borrowed £300 in gould of me jest as the Warr Comencd & Now I Can Nither get Intrust nor principall Nor Even Security . . .

if She [Rachel Wells] did not fight She threw in all her mite which bought ye Sogers food & Clothing & Let Them have Blankets & Since that She has bin obliged to Lay upon Straw.

Despite Abigail Adams's plea to 'Remember the Ladies' (see p.198), the new Revolutionary Constitution did not give women suffrage. Full political identity required a willingness to take up arms for the republic. Women were considered physically unfit for this task. Full political identity required the individual to own property. When women married, everything was owned by the man (single women were social outcasts). Furthermore, political theorists argued at the time that to give women the vote would merely be giving their husbands two.

Devil's Music By the turn of the century racism excluded blacks from well-paid jobs and poverty pushed them into the ghettos of Harlem. Male college graduates were forced into manual labour, or work as porters. Black women, most migrating from the poor South, were exploited but had more options – laundry, maids, cleaning and cooking. Consequently, for a long time black women in Harlem outnumbered black men (in 1919 the ratio was 100:85).

BILLIE HOLIDAY

'There's no damn business like show business,' said Billie Holiday in *Lady Sings the Blues*. 'You smile to keep from throwing up.'

Lady Day is known as much for her untimely death and tragic life of drug addiction and exploitation by men, both black and white, in both her personal and professional life, as for her singing.

She was born, probably in 1915, in Baltimore: 'Mom and Pop were just a couple of kids when they got married. He was eighteen, she was sixteen, and I was three.' Her mother, Sadie Fagan, a factory worker making army overalls and uniforms, pre-empted postwar layoffs by moving to Harlem with her daughter, hoping for more secure work as a maid. Sadie fell ill, the rent was overdue, and Billie trawled clubs for work as a dancer. A few clumsy steps at the Log Cabin proved that this was not her forte, but she said she sang too, and they gave her a job. Musician and writer Spike Hughes recalled seeing her shortly after at Monette's supper club: 'a tall, self-assured girl with a rich golden-brown skin . . . Billie was not the sort you could fail to notice in a crowd at any time; in the cramped low-ceilinged quarters of a Harlem speakeasy she not only registered, but, like a gypsy fiddler in a Budapest café, she came over to your table and sang to you personally. I found her quite irresistible.' She had 'arrived' in Harlem and was soon 'discovered' and promoted by white downtown. In 1958 Frank Sinatra wrote in *Ebony* magazine: 'With few exceptions, every major pop singer in the US during her generation has been touched in some way by her genius.' In May 1959 Billie Holiday made what was to be her last public appearance at the Phoenix Theatre in Greenwich Village. Master of ceremonies Leonard Feather recalled: 'I looked into her dressing-room to say hello, and saw her seated at the make-up table coughing, spittle running unchecked down her chin.' She could barely walk to the microphone. Six days later she collapsed in a coma suffering from 'drug addiction and alcoholism'. While on her hospital bed she was arrested for possession of heroin, and because she was too weak to be moved she was placed under police guard. Her maid said: 'It was . . . like the last straw that the system could do to her.' She died on 17 July 1959. Malcolm X wrote of Billie Holiday: 'Lady Day sang with the soul of Negroes from centuries of sorrow and oppression. What a shame that proud, fine, black woman never lived where the true greatness of the black race was appreciated.'

With little or no work, there was plenty of time for music, which had thrived in the male black community since the first African slaves were shipped over in the 1600s. By the 1890s, Ragtime was influencing white popular music and then in the 1920s blues and jazz. The WASP Establishment was, to say the least, suspicious of the new rhythms that were pounding in Harlem and seducing their children.

'Jazz music causes drunkenness', said Dr E. Elliot Rawlings, a spokesman for the medical profession. 'Reason and reflection are lost and the actions of the persons are directed by the stronger animal passions.' Parents begged rebellious sons and daughters not to go. The lyrics written in 'the Negro brothels of the South', said Fenton Bott, head of the National Association of Masters of Dancing, were 'an offense against womanly purity, the very fountainhead of our family and civil life'. The General Federation of Women's Clubs tried to have the music repressed, and by 1929 it had been banned from New York's public dancing halls.

The rhythms, however, were persistent and brought some women to fame, others also to ruin (see boxes on Billie Holiday and Ella Fitzgerald).

ELLA FITZGERALD

In 1934, sixteen-year-old Ella Fitzgerald had a bet with two school friends and lost: she had to go up on stage at the Harlem Opera House Amateur Night. She gripped the microphone, wobbling on 'the skinniest legs you've ever seen', and got catcalls from the audience: 'Hey, honey, where'd you get them clothes?' She sang 'The Object of My Affection', and 'three encores later, I had the twenty-five-dollar first prize'.

Ella's family had moved from Virginia to the Bronx, hoping for a better life. Ella, like her school friends, did all she could to help the family finances: she 'took numbers' for the illegal gangster-run lottery and acted as lookout for the local whorehouse, knocking to let the girls know when cops were prowling. 'Oh yes, I had a very interesting young life.'

After a spell in an orphanage, she learned to type to finance more competition entries. Soon the 'gawky girl from Yonkers with a voice like a bell' was known all over Harlem, then the world. She has sung more than two thousand different songs, made 70 albums, been voted best singer by musical journals from Melody Maker to Playboy, and was always sent yellow roses by Frank Sinatra when they performed together. She has been given honorary doctorates by several universities, and aggravation by scholars: 'Listen brother, I sure get all shook up when folks start theorizing about my singing. I just tell 'em to sit back and relax. Yeah, that's it, relax. I just sing as I feel, man. Jazz ain't intellectual.' Over six decades Ella Fitzgerald's popularity has survived the demise of the Swing era big bands through Broadway musicals, bebop, rhythm and blues to heavy metal. 'We don't have the Cole Porters and the George Gershwins any more, but we do have the Burt Bacharachs, Stevie Wonder and people like Paul Williams. I dig his lyrics. I also dig Marvin Gaye. When I sang his "What's Goin' On?" some people said, "Why are you doing that? It's a protest song!" I told them, "I don't find it that way. To me it's just good music."

MUSEUM MILE

This strip includes some of New York's most exclusive apartment blocks, a handful of nineteenth-century mansions, and several museums, most notably the sprawling Metropolitan Museum of Art, the helter-skelter Guggenheim, and one of the most beautiful private museums in the world, the Frick Collection.

A room with a park view has been *de rigueur* amongst New York's phenomenally rich since the end of last century. In *A Walk Up Fifth Ave* Bernard Levin reports that Mrs 'Marylou' Vanderbilt Whitney honours the tradition by keeping one of her – ooh – seven or eight bijoux residences on the 21st floor at number 825 Fifth Avenue, although, he says she finds it a weeny bit small for the dinners she likes to throw for four or five hundred old-monied friends. The clash of old and new money is embodied in the Metropolitan Club at 61st Street, a huge over-the-top Italian Renaissance palace that was built by Pierpont Morgan and his contemporaries when they were snootily barred from the downtown clubs because they did not have inherited money.

If it's a nice day and you have boundless time and energy, walk from museum to museum. Be warned, though, that the vast Met alone merits several trips. It's best to target one or two museums, then go for a wander in the park. A good place to start is Grand Army Plaza.

Grand Army Plaza

5th Ave (bet. W 58th and 60th Sts).

This features a fountain named after Joseph Pullitzer, a Statue of General Sherman and, most days, groups of young body-poppers or breakdancers performing for cash from tourists. If there are no dancers, the Plaza, designed by Hardenberg in 1907 in the French Renaissance style, has only occasional appeal: the cream of New York society lark in the fountain when soused after coming-out parties and charity balls. Horse-drawn carriages line the Central Park South side of the Plaza, and where there's horses, however prettily trussed up and harnessed, there's horse manure. As you pass the sulky blinkered mares the stench, especially in the summer, can be overpowering.

Temple Emanu-El

1 E 65th St (at 5th Ave). Open 10 a.m. (noon Sat) to 5 p.m.: worship services Fri 5.15 p.m. (organ recital at 5 p.m.) and Sat at 10.30 a.m.

The interior of this 1929 grey limestone grandiose Byzantine-Romanesque Reform synagogue (the largest in the States) is awesome. The tiny entrance on 65th Street opens into a gargantuan cavern where rows of pews, which can seat 2,500 worshippers, seem to stretch on for ever.

Frick Collection

1 E 70th St (at 5th Ave), tel. 288 0700. Open Tues–Sat 10 a.m.–6 p.m., Sun 1–6 p.m., closed Mon: admission Tues–Sun $1/50c senior citizens and students, $2 Sun; price includes, if you wish, European art lecture on Thurs at 3 p.m. or Sat at 4 p.m., and weekly concerts of classical music, tel. 288 0700 for information or pick up a leaflet. Children under 16 not admitted, over 16 must be accompanied by an adult.

Many people cite the Frick as their favourite New York museum. Its appeal is twofold. First, its layout is informal: ropes, cases and labelling are kept to a minimum, so that exhibits are displayed as if in a lush private home. Second, the Frick boasts a prestigious, curious collection: chocolate-box Bouchers in the West Vestibule precede Vermeers in the South Hall; grand Titians flank a fifteenth-century Bellini in the Living Hall; and the Dining Room surrounds you with society misses by Gainsborough. The Garden Court is one of the most peaceful resting places in the city.

Mr Frick, the Pittsburgh coke and steel industrialist (1849–1919), was not so appealing. Hugh Brogan describes him as a greedy, selfish philistine who broke with partner Andrew Carnegie because Carnegie went soft on strike-breaking. Frick told a go-between: 'You can say to Andrew Carnegie that I will meet him in hell (where we are both going) but not before.'

This low grey mansion, built towards the end of Frick's life by Thomas Hastings, became a museum after the death of his widow in 1931. It is still maintained by Frick's bequest. The selection of paintings illustrates how through the ages patrons and their money have dictated – or at least heavily influenced – artists' subjects. In fifteenth-century Italy the Church was all-powerful, and biblical themes dominated; lords and barons in eighteenth-century England demanded portraits of wives and lovers; pre-Revolutionary French royal mistresses desired decor for their boudoirs.

Enter through the East 70th Street side door between pillars topped by a lounging stone nude. Porters with the manners of butlers will graciously relieve you of excess baggage, coats and cameras. To the right of the entrance hall there's a gift shop (well stocked with postcards), and stairs to the basement's temporary exhibitions room.

Go left for the museum, which has been kept as it was when the Fricks lived here. Life here must have been odd. Coming downstairs of a morning, the aged couple would have trudged past the marble gilt pipes of the biggest organ in any American private house on the landing, and through the dimly lit *South Hall*, where invaluable works of art are slung above priceless artefacts including a 'secretary' Riesener made for Marie-Antoinette. Two Vermeers, 'Officer and Laughing Girl' and 'Girl Interrupted at her Music', catch Dutch seventeenth-century couples at intimate moments, while Boucher's eighteenth-century flushed, saucily smiling French wife luxuriates on a chaise-longue, tickling her ear suggestively. The portrait 'Madame Boucher' was painted when she was twenty-seven and mother of three, shortly before she took up the brush herself to money-spin by reproducing in miniature Boucher's big sellers.

It seems that Frick liked François Boucher (1703–70), who hit fame when Louis XV's mistress *Madame de Pompadour* took him under her wing and introduced him to Louis's court, for a whole room is devoted to him. Off the South Hall, the **Boucher Room** is panelled with eight twirly floral canvases Madame de Pompadour commissioned for an estate near Chartres in 1746. Chubby children representing the arts and sciences mimic adult occupations with some comic touches: one boy in breeches panics as his experiment explodes in 'Chemistry', while another peers through the wrong end of a telescope in 'Astronomy'. Eighteenth-century French courtiers expected women in de Pompadour's position to patronise the arts, and she was heavily criticised for frittering funds on transient decor instead of investing in buildings. She nevertheless remained committed to Rococo decorations, and in the **West Vestibule** there's more Boucher: 'The Four Seasons', which she commissioned as over-doors. Rumours that the coy muffled lady on a sledge in 'Winter' might have been modelled on de Pompadour are confusing, since by 1750 all Boucher's women tended to resemble his wife. Next door are some works by one of his pupils, Jean-Honoré Fragonard.

The airy **Fragonard Room** displays 'The Progress of Love'. The series, which the Frick ranks 'among the outstanding achievements of French decorative painting', elicits giggles from some visitors. A fair damsel and her maids flee past spongy trees in 'The Pursuit'; a spaniel waits by the feet of lovers nuzzling necks over 'Love Letters'; and two flighty cherubs lock lips in 'Love Triumphant'. Commissioned by Louis XV's last mistress, *Madame du Barry*, the series was rejected in 1774, probably because the central figures resembled too indiscreetly the King and Madame du Barry – of whom courtiers disapproved, for the petite blonde beauty was the illegitimate daughter of an innkeeper.

When Frick retired to the sombre **Library**, imperious eighteenth-century English onlookers would have included Thomas Gainsborough's 'Grace Dalrymple Elliott'. The Prince of Wales, who probably commissioned this portrait, was just one of her many influential titled lovers. When the picture was exhibited at the Royal Academy in 1782 prudes approved, thinking the high colouring and expression (a wandering eye and slightly parted lips) appropriate to a woman of Grace's sullied reputation.

While Frick worked late in the Library, poring over papers from his coke and steel businesses, Mrs Frick would have spent her evenings on the elaborate Boulle furniture in the **Living Hall**, where a curvaceous bronze nude Neptune rides a sea-monster (by Severo Calzetta, Paduan, sixteenth century) on the table facing Giovanni Bellini's fifteenth-century 'St Francis in Ecstasy'. This shows St Francis receiving the Stigmata – the wounds of Christ's crucifixion – in 1224 during a retreat on a green-tinged desert Mount Alvernia. The Titian on his left shows a young 'Man in a Red Cap', lost in reverie, idly fingering his sword hilt, which glints by the soft dappled fur of his cloak.

After the **West Room**, where you'll find Vermeer's absorbing mid-seventeenth-century picture of two women colluding with a letter, 'Mistress and Maid', all rooms overlook or lead to the Garden Court. In the **North Hall** pass French Jean-Auguste-Dominique Ingres's 1840s portrait of the 'Comtesse d'Haussonville', Louise, a sexy French princess who married a diplomat at eighteen and wrote a number of books, including a life of Byron. Then relax in the foliage by the pool in the **Garden Court**.

Before you leave the Fricks' mansion, use their public phone booth, which is wood-panelled with a perky seat and soft lighting that comes on when you click the door shut.

Metropolitan Museum of Art

5th Ave (at E 82nd St). Open Fri & Sat 9.30 a.m.–8.45 p.m., closed Mon, Sun & Tues–Thurs 9.30 a.m.–5.15 p.m.; suggested admission $6 adults, $3 students and senior citizens, children under 12 free (if you offer only one cent for admission, cashiers may be ungracious but must accept it and give you the entry badge); phone 879 0421 for general information and 535 7710 for recorded information; pushchairs permitted every day except Sun, and sometimes barred from special exhibitions (phone ahead to check).

The Met boasts an 'encyclopedic survey of 5,000 years of man's art', but if you think 'encyclopedic' means easy reference, abandon your illusions. The guides, who have been doing tours for as long as twenty years, often cannot find paintings and have to ask the guards: 'Is it gone for cleaning, or on loan, or to another room?' Only a quarter of the collection can be shown at any one time. Even the information on paintings' labels is not consistent through the museum, because there are nine different curators. To describe the museum as 'daunting' is a vast understatement, but it is *a must* on anyone's itinerary.

The Beginnings The museum started small when, in 1870, financier and industrialist members of the New York Union League Club pooled 174 works of art (mostly Dutch and Flemish), thereby establishing a higgledy-piggledy private gift tradition. The most generous donors demanded a wing to themselves, so if visitors want to study a particular theme or period, they might have to go to five different galleries in different parts of the museum. Even the building was a group venture. The 1880 heart is by Calvert Vaux (who designed Central Park); the 1906 wings are by McKim, Mead and White; and the monumental 1902 Renaissance façade in grey Indiana limestone was designed by Richard Morris Hunt. The sweeping front steps throng with people, many spreadeagled, chatting and reading; cloth banners with holes in (to counter wind disturbances) drape into the three central arches declaring current temporary exhibitions.

Tackling the Met Go through the main doors and you'll see in the middle of the **Great Hall** a huge splurge of flower arrangement, fresh every Monday, that Lila Acheson, founder and publisher of the *Reader's Digest*, arranged for in her bequest. Beneath the rhododendrons or lilies or whatever is in season you will find the Polomint-shaped Information Desk. Take a selection of leaflets and go to the circular bench on your left, where you can sit while you plan your approach.

Because City funding has been cut, collections are open only on a rotating basis (half and half, morning and afternoon). If you want to see something specific, it's wise to phone ahead. Note too that even armed with every floor plan available, you can still get lost. You should, ideally, set aside at least a day to explore the museum, and you should give yourself breaks. Picnic in the park or patronise the museum café, sunbathe on the Lila Acheson Wing roof garden, or relax in the light-filled American Wing Engelhard Court.

A good way to orientate yourself is to take one or more of the wide selection of generally very good tours, and later return to favourite exhibits. Alternatively, you can concentrate on the current temporary world-touring exhibitions. Or take the lucky-dip approach: strike out blindly. Whichever option you choose, take care not to trip on students and amateurs at easels reproducing great masters. And grasp the handrail firmly on the slippery stone central steps – one visitor broke a leg recently.

The museum's nineteen departments can be divided into four major subheadings: American Art; European Art; 'Primitive' Art; and Ancient Art. Ancient Art includes the crammed Egyptian wing,

Greek and Roman Galleries that are second only to those in Athens, and galleries that contain possibly the largest display of Islamic Art in the world. Lesser galleries include the Costume Institute and Arms and Armour. Several books have already been devoted to the Met's contents. The next few paragraphs will focus on the collections most visitors come to see: the American Wing and European Paintings. Women are rarely the artists, frequently their models. Some contrasting and notable examples are presented here (see box).

Still in the Great Hall, you will find – as well as the Information Desk – the cloakroom, the meeting-point for tours, and two of the Museum's lavishly stocked **gift shops** (selling art books, Christmas cards, and jewellery reproductions of some of the ancient exhibits). Look above the Membership Desk and you'll see Rosa Bonheur's 'The Horse Fair' (1853) (see p.171). It's a large painting which, despite poor museum lighting, bursts with life – men shout, horses snort and whinny, hoofs stamp. The animals come at you from the left, one black stallion rearing wild-eyed, before they veer round tamed, and trot into the left of the picture.

Go up the central stone steps to the European Paintings.

European Paintings

More than 40 galleries including the André Meyer and the Lehman Pavilion show European paintings dating from the thirteenth to the twentieth century. A large number of galleries are devoted to Italy and the Renaissance; there are Dutch, French, Spanish, English, Flemish and German galleries. The 'greats' include Rembrandt's 'Aristotle with a Bust of Homer' and five Vermeers.

In the **Lehman Pavilion** you will see representations of the Annunciation, amongst them one by the Florentine Botticelli and one by the Flemish Hans Memling (both fifteenth century). For the same biblical story – Archangel Gabriel informs Mary that God has chosen her to bear his son – the artists have imagined completely different scenes.

Two Annunciations   Hans Memling, a popular and prolific artist who spent most of his life in Bruges, cloaks the angel in rich red and gold cloth, gives him two angel assistants, and brings them all into Mary's typical wealthy burgher's Bruges bedroom. In the tradition of earlier Flemish painters, including Jan van Eyck and Robert Campin, Memling uses everyday household objects symbolically: the brass candlestick and the half-filled glass bottle represent the shining glory and clarity of the Virgin, and the lilies her purity. The angel raises his hand as he says: 'The Holy Ghost shall come upon thee'; the Virgin, clad in plain white, holds her hand to her breasts demurely.

In Alessandro Botticelli's more tranquil and ethereal 'Annunciation', the solitary angel and Virgin are separated by a wall of pillars, but linked by their mirrored kneeling postures. The angel hitches up his creamy tabard with one hand and bears lilies with the other, but he doesn't speak because God's words are carried on beams of light slanting over his head towards the Virgin, who is by an upright bench in a pleasant but sparse front room or hall. This painting is considered important partly because it is rendered in perspective, not in 2-D. It was the development of perspective, which many say started with Giotto in the thirteenth century, that made Italian – and especially Florentine – art so famous and influential during the second half of the fifteenth century.

As you go through around 40 **Thirteenth to Eighteenth-Century Paintings** galleries, which are arranged roughly in chronological order, you will see more biblical stories, among them two especially human treatments: Giotto's of the Three Kings' visit, and David's of the Flight to Egypt.

A Flight and a Visit Florentine Giotto probably painted 'The Epiphany' around 1320, when he was at the height of his powers, acclaimed throughout Italy for his ability to breathe life into stories. Mary, reclining in the stable, looks knackered, having just given birth. The eldest magus doffs his crown, kneels and impetuously lifts the swaddled baby from the manger. Joseph bends forward, as if to warn: 'Careful!' Giotto takes artistic licence with chronology and puts angels in the background singing the news to the shepherds.

'The Rest on the Flight to Egypt' by Flemish Gerard David (1424–1523) also juggles chronology and is also tempera (oil and egg-white) on wood. David imagined Joseph and Mary's flight and gave the weary mother and child a pit stop on a sandy rock. He presents Mary as mother, not icon, by omitting halo and by depicting her breastfeeding. The child looks askance at the viewer from the right nipple. Far behind, in the extensive wooded landscape, David incorporates a comic scene: Mary and the child on a donkey and Joseph absurdly running to catch up.

Venus and Adonis Twice Gallery 8 holds Italian Titian's 'Venus and Adonis' and Gallery 27 has Flemish Rubens's version, in tribute to Titian's.

Titian (1488–1576) often drew on Ovid's *Metamorphoses* for his mythological paintings, but this scene – in which Venus's mortal lover is about to depart on his fatal boar chase – is nowhere in the text. Its suggestion of recent sex and imminent death is potent. Here Venus, who in Titian's other depictions reclines regally and brazenly nude, has her back to the viewer. Her necklace is displaced and her limbs are animated: she is trying desperately to restrain an impatient Adonis. His dogs are straining at the leash, his spear is grasped firmly and he is trying to stride away, oblivious to the ominous black clouds that are beginning to block the sun's rays. Cupid hides behind a rock, clutching a dove.

Rubens's (1577–1640) scene is more sensuous. Venus's full, languid body is the main focus of the picture; her lover and his dogs are ambivalent, even reluctant, about departure: Cupid, who has tossed down his arrows, seems to be grasping Adonis's leg in affection, not desperation.

A Penitent Magdalen   Georges de La Tour is best known for his austere candlelit scenes, often of women, most famously his four depictions of the penitent Magdalen. 'The Penitent Magdalen' at the Met, probably painted between 1638 and 1643, shows her at the moment of her conversion. Recognition of the wickedness of her prostitute's life (she has thrown down her jewels) requires her to accept death, symbolised by the skull in her lap over which her hands are peacefully folded. The silver mirror, symbolising luxury, is black and empty except for the reflection of a self-consuming candle that represents the frailty of human life. This is a haunting, moralistic picture that is most striking visually for the contrast of bright, flickering candlelight and deep black shadows. Nearby is the more humorous 'The Fortune Teller', one of de La Tour's rare daylight scenes, in which the young man having his fortune told is also having his pocket picked. De La Tour, who was born in 1593 in the independent duchy of Lorraine, was patronised by dukes and kings, then forgotten about for two centuries before being acclaimed as a brilliant and original artist.

Two Women at the Academy   Nearly at the end of the thirteenth- to eighteenth-century galleries, two women painters are represented, both of whom were admitted to the French Royal Academy at a time –1783 – when the number of women artists eligible for membership was limited to four. *Adélaïde Labille-Guiard*'s 'Self-Portrait with Two Pupils' (1785) is a propaganda piece, arguing in favour of women's places at the Academy (see box). But it betrays mixed feelings: she wants to be taken seriously as an artist and treated as equal to men, yet while she is taking up paint with her brush from a palette, she is dressed not in painter's garb but as a Society lady, in a frilled silver-grey silk gown and a feathered straw hat. Labille-Guiard (1749–1803) was apprenticed first to a miniature-painter: later, in 1769, she studied pastel with Maurice Quentin de La Tour. She achieved success at court and, after painting portraits of Louis XVI's sisters, was dubbed *Peintre des Mesdames*. She was able to stay in France throughout her life because she sympathised with the Revolution, unlike Louise Elisabeth Vigée-Lebrun.

Vigée-Lebrun (1755–1842) hit big after Marie-Antoinette

became a fan in 1779 and commissioned portraits of herself and her courtiers. The wan dark-haired sitter for 'Madame de la Châtre' (1789), daughter of Louis XV's *premier valet de chambre* and wife of a count, rests on a sofa with a book in her hand, wearing a white muslin dress. The dress is of note because Vigée-Lebrun professed in her memoirs to like the cut – elaborate by today's standards – for its classic simplicity. She took to wearing such dresses herself, and pressed other sitters to wear them too. Her glamorous ten-year career was ended by the Revolution. During her flight she painted portraits to support herself and her daughter.

MARY CASSATT

As a woman artist in the late nineteenth century, Mary Cassatt had a hard time. 'I am not willing to admit that a woman can draw that well,' declared Edgar Degas in 1891, when they had already been friends for ten years.

Cassatt was born in 1844 into a prosperous well-connected Pennsylvania family. She enrolled at the Pennsylvania Academy of the Fine Arts, found that freedom of expression and originality were ruthlessly suppressed, and – overcoming the resistance of her father, who thought she should marry, like all the other girls of her social class – left for Europe to study the old masters independently. She found that the Paris Salon was also restrictive, so Cassatt showed with the Impressionists, who said 'no juries, no prizes', demanding the right to exhibit without judgement. She met Degas when he was forty-three and she was thirty-three. There has, of course, because of their intense friendship, been speculation: did they have an affair? No one knows; she burnt his letters. Neither married. Cassatt wrote in her memoirs:

> Oh, I am independent! I can live alone and I love to work. Sometimes it made [Degas] furious that he could not find a chink in my armour, and there would be months when we just could not see each other, and then something I painted would bring us together again and he would go to Durand-Ruel's and say something nice about me, or come to see me himself.

Mary Cassatt lived in France for more than twenty-five years before revisiting America, which she did in the autumn of 1898. She was renowned and respected in Paris, yet her arrival got only a brief mention in a Philadelphia newspaper: 'Mary Cassatt, sister of Mr Cassatt, president of the Pennsylvania Railroad, returned from Europe yesterday. She has been studying painting in France and owns the smallest Pekingese dog in the world.' Her dog was a Belgian griffon.

Cassatt returned to France, but despite success she felt cut off and lonely, especially after 1917, when Degas died. For the last ten years of her life she didn't paint, but always maintained an interest in the subject. Forbes Watson wrote: 'one couldn't listen to her, pouring out her ardor and understanding, without feeling his conviction in the importance of art to civilization intensified.' Cassatt died at Château de Beaufresne in 1926.

Women with Parrot The André Meyer galleries have two paintings called 'Woman with a Parrot', both painted in the 1860s by

Frenchmen: one by Gustave Courbet and the other by Edouard Manet, Manet's probably in direct allusion to the controversial work by his rival. The pictures couldn't be more different. When Courbet's was shown at the Paris Salon of 1866 critics lambasted him for 'lack of taste', for the 'ungainly pose' of the model (sprawled naked on a sheet), and for her outrageously 'dishevelled hair' – she caused such uproar because she was a recognisable type (a courtesan of the demi-monde) rather than a distant mythical figure. The woman's sensuality is emphasised by the tapestries around her and by the bright plumage of the parrot, fluttering discreetly at the top edge of the picture on her raised fingertips. Manet's parrot, by contrast, is grey, the background is dun, and his model is fully clothed in a shapeless tent dress with her hair pulled up severely in a band. A half-peeled orange has been discarded at the bottom of the parrot stand, and it has been suggested that the picture is an allegory of the five senses: taste represented by the orange, smell by the violets she is holding to her shoulder with her right hand, touch and sight by the monocle she is holding with her left, and hearing by the talking bird. Manet was later adopted as the father of the Impressionists.

ROSA BONHEUR, ANIMAL PAINTER AND CROSS-DRESSER

Twice a week for a year and a half, Bordeaux-born Rosa Bonheur, the most famous woman artist of the nineteenth century and one of the greatest animal painters in history, went to the horse market of Paris on the tree-lined Boulevard de l'Hôpital and sketched for 'The Horse Fair'. Not wanting to attract attention, she asked the Prefect of Police for 'the authorisation to wear masculine clothing'. Bonheur's cross-dressing was cause for much quizzing. Daughter of an impoverished drawing master, Rosa was labelled a tomboy early on, but throughout her life she maintained that short hair and trousers were for convenience only. She deplored 'women who renounce their customary attire in the desire to make themselves pass for men', she told an interviewer. 'If I had found that trousers suited my sex, I would have completely gotten rid of my skirts, but this is not the case,' she said, reiterating that her garb simply facilitated her work. 'Remember that at a certain period I spent whole periods in the slaughterhouses . . . I had no alternative but to realize that the garments of my own sex were a total nuisance.' She went on: 'if you are even the slightest bit put off, I am completely prepared to put on a skirt, especially since all I have to do is to open a closet to find a whole assortment of feminine outfits.'

'The Horse Fair' was shown at the Paris Salon in 1853 when Bonheur was thirty-one, and later Queen Victoria arranged a private view at Buckingham Palace. The *Daily News* praised the work in 1855: 'The animals, although full of life and breed, have no pretensions to culture.'

American Wing

This includes the decorative arts (for example, Tiffany stained glass and a Shakers' Retiring Room) and paintings from the Early Colonial Period through the Federal Period and Revival Styles to the nineteenth century, the most notorious of which is 'Madame X' by John Singer Sargent, who trained at the Paris Salon.

Notorious Madame X   The portrait was originally called 'Portrait de Mme . . . ' to protect the modesty of the subject, but at twenty-five Mme Gautreau, born in New Orleans but married to a French banker, was already *the* most notorious Paris beauty. Sargent met her around 1881 and, impressed by her seductive charms and theatrical use of heavy make-up, determined to paint her. When the portrait was shown at the Salon in 1884, press and public were scandalised by her shameless figure-hugging black dress that had nothing but delicate strings of brilliants for shoulder straps, and by the violet tones of the copious amounts of skin it revealed. Sargent had hoped the picture would earn him patronage in Paris. Instead it became a scandalous symbol of the lady's piquant reputation. When he sold it to the Metropolitan in 1916 he is reported to have said: 'I suppose it is the best thing I have done.'

American Woman Impressionist   Mary Cassatt (see p.170) was also based in Paris, at around the same time, but she shunned the Salon, becoming the only American artist in the renegade Impressionist group. Her work, which is well represented at the Metropolitan, is characterised by domestic scenes – women and children sitting in dining-rooms, drawing-rooms, bedrooms, balconies, private gardens – while her male contemporaries were painting scenes in, for example, brothels and restaurants, where 'respectable' women could not go.

ART AND FEMINISM

Feminist art historians have been questioning the litany since the early 1970s. Some set out to find forgotten or underrated women artists, including Mary Cassatt and Rosa Bonheur in the second category; others, including Linda Nochlin, ask: 'Why are there no great women artists?' (*Women, Art and Power and Other Essays*, Thames & Hudson). Griselda Pollock writes in *Vision and Difference* (Routledge): 'Women have not been omitted through forgetfulness or mere prejudice. The structural sexism of most academic disciplines contributes actively to the production and perpetuation of a gender hierarchy', and goes on to suggest that Marxism (questions of class) as well as the women's movement should be considered in forging a new art history.

ART AND GREATNESS

In asking, 'Why have there been no great women artists?' (*Women, Art and Power and Other Essays*', Linda Nochlin knocks the notion that 'great' men are simply 'born genius', saying that 'greatness' is largely down to training in accepted institutions, from which women have historically been barred. She goes on to wonder: 'What of the small band of heroic women, who, throughout the ages, despite obstacles, have achieved preeminence?' Are there any qualities that characterise them as a group? 'Almost without exception, [they] were either the daughters of artist fathers, or, generally later, in the nineteenth and twentieth centuries, had a close personal connection with a stronger or more dominant male artistic personality.' She puts Rosa Bonheur and Mme Vigée-Lebrun in the first category and Mary Cassatt, for her friendship with Degas, in the second.

Guggenheim Museum

1071 5th Ave (at 89th St), tel. 360 3500. Open 11 a.m.–4.45 p.m., closed Mon. Tues 5–8 p.m. pay as you wish. Otherwise, $7 adults, $5 senior citizens and students, under-12s free; or get a day pass that admits you to the SoHo branch as well for $10 adults, $7 senior citizens and students.

Frank Lloyd Wright's ideal of 'organic' architecture was ridiculed when it opened in 1957 for resembling an upturned oatmeal bowl. Artists Willem de Kooning and Robert Motherwell complained that the interior's low cream walls and curving ramp were 'not suitable for a sympathetic display of painting and sculpture'. Perhaps this was Wright's intention. He considered architecture the mother art which paintings and sculptures should merely adorn, and once wrote: 'Let us dispose of the insufferable insubordination of the picture . . . I should like to strike the pictorial deathblow.' The original building is still stunning; viewing art that is straight when you are sloping requires skills you can have fun developing; and the recent renovation has doubled the space available to hang exhibits from the rambling, impressive permanent collection.

The most obvious feature of the 1990 renovation is the pale-green limestone ten-storey rectangular **annexe**, which cruel critics say, stuck next to Wright's original oatmeal bowl, makes the whole look like a huge toilet. Applauded restoration work includes the cleaned skylight which allows daylight to flood into the rotunda, and at night spotlights flood out.

How It Started The collection dates back to 1927, when Solomon Guggenheim met a German baroness called Hilla Rebay von Ehrenwiesen, who was obsessed with Rudolf Steiner and 'non-objective' art.

Hilla Rebay had trained in traditional portraiture, until in 1916 her lover, the Dada artist Jean Arp, gave her a copy of Kandinsky's treatise *On the Spiritual in Art*, which advocated 'non-objectivity'. Rebay, an immediate convert, interpreted 'non-objective art' as meaning paintings that were pure artistic invention rather than abstracted real objects and were therefore literally 'without object'. For Rebay, non-objectivity was history's greatest first step 'from the materialistic to the spiritual'.

PEGGY GUGGENHEIM (1898–1979)

During her stormy marriage to Max Ernst, Solomon Guggenheim's niece Peggy danced round the dinner table in nothing but a see-through green raincoat to encourage the suppressed desires of guest Marcel Duchamp. This kind of behaviour was typical of the woman who built up one of the finest private collections of twentieth-century art in the world.

In 1921, bored young Peggy Guggenheim inherited a fortune which she took to Europe, where she gained notoriety for having lots of affairs with lots of artists, and at the age of forty she found her milieu: art patronage. Samuel Beckett got her interested in what he called 'living art', and Marcel Duchamp helped her to draw up a hit list of paintings, including work by Jean Cocteau and Surrealist Yves Tanguy, to fill the Guggenheim Jeune Gallery, which opened in London in 1938. Throughout 1940 she kept her resolve to 'buy a picture a day', including works by Mondrian, Léger, Braque and Picasso, so that she could open the Art of This Century Gallery in New York on 57th Street, which she had designed with curved gum-wood walls and pictures mounted on baseball bats. For its 1942 launch she wore one earring by Tanguy and one by Alexander Calder 'in order to show my impartiality between Surrealist and Abstract art'. Then she decided to ship her art to the Palazzo *Venier* dei Leoni in Venice, which opened to the public in 1949. She based herself in Venice but continued avidly to discover artists, including in 1953 a New York carpenter, Jackson Pollock; and she resolved in 1969 to bequeath her 300-strong collection to the Solomon R. Guggenheim Museum in New York. In later life she looked stunning with silver hair, a deep tan, Egyptian-style robes and four shaggy Lhasa terrier companions.

Rebay moved to America in 1927 with a commission to paint the portrait of Solomon Guggenheim, a would-be art collector who had money but lacked direction, and she made herself his art adviser. They travelled Europe buying up paintings, and by the mid 1930s there was no more hanging space in Guggenheim's suite at the Plaza Hotel, so in 1937 he established the Solomon R. Guggenheim Foundation with Hilla Rebay as the first director, and rented a former car showroom in 1939 which Rebay draped with pleated grey velour and velvet, and infused with the smell of incense and the strains of Chopin and Bach. The museum was a runaway success, so in 1943 Rebay campaigned to raise funds for a permanent building. She decided that Frank Lloyd Wright's quest for organic forms made him a kindred spirit, and wrote him a passionate letter: 'I need a fighter, a lover of space, an originator, a tester, a wise man . . . I want a temple of spirit – a monument! And your help to make it possible.' He agreed, but the project proved a long haul and, in the end, intensely disappointing for Rebay.

In 1951 art critic Aline Louchheim queried the museum's status as tax-free if it showed only non-objective art. The trustees immediately demanded Rebay's resignation to prove the museum's commitment to a wider remit. Rebay's friend Wright died in April 1959, just six months before the museum's official opening, and Hilla Rebay, impotent as Director Emeritus of the museum, died in 1967.

What You'll See Today   The bulk of the Guggenheim's permanent collection is made up of three bequests: Solomon R. Guggenheim's, of which the core is the largest Vasily Kandinsky collection in the world and 70 Paul Klees; Peggy Guggenheim's 'Art of this Century', a collection of Abstract, Surrealist and Cubist works selected with the help of Peggy's friend Marcel Duchamp; and the collection bequeathed by Justin K. Thannhauser, which is mainly French Impressionist and represents Picasso particularly well.

Exhibitions in the **large rotunda** change regularly. You might see a touring exhibition, selections from the permanent collection, or a commissioned site-specific exhibition – for example, a 'truism' by Jenny Holzer (see p.145) written down the quarter-mile-long helter-skelter ramp. The **small rotunda** houses highlights from the Thannhauser collection. And the great advantage of the much-criticised airy **annexe** is its size – the annexe can show works from the permanent collection, including big pieces by Francis Bacon and Roy Lichenstein, that could not fit on the walls of the rotunda. You can reach the large rotunda's ramp at all levels from the annexe. A unique and some say gut-twisting experience is to stand at the top of the ramp and look down. On the ground floor of the museum there's a Dean and Delucca **restaurant** and a **store** selling Kandinsky scarves and the biggest collection of Lloyd Wright books in New York.

National Academy of Design

2 E 91st St (at 5th Ave), tel. 860 6868. 1083 5th Ave, Tues noon–8 p.m. Wed–Sun noon–5 p.m.; $3.50, $2 students, senior citizens and under-16s, free Tues 5–8 p.m.

This is a pleasant place to visit if you've finished at the nearby Guggenheim and still have energy left. The topical programme of lectures and critiques often includes workshops for children. Examples in the past have included 'Babar at the Academy' on

Babar's 60th anniversary (phone 369 4880 for information).

This revered New York institution was founded by Samuel F.B. Morse, an itinerant portrait painter, in the early nineteenth century as an exclusive art school which would also hold exhibitions, mostly of American artists, when Paris was the centre of the art world. A one-hundred-and-fifty-year-old tradition has it that members must present a portrait of themselves, and that associated academics should donate at least one work. These pictures form the mainstay of the Selections from the Permanent Collection, which usually includes works by John Singer Sargent, Winslow Homer, Augustus Saint-Gaudens, and Morse himself.

UPPER EAST SIDE

This is where the City's rich elite live and shop. It is safe both day and night for women because of what architecture critic Jane Jacobs calls its 'watching eyes': the eyes of the braided-peak-capped doormen at canopied entrances of posh apartment blocks. Go shopping at Givenchy, go flirting at singles bars, lunch at the star-studded Le Cirque (see p.279) and buy trendy children's clothes at Chocolate Soup (see p.340) after an art exhibition at the Whitney.

History Mrs Astor built a mansion at 65th Street on Fifth Avenue in 1896, and her high-Society friends followed. Their homes became showcases for all the latest fads and gadgets. One simply *had* to have an elevator; elaborate intercom systems replaced dated ropes and bells; and several dumbwaiters per mansion made life easier for the frilly-capped maids and sleek butlers. By the turn of the century, bathrooms were transformed. Indoor plumbing was flaunted. Previously, bathrooms had been lavishly panelled in dark wood to disguise their function; now they were filled with elaborate ceramic fixtures, imported tiles and gold-plated pipes, and hosts showed off showers that sprayed water in several directions at once.

Sara Delano Roosevelt was more interested in connecting doors. Disapproving of her son Franklin's marriage to plain, virtuous Eleanor, she built adjoining houses for herself and the newly-weds (No. 49, still standing) to reassert her authority. 'You were never quite sure when she would appear, day or night,' said Eleanor (see p.179) of her mother-in-law, who interfered not only with Eleanor's marriage, but with her children. 'Your mother only bore you,' she often told them.

In 1920 the *New York Times* described the Upper East Side as 'a string of pearls: each pearl is a double block of millionaires, and Madison Avenue is the string.'

The distribution of wealth hasn't changed much, but the clothes of its spenders have. Today you won't see bustles and parasols; you'll see trim trousered women, perhaps in berets and dark glasses, taking beribboned snapping dogs for walkies in special pooch trolleys. They have busy schedules – pedicures, manicures, facials, coming-out balls to arrange for their daughters, and luncheons at the Colony Club (564 Park Ave), which has been the exclusive meeting-place for women on New York's social register since 1915, when women were systematically barred from men's clubs.

A shopping tour of the Upper East Side is a must – not for buying but for people-watching. Start at the exclusive Bloomingdales, where you must brave an assault course of scent-squirting assistants delivering sales patter without moving their fire-red lips. Wind north past Cher and Jackie Onassis buying powder puffs at Boyd's Chemist (see p.327). Stop on the way at the Barbizon (see p.243) for tea and a view that inspired Georgia O'Keeffe, or at Serendipity ice-cream parlour (see p.278) for children aged eight to eighty. Venture to the eastern edges of the Upper East Side for white iced ginger cake from a German deli.

Yorkville The Upper East Side working class is squashed into a strip by the river between F.D.R. Drive and Lexington from 77th to 96th Streets, known as Yorkville, shrinking home to New York's immigrant German community. Early this century, 86th Street was crammed with beer gardens, lederhosen and pastries and dry-good stores. Today, most of the Yorkville streets are lined with cheap chain stores and fried chicken and pizza parlours. Only a handful of traditional delicatessens remain. Try Schaller and Weber on 1654 Second Avenue (bet. 84th and 85th Sts) and Bremen House at 218 East 86th St (bet. 2nd and 3rd Aves); for cakes and pastries, go to Café Geiger (see p.278).

Whitney Museum of American Art

945 Madison Ave (at 75th St): closed Mon; Tues 1–8 p.m., Wed–Sat 11 a.m.–5 p.m., Sun noon–6 p.m.; $5, students with ID free, free for everyone Tues 6–8 p.m.; free gallery talks on Tues (1.30 p.m., 3.30 p.m., 6.15 p.m.), Wed–Fri (11.30 a.m., 1.30 p.m., 3.30 p.m.).

The building is a top-heavy Brutalist mass that thrusts out towards the street over a drawbridge-type walkway. Its apparent absence of windows (angled trapezoidal windows allow inmates to see out, but outsiders can't see in) gives the Marcel Breuer and Hamilton Smith 1966 structure a sinister air.

The Founder Wealthy socialite Gertrude Vanderbilt Whitney opened the museum in 1931 to support young artists and increase awareness of American art. She owned 500 works by realist artists, including Edward Hopper, which formed the nucleus of the collection. Now the museum has a permanent collection of over 8,000 works and it is perhaps best known for the Whitney Biennial (between March and June on odd-numbered years), which aims to give a provocative overview of the work being produced by contemporary artists, including a significant strand for film-makers and video-artists. The show is often panned by critics and always teeming with visitors.

GERTRUDE VANDERBILT WHITNEY

New York women of wealth and social standing have long been expected to at least dabble in art patronage, so Gertrude Vanderbilt Whitney was applauded when she founded the Whitney Museum in 1931, but she was ridiculed when she first studied art herself. She went on to become one of the best-respected American sculptors of her time.

Born in New York in 1877, Gertrude was the great-granddaughter of the railroad magnate Cornelius Vanderbilt. She married rich banker and sportsman Harry Payne Whitney in 1896 and devoted herself to art, spending time at the turn of the century studying in Paris under Auguste Rodin. In 1907 she opened her first studio in a converted stable in Greenwich Village's MacDougal Alley, but when World War I broke out she immediately gathered a group of doctors and nurses and left for France to establish a hospital near Soisson, for which she was decorated by the French government. The war informed her work – later sculpture titles included 'In the Trenches', 'Gassed' and 'His Bunkie' – and fierce patriotism became embedded in her nature.

Her husband died in 1930 but Gertrude declared that the Whitney Museum of American Art would go ahead as scheduled, and at the opening she declared that she had collected American art when few others thought it worthy because she 'believed in our national creative talent. Now I am making this collection the nucleus of a museum devoted exclusively to American art – a museum which will grow and increase in importance as we ourselves grow.' In 1941 a seven-foot bronze statue by Gertrude Vanderbilt Whitney of New York's first Dutch governor, Peter Stuyvesant, was unveiled in Stuyvesant Park, where it still stands today; the next year Gertrude died in a New York hospital surrounded by her family.

On the **ground floor** beyond the **information desk** near the lifts you'll see sculptor Alexander Calder's miniature animated 'Calder's Circus' with cork and wire wild horses and a gyrating cloth belly dancer.

The **second and fourth floors** have regularly changing mixed shows and retrospectives of established American artists; the **third floor** usually showcases the Whitney's permanent collection. Ed Keinholz's grim 'The Wait' is usually on display, an installation in which an old woman represented by a sheep's skull in a bottle sits surrounded by yellowed photos, fraying bric-a-brac, and a caged bird whose depressed cheeps haunt adjacent rooms. Women artists represented in the Whitney's permanent collection include Alice

ELEANOR ROOSEVELT

President F.D. Roosevelt's wife Eleanor had many causes for unhappiness throughout her life, but she transcended them all and became perhaps the world's most famous woman diplomat and humanitarian.

Born into a powerful New York family in 1884 to a mother who nicknamed her 'Granny' for being so dull and an adoring but impetuous father, Eleanor was orphaned before she was ten years old. While she was raised by her maternal grandmother she threw herself into learning, and shortly after she had dutifully 'come out' at seventeen in New York Society, she plunged into settlement work, helping the immigrant poor at the Rivington Street Settlement House, located in the heart of New York's Lower East Side slums. This made her a social oddity and intrigued a distant cousin, Franklin, who began courting. She felt unworthy, but mutual friends thought dashing F.D.R. was the lucky one.

F.D.R.'s mother Sara Delano Roosevelt did not. She insisted that Eleanor give up work at the settlement house for fear that she would bring home contagious diseases, and she persuaded the couple to keep the engagement secret for a year, saying that a long engagement would give them time to examine their feelings – or, she hoped, cool their affections. To Sara's immense disappointment, the marriage went ahead in March 1905 and during the voyage-honeymoon Eleanor suffered not seasickness but morning sickness. Baby Anna was born in 1906, 'just a helpless bundle', and Eleanor was frightened. She wrote later in her memoirs: 'I had high standards of what a wife and mother should be and not the faintest notion of what it meant to be either a wife or a mother.' She let her mother-in-law dominate. From 1906 Eleanor suffered ten physically and emotionally draining years, during which she bore six children (one of whom died), undertook a heavy regime of war work throughout World War I, and discovered that her husband was having an affair with his secretary, Lucy Mercer. F.D.R.'s political career was at a critical stage, so Eleanor agreed not to divorce him, but the betrayal aggravated psychosomatic illnesses that led to gum deterioration which gradually caused the protuding, crooked teeth that were so often caricatured. There is speculation that F.D.R.'s infidelity pushed Eleanor into a lesbian affair with journalist Lorena Hickock. Certainly, F.D.R. and Eleanor developed a fond but distant working relationship, and this gave Eleanor space to establish her own political identity. She fought for women's suffrage, ran a school for girls where she taught pupils to be aware of social injustice and think for themselves, and after her husband was crippled by polio in 1921 she became 'his legs', encouraging and facilitating his political advance as a Democrat. He was elected Governor of New York in 1928, and in 1933 Eleanor went to the White House as First Lady. When she returned to New York State after her husband's death in 1945 she became America's only woman United Nations representative (see p.126), and in her eighties she showed no signs of cutting down her public activities. Asked where she got her energy from, she replied: 'I don't have any more energy than anyone else. But I never waste any of it on regrets.' Eleanor Roosevelt's last major official position was to chair President Kennedy's Commission on the Status of Women in 1961. After attending a Democratic rally in 1962 she said: 'I don't feel very well,' and was hospitalised. She spent her last days at home surrounded by her children, and died of tuberculosis on 7 November.

Neel's portrait of Andy Warhol: Warhol sits erect but worn on a sofa, his naked ageing torso visibly scarred and bandaged after

Valerie Solanis's attempt on his life (see p.136). Neel, who lived and first painted in Spanish Harlem in the 1940s, paints New York portraits in the realist tradition. Many say that her works – including a number of nude portraits of pregnant women, with ballooning bellies and distended nipples – hint at impending menace. Neel, it seems, is genuinely puzzled. The feminist art historian Linda Nochlin, who sat for a portrait in the 1980s, reports Neel saying: 'You know, you don't *seem* so anxious, but that's how you come out.'

If the 1927 'Black Iris' of Georgia O'Keeffe, also a realist, is not on display, then a similar work will be. Although O'Keeffe swore that her flowers were just flowers, feminists disagree. Her magnified depictions of plant forms and bones, they say, are striking natural symbols of the female genitalia and reproductive organs.

Louise Nevelson's work, by contrast, is not obviously 'feminine', either in subject or in style. Creator of spiky metal abstract sculptures, Nevelson (see p.64) wears 'feminine' false eyelashes and says she married at seventeen, despite her certainty that she could not live without creating, because 'the world said you should get married'.

The spaces throughout the museum are versatile and alter dramatically for each show. Only the dimly lit Swedish-look pine stairwells between floors remain constant.

Go down to the concrete pillared basement and take afternoon or savoury tea at Sarabeth's flowery-tableclothed restaurant for around $14.

CENTRAL PARK

Harper's magazine described it as 'radiant in the magic of atmosphere and taste' in 1876. Its designers, Olmsted and Vaux, wanted it to contribute to 'the greater happiness of each . . . rich and poor, young and old, Jew and Gentile'. Today it regularly makes headlines for gang rapes and vicious murders; mothers in gardenless apartments would go mad without it; businessmen and women pound its customised joggers' paths before pounding the board table; all-American kids skate and rollerblade and whack softball while couples get passionate on patchy bits of grass. Central Park is still, as Olmsted wished in 1870, 'a ground to which people may easily go . . . where they may stroll for an hour' and feel 'nothing of the bustle and jar of the streets'.

Conception In 1844 newspaper owner William Cullen Bryant became worried that buildings might soon cover every inch of Manhattan Island. Developers thought he was barmy to propose protecting wasteland in the middle of wasteland from prosperous urban growth, but Bryant campaigned relentlessly through his paper, the *New York Post*, and put parkland firmly on the forthcoming 1851 mayor electoral campaign agenda. By 1853 the winning candidate, Mayor Ambrose Kingsland, was committed to setting land aside for recreational use, not profit. He commissioned Olmsted and Vaux to landscape an 840-acre swamp that Olmsted described as a 'pestilential spot where miasmatic odors taint every breath of air'.

Over sixteen years, gangs of men with picks, shovels and teams of horse-drawn wagons rearranged nearly 5 million cubic yards of stone and dirt and added nearly 600 species of trees to the original 42. Olmsted and Vaux's design imitated nature, featuring a lake-shaped reservoir, craggy outcrops of rock and pastures scattered with grazing sheep.

When the Gates Opened   New York's High Society were the first to rush through the gates, to show off their latest toys. Elegantly bustled, coiffured ladies lined up near the entrance in victorias, broughams, phaetons and barouches, pitilessly eyeing the rigs of their rivals. For men, trotters were all the rage – they whipped through the park to the raceways of Harlem. In winter, young Whartons, Astors and Vanderbilts spent time between fashionable balls and parties tobogganing down the landscaped slopes, and in summer they took to bicycle riding. Despite desperate parental cries that the sport was unbecoming for respectable young ladies because of undue freedom of dress and movement, by the 1890s Central Park was teeming with lady cyclists.

The 1930s Depression brought darker days, when the emptied reservoir became the biggest of many 'Hoovervilles' (named after President Hoover), where the unemployed and down-and-outs built shanties and slept beneath sheets of newspaper, dubbed 'Hoover blankets'.

Today there are still echoes of Hooverville. By tree trunks at the edges of the park you'll see carefully constructed mounds of blankets with pillows of cardboard to support the sleeping heads that often have Walkman phones plugged in to block noise. Dayglo-lycra-clad bionic women jog past oblivious, bleached ponytails bobbing; others walk, a newer, more chic fad that is performed with a writhing waddle and weights strapped to ankles, to tone up buttocks. Children on the end of nannies' tired arms point and jeer and squabble. Bored professional dog-walkers tie their ten or twelve yapping, snarling Alaskan husky and Chihuahua wards to railings and at some point, if they're decent upright citizens, they'll use plastic spade Pooper Scoopers to scoop their dogs' poop into specially labelled disposal receptacles before taking the exotic breeds back to their luxurious Upper East Side apartments.

What There Is and How To See It   This is a big park, so if you want to 'do' it all at one go, hire a **bike** (from the Loeb Boathouse, $6 for first hour on a basic bike) or take a horse-driven buggy (around $15 for half hour from Central Park South). Perhaps the best way is to see it **by foot** in leisurely chunks between visiting the Upper East or West Side's sights and museums: for example, Trump's Wollman Rink after Fifth Avenue; the Zoo after the Frick collection; and boating after the Metropolitan Museum of Art. For orientation, just find a lamppost – each bears the number of the nearest street. After dark it's illegal to enter on foot. For **safety**, observe general rules on page 20; avoid going above the reservoir midweek, since although the Harlem section is the target of restoration projects, it can still be ominously quiet; go pretty much anywhere on weekends when everywhere teems with families and sports events; always be wary of quiet corners – the wild garden called the **Ramble** (74th–79th Sts bet. East and West Drives) in particular is a notorious hiding-place for gay-bashers and rapists. The section below the reservoir has most places of interest. For a **rest**, go to the **Tavern on the Green** (see p.277) for Pina Coladas on the patio. For details of the many children's parks, see p.338.

Visitors' Information at The Dairy

Level with 64th St (bet. East Drive and Center Drive).

In 1870 this Gothic building was briefly a sylvan dairy where European-style milkmaids and a herd of cows gave children a rare treat: fresh milk. It reopened in 1981 as a Visitors' Centre, with an information desk, exhibitions, a sales desk, and (on weekends) tours by the Urban Park Rangers. Tel. 397 3080 for information and 360 1333 for special events.

The Carousel

65th St (at Center Drive).

The original 1871 merry-go-round was driven by horses walking a treadmill in an underground pit. The present carousel, featuring 58 hand-carved horses, was built at Coney Island in 1908 and moved here in 1951.

Wollman Rink

59th St (at 6th Ave).

Come here for ice-skating September to late April or roller-skating in the summer months (see p.315 for times and prices), and credit real-estate and casino millionaire Donald Trump for its 1986 reopening. Trump took over when bureaucracy thwarted City attempts to rebuild it. He sometimes turns up graciously to accept the thanks of skaters on nippy winter weekends.

Central Park's Zoo

64th St (at 5th Ave). Open 10 a.m.–4.30 p.m.; adults $2.50, senior citizens $1.25, children 3–12 50c, children 0–2 free; tel. 408 0271.

This is a hot spot for women with children. There's a special pram-parking area; women spread out nappies, pins and babies on benches.

The informatively and entertainingly labelled 1988 collection of animals is based around three climatic regions: the Tropic Zone, the Temperate Territory, and the Polar Region. Monkeys swing in a fake African environment, bats flap in naturalistic caves, alligators lurk in a rather plush swamp. Glass and minimum caging let children get close to the animals safely. The barking sea lions are popular, and the polar bears do an elegant backstroke. If you don't want to pay, bear in mind that the Zoo is sunk below park level. You can see a large amount from the surrounding walkway.

Central Park's Children's Zoo

65th St (at 5th Ave). Open 10 a.m.–5 p.m.; admission 10c.

The sign says '10c for zoo and restrooms'. The dingy rest rooms are more appealing than the zoo-cum-adventure-playground, which boasts 'a walk into the jaws of Jonah's whale', 'a tour of Noah's Ark', a nose-to-nose meeting with sniffling Stardust the Llama or pathetically cawing Edgar the Raven. The live animals are moth-eaten, the models are tatty.

Walk up the Mall, past the **Naumburg Bandshell**, which hosts summertime concerts of jazz, folk dancing and theatrical performances (tel. 360 2756).

Bethseda Terrace

72nd St (at Terrace Drive).

This, the only formal area, is generally considered the centre of the park. Mothers lounge and joggle their strollers (pushchairs) on the ledge around the Bethesda fountain on top of which Emma Stebbins's romantic winged statue, Angel of the Waters, has settled. The paving juts out into the lake, where you might see the Loeb Boathouse's one Venetian gondola, complete with fully trained gondolier, poling its way through the rippling waters.

72nd St (at 5th Ave).

This pond hums with whizzing motorboats; the edges are dominated by their earnest child operators. To the west there's a bronze statue of Hans Christian Andersen, and to the north an Alice in Wonderland statue – Alice and her Mad Hatter's Tea Party compatriots regularly become a climbing frame for rampaging infants.

The nearby Claremont stables (see p.315) supply a steady stream of prim ladies tapping crops on withers and rising and sitting in gleaming saddles.

UPPER WEST SIDE

The Upper West Side has five main attractions: the Lincoln Center for classical music and opera; the Natural History Museum, which is a favourite for women with children; the impressive even though still unfinished Cathedral of St John the Divine; Columbia University, where, at Barnard College, subsequently eminent American women chewed pencils at desks; and the New York Convention and Visitors' Bureau, which should be one of your first stops when you arrive in the City.

The sights are widely spaced, so you should use public transport or cabs. It's too far to walk.

The Upper West Side is a mixture of posh and downbeat. At the turn of the century, members of the upper-middle class built town houses along Riverside Drive and Central Park West. Riverside Drive, with its river view, nearly made it as *the* most desirable address, but Fifth Avenue, which boasted the Astors and the Vanderbilts amongst its residents, kept the edge. In the 1920s many of the four- and five-storey houses were knocked down and replaced by fifteen-floor apartment blocks. The genteel hotchpotch curves the length of Riverside Drive. Off Columbus Avenue some of the brownstones are painted cheery pinks and soothing greens, and the tree-lined pavements behind the Natural History Museum are sometimes used for fashion shoots.

A 1940s urban renewal programme cleared twelve blocks of slum tenements for the Lincoln Center, and nowadays there's a thriving singles bar scene up to 83rd Street, cafés spill on to the sidewalk, mothers parade their children in strollers, dog hairdressers do a roaring trade, and launderettes are decorated with copper bedpans and gilt-framed copies of Great Masters. Women dripping with diamonds pour out of Metropolitan Opera opening nights.

Yuppy West Siders swear their patch is superior to that of East Side yuppy rivals. Central Park West is, they say, wider and so much more pleasant than choked Fifth Avenue. Certainly, the West

Side escaped the worst ravages of waves of developments. You'll see few high-rises.

Further north, the area is still in transition. Some of the run-down tenements and middle-income apartments are becoming desirable residences; cafés and antique shops are springing up, particularly along Columbus Avenue; the University inevitably attracts musty bookshops and trendy bars (for example the West End, see p.291). But the elegant cathedral and the friendly bustling university campus border Harlem's grim projects. The rule is simple: if you're at all worried, don't go much north of Cathedral Parkway on foot.

After a trip to the Park, the Children's Museum or the Natural History Museum, take your children to Café Lalo (see p.276) for cake and coffee. Or, for some social anthropology, go to Zabar's Deli (see p.276), favourite grazing ground of rich dandy West Side women.

Lincoln Center for the Performing Arts

West 66th to 62nd Sts (bet. Columbus and Amsterdam Ave). Hour-long tours leave on the half-hour daily between 10 a.m. and 5 p.m.; $7.50 for adults, $6.50 for senior citizens and students, $4.50 for children.

Uninviting from the street, this five-building complex consists of some of the lowest new buildings in New York. They are designed to look Greek; their façades feature pillars, they are square and grey and spread out on a raised flagstone platform. 188 slum tenements were demolished and 1,600 people rehoused to accommodate it. Built as New York's cultural centre, it is home to the Metropolitan Opera, the New York Philharmonic, the annual New York Film Festival and a branch of the City Library. You can come to a performance (see p.311) or, during the day, you can take an official guided tour of the complex.

To find the tours, which start in the basement, enter through a labelled door in the side of the Metropolitan Opera House, go down the steps and follow the arrows. Pay your money and have a plastic badge clipped on. The guide says hello, what country are you all from? and you're off. The tour is too speedy. It goes briefly through a 'NO PUBLIC ALLOWED' area, but otherwise you could see everything by entering the foyers and/or going to a performance.

Construction The idea for a place where plays, operas, ballets and concerts could all be performed at the same time germinated in the 1950s. In 1956 J.D. Rockefeller took charge of the committee and Wallace K. Harrison, who designed much of the Rockefeller Center, was appointed. His design was influenced by the Radiant

City and City Beautiful ideas of architects like Le Corbusier, in which people are isolated from traffic and culture from work. The result is that at night, the complex is deserted and, though probably safe, still eerie.

BEVERLY SILLS

'Bubbles' Beverly is not sure if she wants to be easy-going girl next door or inaccessible prima donna, but she is sure she's interesting. She has written not one but two autobiographies.

She was born into a middle-income Jewish Brooklyn family. Her mother was opera-mad and her father, who worked for Metropolitan Life Insurance, was a hard taskmaster. 'I once scored 98 on an arithmetic test, and I remember his saying: "I don't like ninety-eights. I only like one hundreds."' His pet name for her was 'Bubbles', because 'I was born with an enormous bubble of spit in my mouth.'

A chubby knock-kneed child, she made her stage debut aged three at the local 'Miss Beautiful Baby of 1932' contest. She sang 'The Wedding of Jack and Jill': 'I wore an outfit with a deep décolleté and I had no doubt I would win.' By the age of seven she was singing every week on radio. By the night of 27 October 1980 her professional career had spanned more than three decades, brought her in contact with 'Princess Di several times', taken her to the world's greatest opera houses, and she was singing her goodbye concert at the New York City Opera. Confetti and balloons filled the hall, the evening cleared more than a million dollars, and next morning she took over as the company's General Director. 'I reported for work at 9 o'clock . . . Prima donnas do not wear inexpensive outfits, so I showed up in a sable-lined raincoat, a cashmere dress, Ferragamo shoes, with a ten-carat diamond ring on my finger.'

'There were problems she hadn't anticipated. The Opera was on the point of bankruptcy, she had to work '15 hours a day, 7 days a week', and not everyone approved of her appointment. 'Did being a diva disqualify me in some way? Even one of my severest critics once wrote that I'd had more impact on the public than any opera singer since Enrico Caruso.' By 1982 the indefatigable Bubbles had raised $6 million. In 1983 she had topped $9 million, and in 1987 she was photographed with 'the powers that be at Lincoln Center', the only woman at the centre of 'my male harem.'

She does not know how history will judge her singing: 'I'm much clearer about the contribution I've made to popularizing opera in America . . . Before I came on the scene, the public regarded opera stars as exotic hothouse plants. I think I changed that. I was a home-grown product the public could identify with. I looked and talked the way they did.'

What career next? She hasn't decided, but whatever it is, 'I've always tried to go a step past wherever people expected me to end up.'

The Center was funded almost entirely by private contributions – and the larger the donation, the more prestigious the acknowledgement. A $5 donation for a hod of bricks wins no public recognition; $1,000 entitles the donor to have their name inscribed on a seat in the Philharmonic Hall; $100,000 and they have their name engraved on a plaque in a lobby. Mitzi Newhouse, wife of the publishing giant Si Newhouse, donated a million dollars and had a theatre named after her.

The Visit   Most of the buildings have gift shops. The outdoor **Plaza** has a fountain in the middle. In the summer, a café spills on to it and there are free lunchtime and evening concerts.

Formerly Philharmonic Hall, Avery Fisher Hall was renamed after the founder of Fisher Radio donated stupendous amounts of money. The auditorium was totally reconstructed in 1976 by architect Philip Johnson in association with an acoustics consultant Cyril Harris. The result is slick high-tech. The doors are soundproof lead, the stage is shaped like a megaphone, and the wood and gold ceiling is staggered for improved sound projection. In the foyer there is a Richard Lippold 'Stabile' – a kind of mobile, only it's stable – made from piano wire. It shows Apollo giving an appreciation of music to Orpheus. Wits on the tour ask the guide: 'That's Orpheus? Well, we'll have to take your word for it!'

The Metropolitan Opera House foyer has a grand swooshing double staircase with two Austrian crystal chandeliers hovering above it and two large, colourful Chagall murals at the top. Chagall planned to make stained-glass windows but was discouraged because it was thought that the area was still too rough – hooligans might chuck bricks. The murals are covered during the day to prevent damage from sunlight. The 3,788-capacity auditorium is lined with plush maroon velvet and African rosewood.

The New York State Theater is now home to the New York City Ballet and the New York City Opera. From 1979 to 1989 the opera star Beverly Sills (see box) was Director.

Museum of American Folk Art

2 Lincoln Square. Open daily 9 a.m.–9 p.m. Voluntary contribution.

Formerly a dank arcade, this space under an apartment building is now a pleasant if small museum celebrating the best of American folk art, including furniture, decorative arts, textiles, paintings and sculpture from the eighteenth century to the present day in changing exhibitions. It is a well-organised and welcoming space; the exhibits are labelled with a wealth of interesting background information. Because the focus of exhibitions is often domestic, they frequently feature work by women. Buy unusual folksy bits and pieces in the shop next door.

Children's Museum of Manhattan

212 W 83rd St, tel. 212 721 1223. Admission: $4 and $2 for workshops (free to children 2 and under).

This caters for toddlers to ten-year-olds. Children can paint, make collages, learn about animation, become newscasters, and outside they can clamber in the Urban Tree House, which is made of traffic cones and old tyres and houses hands-on exhibits to teach 'reduce, recycle, reuse and rethink'. Children love it.

American Museum of Natural History.

Central Park West (at 81st St). Open daily 10 a.m.–5.45 p.m., 8.45 p.m. on Fri and Sat. Suggested admission $5 adults, $2.50 children.

The building resembles clichés of Colditz; inside, the exhibits include moth-eaten stuffed animals and a laughably unreal fibreglass blue whale; all over, the atmosphere is jolly chaos. Most days there are hordes of mothers and children in here. The strollers take on lives of their own, and the entrance usually resembles a crèche. It's a great place to go with children, or, if you're tired of sophisticated New York and you want to regress, go on your own.

The 700-ft-long façade features cylindrical pointy turrets, a bridge that originally let carriages in, and dour statues of the explorers and naturalists Boone, Audubon, Lewis and Clark. Work began in 1872 with Calvert Vaux designing, and bits were added up till 1933. The American Museum of Natural History is, says the *Guinness Book of Records*, the largest of its kind in the world. It holds 35,000,000 exhibits, ranging from Invertebrates, Mammals and Peoples to Meteorites and Crystals, including the Star of India, the largest blue sapphire ever found.

As part of the museum's current revamping, the star attractions – the dinosaur skeletons – are being remodelled. Locals fear the loss of charm; the museum hopes to lure more tourists and dispel the musty hopeless image. Watch work in progress on the dinosaurs until 1996, when you'll see a giant Tyrannosaurus with its head lowered to attack prey, a 50-ft-tall Barosaurus defending its young against an attacking Allosaurus, and the moving wings of a Deinonychus.

The **Discovery Room** (open weekends only; tickets at the first-floor information desk) is great for children aged four–ten. Touch and smell the wonders of nature, and on Saturdays come for the special magician, puppeteer and storytelling shows. Children of all ages can go to the **People Centre** on the second floor, where live dance, music and craft programmes illustrate facets of different cultures. The first-floor **Naturemax Theatre** (adults $5.00, children $2.50, senior citizens $3.75) shows changing programmes of nature films on a four-storey-high screen. And on the north side of the museum on the first floor, again mainly for children, there is the **Haydn Planetarium** ($5 adults, $2.50 children; admission covers entrance to museum; separate entrance on 81st St; shows Mon through Fri 12.30–4.45 p.m., Sat–Sun noon–5 p.m.). In the ground-floor **Guggenheim Space Theatre**, hear Henry Fonda and Walter Kronkite waxing lyrical while a 360-degree space-screen covers topics including 'Rocketry', 'Earth', and 'Solar Systems'. In the upstairs **Planetarium** Vincent Price's voice accompanies a sky show of 'The End of the World', 'The Sky at Christmas' or 'The Drama of the Universe', depending on the season. There are two **Junior Shops** for gifts and knick-knacks ranging from Mexican crafts to microscopes and petrified wood (floors 1 and 2). For free museum highlights tours, assemble at the second-floor information desk.

If it's not too late, round off your trip with a walk in the park.

Cathedral Church of St John the Divine

Amsterdam Ave (at W 112th St). The Cathedral is open 7 days a week 7 a.m. to 5 p.m., three services a day and seven on Sun. Pre-school childcare is provided from 9.45 a.m. to 12.45 p.m. on Sun (ask an usher or guard for directions).

This is, after more than a century's building work, still only two-thirds finished (completion is scheduled for 2050), but it is already a major tourist attraction. Coachloads of camera-clicking sightseers tumble in and out to *ooh* and *aah* at 'the largest Gothic cathedral in the world', which can fit both Notre Dame and Chartres or 10,000 worshippers inside at any one time.

Construction Work on the Cathedral Church of the Episcopal Diocese of New York began on 27 December 1892, the Feast Day of St John, under the direction of C. Grant LaFarge, who decided the dominant style should be Romanesque-Byzantine. He managed to build only an elegant choir and a grand airy narthex before Ralph Adams Cram took over in 1911 and the Cathedral went Gothic. Cram was responsible for the awesome jagged main façade flanked by two square towers (the west front) and for the nave behind it. The west towers, the transepts and the crossing have yet to be completed. The Cathedral's exterior is highly detailed. A bronze Angel Gabriel toots his horn from on top of the ambulatory chapels while assorted saints chat, contemplate and agonise in custom-made bobbled turrets by the windows of the sanctuary. A fully robed, grave Christ sits in Majesty in the tympanum above the great doors of the west front while the doors themselves, each 18 feet high and weighing 3 tons, have bronze relief panels showing scenes from the Old and New Testaments: fiery horsemen from the Apocalypse, a buoyant ark, assorted winged animals, coy Eve and Adam, and a wicked, coiling snake. The doors were cast in Paris at the same foundry that cast the Statue of Liberty. St John stands between them, looking pained.

The Visit   In the **narthex**, go to the information desk for tourist leaflets and photocopied details of the Cathedral's community activities, which include soup kitchens, an ensemble for early music, shelter for the homeless, meetings for incest survivors and pop AIDS benefits. Down both sides of the nave there are bays, each with a name. In the **Arts Bay**, for example, 'Poets' Corner' is 'dedicated to American Literature'. The various floor inscriptions include 'Live all you can; it's a mistake not to', for Henry James; 'Out of space – out of time', for Edgar Allan Poe; and 'Thy will be done in art as it is in heaven', for Willa Cather. On the south side of the nave in the **St Francis Bay** you can see tanks full of mud and algae in an exhibition that illustrates the life forms of the Hudson Valley.

On a column in the middle of the **nave** there is a small plaque which shows a bishop with his hands tied behind his back. This marks the spot where, in 1973, angry women protested for the right to become priests while five men were in the process of being ordained. With the support of the then bishop of New York, Bishop Moore, the fight continued, and in 1976 women were officially admitted to the priesthood in the Anglican Church. Indeed, it is claimed that one in five full-time clergy in America are now female. At the Cathedral, scene of the first most vocal dissent, all the hymns for the children's services have been altered so that God is always 'God' and never 'her' or 'him'.

The chapels off the north and south ambulatories contain a mixture of permanent and changing exhibitions. You will always be able to see nineteenth-century gold-embroidered priest's stoles and a fiddle-back chasuble in tall glass cases. The photographic exhibition in the **St Boniface Chapel** may or may not be Richard Sandler's images of New York's gross poverty and wealth (in one, a man holds up a billboard that reads: 'God really loves homosexuals; God really hates homosexuality').

Throughout the Cathedral, depictions of holy men and women are mixed up with characters from the history of America. Stained glass windows in **St Alban's Chapel** show white-wigged men and scrolls of paper in the signing of the Declaration of Independence. In the vaulted **Baptistry** one of the eight niches contains Peter Stuyvesant.

The Cathedral's extensive **gift shop** is nomadic. It is most often in the north transept. You might find the Dean's wife at the cash till.

Before you leave, go to the very noisy **yard and workshop** (beyond the north transept). Under a multiracial programme devised in 1979 by Bishop Moore and Dean Morton to help 'at-risk kids', 60 youths from Harlem, who would otherwise be unemployed, are trained in the art of stonemasonry. Simon Verity, who, the Cathedral proudly declares, used to carve for the Queen of England, is the master-carver. He oversees a business. There is some romantic tap-tapping with chisels, but mostly trainees wear space-age goggles and manipulate state-of-the-art technology, including robotic carving machines.

Rats have no respect for religion. On your way out you might notice, on the edge of the spacious lawns of the Bishop's Garden, a skull and crossbone sign tacked on to a lamppost: 'DANGER, RAT POISON was placed in this area'. The posters warn you to keep dogs on a leash and watch children at play; they carefully detail the type of poison and its antidote; the information is repeated in Spanish; and some of the posters feature graffiti, for example: 'Rat Poison kills more than rats – think about it!'.

Columbia University and Barnard College

W 114th St–W 120th Sts (bet. Amsterdam Ave and Broadway). Stroll about the campus or, if you'd like to see the insides of some buildings, take a free guided tour from 10 a.m. to 2 p.m. late May–August and at 3 p.m. through the academic year. Meet at Room 201, Dodge Hall, corner of 116th and Broadway.

Columbia is one of America's most prestigious Ivy League Universities. It has some pretty buildings, and it has good views of Manhattan, but the only real reason to go is if you're enrolled as a student.

MORNINGSIDE'S LAYOUT

Jane Jacobs blames the odd state of Morningside Heights on urban planning. In *The Death and Life of American Cities* she wrote:

According to planning theory it should not be in trouble at all, for it enjoys a great abundance of parkland, campus, playground, and other open spaces. It has plenty of grass. It occupies high and pleasant ground with magnificent views. It is a famous educational centre with splendid institutions . . . it has no industry . . . Yet by the early 1950s Morningside Heights was becoming a slum so quickly . . . that the situation posed a crisis for the institutions. They and the planning arms of the city government got together, applied more planning theory, wiped out the most run-down part of the area, and built in its stead a middle-income co-operative project complete with shopping centre and a public housing project, all interspersed with air, light, sunshine, and landscaping . . . After that, Morningside Heights went downhill even faster.

UPPER MANHATTAN

Some Background Columbia was founded in 1754 and built on a buckwheat field. It educated some of the nation's most historically significant men, including first Secretary of the Treasury Alexander Hamilton and President Franklin D. Roosevelt; it bred political dissent in the 1960s, when students demonstrated against the Vietnam War on the library steps; today it has 18,000 eager graduates and undergraduates milling between library and lecture hall in baseball caps and sweatshirts. It didn't admit women until 1983. The affiliated Barnard College (on a separate campus across Broadway), however, was founded as one of the first independent colleges for women in 1889, at a time when women were poorly educated or not at all, and certainly not beyond childhood (see box).

EDUCATION IS LIBERATING

After the Revolution some educational opportunities opened up for women, but only within strict social boundaries, as the Columbia College commencement oration titled 'Female Influence' made clear in 1875 when it described the ideal educated woman. She would not be masculine or threaten the sanctity of marriage: quite the contrary. She would feed the 'nutritive fluid' of her learning to a sprightly fireside band of babes and 'generous youth just ripening into manhood'.

Nineteenth-century suffragists held less romantic views. They saw education as a key to breaking down, in Carrie Chapman Catt's words, 'all artificial barriers which laws and customs interpose between women and human freedom'. Educated women could get jobs. Upper- and middle-class women left wifely and motherly duties and flocked into New York, boarding at women's hostels such as Pan Hellenic House (see p.134). By the 1920s the number of women employed in the professions had increased by over 450,000 and in business by over 100,000. Women became editors in publishing houses, sold real estate, practised pharmacology, and took up important positions in department stores. But other statistics showed that women were still largely confined to 'female' occupations. The number of women in medical schools actually diminished from 1,280 in 1902 to 992 in 1926. Then the Depression fostered a wave of reaction against change in women's traditional roles. The Barnard placement office reported that only one-third of the class of 1932 desiring jobs secured paid work, and most of that was part-time. Even at the beginning of World War II, public opinion, remarked a Women's Bureau official, would not 'countenance the use of women as long as men could be found to do the emergency work'. But soon men ran out. A beautician overnight became a switchwoman for 600 Long Island Railroad trains; Josephine Miklos, an Austrian aristocrat and designer of perfume bottles, took a job as a precision toolmaker in Hoboken's shipyards. Women's colleges did their part for the war effort by training students for wartime work and by encouraging students to enlist in civil defence activities. Barnard offered courses in auto repair, map-reading, and aeroplane-spotting.

Barnard College The college's namesake, Frederick A.P. Barnard, was dead by the time Barnard College opened. Barnard, the tenth

President of Columbia University, became a champion of higher education for women in the 1860s, suggesting in annual reports between 1879 and 1889 that women be admitted to Columbia College. His colleagues didn't like the idea of co-education one bit. Some thought women weren't worth training, others genuinely worried about the effects of academic life on frail, feminine physiques. In 1883 a petition signed by 1,000 citizens pressured Columbia's trustees into authorising an experimental 'Collegiate Course' that would enable women to receive the bachelor's degree – at least in theory. The odds were against women from the start, since they were barred from the lectures on which the final examination papers were based and received only occasional, irrelevant assignments. Female students weren't told this. Miss Annie Nathan, a small, pretty eighteen-year-old, had diligently studied everything she could wrest from teachers, so when she sat down in the exam room she was outraged and explained her objections in the margin: 'The professor had a sense of justice – or possibly, a sense of humour – for he passed me.' From then on Annie Nathan gave practically all her time to fighting for equal education opportunities for women, and hit on a winner when she suggested a separate college for women. The Columbia trustees approved the resolution in April 1889, but awarded no funds. J. Pierpont Morgan gave $5,000, the only generous contribution, and on a skimpy budget Barnard opened in October 1889 in a rented brownstone house at 343 Madison Avenue with thirty-six enrolled students before moving nine years later to the present site.

'PUNK' MEAD

The 1920s were the golden age for the new anthropology, and the dumpy, bespectacled, thrice-married Margaret Mead (1901–78) became its guru. She has since been accused of imposing her own ideological beliefs during fieldwork on her findings. Her best-known work, *Coming of Age in Samoa*, gained near-bestseller status because it simultaneously evoked romantic faraway places and confirmed widely-held beliefs about the ideal society, which kept woman at home as happy housewife. Betty Friedan later castigated Mead for enthusiastically endorsing accepted views of femininity in her work while ignoring them in her own life.

Born in Pennsylvania to an economist father and a keen gardener mother, Mead always insisted that her 'true age' was eleven, and remained fond of her father's pet name for her, which was 'Punk'. Her avowed aim in life was to become famous. One way to do this was to achieve in a world that was male-dominated. Anthropology fitted the bill. Amongst other things, Mead was an innovator in the use of photography as an anthropologist's tool.

Even up to the last year of her life, when cancer limited her activities, she rose at 5 a.m. each day to read books, articles, newspapers and students' theses before starting on her own work.

Today Barnard has over 2,000 students and is respected nationally for its Anthropology Department, which was founded during World War I and spawned the now infamous anthropologist Margaret Mead (see box). Other noteworthy Barnard alumnae include Zora Neale Hurston (see p.200), Joan Rivers and Laurie Anderson, and during the 1970s professors included feminist Kate Millett, author of the influential *Sexual Politics*.

A Visit The Columbia campus fills seven blocks between Amsterdam and Broadway. At its centre the **Low Memorial Library**, designed by McKim, Mead and White, is impressive. Domed and fronted with a colonnade, it sits on top of a flight of white marble stairs.

THE NORTH, INCLUDING HARLEM

The area north of Central Park has a wildly contrasting mixture of things to see, including burnt-out ghettos and genteel Sugar Hill in Harlem; Napoleonic relics in the Morris Jumel Mansion; and an eccentric branch of the Metropolitan Museum of Art, the medieval Cloisters. All these things and more are worth visiting – the only question is how. The subway to Fort Tyron Park and the Cloisters is a clean, efficient express service. As for the rest, some New Yorkers will not set foot in Harlem, while others happily hop on the subway and rattle their way up to Sylvia's soul food restaurant for Sunday brunch (it gets crowded when the churches empty, so arrive early). Washington Heights around Morris Jumel Mansion and Harlem's Sugar Hill, which is the site of Hamilton Grange, are considered safe by pretty much everyone, although many women prefer to take the bus. If you're at all unsure about Harlem, especially if you're alone, the ideal way to see it is with a tour group. One of the oldest and best is Harlem Spirituals Inc. (see p.199 for details).

Fort Tyron Park & The Cloisters

Open Tues–Sun 9.30 a.m.–5.15 p.m. (March–Oct) and 9.30 a.m.– 4.45 p.m. (Nov–Feb), closed all Mons; suggested admission $6, $3 senior citizens and students, and free for under-12s (admission includes entry to Metropolitan Museum). Tel. 212 923 3700 for details of concerts (from William Byrd to the madrigals of fifteenth-century Italy's Guillaume Dufay) and lectures.

To get there by subway, take the IND Eighth Ave A train to 190th St, exit station by elevator and follow Margaret Corbin Drive; or take the M4 (Ft Tyron Park–The Cloisters) to the last stop; or take the hourly shuttle from the Metropolitan Museum.

High above the Hudson in a woody park, a square stone tower rises from a glued-together assortment of cloisters. This is the medieval branch of the Metropolitan Museum. A wonderful, crazy place to go, it still conjures the echo of sandal-footed monks bustling to and from prayers and meditation.

A monastery cloister is by definition a wholly male preserve, yet this one features a myriad of women in the form of the Virgin Mary, some tender and maternal, others holy and distant. You'll see more Madonnas crammed here than anywhere else in New York because the city is, like the rest of America, predominantly Protestant. For an informed and entertaining exploration of 'the myth and the cult of the Virgin Mary', read Marina Warner's *Alone of All Her Sex*.

Construction   Around the turn of the century, American sculptor George Grey Barnard developed a passion for shipping bits of Europe's disintegrating medieval buildings back to America. He built his very own medieval monument, merging sections from four medieval cloisters – one Romanesque and three Gothic – to house his smaller relics – or 'stones', as he called them. To achieve the authentic 'aged' look, he hosed down walls while the mortar was still wet. In 1914 his museum opened to a public that had little knowledge of medieval art. In 1917 a New York newspaper described an 'early-twelfth-century Madonna' that was actually a fourteenth-century statue of a deacon saint. When Barnard put the museum up for sale in 1926, John D. Rockefeller gave the Metropolitan Museum enough funds to buy Barnard's collection, and to improve its presentation. This included buying the land directly opposite and slapping a protection order on it so that the view from the Cloisters would always be aesthetically pleasing.

Mr Rockefeller and his wife then added to Barnard's collection so that the museum now shows sculpture, metalwork, tapestries, stained glass, manuscripts and panel paintings.

The Visit   If you arrive by subway, during the elevator journey to the surface you might notice the eyes of any New Yorkers widen. They're not used to travelling through this amount of rock. As you come out of the subway on to the street, take a left turn and, if you don't want a ten-minute walk through beautiful parkland, take the M4 bus one stop.

Ground Floor   Once in the main entrance hall, work your way round anticlockwise and you can pass through several centuries of medieval stonemasonry from all over Europe in a matter of minutes: go from a nineteenth-century Catalan chapel straight into thirteenth-century French cloisters back through a twelfth-century

Burgundian Romanesque Hall and into a Benedictine chapterhouse before you reach the **Early Gothic Hall**, where curvaceous fourteenth-century Virgins grin at you from every wall and two thirteenth-century statues of angels wear the famous 'Rheims smile' (coy and saucy).

It is hard to pick out highlights because there are so many, but take time to appreciate the view across the Hudson from the **Saint-Guilhem-Le-Désert Cloister**. And don't miss the **Langon Chapel**, where you will find the Autun Virgin and Child, the child sadly without his head. The Virgin and her infant's body were carved from a single block of birchwood, but Christ's head was stuck on with a piece of dowel that was not, it seems, quite sturdy enough. Both Virgin and Child are in rigid frontal poses, the God-child grasping a book symbolising knowledge or wisdom while his mother begins to roll her eyes heavenwards. The statue would have been venerated while displayed on an altar, carried in processions, and used in biblical dramas re-enacted in the church. You could spend hours absorbed by details in the **Nine Heroes Tapestry Room**, which features five of the original nine heroes, including David with a golden harp and King Arthur. The heroes sit in state, guarded by lesser personages such as warriors, cardinals and bishops. Directly above them, safely behind ramparts, are nine heroines, among them a court lady who looks especially bad-tempered, despite the purring pet cheetah and lovely maidens valiantly plucking musical instruments. The tapestries, designed as insulation against damp and as an ostentatious statement of wealth, were probably commissioned for Jean, Duke of Berry, brother of the French king Charles V.

Last stop on this floor is the darkened **Campin Room**, where the famous Annunciation altarpiece by Robert Campin is surrounded by domestic objects from the period, including a curious bronze chandelier and a fifteenth-century birdcage. The left-hand side-panel of Campin's altarpiece depicts the kneeling husband and wife donors, and on the right St Joseph is in his workshop drilling holes in a bit of wood, having set up a mouse-trap on his workbench. The central panel represents the Annunciation: the Archangel Gabriel announces to the Virgin Mary that she has been chosen by God to be the mother of his son.

Lower Level   After the **Late Gothic Hall**, backtrack to get to the lower level (stairs in the Boppard Room and Early Gothic Hall), which houses the eerie tomb-filled French **Gothic Chapel** and two airy ivy-clad cloisters. The long **Glass Gallery** and the **Treasury** contain a host of beautiful objects commissioned by bankers and merchants to adorn their homes and declare their faith. Weave through fifteenth- and sixteenth-century statues in wood, stone, alabaster and ivory, pore over lavishly illuminated manuscripts, and wonder how on earth big human hands managed to carve out the tiny representation of the Passion inside the German fifteenth-century boxwood rosary bead.

Afterwards, enjoy the spacious Fort Tyron Park. It has the Maple Leaf Café and – near the M4 bus stop – a playground for children.

WASHINGTON HEIGHTS

Washington Heights' Jumel Terrace Historic District, a neighbourhood of charming well-kept nineteenth-century row houses complete with curvy black streetlamps, surrounds the Morris Jumel Mansion. Paul Robeson, singer of 'Old Man River', lived here. The immediate area is safe because nearby Columbia Presbyterian Centre has constant tight security.

Morris Jumel Mansion

1765 Jumel Terrace (Edgecombe Ave at W 160th St). Open Tues–Sun 10 a.m.–4 p.m., admission $3 adults, $1 senior citizens and students, children under-12s free, tel 212 923 8008 to arrange a tour (run by the Daughters of the Revolution). Bus M3 (to 160th St, Morris Jumel Mansion), or take one of the Harlem Spirituals Inc. tours that include the mansion (see p.199).

Surrounded by garden and overlooking the Harlem River, this is an almost bucolic enclave. The house was built in 1765 by the British Colonel Roger Morris and his American wife, Mary Philipse Morris, as a summer villa in the country. The house is brick encased in wide planks of wood with a porch and balcony you could easily imagine a rocker on, and at the bottom of the steps there's a small cannon.

The Revolution   Morris Jumel Mansion, with its sweeping views and size, was a perfect lookout post. The loyalist Morrises fled with the outbreak of Revolution and Washington seized their property as his military headquarters. In 1790 he threw a Cabinet dinner for, amongst others, Jefferson, Hamilton, and John Adams, who came with his outspoken wife Abigail (see box).

Eliza Takes Over   In 1810, Stephen Jumel bought the mansion for his wife, thereby scandalising New York Society. Although Jumel was a wealthy, respectable French émigré wine merchant, his notorious beautiful Rhode Island wife Eliza Bowen was previously his mistress and a prostitute. In 1815 Eliza and Stephen sailed for Europe – not in shame, as New York hoped, but to befriend Napoleon Bonaparte, who showered them with gifts after their offer of safe passage in their ship the *Eliza* after Waterloo. Back home, Eliza flaunted her Napoleonic connections by lavishing her house with relics, amongst them the mysterious 'Jumel wings': a carved and gilded eagle (now, unfortunately, not at the mansion). It was fashionable at the time to adapt carved ornaments – such as the wings – to decorate curtain pelmets. In 1882 *Harper's Weekly* reported the 'array of strange furniture, which Madame Jumel brought with her from France . . . the rooms are crowded with curious and useful articles, and the walls are adorned with expensive paintings'.

In 1832 Stephen Jumel died and Eliza really cocked a snook at New York society a year later by marrying the Vice-President of America, the well-connected Aaron Burr. The marriage was conducted in her front parlour. Burr was twenty years her senior. The marriage lasted only six months, and Burr died on the day of their divorce, but Eliza had what she wanted: she had been born in poverty; she died aged ninety-one in 1854, one of the wealthiest women in America.

ABIGAIL REMEMBER-THE-LADIES ADAMS

When her husband John Adams was debating the new American Constitution in a smoke-filled Philadelphia room, Abigail wrote from her parlour: 'Remember the Ladies, and be more generous and favourable to them than your ancestors. Do not put such unlimited power into the hands of the Husbands. Remember all Men would be tyrants if they could . . .' John laughed and wrote back that he knew 'Indians slighted their guardians, and negroes grew insolent to their masters,' but, he said, 'your letter was the first intimation that another tribe, more numerous and powerful than all the rest, were grown discontented.'

Abigail Adams was a tiny woman, less than five feet tall, with dark hair, piercing eyes and a forceful personality that belied her size. Women got no formal schooling in the eighteenth century, so Abigail taught herself to write in a big and bold hand. Her son found her unorthodox spelling and random punctuation hilarious, and she wrote back that he was a 'sausy lad . . . As to points and commas I was not taught them in my youth, and I always intend that my meaning shall be so obvious as that my readers shall know when they ought to stop.'

Abigail had more power than most women of her generation could hope for. She managed all the family property and investments, and she was in a position to dog her politician husband and friends with her views on equal legal status for women and freedom for slaves. She did not, however, think her sex should have the vote, and she became increasingly obsessed with 'delicacy' and moral purity. When her husband was made President she feared that she was too brash and would not live up to Martha Washington's pretty example as First Lady. And in the end, for all her brashness, she held little sway. The finished Declaration of Independence did incorporate Revolutionary principles, but in 1776 a piqued Abigail Adams wrote to her husband, one of the signatories: 'I cannot say, that I think you are very generous to the ladies for, whilst you are proclaiming peace and goodwill to men, emancipating all nations, you insist upon retaining an absolute power over your wives.'

Today The rooms have been restored to periods dating between 1765 and 1835. You can roam freely from attic to scullery base-ment (although parts of every room are roped off to protect the fur-nishings). The long octagonal **Drawing Room** served as the Council Chamber for General Washington. The **Parlour** features Madame Jumel's chandelier. The **Dining Room** is more informal, and in the **Hall** her grandfather clock still chimes the hour. Upstairs, take a look at the lavishly draped **Bedroom** and in particular at the bed – Napoleon's – which the Jumels acquired from Empress Josephine's niece. Eliza's obituary is in the attic.

Lectures and concerts are held here regularly. You are allowed to picnic in the colonial herb and rose gardens.

HARLEM

Take a tour. One of the oldest and best is operated by Harlem Spirituals Inc., 1697 Broadway, Suite 900, NY 10019, tel. 212 302 2594. Prices range from $27 to $60. You get a lot for your money. $27 Sunday tours last 5 hours and incorporate 'an authentic church service' with 'stirring gospel music' as well as conventional sights, a good guide patter and a brief look inside the Apollo Theatre. Week-day tours concentrate on social history and culture, and include Morris Jumel and Hamilton Grange as well as lunch. The more expen-sive 7 p.m. to midnight Soul Food and Jazz tours 'relive the Harlem of the Twenties'. They include a meal, drinks, music and clubs.

The sights are too widely spaced for walking, which is in any case ill-advised as you might stumble inadvertently into no-go areas. The consensus is: days are fine (though, as always, watch your purse); nights, whether you're black or white, *don't go* unless you're with someone who knows the area *very* well.

Some History In the nineteenth century Harlem was a fashion-able white suburb. Trotting races on Harlem Lane were all the rage, and after 1900 the bicycling fad took over. Then in 1904–5 the real-estate market collapsed, middle-class whites moved out and the Afro-American community moved in. Harlem became the 'black metropolis', and by the 1920s bohemian Greenwich Villagers were heralding the 'Harlem Renaissance'. Black fiction was 'in', and writ-ers like Zora Neale Hurston (see box) gained near-celebrity status. Young WASP tearaways flocked north in the evenings for bootleg liquor and the rhythms of Duke Ellington, Cab Calloway and Count Basie at the Cotton Club or Connie's Inn (both of which barred blacks admission).

Writer Langston Hughes deplored the voyeurism of white men and women, who ogled black revellers at clubs as if they were 'ani-mals in a zoo'. He said that most Afro-Americans had never heard the term Harlem Renaissance, 'and if they had it hadn't raised their wages any'.

The 1929 Crash stopped the stream of tourists, and most of Harlem became a slum. To pay the rent, residents took in boarders and lodgers. They turned to prostitution, pimping, hustling, dope-dealing and gambling. Poverty, overcrowding, health problems and high crime rates became endemic.

ZORA NEALE HURSTON

In her day Zora Neale Hurston was loved more by whites than by blacks for her 'amusing' research into exotic 'Negro' culture.

She was born in 1901 in Eatonville, Florida, an all-black village in central Orange County. Her father was a Macedonia Baptist Church preacher; her mother told her to 'jump at de sun', let no one 'squinch' her spirit, 'for fear that I would turn out to be a mealy-mouthed rag doll by the time I got grown'. When Zora was nine her mother died. Work as a maid in a travelling Gilbert and Sullivan troupe took her to Washington, where she finished high school, then to New York, where she became a star of the 'Harlem Renaissance'. She studied black American folklore at the Anthropology Department of Barnard College, and persuaded patron Mrs R. Osgood Mason to finance 'field trips' to Florida, Alabama and Louisiana. Big-boned and beautiful, with high cheekbones and sparkling eyes, she went places scholars feared. She dressed in a $1.98 mail-order dress, packed a pearl-handled pistol in her purse and roamed dusty roads in a Chevrolet coupé. She described in *Mules and Men* (pub. 1935) how she was forced to toss a live black cat in a boiling cauldron and, after the flesh had dropped away, pass the bones through her mouth until one tasted bitter; in New Orleans she lay naked on a conjurer's couch for 69 hours with snakeskin touching her navel before having a streak of lightning painted down her back and drinking wine mixed with the blood of all those present so that she would be accepted by the spirit: 'I could have been maimed or killed on most any day.'

By 1935 she had won a Guggenheim fellowship to study magic practices in the West Indies, and by the age of fifty she had had seven books published, produced a Broadway concert, written movies for Paramount Studios, received honorary doctorates, swapped stories with Ernest Hemingway and graced the covers of all the major national papers. Today she is hailed by Toni Morrison as 'one of the greatest writers of our time'.

Men could turn to music, but the new jazz of the 1940s called bebop was rarely lucrative and it continued to marginalise women. In *As Serious as Your Life*, Valerie Wilmer describes how women were either wives struggling to pay the bills or nurturing mother-figures – for example, it was at the apartment of beautiful singer and pianist Mary Lou Williams that Dizzy Gillespie, Charlie Parker, Thelonius Monk and Bud Powell 'gathered for appreciation, help and understanding' before going to clubs like Minton's on West 118th Street, where they developed bebop during the after-hours jamming sessions. And when women did manage to get in bands, they were often the butt of men's jokes. It is said that Donna Lee, a bassist with Charlie Parker, was told when she complained of blistered fingers to cut open the blisters and pour whiskey in to turn them into callouses, and that only minutes after she had complied she was suddenly told to go on stage and play. Apparently Parker laughed in the audience for thirty minutes while blood dripped from her fingers.

Women's avenue of expression has more often been writing. In the 1940s, protest writers who offered a bleak naturalistic view emerged, including Ann Petry (see box), and in the 1950s Rosa Guy (see box) co-founded the Harlem Writers' Guild to help black writers.

In the 1970s the Black Power movement centred not in New York but in Los Angeles, where the Black Panther Party emerged, and by the 1980s crack had hit Harlem, frequently taking women and children as its victims – teenagers were killed in drugs disputes; women became addicts, then thieved to support the habit; and mothers gave birth to 'crack babies'. Rap artists came out of Harlem's Sugar Hill in the 1980s, but women had to wait until the 1990s for their break in the pop world (for example Queen Latifah, see p.298).

PROTEST WRITERS ANN PETRY AND ROSA GUY

Ann Petry, who was born in Connecticut in 1908, took a degree in pharmacy so that she could work at the family drugstore before she married in 1938 and moved to New York, where she became a journalist. In 1941 she became editor of the Harlem *People's Voice* women's page, and in 1944 she started creative writing studies at Columbia University. She described her novel *The Street* (pub. 1946) as a summing-up of her six years' experiences of Harlem – characters are driven off her novel's street, which assaults them: 'There was a cold November wind blowing through 116th Street. It rattled the tops of dustbins, sucked window blinds out through the top of opened windows.' The *New York Times* wrote on publication: 'You won't forget that Harlem Street. You see it at all hours of the day and night, in all weathers. You hear the blaring radios and the dreams of people living and dying with a kind of hopeless violence.'

Rosa Guy born in 1925 was raised in Harlem, left school at fourteen and became politicised when she realised that the only work open to her was a poorly paid factory job. She became involved with the unions at her workplaces, and then with the larger struggle for black freedom. She began to write. After repeated rejections, her novels for teenagers were accepted, and finally a novel about Harlem life from the 1920s to the 1950s, *Bird at My Window*, of which the *Chicago Tribune* said: 'She has translated into living terms Thoreau's inspired phrase "quiet desperation".' She shared many experiences with Ann Petry, but her vision admits hope and real pleasure:

Electricity had changed night into day, and folks stood out enjoying it. In such numbers! Talking, laughing . . . lining up to enter glittering showplaces. Coloured folks too! Right out there in that brightness – wearing bow ties, boaters, slick-looking spats, sporting canes – laughing, talking loud, belonging – and sounding free.

Today, as Bedford Stuyvesant-born poet June Jordan poet points out, one of the few places offering work to young Afro-Americans in Harlem is the army recruitment offices. And suspicion is growing that the borough's political representatives are not only failing to get their men and women out of the ghettos but indirectly keeping them in. Congressman Charles B. Rangel presides over a Harlem constituency where life expectancy is lower than in Bangladesh, and alcohol- and tobacco-related illnesses are the leading cause of death. Rangel's main sponsors include the liquor company Seagram and the cigarette company Philip Morris; Rangel has been instrumental in achieving *lower* taxes on alcohol and tobacco.

Visiting Harlem   Although Harlem is statistically less dangerous than Brownsville, Brooklyn and parts of the south Bronx, it is best to see most of it from the security of a bus, which will take you down once desirable avenues now lined with burnt-out brownstone apartment blocks where the only colour is schoolyard walls graffitied with primary-colour memorials to 1980s victims of drug violence.

WEST 125TH STREET

The Apollo Theatre in the middle of West 125th Street, Harlem's main artery, still boasts a busy Amateur Night (see p.298), but the 'Beautification of Harlem' mural next to it looks like a sick joke. The primary yellows and reds of its painted bulldozer and flowers constitute the only colour on Harlem's gloomy main shopping street. Cashiers shouting out of cheap shoe stores drop the price of sneakers further with each step away you take; street vendors hawk pirate videos of movies released that week; jumbles of indoor stalls sell plastic jewellery and toilet cleaner.

Round the corner, opposite Sylvia's Soul Food restaurant (see p.280), there's a more inviting sprawling Senegalese market, where African-print-saronged women chat while children dance and play around the waste bins.

Studio Museum in Harlem

144 W 125th St (Lenox Ave and Adam Clayton Jr Blvd); Wed–Fri 10 a.m.–5 p.m., Sat 1–6 p.m.; $2, students $1. See p.199 for tour.

Established in the mid 1960s as a working space for artists, the museum has ten to twelve shows a year, highlighting the work of prominent and emerging black artists, often local. Tel. 212 864 4500 for details of year-round education programmes, including the 'Vital Expression in American Art', which offers lectures, concerts and poetry readings.

Black middle-class Sugar Hill, so-called because it's 'the only sweet place to live in Harlem', is high and airy and almost entirely residential, spread with a mixture of brownstones and five-storey redbrick houses with Dutch-style gables.

Schomburg Centre for Research in Black Culture

515 Lenox Ave (at 135th St) Mon–Wed noon–8 p.m., Thurs–Sat 10 a.m.–6 p.m.; free; tel. 212 862 4000; see p.199 for tour.

This is primarily a research centre, with the largest library of black and African culture in the USA, but there are often small shows by African and black American artists.

Abyssinian Baptist Church

132 W 138th St (bet. Lenox Ave and Adam Clayton Jr Blvd); see p.199 for tour.

New York's oldest black church (founded in 1808), this is famed for its Sunday Gospel services (tel. 212 862 7474) and for its former pastor, the Reverend Adam Clayton Powell Jr. In the 1930s he pressed white-owned industry to provide jobs for blacks; he later became the first black on the City council and then New York's first black representative at Congress. He died in 1972 surrounded by scandalous allegations of misappropriation of funds. In the memorial room at the back of the church, artefacts trace his life.

The church is New York bluestone with a Tudor-Gothic window in the front.

Hamilton Grange

287 Convent Ave (at 141st St); open Wed–Sun 9 a.m.–5 p.m.; closed Mon–Tues; free; catch 8th Ave IND Express subway to West 145th St or catch Broadway bus 4 to West 145th St and Convent Ave, or Convent Ave bus 3 to 142nd West, or see p.199 for tour.

This charming 1802 wooden Federal-style two-storey frame house was the home of Alexander Hamilton, but only briefly. Hamilton died in the summer of 1804 after Aaron Burr shot him on the duelling fields of Weehawken, New Jersey.

Hamilton, Careerist Alexander Hamilton was 'the most restless, impatient, artful, indefatigable, and unprincipled intriguer in the United States', wrote John Adams, the second President of the United States and a member of Hamilton's own political party.

In 1768, at the age of thirteen, illegitimate Hamilton was a 'grovelling' clerk in Scotland. Eight years later he was General Washington's Revolutionary right-hand army man. He fought for federalism – that is, uniting the separate States – agreeing with Benjamin Franklin, who said: 'We must hang together, or assuredly we shall all hang separately.' After two decades of a glittering political career, Hamilton's party was defeated by the Republicans, led by Jefferson. Hamilton turned to the simpler pleasures in life: his family and a little law practice in New York City.

Hamilton, Family Man Hamilton married Elizabeth Schuyler during the Revolution. In 1797 he wrote: 'It is impossible to be happier than I am in a wife', and in 1798 he wrote to his 'Betsy': 'I have formed a sweet project . . . in which I rely that you will co-operate with me cheerfully.' The project was Hamilton Grange, a bijoux country home, and Elizabeth's co-operation meant supervising construction and landscaping operations, as well as entertaining his guests and educating their five children. Hamilton wrote to a friend: 'A garden, you know, is a very usual refuge of a disappointed politician. Accordingly, I have purchased a few acres about nine miles from town, have built a house, and am cultivating a garden.' The 13 gum trees he planted to symbolise each of the colonies are long gone.

Hamilton's House Today The house was originally a few yards further down the road. It was moved here wholesale in 1889 as a parish house for the church it is squashed behind. Currently bare floorboards and cobwebs throughout, it is being turned into a museum. Exhibits will include the pianoforte of Alexander's mother, Angelica; the floaty, musty summer dress of wife Elizabeth; 1870 photographs of the grounds; and a slide show.

Aunt Len's Doll and Toy Museum

6 Hamilton Terrace (at W 141st St); directions as for Hamilton Grange.

Former schoolteacher Mrs Lennon Holder Hoyte started collecting dolls and bears in 1962. She has over 5,000: china, plastic, big and small. She's old. Even if you've made an appointment she may not keep it, but if she does, it's worth the trip.

EL BARRIO

Make a trip to the marvellous Museo del Barrio, but don't wander idly East of Fifth Avenue.

The Hispanic community, which today makes up a quarter of

New York's population, has historically centred in East Harlem, or 'El Barrio', which is now largely Puerto Rican. Many shop signs are written in a mixture of Spanish and English known as 'Spanglish'. The streets are dirtier and the atmosphere is more intimidating than in Harlem. If you're going uptown via Madison Avenue by bus or subway, which goes overground at 96th St, the change after the affluent Upper East Side is abrupt.

Relations between blacks and Puerto Ricans have historically been distant, although the two groups united in the 1980s to elect David Dinkins, the city's first black mayor. You still see photocopied peeling fliers on broken windows of deserted buildings saying: 'Elect Dinkins – for all of us'.

The biggest influx of Puerto Ricans came in the 1950s.

Operation Bootstrap   The small island of Puerto Rico was 'discovered' by Columbus in the fifteenth century, the Spanish arrived in the sixteenth century, and after the 1898 Spanish–American War Puerto Rico became 'a commonwealth' of the United States, which decided that Puerto Rico's financial staples – sugar cane and pineapple – were not lucrative enough. In the 1940s Operation Bootstrap was implemented to industrialise agrarian Puerto Rico. The Museo del Barrio's picture by Marina Gutierrez presents visually the human effects: in 'La Isla del Encanto' ('The Island of Enchantment') fish jumping at the top are replaced by fighter planes at the bottom to show how US military restrictions strangled local industry; factories churn out pollution; and a woman spurting blood represents the mass sterilisation programme the US maintained throughout the 1940s and 1950s. Puerto Ricans who made money at the factories sent their children to New York for 'a better life', and those who lost their jobs came themselves. Most were kept in the poverty trap by language barriers and prejudice – landlords, for example, continue to refuse Hispanics properties on the assumption that they will stay jobless and default on payments. Even when El Barrio receives State and City help – designed to fund social services in poor areas – the money often falls into the wrong hands.

Women in the Community   Latina women feel that the whole community would benefit if they had more power, but Lucy Cruz, the first Latina elected to the New York City Council, says her fiercest opponents were Latina men. Some of the problems that have kept the Latina feminist movement small are endemic to all poor New York areas; others are specific to the Hispanic community. Hispanic gender stereotyping ordains that girlfriends can be fought over in gang gunfights and matrons run the bodegas (grocery stores) that often serve as local bases for conflicting camps in the drug wars, but men run the gangs and drug trafficking. The Catholic veto on condoms contributes to the fast-increasing numbers of Hispanic women with AIDS. And women's pin-money jobs in, for example, the garment industry and cleaning work leave them negligible time or energy for political organising.

Latinas don't think established national feminist organisations like NOW (the National Organization of Women) can address their needs, but see new hope in international networking – with the strong feminist movement in Latin America, for instance – and in education. Indira Briones, a student at Hunter College, hopes that 'the younger generation of Latina women who are attending colleges and universities will start projecting themselves politically'. Academics, including Saskia Sassen of Columbia University, are beginning to document the plight and contribution of Latinas as immigrants and workers. And Latinas are, gradually, getting a voice in the workplace – most notably in the form of Ida Torres, who has been fighting for women's rights at work since the 1960s and became the first female President of the Hispanic Labor Committee and the first woman Secretary/Treasurer of the United Storeworkers' Retail Wholesale and Department Store Union.

El Museo del Barrio

1230 Fifth Ave (at 104th St); take bus M1, M3 and M4; open Wed–Sun 11 a.m.–5 p.m.; suggested donation $2, $1 students, under-12s free.

This vast ramshackle stone building behind railings, which was originally a 1920s children's shelter, now houses the only museum in the country to specialise in the arts and culture of Puerto Rico. Ongoing restoration won't close off any exhibits but may eventually raise the requested admission price.

Go through the bleak courtyard, and inside the main entrance hall is lined with tiles depicting fairy tales. Of the museum's 10,000-strong collection of objects, the exhibition of 'santos' (saints) is especially prized. One of the oldest Puerto Rican sculptural traditions, the small wooden santos have been carved through the centuries for worship in family homes. 'El Chadelier, La Cama' ('The Bed', 1987) is a pink-and-white-lace full-size four-poster bed laden with baubles and trinkets that hold personal significance for its creator, Pepon Osorio, as well as stitched 'capias' (souvenirs) that are traditionally given in Puerto Rico at weddings, baptisms and anniversaries. His piece 'The Corolla Club' ('El Club Corolla', 1989) – a car windscreen lavishly decorated with images of Christ, rubber angels and bottles of air freshener – salutes the car as prized signifier of potency for Puerto Rican males.

The museum is airy and well laid out with – for the moment –

two main exhibition spaces. Afterwards you could cross 5th Avenue to the Conservatory Garden, Central Park's only formal garden, which has a beautiful ivy-covered paved platform to relax on, before plunging back into Manhattan.

THE OUTER BOROUGHS

Don't let Manhattanites put you off – the Outer Boroughs have a lot to offer. Treat them as day trips. For children there's the Staten Island Children's Museum and Coney Island's Aquarium; for culture vultures there's the Brooklyn Museum and performances at the Brooklyn Academy of Music; and for those after a bit of history there's Alice Austen house and Richmondtown Restoration. But unless you're with someone who knows the Outer Boroughs very well, stick to the sights mentioned here. There are neighbourhoods, particularly in the Bronx and Brooklyn, where racial and class tensions are extreme, and outsiders are seen as aggressors.

BROOKLYN

Women who live here say you *must* come, it's *lovely*; Manhattanites say it seethes with guns and drug-related violence. Tread the middle ground and you can enjoy a museum many prefer to the Met, one of the most exciting modern dance venues in New York State, baby Beluga whales, and a sleepy genteel historic district – all without broaching the dangerous areas (most notably Bedford Stuyvesant, known as 'Bed Sty', Crown Heights and East New York).

Lots of hip New Yorkers live in Brooklyn for its relatively low rents in spacious brownstones along tree-lined avenues. They just flip over the novelty of a garden, which facilitates barbecues and drop-in culture, but they still go to Manhattan for work and *real* entertainment, so you won't find the fabled community atmosphere unless you're staying with Brooklyn-based friends.

Children love Coney Island, but the Brooklyn Children's Museum (145 Brooklyn Ave at St Mark's Ave, tel. 718 735 4432) is largely geared towards community work – stick to the Manhattan and Staten Island Children's museums (see pp.188, 221).

For culture vultures, a performance at the Brooklyn Academy of Music, the place that schooled mad genius Isadora Duncan, is a must (see p.311). Nearby Flatbush, a grimy stretch of high street, is not especially dangerous, but nor is it inviting, especially at night.

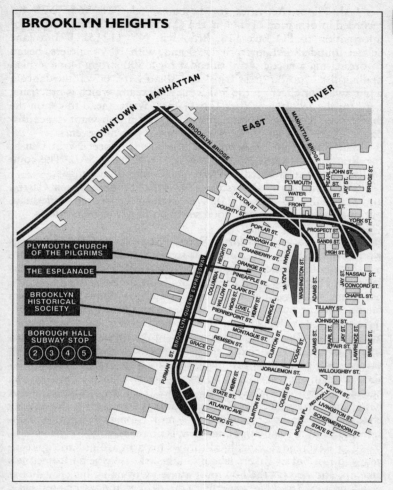

PLYMOUTH CHURCH
OF THE PILGRIMS

THE ESPLANADE

BROOKLYN
HISTORICAL
SOCIETY

BOROUGH HALL
SUBWAY STOP
② ③ ④ ⑤

Dyke Slope Brooklyn's Park Slope area has had a large lesbian community since the 1970s, but it was largely closet until 1990 when SAL (Slope Activities for Lesbians) revved into action. Today, many Manhattanites still haven't heard of it, but they will. 'Dyke Slope' as it's fondly known is now home to the renowned Lesbian Herstory Archives (see p.14); the Prospect Park based women's softball team have lesbian league ambitions; and a straight bar, the Roost, is fast being colonised by 'lesbian jocks'. If the Manhattan lesbian scene (see p.13,285,295) is too fast, or you fancy a change, try one of the following.

SAL (Slope Activities for Lesbians, tel. 718 965 7578 for recorded information or look in the *QW* magazine listings, write for information to PO Box 118, Brooklyn, NY 11215). Debra Jane Seltzer founded SAL in April 1990 and, with 10 volunteers, began co-ordinating a hectic social calendar for a 500-strong Slope lesbian mailing list – go on 'field trips' to lesbian bars, bowl/dine/dance a night away, or cheer on the SAL volleyball team, which is practising hard for the 1994 New York Gay Games. Write ahead to get on the mailing list (enclose $10 annual fee, or $20 if you want dance discounts); give 24 hour notice to reserve places on any events.

The Roost (on 7th Avenue at 8th Street). Queer Night Out at the Roost is sponsored each Tuesday at 9pm by SAL. The joint really jumps after women's softball games on summer nights.

The Community Bookstore (143 7th Avenue between Carroll and Garfield, 718 783 3075). Not exclusively women or lesbian, but this bookshop carries a good selection of gay/lesbian titles.

Religion's New Patrolling Role In places white authorities won't police, the black Church has stepped in to tackle social problems, including housing shortages and schools. Brooklyn's Thomas Jefferson High School, where students punch in with identity cards, has come to symbolise the worst ravages of New York's urban blight. The surrounding streets are so tough the school has a 'grieving room' for students to mourn the often violent deaths of friends and relatives. In 1987 Jefferson was ranked the most dangerous school in the city; in 1988 the city, parents, teachers and pupils vetoed a proposal to install metal detectors; in 1991 a student was shot dead in the corridor, and metal detectors went back on the agenda. It was once a respectable school (Danny Kaye dropped out here, and actress Shelley Winters graduated in 1935), but lots of children carry guns or knives now – and Thomas Jefferson is typical. The Church's self-appointed task is not easy.

The Reverend Youngblood throws his arm around an eighteen-year-old just out of Rikers Island jail, he asks *why* he cut someone's face up, and he says the boy must atone by bringing his crowd next week to the Brooklyn church: 'You deliver the associates here, man'. Youngblood was warned when he came from New Orleans that Bedford Stuyvesant was 'one of God's Alcatrazes'. He and his colleagues battled on. Now welfare supervisors worship next to brothers on welfare; an 'affordable housing' programme is up and running in Brownsville; Youngblood is negotiating with the City to start a Church high school; and the 'ministry for children' pays to send 30 teenagers to private group-therapy sessions in Queens.

Women, however, tend to get short shrift, partly because they make up the bulk of the congregation (they're already saved).

ISADORA DUNCAN (1878–1927)

Born when 'Venus was in the ascendant', Isadora Duncan professed to have had a 'religious and awe-inspiring' effect on men in a life that was 'more interesting than any novel and more adventurous than any cinema'. Auguste Rodin described her as 'the greatest woman the world has ever known'. Oh, yes – and in her spare time she was a dancer, famed as a pioneer of a revolutionary language of movement and expression that was inspired by the spirit of Classical Greece.

Born in 1878 in San Francisco, Isadora Duncan lived most of her life in London, Berlin, Paris and Russia, but her time in New York was formative. She dragged her whole family along and described her Manhattan experience in her autobiography with a charming lack of self-effacement and some interesting social comment. They arrived at a boarding house off Sixth Avenue. 'There was a strange collection of people in this boarding house' who had one thing in common: 'none were able to pay their bills and they lived in constant proximity to ejection.' Isadora and her family took a studio and emptied it of furniture so that she could dance. An influential composer called Ethelbert Nevin was soon enchanted by her and arranged performances in Carnegie Hall. She was thus launched on New York Society:

'Many society women were in the audience, and my success led to engagements in different New York drawing rooms . . . I was invited by Mrs Astor to dance at her villa in Newport . . . Mrs Astor represented to America what a queen did to England. The people who came into her presence were more awed and frightened than if they had approached royalty. But to me she was very affable. She arranged the performances on her lawn, and the most exclusive society of Newport watched me dance on that lawn. I have a picture taken of this performance which shows the venerable Mrs Astor sitting beside Harry Lehr, and rows of Vanderbilts, Belmonts, Fishes, etc., around her . . . [However] our visit to Newport left an impression of disappointment. These people seemed so enwrapped in snobbishness and the glory of being rich that they had no art sense whatever. In those days they considered artists as inferior – a sort of upper servant . . . I began to feel a strong wish to find some more congenial atmosphere than New York . . . to speak the truth, in all my experience of New York I had found no intelligent help or sympathy for my ideas.

In 1927, in the South of France, she was strangled by her flowing red scarf, which had become caught in the wheels of her Bugatti.

Tuesday nights are 'men's ministry' nights, when Youngblood uses swear words and disparaging comments about 'gay brothers' to dispel the idea that Church and God 'effeminize' worshippers. Meanwhile, behind the smokescreen of male gang violence, the women drug abusers, many of whom are single mothers with AIDS, multiply.

CONEY ISLAND

Anyone who loves seedy seaside funfairs must come here, and the Aquarium is riveting for everyone – especially for children.

This was originally a sandy island hopping with rabbits; the Dutch named it Konijn Eiland (Rabbit Island), which went into popular parlance as Coney Island. In the 1830s Coney Island was a *très chic* resort; by the turn of the century rollercoasters and the new Ferris Wheel had appeared and the clientele had become working-class. Crowds of 100,000 on sunny days flooded in to cheer girls going up in balloons showing a saucy amount of leg, and daring punters dropped screaming from the parachute jump. The area declined after the 1950s. Today, Surf Avenue midweek is a rather eerie mixture of lone kids hanging out and yellow booths selling beach balls, plastic sunglasses, cheap beds, second-hand clothes, or with signs saying 'Checks Cashed' – a sure sign of a poor neighbourhood. Look inland and it's all Projects. Go straight to the Aquarium and the boardwalk and you'll have a great time.

Getting There   Take the B, D, F or N line to the Stillwell Avenue Coney Island Stop for Surf Avenue and the D or F line to West 8 St NY Aquarium stop for the Aquarium. The advantage of going midweek is that it's empty; the advantage of weekends is safety in numbers. The subway journey is considered safe, but it can be unsettling – you might spot youths graffiti-ing the seats not with pens but with razor blades.

The Boardwalk and Funfair

This is a real American **boardwalk**. Long low metal stalls along the edge sell ice-cold beer and clams. A sprout of pier is lined with men and kids fishing for soft-shell crabs. A Slav couple with all-gold teeth cut your silhouette portrait for $2 in two minutes. Male joggers catcall passing women joggers. Mothers from the country's largest community of Russian émigrés – 20,000 strong – in Brighton Beach's 'Little Odessa' chatter in Russian on benches and shout out when their children stray too far.

Stroll the boardwalk and breathe in the sea air, then go to the **Astroland Amusement Park** (open Memorial Day to Labor Day). Pass a rusted rollercoaster skeleton, go into a museum that boasts the Mermaid Parade (open only weekends), and then try a mixture of new and old rides in the Park before seeing the only travelling Freak Show in the States.

The stretch of whitish beach is pleasant to look at, but there's a no-swimming rule and don't go barefoot – washed-up broken bottles are everywhere.

New York Zoological Society, New York Aquarium

Surf Ave (at W 8th St), Coney Island, tel. 718 265 3400. Open daily 10 a.m.–4.45 p.m., till 7 p.m. holidays, summer and weekends. $5.75 adults, $2 senior citizens and under-12s, under-2s get in free.

Gaze into the jaws of a white-tip shark, watch a serene shoal of gold-specked piranhas and chortle indulgently over the Baby Beluga Whale, also called the Canary of the Sea for its twittering song-like call.

The oldest aquarium in the States, this has 10,000 aquatic animals to keep children and adults of all ages entertained for hours. Check your pushchair in at the Stroller Park before going to the Discovery Cove's gift shop and educational exhibits (stand under a simulated crashing wave, examine a salt marsh). At the Aquatheatre show wave at the walrus and watch sea lions demonstrate comically why seals are *far* inferior. And finish off with a sticky pizza at the sea-view cafeteria.

For those worried about the political correctness of an aquarium, this one's keen to assure visitors that theirs is OK: the New York Aquarium helps with research into marine pollution, and it is part of a programme that rescues and rehabilitates stranded marine mammals and turtles.

THE BROOKLYN MUSEUM AND AROUND

Getting There By subway from Manhattan, take the 2 or 3 Lexington Ave Express to Eastern Parkway/Brooklyn Museum stop, which is in the museum's drive. Or, for the scenic route, cross the Brooklyn Bridge on foot, take the Tillary path where the pedestrian walkway splits, from the bottom take a right turn and on the corner of Tillary Street and Cadman Place take the 41 bus up Flatbush to the Grand Army Plaza (ask the bus driver to point out the museum).

The Brooklyn Museum

200 Eastern Parkway (at Washington Ave), tel. 718 638 5000. Open Wed–Sun 10 a.m.–5 p.m. Suggested contributions $4 adults, $2 students, $1.50 senior citizens; under-12s go free.

Renowned for its Egyptian collection and with wonderfully evocative period rooms, this museum is also unusually children-friendly. Almost all gallery space is accessible with pushchairs; 'Arty Facts' is a combination gallery visit and art workshop that happens 11 a.m.–12.30 p.m. every Saturday and Sunday for children aged four to seven (free with museum admission); and there's a special children's gift store, 'Artsmart'. Make it a day trip by relaxing in the neighbouring Botanical Gardens afterwards.

Housed in a grand beaux-arts building (McKim, Mead and White, 1893–1924), the museum gained brief infamy in the early 1980s when Judy Chicago's *Dinner Party* was shown here. People queued round the block to see the 39 ceramic plates that featured heads of famous women (including Sojourner Truth, see p.52) and were crafted to represent female genitalia. Chicago said the piece was a reinterpretation of the Last Supper 'from the point of view of those who have done the cooking throughout history'. The *Dinner Party*'s gone, and so have the queues, which is sad for the museum but great for the visitor. Unlike the Metropolitan Museum (the only one bigger than Brooklyn's in New York State), the Brooklyn Museum has space to breathe.

Orientation The airy **Grand Lobby** showcases contemporary artists, and beyond that you'll find African, Oceanic and New World Art. The **second floor** displays Asian work and highlights from the Egyptian collection are on the third floor. Twenty-eight period rooms on the **fourth floor** precede Paintings and Sculpture on the **fifth floor**. Bring a picnic and eat it in the Memorial Sculpture Garden, which remains tranquil despite overlooking a car park, or go to the **Museum Café** (open 10 a.m.–4 p.m.) for 'The Minimalist' cream cheese sandwich or 'The Cubist' egg and bacon sandwich, both for under $5 (you know it's good because the staff eat there).

Fashionable Dress Many of the museum's 1.5 million objects have a Brooklyn slant, including Georgia O'Keeffe's painting of the Brooklyn Bridge and a dress worn by Mrs Washington A. Roebling, the woman who oversaw the Bridge's construction after the chief engineer – her husband – was incapacitated (see p.81). The gown on show was commissioned by Mrs Roebling, probably from the House of Worth and certainly from Paris, because American fashion dictated that only a European dressmaker could do justice to the great honour she was to receive: presentation at a Europe Court. In 1896, all trussed up in a gold gown with cloth orchids swishing about in the train, Mrs Roebling glimpsed not only Queen Victoria but the Empress of Russia.

Europe is a recurring theme through the costume collection. A 1934 oyster silk crepe flapper dress is displayed as a typical Henri Bendel purchase. Bendel attracted the most fashionable women in America to his New York store (see p.320) simply because he was the largest buyer of French designers, including Chanel and Schiaparelli. A Schiaparelli necklet is also on show. It was worn by one of the most stylish and daring American women of her day, the Standard Oil heiress Millicent Huttleston Rogers. Like a chameleon, she altered her appearance to fit her environment, wearing Tyrolean attire in the Austrian Alps, Southwest American Indian garb in New Mexico, Provençal dress on the Riviera, and sophisticated designer clothes in the great metropolitan centres of the world. One can only speculate on the occasion to which she wore this Schiaparelli clear plastic necklet, on which nineteen embossed and polychromed insects chase one another, apparently on the wearer's flesh. The rather hideous dress worn by Austine Hearst, the wife of William Randolph Hearst Jr, to the 1953 Eisenhower Inaugural Ball is exceptional because it was commissioned from – not quite an American but at least an Anglo-American. The designer, Charles James, renowned for missing deadlines, came to think this white satin and black velvet 'Abstract or Four-Leaf Clover Ball Gown and Petal Stole' the pinnacle of his dressmaking.

Botanical Gardens

1000 Washington Ave (bet. Empire Blvd and Eastern Parkway), tel. 718 622 4433. Tues–Sun 10 a.m.–5 p.m. Free.

Fifty acres of botanical garden which is different for each season and always wonderful. There is an especially peaceful Japanese hill and pond garden, one of the largest public rose collections in America, a Fragrance Garden for the blind, and a children's garden.

BROOKLYN HEIGHTS

Manhattanites occasionally come to Brooklyn Heights – because it has a great view of Manhattan from the Bridge, the Esplanade and the exclusive River Café (see p.281). Brooklynites bring visitors with pride, for Brooklyn Heights is a pocket of beautifully preserved nineteenth-century grandeur (in Manhattan most of this was razed for skyscrapers). Brownstones and carved Romanesque Revival private residences rise regally on quiet tree-shaded streets. It's lovely to stroll around if you've a spare afternoon.

THE QUAKER BEECHERS AND THE CULT OF TRUE WOMANHOOD

Always prepared to question the status quo if it seemed unjust, Quakers in the nineteenth century were a force to be reckoned with. Henry Ward Beecher's family won untypical renown but was typically troublesome.

The Reverend Lyman Beecher instilled a strong sense of religious mission and social responsibility in his eleven children, and all seven sons – including Henry Ward Beecher – followed him into the ministry. *Catharine Beecher* became a pioneer in women's education and home economics, while *Isabella Beecher Hooker* became a prominent suffragist and *Harriet Beecher Stowe* a popular novelist (she wrote more than 30 books and the 1859 bestseller *Uncle Tom's Cabin*). All the siblings were passionate about their beliefs, and not necessarily in agreement.

In the nineteenth century women were responsible for creating a haven of domestic bliss after the men's day out earning money in the cut-throat world of business. This was identified in 1966 by, amongst others, historian Barbara Welter as the 'Cult of True Womanhood'. In *Woman's Offices and Influences*, J.H. Agnew explained: the woman's heart is 'a great reservoir of love, the water-works of moral influence, from which go out ten thousand tubes, conveying the ethereal essences of her nature, and diffusing them quietly over the secret chambers of man's inner being'. Catharine Beecher disagreed. When it was thought that to call housewifing anything other than spiritually uplifting was common and degrading, her 'Treatise on Domestic Economy' said that women's housewifing was hard work comparable to men's 'business' and should be valued accordingly.

Harriet Beecher Stowe, by contrast, held views that were absolutely in accord with convention. When she moved to Maine in 1850 she wrote to her sister-in-law, Sarah Beecher. Harriet described with excitement how she had 'made two sofas – or lounges – a barrel chair – divers bedspreads – pillowcases – pillows – bolsters – mattresses . . . painted rooms . . . revarnished furniture', meanwhile lobbying the landlord to install a new sink, giving birth to her eighth child, reading all Walter Scott's novels and writing herself to support the family, because her husband's salary was meagre. 'And yet,' she wrote, 'I am constantly pursued and haunted by the idea that I don't do anything.'

Harriet's life was obviously hard work, so why did she and other women endorse the nineteenth-century pastoralisation of housework? For one, they were not immune to the values of their community, and Catharine Beecher argued that their endorsement was a protective strategy. In her 'Essay on Slavery and Abolitionism' she wrote: '[T]he moment woman begins to feel the promptings of ambition, or the thirst for power, her aegis of defence is gone. All the sacred protection of religion, all the generous promptings of chivalry, all the poetry of romantic gallantry, depend upon woman's retaining her place as dependent and defenceless, and making no claims . . . '

Harriet Beecher Stowe is an exception because she managed to tread both the 'Mommie Track' (see p.19) and the career path, and still appear to be a role-model for the 'Cult of True Womanhood'.

Getting There   If you want to cross the Brooklyn Bridge (about a 15-minute walk), find the Manhattan end of the pedestrian walkway at City Hall Park and exit at Camden Plaza West, which goes under the elevated highway (it's a little complex, so if you're unsure ask a passing commuter). At the bottom take a right turn up Henry Street and you're in the oldest part of Brooklyn Heights. If you prefer speed to breathtaking views, take the N or the R line to Borough Hall stop.

If you've come via the bridge, meander past the Plymouth Church of the Pilgrims, along the Esplanade, and end up at the Brooklyn Historical Society. If you've come by subway, reverse the process.

If you don't want to do any of this but you still want to see Brooklyn, see p.48 for tours.

Plymouth Church of the Pilgrims

Orange Street (bet. Henry and Hicks St).

Abolitionist Henry Ward Beecher's impassioned oratory brought Mark Twain, newspaper man Horace Greeley, and even Abraham

Lincoln, to worship in this simple 1849 brick meeting-house. Ward Beecher (see box) held mock slave auctions here and used the money to buy slaves' freedom.

The Esplanade

Clark St leads towards the river and the Esplanade.

Called the 'Promenade' by locals, this quaint cobbled stretch is lined with romantically ivy-hung buildings and benches to sit on while you enjoy the view.

Brooklyn Historical Society

128 Pierrepont Street (corner of Clinton St), tel. 718 624 0890. Open 10 a.m.–4.45 p.m.; library and gallery closed Mons and the month of August.

If you want to know more about Brooklyn, this is the place to come. Ask any questions at the desk, browse their large collection of Brooklyn-related books, documents and artefacts, and if you're lucky you'll coincide with one of their walking tours, which are irregular but good and cost around $8 (phone ahead if you can for schedules).

STATEN ISLAND

Known variously as commuter land, that place with the cheap ferry, and Manhattan's rubbish dump, much-maligned Staten Island has a lot to offer, not least a welcome change from Manhattan's clamour and high-rises. Treat it as a day trip – or two – and you'll have a great time. Enjoy that cheap ferry, treat your children to educational fun at the children's museum, mellow out with Tibetan art, see one of America's first woman photographer's Victoriana clutter, and watch basket weavers at work in New York's only seventeenth-century Dutch village.

Staten Island was ceded to Manhattan as a prize in a 1687 sailing contest sponsored by the Duke of York. Today residents resent paying high taxes to be used as a tip. Ninety per cent of Manhattan's garbage – 100,000 tons a week – is piling up on the island's notorious Fresh Kills landfill, and in 1990 Staten Islanders created a charter commission demanding independence. The heated debate doesn't affect what you'll see as a visitor: on the ferry, cloth-capped men offer shoe-shines to commuters; on buses, children with their first names monogrammed on baseball jackets taunt each other; the streets are a mish-mash of 'checks cashed here' stores and ice-blue, pale-green and sunflower-yellow wooden houses, complete with porches for rockers and mailboxes on stalks, that date back to the Civil War. For diner-food to fuel your trip or to relax after-wards, go to Lil's Diner. Run by two women, one a policeman's widow, Lil's serves a mixture of classic diner food and good ole' Southern food (95 Stuyvesant Place, straight up from the ferry, tel. 273 955). Friendly service, high quality, low prices.

ALICE AUSTEN (1866–1952), SOCIETY PHOTOGRAPHER AND REBEL

Alice was only ten or twelve when her uncle, a Danish sea captain, brought a camera home from his travels. Precocious Alice persuaded him to show her how to use it and then to give it to her. She was 'of gentle birth', and the half-hour it took to set up the glass plates and cumbersome equipment was really not considered a ladylike hobby. She took what she called her 'larky' photographs of Society friends and family, she took pictures of immigrants at Ellis Island, and – in the days when women did NOT show their ankles – she climbed fences to photograph automobile races. Acclaimed now as a recorder of 'social history', Alice just did it for fun. The only paid job she ever agreed to do was illustrate with photographs how proper ladies should ride a bicycle, a crucial section being how to mount discreetly.

Alice, who remained single, was left enough money by her grandfather never to have a financial worry in her life, but she invested unwisely and lost it all in the Stock Market Crash of 1929. She and her intimate friend of 55 years, Gertrude Tate, tried to support themselves by starting a restaurant at Clear Comfort. The venture failed. Alice was by now a crotchety old woman crippled by arthritis, called 'the witch' by locals, and she was forced to sell up. She went into the poor house, where she was discovered by the editor of *Life* magazine, who wanted to use some of her photographs. She was moved to a private nursing home and was still alive when her work was published to much acclaim in several magazines.

Getting There   Unless you're coming from Brooklyn (in which case cross the Verrazano-Narrows Bridge), the only way is by ferry. To reach the Manhattan terminal catch the 1 or 9 subway line to South Ferry, turn right out of the exit and the low round metal building under immaculate skyscrapers next to ramshackle metal blue harbour buildings is the Staten Island Ferry Terminal (tel. 718 390 5253 for schedule information). The round trip costs 50c. On the 25-minute journey, you mustn't miss the view as the ferry leaves Manhattan, but also look around you. Men with suits in zip-up hang bags read newspapers next to squawling families on their way back from shopping outings. When you arrive, pass through the turnstiles and you'll see several exits up passageways, each leading to bus stops. To find your bus, look for the blue signs at the passage mouth.

Alice Austen House

2 Hylan Boulevard (at Bay St), tel. 718 816 4506. Suggested admis-

sion $2. Hours Thurs–Sun noon–5 p.m. 51 bus along Bay St to Hylan Blvd. Walk down towards the river.

Past wooden houses with gnomes and anchors in their gardens, 'Clear Comfort' is a fairy-tale white house with three gabled windows, ivy hanging over the verandah and a view of the Narrows. It was home to Alice Austen, who was a contemporary of Jacob Riis and one of the first American woman photographers (see box).

Enter to the sound of a cowbell ringing over your head and first watch the video about Ms Austen's life (rather wacky music, but informative narrative). The parlour's Victoriana clutter has been reproduced as it was when she lived here, including ginger jars in cabinets and a Delft tiled fireplace. What was the ground-floor bedroom has changing exhibitions, and the gift shop sells replica Victoriana, including elaborate photograph frames. Phone ahead for special events which usually have a Victorian theme (Victorian Tea Dances for $30, Victorian dress optional).

Jacque Marchais Center of Tibetan Art

338 Lighthouse Ave (at Windsor Ave), Richmond, tel. 718 987 3478. Hours Wed–Sun 1–5 p.m. April–Nov; Dec–March, open by appointment. Costs $3 adults, $2.50 senior citizens and $1 children. Bus 74 from ferry to Lighthouse Avenue, when you walk up the hill (about 30–40-min bus ride).

Mrs Jacqueline Norman Klauber spent her late-nineteenth-century Midwest childhood playing with Tibetan figurines instead of dolls. When she grew up she took a more romantic French name – Jacque Marchais – to promote her career as a New York art dealer and used her rich husband's money to buy up art from the Orient, for which in the 1940s she built this peace-inducing reproduction Buddhist temple on a hill surrounded by garden. Today the biggest collection of Tibetan art in the Western hemisphere, the Center impressed His Holiness the 14th Dalai Lama in 1991. Come at the beginning of October and you'll see monks in saffron robes perform traditional ceremonies (phone ahead for the exact date). Special programmes (a series of lectures, shows and demonstrations costing an additional $2) include Zen Martial Arts, Banana Princess Puppet Show and Goddesses in Tibetan Buddhism.

Richmondtown Restoration

441 Clarke Ave (bet. Richmond and Arthur Kill Rds) Richmond, tel. 718 351 1611. Hours: Jan–March, Wed–Fri, 1 p.m.–5 p.m.; April–June, Wed–Sun, 1 p.m.–5 p.m. Admission $4 adults; $2.50 senior citizens, students, children 6–18 (pushchairs barred from *most buildings). 30–40-min journey from the ferry on the S74 bus. Look out for a sign on the left saying Richmondtown Restoration or ask the bus driver.*

Richmondtown started in the 1690s as a crossroads settlement called Coccleston, convenient meeting-point for gentry and island farmers. Now a 30-acre museum complex; its 25 historic buildings include a two-room privy, the first elementary school in the country, a courthouse, stores and homes, all as they were two or more centuries ago. In some craftsmen wearing big boots, braces and kerchiefs chat to you while weaving baskets or beating out tin pots; in others, light streams into the elegant parlour and a fire burns in the basement kitchen hearth; and the General Store (which stopped selling only in 1915) is chock-a-block with candies, hardware and spices, and – because it was a social centre – in front of the cast-iron coffee mill there's an upturned barrel with a chequerboard on top.

Phone ahead to ask about traditional music Tavern Concerts and summer demonstrations of Early American trades and crafts, including fireplace cooking and wool spinning (free with admission to grounds).

Snug Harbor, with Children's Museum

1000 Richmond Terrace (bet. Fillmore and Clinton Sts). Open daylight hours. Tel. 718 448 2500. No fee for grounds. S40 bus from ferry to Richmond Terrace and ask for Snug Harbor.

Now an 83-acre cultural centre, Snug Harbor was founded in 1801 by Richard Randal as a home 'for aged, decrepit and worn out sailors'. It was in its heyday one of the richest charitable institutions in the world.

After a bus journey that runs parallel with a disused railway line and big red barges loaded with garbage on their way to the landfill, the first sight of Snug Harbor is a surprise. A line of five sombre main buildings with grand Greek pillars face the bay, and they're only the front of a complex of Greek Revival and Italianate buildings that includes a Botanical Garden, a Music Hall and a row of pre-Civil War cottages that house artists-in-residence. Enter the West Gate and follow the path to the well-signposted Visitors' Centre. If it's a weekend you can pick up a tour, otherwise peruse a map and leaflets. Just next to the **Visitors' Centre** is the basic and friendly **Melville Café** (chew $2.95 Mahogany Chicken Wings in primary-coloured surroundings). Down the corridor you can see browned black-and-white photographs of bearded old sailors sitting rigid with sticks on benches. Their reading room in the vaulted **Great Hall** now hosts events. The **Newhouse Center for Contemporary Art** still has, above the inside doors, original stained-glass windows depicting ship and harbour scenes, and written on the balustrade round the mezzanine level is 'rest after dangerous toil'. The overall feel of the place is: some lovely buildings but a bit of a mess – patchy grass, litter, fenced-off areas scattered with sand and workmen's spades. The children's museum is the main attraction.

Women who find the Manhattan Children's Museum a bit snooty Upper-East-Sidey come here for **The Staten Island Children's Museum** (Wed–Fri 1–5 p.m.; weekends/holidays 11 a.m.–5p.m.; Summer Tues–Sun 11 a.m.–5 p.m., tel. 718 273 2060, admission $3 or free for under-2's). The entry is framed by a giant pair of red neon hands, and a stroller park is right inside the door. Everything has a high learning content, and it is all low-tech so the exhibits never 'go down'. The needs of all the family are taken into account. Exhibition rooms are separate so that mothers and grandmothers won't get a headache from chirruping infants. Older children won't get bored because they'll be asked to join in as helpers – if, that is, you can wrest them away from 'News to Me', a permanent participatory radio and TV studio upstairs. If you're around for the first Saturday in May, come for the Magic Meadowfair, when 10,000 flood in to see magicians and sorcerers' apprentices.

QUEENS

GAY QUEENS

Gay activism and the dull sprawling suburb of Queens were an unimaginable combination until two things happened: a vicious murder in July 1990 and the rejection of a school curriculum in May 1992. Both happened precisely because it's a dull suburb.

For more than 25 years Queens has housed a gay community made up mainly of working-class and older gay men, including many Latinos, who chose Queens for its low rents, and for the privacy that goes with suburbia. Few belonged to or even approved of radical organisations like Queer Nation or Act Up (see p.28). Latino Julio Rivera, a part-time bartender who, friend Alan Sack said, loved to dress well and 'play macho', was typically apolitical. In July 1990 three men went to the only cruising strip in the gay area (which is around 75th Street between 37th Road and 37th Avenue) to find a gay man to attack. Rivera, who was repeatedly stabbed, bled to death in a desolate Jackson Heights schoolyard. Suddenly, closeted gay men and lesbians decided their sexuality was political. Queens Gay and Lesbians United formed; vigils and marches were not only organised but well attended; the New York City Gay and Lesbian Anti-Violence Project came to consciousness-raise about the escalation in the number of anti-gay violence cases reported (an increase of 129% between 1989 and 1990). Two years later, the same Anti-Violence Project came back to accuse a Queens' school board of contributing to the atmosphere of fear and prejudice that homosexuals endure.

In May 1992 the nineteen-member board of Queens' School District 24 unanimously decided that the Board of Education's new curriculum threatened the moral codes of families in their area. The booklet in question, *Children of the Rainbow*, which recommended giving first-graders 'a healthy sense of identity by including references to lesbians and gay people in all curricular areas', was rejected along with books like *Heather Has Two Mommies* and *Gloria Goes to Gay Pride*, as were any mentions of masturbation, abortion or contraception. The United Federation of Teachers is currently fighting the decision which, along with the Rivera killing, gave public voice to gay communities outside New York's traditional gay centre, Greenwich Village. Rafael Ruiz-Ayala said of the Rivera killing: 'One thing it did was put a brown face to gayness in the city of New York. There are a lot of people who think that Latino gays are twice the scum of the city. This has created a new awareness. It acknowledges you exist.'

Why come to Queens? Not for the gay scene, which is still largely underground and in any case mainly male; and not for the architecture, which is dull two- and three- storey run-down clapboard suburban homes. Come for the American Museum of the Moving Image, for the Isamu Noguchi Garden Museum, for Shea Stadium if you're a sports fan (see p.314), and for the nightlife of Queens' Greek Astoria area.

The largest Greek population outside Athens is concentrated on Queens' Broadway between 30th and 35th Streets. Walk down Broadway past the Chase Bank (at 35–12) with a sign reading 'Omiloume Ellenika' ('Greek spoken here'), pass stores full of vine leaves and tarama and stop off at one of the plain cafés that sell cream-filled ekmek, coconut kaidaifs and tiny lethal coffees to Greeks, bridge-painters and cabbies till the early hours. 'You can't imagine what it is to walk in the streets of Astoria and hear nothing but Greek; it's like being in Athens,' says Fannie Petallides-Holliday, publisher of the Greek daily Proini (The Dawn) – but that's changing. Greeks first came to Astoria after World War II, the peak was in 1976, and now Hispanics and South Americans are the largest groups in the area. Greeks are beginning to move out, but their restaurants will stay. Go to Taverna Vraka (23–15 31st St bet. 23rd and 24th Aves, tel. 718 721 3007), which is more nightclub than Cypriot restaurant. Piano and bouzouki boom into action, and out comes the boss himself, pirouetting ferociously in traditional Greek boots and bloomers until he's carrying a precarious stack of eight filled glasses accompanied by the wild whooping of patrons who finally abandon tables to join the handker-chief dance and quickstep (you can have a meal or just a coffee).

Apart from its Greek community, Queens is famous as America's pre-Hollywood home of the film industry. Rudolph Valentino and Gloria Swanson starred in silents and Edward G. Robinson made the early talkie Hole in the Wall at the Kaufman Astoria Studio, which is still in business (one of Sidney Lumet's favourite locations) and now a historic landmark (34–12 36th St bet. 34th and 35th Aves). Housed within is the – sadly, rather small – Museum of the Moving Image.

American Museum of the Moving Image

35th Ave (at 36th St), Astoria, Queens. Subway R (except week-ends) and G to Steinway St, exit at 34 Ave end of the station, walk along Steinway St to 35th Ave, turn right and walk on to 36th St. Tues–Fri noon–4 p.m., Sat and Sun noon–6 p.m. $5, students and children $2.50. No pushchairs permitted. Film and exhibition information tel. 718 784 0077.

This opened in 1988 as the only museum in the United States devoted to the art, history and technology of motion pictures, television, and video. It's well worth the trip to Queens. Magic mirrors put you in Vivien Leigh's *Gone With the Wind* gown, revolting special effects have their workings exposed (see the vomit machine from the *Exorcist*), and directors explain their craft over clips from their films. Go for a break to the café where Valentino ate, and check out film screenings in the lavish mock-Egyptian movie house, Tut's Fever, where James Dean comes out of a sarcophagus.

The ground and second floors house temporary exhibitions, and the first-floor permanent exhibition ranges from indulgent lavish souvenir posters and 1930s and 1940s memorabilia to present-day original sets and costumes.

Isamu Noguchi Garden Museum

32–37 Vernon Blvd (at 33rd Rd), Long Island City. Wed and Sat 11 a.m.–6 p.m., Apr–Nov. Suggested donations $2. Don't go by subway, which leaves you with a 15 -min walk. Take the Saturday shuttle bus from outside the Asia Society at 725 Park Ave (at 70th St) every hour on the half-hour 11.30 a.m.–3.30 p.m., $5 round trip, tel. 718 721 1923 for information.

Relaxing and lovely but a long haul to get to, this museum is exceptional because it was created by the artist, Isamu Noguchi (1904–88), for his work. Renowned for his 'Akari' light sculptures and as controversial creator of set designs for Martha Graham (see p.312), Noguchi was a man with several visions: 'The museum shows in particular, my own part in the widening ideas of environment starting in 1933; my experimental approach to structure and the theatre during the '40s; and my search for a sculpture outside the confines of the studio since then.' Over 300 works are housed in a garden and 13 airy galleries. For devotees of his work.

THE BRONX

You'll hear plenty of bad things about the Bronx, so here are some good things: Yankee Stadium, Bronx Zoo, the Botanical Gardens and new conciliatory moves in high schools.

A big problem in any neighbourhood that attracts large numbers of immigrants is alienation. Teachers at Roosevelt High School in the Bronx have devised a programme which, they hope, will help bridge the culture gap and eliminate the language barrier. Roosevelt is in the quiet Belmont area, which was until recently predominantly Italian. Today, of the 3,059 students 62% are Hispanic, 29% are black, 8% are Asian and 1% are white, and 1,000 students are listed as having limited proficiency in English. Classes have been scheduled that put teachers at desks while students tap the blackboard, teaching tutors their native language. Students feel good about themselves, teachers gain understanding of students' difficulties and are better able to communicate with parents on parents' days. The programme of role-reversal classes has been so successful that other schools are following suit.

But it is not possible to gloss over the bad in the Bronx completely. A handful of decayed, empty 1920s Art Deco apartments on the main artery, Grand Concourse, speak sadly of the borough's brief desirable period. Today, although it's not all decimation, large parts – mainly the south – have been ghettoised and are dangerous. They're no-go areas partly because of arbitrary killings at the hands of trigger-happy teenagers. Statistics tell a grim story: 73% of homicides in 1990 involved the use of handguns (in 1960 the figure was 19%); fifteen to nineteen-year-olds are more likely to be arrested for murder than any other age group; and statisticians have been obliged to come up with an entirely new category to chart the number of innocent bystanders killed (the number is rising steadily – 22 in 1990, and 29 in 1991). News stories such as the following are common: 'Police officer on his way to work was stabbed six times yesterday after he told three teenagers to stop scrawling graffiti on a southbound D train in the South Bronx.'

The question of *why* places like the Bronx continue to deteriorate is a subject for hot debate, but many blame comfortable white authority's repeated insensitivity. For example, New York City's Department of Cultural Affairs recently commissioned two sculptures for a South Bronx police station. One of the sculptures was a hooded figure petting a pit bull; another was a black man holding a basketball with one foot on a boom box. They were removed immediately. 'We were stunned,' said a senior Bronx police officer, horrified by the coarse racial stereotyping. 'The message the art would have sent was, at the very least, insensitive. At most, it could have caused a riot.'

President Jimmy Carter made noises about cleaning up the Bronx; Reagan and Bush between them effectively destroyed the public benefit system; Mayor Dinkins simply had too much on his plate: no improvement in the Bronx. And there is one advantage none would admit to leaving ghettos as they are – the violence is contained. Manhattanites even thrill to the *frisson* of danger, if it's from the safety of Park Avenue apartments. Leonard Bernstein threw a party for the radical activist group the Black Panthers in the 1970s. The Panthers announced to socialites and celebrities from one of two grand pianos their plan to destroy all such plush Park Avenue apartments in the cause of black freedom.

You can glimpse the Bronx's no-go areas during the subway journey to Yankee Stadium or on the bus ride to the Zoo, but it's not thrilling – only depressing. It is much as Tom Wolfe's *Bonfire of the Vanities* describes: empty, windowless apartment blocks, 'a long low building with scalloped dormer windows . . . like something from a storybook Swiss chalet' but blackened, a three-legged chair with 'a burnt seat with the charred stuffing hanging out in great wads, rammed halfway through a cyclone fence'. The only colour is graffiti splashes saying 'Crack is wack', 'Crack kills'.

BAD GIRLS

In the South Bronx and similar New York neighbourhoods girls are turning increasingly to violence for two reasons: fashion and personal protection.

In many urban high schools a girl's 'gear' determines her popularity, and if she has no money she resorts to theft or violence. Aleysha from the Bronx told the *New York Times* how she sees things, wants them and pulls a knife to get them. A female youth group in Crown Heights, Brooklyn, talked about carrying guns after being caught in crossfires, and about forming gangs as the best way to get the same protection boys give each other from the random violence in the subway system and in their neighbourhoods. Girl gangs' violence is usually directed at other girls and often caused by jealousy of clothes or boyfriends. In 1990 roving gangs terrified Upper West Side women with random pinprick attacks. In 1991 fifteen-year-old Maribel Feliciano was stabbed to death on the subway for refusing to hand over a pair of gold hoop earrings.

There has been little research on girls' violence, but Anne Campbell of Rutgers University estimates that about 10% of gang members across the country are girls. In the four years between 1986 and 1990 the number of girls arrested for felonies in New York City went up by 48%.

Yankee Stadium

E 161st St (at River Ave, Highbridge), tel. 718 293 6000. 4 train to 161st St station. When you get off the train you can see the stadium, which you reach by going up blue metal stairs then down. Go *in the door marked Bleechers for the equivalent of the terraces; tickets $5.50. Baseball season May–Sept.*

Come to a game even if you're not a sports fan, and experience some all-American culture. Built in 1923 by a brewery magnate for the team he owned (the Yankees) and known affectionately as 'the house that Babe Ruth built' ('the Babe' scored 60 home runs in 1927), the Yankee Stadium is one of the few ball parks that still has a live organist instead of Muzak. If you're keen, go to the bleechers to share a community atmosphere with committed fans. The bleecher audience is mainly male, but there are women regulars and some men proudly bring their infants. If there's any sign of trouble, the audience shouts for order. At high points in the game there's wild hand-slapping and a man runs to the railings with a sign saying 'BOOM'.

The safety in the numbers that throng to see the game makes the subway journey comfortable and offers a chance to see the Bronx from the train, which runs overground for much of the journey. Go straight from the subway station to the game, then straight back to the subway, and don't wander.

Bronx Zoo

Bronx River Parkway, Fordham Rd, Bronx, tel. 718 367 1010. Open 10 a.m.–5 p.m. daily, to 5.30 on weekends and holidays. $5.75 and $2 for children 2–12 and senior citizens. BxM11 Liberty Line express bus service from Madison Avenue at 28th, 37th, 40th, 47th, 54th, 63rd, 84th or 99th St; tel. 212 652 8400 for schedule; and have the $3.75 fare ready in change.

This is a summer day trip for families who need a break during a long stay in Manhattan, and for lovers of safari parks. Four thousand animals from all over the globe roam more or less free through 265 acres of parkland, the largest urban zoo in the United States. Much of the parkland is fake but convincing. In Jungle World many trees are plastic and steel, and some of the Himalayan Highland rocks have heated coils built in so that the snow leopards have warm spots to rest – they are conveniently sited for visitors' viewing. Ask to see recent newborns which included in 1991 a polar bear, a wallaby, birds of paradise and Vietnamese potbellied pigs. For $1.25 (75c children) take the Bengali Express monorail train through dark forests and past elephants and rare sika deer wandering a barren Asian wilderness. Take youngsters to the children's zoo ($1, 75c children) where they can climb a spider's web, escape like a lizard down a tree, or try on a pair of Fennec Fox simulated ears. The Cafeteria, Zoobar and Pub all sell food, and the first two have bring-your-own picnic table areas.

In winter some animals are caged and the monorail doesn't run, so visit between May and October to get the best of it.

If you've come as far as the Zoo, make time to slip across the road into the back entrance of . . .

The New York Botanical Gardens

200th St (at Southern Blvd, Bronx Park), tel. 718 220 8700. Hours Tues–Sun 10 a.m.–5 p.m., last admission 4 p.m. Admission to grounds, free; admission to conservatory, $2.50. If you're coming from Manhattan, take a shuttle bus from the Metropolitan Museum, $7 round trip (tel. 212 220 8700 for schedule and reservations).

The Brooklyn Botanical Garden is easier and cheaper to get to, and some say better – but the Bronx Gardens are bigger. Go to the Museum Building for a map to the 250 acres of grounds which include 40 acres of virgin hemlock forest and a conservatory modelled after the Great Palm House at Kew Gardens in London. Hours of walking in beautiful surroundings. Take a picnic or use the Lorillard Snuff Mill café.

HOTELS

New York hotels have been catering for businesswomen since the 1970s. In almost all mid-priced to expensive hotels you'll find skirt as well as trouser hangers, his and hers bathroom amenities, powerfully magnifying make-up mirrors, good security (peephole, dead chain and bolt) and low-calorie salad options on room service menus.

CHOICES FOR BUSINESSWOMEN

With the exception of cheap hotels, any you pick is likely to be as satisfactory as the next, but hotels that are particularly well geared up for businesswomen travellers include **The Grand Hyatt Hotel** (see p.236) for its research into the needs of women business travellers, the **Righa Royale** (see p.233) for its elegant suites that can easily be used for business meetings, the **New York Hilton** (see p232) for its Concierge floor, and the **Mercer Hotel** (see p.231) for its desirable Downtown location and health spa.

Children haven't been so well catered for, but that looks set to change. In 1988 the Grand Hyatt Hotel's Travel Futures Research Project identified a new and potentially lucrative group called 'Family Tieds'. Family Tieds are the growing number of businessmen and women who take their children with them to reduce family stress, and have low cost as a priority. More hotels are doing special reduced family packages. In general, suite hotels are best (see below) if you have children, or if you're a woman alone who doesn't want to rely on restaurants and room service.

Because New York is principally a convention rather than a tourist city, high and low seasons correspond not with temperature but with the number of business travellers. You can get cheap deals at weekends, in the summer and just after Christmas. You should always haggle for discounts – hotels expect this, thanks to the recession. And you must book ahead. All the major sales conventions are held in New York and if your visit coincides with one, cheap deals will not be your concern – you simply may not be able to find a bed. You should also check the tax, which will not be included in the quoted rate and will add anything between 18% and 22% to your bill (depending on room type).

Be wary, though, of economising by checking into a cheap hotel on spec. Many in New York are homes to mixtures of failed entertainers and alcoholics who checked in thirty years ago and never checked out. You might enjoy your stay in one of these eccentric 'residential hotels' that cater for people who can't be bothered to cook or clean, or you might find your sleep interrupted by wails of a patient confiding bleakly to his analyst, the warbles of an aspiring singer or the sad pluckings of a once-famous ukelele player.

When you choose your hotel, bear in mind that if it's cheap and in an old building, there can be two problems. One is the pipes, which can be incredibly noisy (light sleepers take ear plugs). Another is cockroaches, which lurk in the heating system and do not necessarily mean that a place is unclean. Indeed, a New Yorker's reaction to a European shrieking at the sight of a delicate big brown bug is likely to be a shrug of the shoulders and 'welcome to New York!'

Tipping is crucial. If you don't tip enough (from bellman to porter to waitress) you will be dead-eyed for the rest of your stay. Tipping is not a perk as far as the staff are concerned. They work for practically nothing, so tips are their wages. Reckon on $2 per bag carried and 15–20% of sundry bills.

Last but not least, don't be surprised if you get a bellboy pressing you to take note of his name and free time with a pointed invitation to 'just call if you need anything *at all*'. If you're not interested in having a toy boy for the night, assume innocence and there'll be no embarrassment on either side.

Unless stated otherwise, all hotels will: take Access, Visa or American Express; have phones, TVs, air-conditioning, baths and showers; have 24-hour reception and a restaurant and bar; have at least basic photocopying and fax business services. Every decent moderate and expensive hotel has access to health-club facilities – it's specified only if those facilities are in-house and cheap or free. Only the cheapest hotels have single beds – in all the rest you get a double for paying a single rate. All prices quoted are, unless otherwise specified, before tax. In all hotels watch out for telephone charges, which can be anything from 60 cents to over a dollar for a local call that would cost 25 cents in a phone booth.

Cheap = $27–$75 per night
Moderate = $80–$150 per night
Expensive = $150 plus.

ACCOMMODATION

Hardly any hotels at all below 14th Street, but here are a handful of gems in unbeatable Downtown locations.

Cheap

OFF-SOHO SUITES

11 Rivington St (bet. Christie and Bowery), New York NY 10002. Tel. 212 979 9808. Fax 212 979 9801.

B or D subway to Grand St, walk north 3 blocks up Bowery to Rivington and turn east; 101 bus from Grand Central Station to Delancey St, walk north one block to Rivington and turn east. You'll spot the hotel by Christmas lights decorating a tree in a tub outside. Six-storey white building with wrought-iron fire escapes down the front.

This is, as it advertises, a good 'traveller's alternative to New York's overpriced, undersized hotel rooms'. A suite with shared bathroom and kitchenette costs only $66 for two people, and a suite that sleeps four costs $99 for the lot of you each night before tax. But the name is crucial: not 'In-SoHo' but 'Off-SoHo', in the Lower East Side, far from SoHo galleries and surrounded instead by industrial kitchenware shops with the Bowery Mission a block away, where shoeless unshaven men slurp soup at benches. It's still a great place to stay, though, as long as you take cabs at night and don't wander too far East. You'll meet students on vacation and wannabe rock stars in the elevator. The newly renovated clean rooms have unobtrusive modern decor (glass tables, Venetian blinds, Swedish-look woodwork) and the downstairs deli and minimarket is open 24 hours (heat up cold food in your microwave if you can't be bothered to cook). Staff are

very friendly and reliable about taking phone messages. Twenty-four-hour reception, phones and TVs in all rooms plus air-conditioning, and special offer of a chauffeur-driven stretch limo to take you to the airport for $35 or $40, depending which airport. Thirty-six suites total.

WASHINGTON SQUARE HOTEL

103 Waverly Place (bet. MacDougal St and 6th Ave), NY 10011. Tel. 212 777 9515. Fax 212 979 8373.

A, B, C, D, F subway to West 4th St–Washington Sq, walk north 2 small blocks to Waverly Place; 2, 3 bus to Astor Place, walk west along 8th St and south down MacDougal St one short block to Waverly Place. The hotel is an eight-storey red-brick building with grey-white stonework. Look for a street-level round ironwork awning with the name on.

This is a romantic and handy location in the heart of Greenwich Village, in a designated Landmark area. The nearby square evokes visions of clopping horse-drawn carriages and elegant Old New York characters out of Edith Wharton and Henry James novels. You can fall out of bed into Little Italy coffee shops and SoHo galleries, then later into jazz clubs, restaurants and bars. Wrought-iron gates at the reception area open up on to a wonderful marble lobby that has a Mediterranean feel and Audubon-type prints of birds on the wall. The standard rooms are not so plush, with worn bedspreads, dingy yellow plastic curtains in the bathrooms, some of which smell dank. Pay extra for a redone 'deluxe' room and you'll get a room about 10ft by 12ft with peach and green sponge-painted walls, bright polyester floral bedspreads, mirrored closets and modern bathrooms. Guests are mainly young European tourists, but you get occasional visiting NYU professors and stars including Bo Diddley, and the proprietors are hoping the newly refurbished rooms will attract business custom. Washington Square can be seedy at night, but the hotel's just far enough away for a woman alone to be able to avoid it easily. No room service, but guests get 10% discount at the restaurant next door (Cajun Chicken sandwiches for $7.95 before discount). Standard rooms cost from $60 single to $105 quad and deluxe rooms cost $70 to $116, all prices including tax. $7 for extra bed. Twenty-four-hour reception. All 160 rooms have TVs, phones and air-conditioning.

Expensive

THE HOTEL MERCER
99 Prince St (at Prince St), NY 10012. Tel 212 226 5656. Fax 226 8224. R subway to Prince St, turn west down Prince St; 6 bus down Broadway to Prince St, turn west into Prince St. The hotel is an 1888 Landmark building on the corner with distinctive large arched windows at the top sixth storey level.

$33 million has gone into making this the first four-star luxury hotel below 14th Street, and its philosophy is particularly suited to women travelling alone on business or for pleasure. André Balzazs and Campion Platt, who know everyone from John F. Kennedy Jr to Harold Brodky, sought advice from renowned media folk including Annie Flanders. Retailer in the 1960s, factory operator in the

deserts of Ethiopia in the 1970s and founder of *Details* magazine in the 1980s, Annie insisted on bathroom lighting that is correct for doing make-up, on full-length mirrors, on velvet to replace masculine fabrics; and she is conceiving for the hotel a health spa and pharmacy with the first full-service homeopathic shop in New York, featuring a leading French homeopath behind the counter (it should be operating by 1993). The lobby will be separate from the brasserie/bar/lounge area and therefore more secure than most, and staff will greet each guest by name. There'll be a chef on duty round the clock so that late-nighters can 'step right into the kitchen' and 'treat it like a home pantry'. Because it's a designated Landmark building, the 'Thirties moderne' decorated rooms (elegant and functional with olive and rust scatter cushions) are big, with the bathrooms a special feature. Balzazs and Platt decided that guests spend a lot of time in the bathroom, and they liked the 'wonderfully sensual open bathrooms' of Bali and Thailand – yours will be nearly as big as the bedroom, and a sliding door will make the two one. The 78 loft-style rooms cost between $195 a night for a standard single to $320 for a double and $425 a night to $2,200 for the suites. Facilities include VCRs in all rooms, secretarial service, packing and unpacking services, foreign newspapers, florist on the premises. In-house fitness centre.

VISTA INTERNATIONAL HOTEL
3 World Trade Center (bet. West and Liberty Sts), NY 10048. Tel. 212 938 9100. Fax 212 321 2107. E subway takes you direct to the World Trade Center and you're in the complex; 1 or 6 bus to Wall St, walk

north to Liberty St then west. Look for the World Trade twin towers.

This is deluxe and caters largely to male business executives because of its Financial District location, but businesswomen will be well served, if outnumbered, and women with children will appreciate the 50-ft swimming pool (pools are rare in New York hotels). The building is a modern chrome-and-glass monolith; the rooms are handsome and comfortable, many with spectacular harbour views. Every service is available that makes the life of the stressed-out executive easier, including organised tours of Chinatown, massage, secretarial help and the American Harvest and Greenhouse Restaurant, which serves decent American cuisine. Single rooms run from $190 to $225, doubles from $215 to $280 and suites from $525 to $1,245 a night. Weekend packages are available. In-house fitness centre.

Central Midtown

The area between Fifth Avenue and Eighth Avenue below Central Park contains most of the hotels. It also boasts MoMa, proximity to the Fifth Avenue shops, and easy public transport access up- or downtown. It is a generally safe area with the possibility of a view of the park in tall hotels.

Expensive

NEW YORK HILTON AND TOWERS
1335 Ave of the Americas (bet. 53rd and 54th Sts), NY 10023. Tel. 212 586 7000. Fax 757 7423.
B, D, F subway to Rockefeller Center, walk up 6th Ave to 53rd St; 5, 6, 7 bus to 49th St, carry on north up 6th Ave to 53rd St. The Hilton is the reflective glass skyscraper with lots of yellow cabs at the entrance.

This Megahotel has everything for everyone: it has two non-smoking floors; it has possibly the best facilities for the Physically Challenged in the city, including rooms for the hearing-impaired complete with strobe lights and audible alarms; it has an on-site hairdresser open till midnight; both Grill 53 and Café New York have highchairs and booster seats and will do half-price meals for children; the Executive Towers is ideal for businesswomen for its speedy check-in and relaxing complimentary breakfast/afternoon tea in a private lounge that can double as a place for informal meetings. Room decor is comfortable modern in no-nonsense greys, mauves and blues. Basic amenities include sewing kit, Camay and the Vidal Sassoon Ultra Care range. Large downstairs lobby mills with Japanese businessmen, American tourists and guests attending conventions (male and female in pretty much equal measure). The 2,042 rooms in the soaring skyscraper cost between $175 and $235 single, $200–$260 double, and suites cost $400–$575 per night. Weekend packages are available. In-house fitness centre.

PARKER MERIDIEN
118 W 56th St (bet. 6th and 7th Aves), NY 10019. Tel. 212 245 5000. Fax 212 247 4698.
B and D to 57th St, walk south to

56th St; 6 or 7 bus to 57th St, walk south to 56th St. The main entrance is set back from the street. Look for milling porters.

Next door to the Russian Tea Rooms (see p.272), the 57th Street atrium entrance to the hotel is like a Hollywood film set, with marble and mirrors, a peach pillared balcony, full-grown trees in pots and a skylight. The city's first French-managed hotel, it has a lot of French visitors (tourist and business equally) as well as New Age executive California clients and a heavenly rooftop swimming pool (indoor and outdoor) in the penthouse health club. Grey, black and yellow decorated rooms have 'overstuffed' sofas, French lithographs and mounted lighting on the walls, and in-room aerobic videos available constantly. Rates run between $200 single/$225 double to $1,500 for the presidential suite, and there is an assortment of special deals that can take you down to $150 single or double a night. In-house fitness centre.

RIGHA ROYAL
151 West 54th St (at 7th Ave), NY 10019. Tel. 212 307 5000. Fax 212 765 6530.
1 or 9 subway to 50th St, walk east to 7th Ave and north to 54th St; 6 or 7 bus to 53rd St and north to 54th St. The tall building is stepped Deco style with a pink-cream marble façade.

This hotel is made up entirely of suites that are designed (successfully) to feel like 475 apartments. They are perfect for businesswomen who want a separate work area that's plush enough also to serve for informal meetings (decor is blue and beige with 1920s bent). Good too for couples with children, since in some the living area has a sofa bed, and the charge is

per room, not per number of guests. There's Crabtree and Evelyn in the bathroom and power showers that will spoil you for life. Formal, elegant pink-brown marble lobby. Relaxed piano bar for the evenings. Twenty-four-hour business centre, and of course Japanese breakfast on room-service menu. Prices from $260 for a standard room to $700 for a deluxe two-bedroom suite. Weekend packages available. In-house fitness centre.

ROYALTON
44 W 44th St (bet. 5th and 6th Aves), NY 10036. Tel. 212 869 4400. Fax 212 869 8965.
4, 6 and 7 subway to 42nd St, walk north to 44th St then west; 1, 2, 3, 4, 5 bus to 42nd St, walk north to 44th St then west. The sign engraved in the grey nineteenth-century façade is too discreet. Look for the fresh flowers in windowboxes and two beautiful bellboys standing guard masquerading as square-jawed hunks in zoot suits.

Shrager says his hotel pioneers the 'art of lobby socialising', meaning that the Royalton Hotel replaces bars and clubs as *the* place to be seen for style-conscious media moguls from Manhattan and all over the world. It's also a marvellous place to stay. Philip Starck designed the 205-room 1898 Manhattan Landmark, mixing 'classic' with 'cutting edge'. It has subdued lighting and a leaping dolphin motif throughout. All standard hotel functions are concealed, so that the lobby-bar looks like a lavish echoey living-room with reception tucked away in a floor-to-ceiling mahogany façade. The rooms are midnight blue and grey with giant white bolster pillows, luxurious round bathrooms, Dean and Deluca 'gourmet goodies' in the fridge, and some have working fireplaces. The gym is 24 hours and the hotel's Restaurant 44 serves very good, if not quite top-class, American cuisine. Ideal for the executive woman alone, but mothers can bring children under twelve free. Cribs are free, but rollaway costs extra $25 a night. Singles $210–$325, doubles $235–$350, suites $350–$1,400. In-house fitness centre.

Murray Hill

This area is, broadly speaking, respectable, safe and quiet at the northern section and not so safe around the bottom section. Hotels near the top boast proximity to Grand Central, the UN, Park and Madison businesses, and Fifth Avenue from the quieter side.

Cheap

ALLERTON HOUSE FOR WOMEN
130 E 57th St (at Lexington Ave), NY 10022. Tel. 212 753 8841.
4, 6 subway to 59th St, walk south down Lexington and west into 57th St; 101, 102 bus to 59th St, walk south down Lexington. Tall dark brick building with grey-white awning sticking out saying Allerton House.

This plain, clean hotel is for professional and business women and students who want the safety of the neighbourhood, low prices and a quiet, undisturbing anonymous atmosphere. No children or visitors are allowed unless they're female relatives. Many of the 500 flower-and-turquoise-decorated rooms with modern bedside cabinets are residential, so book ahead. The chintzy, airy lobby operates 24 hours and feels secure. The sunroof with benches is open through the summer, and although there is no room service, there's an Irish bar and restaurant next door where you can get chicken and leek pot pie for $9.95. Rates are $35 a night with running water, $40 with connecting bath, $50 with private shower or bath and $65 for a twin-bedded room.

CARLTON ARMS HOTEL
160 E 25th St (bet. 3rd and Lexington Aves), NY 10010. Tel. 212 679 0680.
6 subway to 23rd St, walk north 2 blocks and east down 25th St; 101 or 102 bus to 25th St. The walk to the hotel takes you under scaffolding and through unsavoury odours along a quiet road. Be careful after dark – take cabs if you can. The hotel is in a five-storey red-brick building over a bicycle shop. Walk up narrow stairs to narrow lobby.

The Carlton is billed as the Artbreak hotel you'll never forget, with every wall a piece of art and practically an entire staff of spaced-out English dudes. One room boasts wall-to-ceiling papier-mâché breasts, another has bongo players made of bin-liners and one down the hall is black Goth covered in skulls. Every room has a basin, but what a basin – covered in centuries of limescale. The windows don't need curtains because they're so dirty, the bed creaks let you know exactly what your neighbour's doing. No phones or TVs in any rooms, no food available in any form, and no money changing. Twenty-four-hour reception means only that the staff live in and might wake up if you ring the bell long enough (guests have own keys), and the security leaves something to be desired (weak locks on doors). This hotel is strictly for youth getting wasted and clubbing all night who like the nearly-Downtown location and, if you're a woman alone, you'll get to know like-minded travellers. Cost for rooms with private bathroom go from $48 for one person to $74 for three and without private bathroom from $40 for one to $65 for three. All rates, except the $48 for one with bath, get a student and foreign tourist discount rate which lops anything from $3 to $7 per night off the bill. Maximum stay 25 nights.

MARTHA WASHINGTON
30 East 30th St.

The Martha Washington advertises itself as 'Exclusively for Women . . . the hotel with the club-like atmosphere.' The block is unsavoury at night. After the marble stairs and 1970s swirling carpet in the lobby, the rooms are dirty and seedy, some have weak connecting doors to strangers' rooms, and while it's true that hotel guests have access to a bar, so does everyone else in the City, for a fee of $10. The bar is one of three glitter-decorated Gothic constructions in the downbeat disco-diorama club next door where, it's said, Madonna began her career.

PICKWICK ARMS
250 E 51st St (bet. 2nd and 3rd Aves),
NY 10022. Tel. 212 355 0300. Fax
212 755 5029.
6 subway to 51st St, walk east; 98,
101, 102 bus to 51st St and east down
51st St. Pass a florist on the corner
and the hotel is a twelve-storey turn-
of-the-century building, white stone at
street level and dark brick the rest.
The hotel's name is written in Gothic
scrawl on a brown awning.

This is good value for the budget woman business traveller. It's secure, clean and cheap with TVs, phones, private bathrooms and air-conditioning in all rooms. It is in a safe area that is handy for the UN, not too far from Fifth Avenue and Museum Mile, and offers easy access Downtown by public transport. Regular clients include many South Americans. The lobby's newly revamped marble look is a bit sterile, but the staff are fairly friendly and after midnight the front door is locked – only people who show room keys to the camera are let in. Some rooms are still a little gloomy but will eventually be revamped in pastel blues and pinks with brass-look side-lamps. The low-priced café is purely functional (eat and get out quick). There's a rooftop garden for summertime and a good Spanish restaurant, Torremolinos, next door, which has a flamenco guitarist Tuesdays–Saturdays with an average meal coming to $35 (children not welcome). The Torremolinos bar is nice when busy but depressing on quiet nights. Traveller's cheques in US dollars will be changed, but not money, and only basic business services are available (photocopying and faxes sent and received at reception). Prices $42–$55 singles and $75–$85 doubles, children under eighteen go free with $10 charge for the cot.

Moderate

GRAMERCY PARK HOTEL
2 Lexington Ave (at 21st St), NY
10010. Tel. 212 475 4320.
Fax 212 505 0535.
6 subway to 23rd St, walk east to
Lexington and south two blocks to
21st; 101 or 102 bus to 14th St, walk
north up Lexington to 21st St and

ACCOMMODATION

west. The hotel is a huge old brownstone. An inconspicuous brown awning at street level marks the entrance. The immediate area is safe and quiet, but at night better to take cabs Downtown than walk.

Once the elegant last home of Stanford White, this Old World mixed with modern-style hotel is a favourite with European publishers and musicians for its nearly-Downtown location, and with families because some of the rooms have kitchenettes and sofa beds. All hotel guests have access to the pleasant green private Gramercy Park, where children can play (just ask the doorman for the key). Electric chandeliers decorate the wood-panelled lobby and the restaurant, which boasts fresh fish daily and good steaks (Hot Shrimps Gramercy appetiser for $12.75 and Fettucini All Casa entrée for $20), but there are no price reductions for children. The long thin piano bar is mellow, with bartenders who pour generously. The 509 renovated rooms, which have blue or flower bedspreads, grey wallpaper and Venetian blinds, start at $125 for a single to $140 for a double, and special one-bedroom family suites start at $160 (add on $10 for each extra adult, children under seventeen go free, suites sleep up to five).

Expensive

BEEKMAN TOWER HOTEL
3 Mitchell Place (corner of 49th St and 1st Ave), NY 10017-1801. Tel. 212 355 7300, Fax 212 753 9366. Grand Central Subway terminal, 6 or 7 subway. Walk East down 42nd St and Downtown along 1st Ave; 15 bus, to 49th St. The hotel towers in front of you, a red-brick Deco construction.

The Beekman advertises itself as 'one of Manhattan's safest and most fashionable addresses'. It is also stunning, considered – alongside the Chrysler Building – one of the city's finest examples of Art Deco architecture. It was built in 1928 by a woman, Emily Eaton Hepburn, widow of the Chase National Bank Chairman, who envisioned Beekman Hill as the ideal site and neighbourhood for a hotel for sorority women launching careers in New York. To survive the Great Depression, the Pan Hellenic House, as it was first known, opened its doors to men. Since it is practically on the doorstep of the United Nations, the hotel's clientele regularly includes visiting dignitaries and politicians. It has been refurbished faithfully to period, that is: twenties Art Deco with plum and aubergine colours throughout and a conch-shell sofa in the amber-wood-coloured lobby. The restaurant has friendly service, very good food, and the layout makes it pleasurable for a woman alone. The romantic Top of the Towers bar is a low-lit comfy-chaired lounge with a tinkling pianist and a panoramic view. Prices from $185 for a studio suite to $375 for a double two-bedroom suite, 396 rooms total. In-house fitness centre.

GRAND HYATT
Park Ave at Grand Central Station, NY 10017. Tel. 212 883 1234. Fax 212 697 3772. 4, 6, 7 Subway to Grand Central terminal, which has a pedestrian link to the hotel; 101, 102, 104 bus to Grand Central. The hotel soars up next to stumpy beaux-arts Grand Central: thirty storeys of shiny glass with 1,407 rooms. The glass revolving doors manned by old-fashioned

uniformed porters are the entrance.

This was one of the first hotels to cater to businesswomen travellers' needs – it installed make-up mirrors, put women near the elevator, and is continually researching what businesswomen want – and you know security's good because the Hyatt has a national contract with the country's baseball teams. Batting stars are installed here by their managers to keep them safe from screaming girl groupies. The sprawling lobby is all chrome and glass filled with Muzak and a spouting fountain surrounded by plastic-look fauna. Room decor is instantly forgettable modern, but the hotel is efficient with excellent service. There's an appealing deal for women with older children: if you don't want them in your room you'll get 50% off a second room. Also ask about special weekend rates. Full business centre operating business hours and Saturday. Choice of 3 decent restaurants. Prices from $190 single to $285 double, suites start at $350.

MORGAN'S
237 Madison Ave (at 38th St), NY 10016. Tel. 212 686 0300. Fax 212 779 8352.
4, 6, 7 subway to Grand Central terminal, walk west to Madison and then south; 2, 3 bus stops right outside. The hotel is a twenty-storey 1929 building with no sign. Look for porters and bellhops dressed by Shamask in blazers sauntering towards you from the grey and ecru high lobby.

No longer *the* 'in' style-conscious executive's hotel, Morgan's is as a result more relaxed, intimate, and now perfect for a woman travelling alone. The friendly staff will greet you by name, French André Puttnam's

Japanese-influenced design masters understated elegance with the low beds, warm grey maple laminate walls and black uplighters. Features in every room include Kiehl pharmacy shampoos, fresh flowers, complimentary continental breakfast, VCRs, and a tape library of over 200 films is available. A number of fashion designers, photographers and celebrities including Cher and Margaux Hemingway are all regulars, so book well ahead. There's no restaurant, but there's 24-hour room service from a full, high-quality kitchen. The hotel is near the Pierpont Morgan Library and Fifth Avenue shops, and well-placed for getting Uptown and Downtown quickly. You can have as many guests in suites as you like at no extra charge, which is good for women with children. Rates for the 112 rooms and suites run from $160 to $380 per night, with a weekend nightly rate of $140 for a room and $180 for a suite.

THE WALDORF-ASTORIA HOTEL
301 Park Ave (bet. 49th and 50th Sts), NY 10022. Tel. 212 355 3000. Fax 212 758 9209.
6 subway to 51st St, walk south one block down Lexington then west; 101, 102 bus to 51st St, walk south one block then west. The Waldorf is a huge gold-embellished H-shaped Art Deco building that covers a whole block and has flags sticking out over the front entrance.

The ornate revamped Deco lobby is a riveting mêlée of snap-happy Japanese and all-American tourists hopping between convention guests who might be flushed ball-gowned seventeen-year-old hopefuls at the recruiting 'Modelling Association of America Incorporate' evening or Poles in traditional embroidered pinnies and

ACCOMMODATION

braids on their way to the annual Kosciuszka Foundation in one of the various elaborate Convention Halls and Ballrooms. The lobby also has the most notable ladies' rest rooms in town: each toilet has its own basin and vanity mirror, so women come here after work to change before dinner events. The rooms in the Waldorf-Astoria can be the size of a broom cupboard or a rambling suite, both in the generic Old Europe decor favoured by New York hotels and costing between $190 singles and $275 doubles. The Waldorf Towers, where presidents and multimillion-dollar pop stars stay and where Cole Porter lived for thirty years, has nearly all suites individually decorated with antiques, chandeliers and lots of gilt and plush velvet for between $260 a night single and $3,000 for the four-roomed Presidential Suite. The Peacock Restaurant is a beautiful wood-panelled room with wonderfully quiet polite service, but the food is average. The leather-and-dim-lighting bar is fine for a woman alone. The size of the hotel (1,692 rooms) affords an anonymity that can be welcome. OK for children, but not a first choice. Weekend packages available. In-house fitness centre.

INTERCONTINENTAL HOTEL
111 E 48th St (bet. Park and Lexington Aves), NY 100017. Tel. 212 7555 5900. Fax 212 664 0079.

6 subway to 51st St, walk south down Lexington to 48th St; 101 or 102 bus to 51st St, walk south down Lexington to 48th St. Entrance has three big awnings with doormen elaborately kitted out in gold-braid outfits.

The efficiency of a big chain hotel combines with Old Style elegance to make business travellers feel there's no-time-wasted but they're in luxury. There's a steam room and sauna, and a super-quick video check-out system that allows you to press a few buttons while cleaning your teeth before the dash to an airport. The sprawling wood-panelled lobby with a latticed brass birdcage under the hotel's original Federal-style Tiffany skylight at the centre is airy, pleasant, and secure because any loiterers would stand out like sore thumbs. Because it's an old hotel (1926), the 691 newly renovated rooms are bigger than usual, with the Old Style elegance continued (some have antiqued fireplaces and Turkish-style carpets). The Barclay Restaurant boasts a 'club-like atmosphere' with chandeliers, and there's a less formal Terrace for breakfast, lunch, dinner and cocktails, and low-lit Bar One Eleven for late-night chatting. Rates run from $215 to $275 single and double. Intercontinental is unusual for having special rates as low as $99 running seven days a week, not just weekends, in low seasons. In-house health spa.

The Theater District and Around

Some women feel uncomfortable about Times Square – if that includes you, avoid it completely – but others thrill to the bustle of the famous neon-flashing crossroads where women in furs swagger to theatre premières and Japanese pop groups mime songs for video cameras with red 'Drink Coca-Cola' as a wavering backdrop. If you plan to take cabs at night anyway, hotels like the Crowne Inn Plaza are a great way of getting luxury for less money. Many of the surrounding streets are at once quietly respectable and convenient for the Theater District and Fifth Avenue.

Cheap

HOTEL CHELSEA
222 W 23rd St (bet. 7th and 8th Aves), NY 10011. Tel. 212 243 3700. Fax 212 243 3700.

The Chelsea is fun to talk about but not a place to stay. The art-filled lobby is almost plush, with a woman in a swing sculpture hanging from the ceiling and gaudy pictures of Andy Warhol all over. But behind the scenes, things get grim. Residents describe the Chelsea as a cathedral to deferred maintenance, saying the owners' idea of renovation is to paint the lift gold with a roller made of toilet roll. The old ironwork railings are bent in several places where a drunk bounced down the stairwell. Some of the transient guests' rooms are perfectly comfortable, some are filthy, and your neighbours could be drunks, heroin addicts, transvestites, film-makers or 'the witch' with tattoos on her face.

Moderate

THE PARAMOUNT
235 W 46th St (bet. Broadway and 8th Ave), NY 10036. Tel. 212 764 5500. Fax 212 354 5237.
1 or 9 subway to 50th St, walk south down Broadway to 46th St; 10, 27 or 104 bus to 42nd St, then north to 46th St. The hotel's arched façade has evergreen trees in pots at every pillar, but no sign. You know you're in the right place only when those handsome men in black suits and T-shirts grab your bags – they're not thieves but bellhops.

This is billed as the 'cheap chic' version of the Royalton. An eclectic selection of jade, tomato and harlequin print chairs in the cavernous lobby are peopled with blonde, tanned visions in tight black leather; stone stairs float down from the overlooking brasserie that twinkles with jewel lights at backgammon-drink tables; electric red, green and blue lights glow in the spaceship-style elevators; bedrooms have blown-up Vermeers for bedsteads and one-armed chain-stitched velvet armchairs; bathrooms have freestanding bijoux industrial basins. Some guests find the walls too thin and the party in the next room too riotous till too late, but those having the party love the Paramount. A club, Les Bandouches, is due to open soon, and the Whiskey Bar is already a happening spot. Children are well catered for in theory, with babysitting services available and an incredible playroom by the set-designer from Pee Wee's playhouse (try the Sylvester and Tweetypie chairs), but the staff have a joke: 'No kids allowed in the lobby', meaning – they wouldn't fit in with the decor. You can get everything from continental breakfast to standard sandwich fare and 1 a.m. cocktails at the Mezzanine Restaurant, and Dean and Deluca have a cappuccino café off the lobby. The Brasserie du Théâtre restaurant should be up and running by spring 1993. Good selection of newspapers in the small lobby shop. Children under eighteen stay free, and they'll get a rollaway bed at no extra charge. Rates run from $110–$170 single to $130–$190 double. The hotel is on a quiet street that feels especially secure because the Guardian Angels'

ACCOMMODATION

HQ is directly opposite. In-house fitness centre.

Expensive

ALGONQUIN HOTEL

59W 44th St (bet. 5th and 6th Aves), NY 10036. Tel. 212 840 6800. Fax 212 944 1419.
B, D, F subway to 42nd St, walk north up 6th Ave to 44th St; 5 bus to 49th St, walk south to 44th St. The dark, grimy 1902 façade is hard to spot – look for curling characters saying 'Algonquin' over a modest front door.

Old Style European grandeur and the Round Table where Dorothy Parker and Robert Benchley gathered to satirise 1920s New York mores draw an itinerant local publishing crowd for lunch and evening cocktails, and a mix of leisure and business travellers for the hotel rooms, from pop stars to loyal, doddery guests of eighty and older. The lobby has a grandfather clock and brocade chairs, the Oak Room hosts cabaret evenings and the Blue Bar offers drinks in a mellow atmosphere. Some rooms feel poky, but they've all been recently refurbished keeping the Old Europe look, including vaguely Edwardian-looking chairs and antiqued barometers on the walls. No minibars in the rooms. Singles run from $165, doubles from $175 and suites from $330 a night. Genteel place for a woman alone; not the best place for children.

HOLIDAY INN CROWNE PLAZA

49th St and Broadway, NY 10016. Tel. 212 977 4000. Fax 212 977 5517.
1 or 9 subway to 50th St, walk south 1 block down Broadway; 10, 27, 104 bus to 50th St, walk south down Broadway. The hotel is a shiny pink skyscraper opposite a blue-movies theatre, which might bother you, but ten to one you'll stop noticing after a day – it's just part of the New York scenery. Avoid Times Square subway at night, and use sparingly during the day.

The appeal is 'a big bang for your buck' (i.e. good value), and friendly service in a city renowned for rudeness: if hopefuls for any post, from concierge to pot-washer (all unionised), don't smile four times or more during the interview, they don't get the job; there's an annual teamwork day when managers are bossed by workers; all staff get a weekend in a room for free in return for filling in questionnaires on how service could be improved. The concierge floor with separate lounge and complimentary breakfast is good for women alone and businesswomen, there's a swimming pool for health fiends and women with children, and Samplings restaurant is for star-spotters – the hotel is conveniently located for big Broadway theatre parties attended by everyone from Isabella Rossellini to Tracy Ullman and Glenn Close. Your rooms will be dusky greys and beige, plain and comfortable no-nonsense modern. The atmosphere buzzes in the lobby-bar area, and is immediately secure and quiet once you've bolted your door. Prices run from $185 single standard to suites starting at $350. In-house fitness centre.

RAMADA RENAISSANCE

2 Times Square (Broadway bet. 47th and 48th Sts), NY 10036. Tel. 212 765 7676. Fax 212 765 1962.
1 or 9 subway to 50th St, walk south down Broadway; 10, 27, 104 bus to 50th St, walk south. The front of the building is twenty-six storeys of

flashing Samsung, Suntory Whisky and Enjoy Coca-Cola ads. Look for a pink neon Ramada Renaissance sign at the east side first-floor level, and the entrance is underneath. Avoid Times Square subway at night, and use sparingly during the day.

Might last, might not, but this elegant new concept hotel is great if it does, with a beautiful butler in spats on almost every floor to unpack your case, bring you breakfast in bed or deliver a glass of juice in the afternoon. There's a fax on the teak-look desk in your fawn-gold decorated bedroom, and personalised headed paper appears miraculously. The Renaissance Lounge and bar-restaurant, '2 x 0', both have romantic bird's-eye views of Times Square. Security is obviously a prime concern on Times Square, and the hotel's strong on this score. To get to the first-floor lobby you must go through a preliminary street-level marble area filled with bellhops and security guards who make it their business to recognise you and say hello. Too early to gauge the clientele yet, but the hotel is wooing jaded business travellers. Weekend rates start at $155 for a Superior room and $205 for a butler, corporate rates at $185 Superior, $235 Butler, and rack rates run from $195 for a Superior single to $260 for a Butler double, with suites starting at $425.

Upper West Side

Here you'll find some of the cheapest places to stay (see also p.245 for hostels) in mainly quiet and safe areas, although you should be careful of the middle section running roughly between 83rd and 102nd Streets. Upper West Side has Central Park, the Lincoln Center and the Natural History Museum.

Cheap

MALIBU STUDIOS
2688 Broadway (bet. 102nd and 103rd Sts), NY 10025. Tel. 212 222 2954. Fax 212 678 6842.
1 or 9 subway to 103rd St at Broadway; 104 bus to 103rd St on Broadway. The five-storey hotel is cream with a flapping blue banner bearing a palm-tree logo and the name, Malibu Studios. It's above 'Regine Kids, clothing and juvenile furniture' shop. Ring the buzzer and go upstairs.

Ideal for the single woman who wants comfort, cleanliness, security, and a cheap room where she can sleep for five hours and spend the rest of her time and money making the most of New York. Regular clients include would-be models, actresses, and budget business traveller guests. The Natural History Museum, the park and the nightlife spawned by Columbia University are nearby, and Downtown Manhattan is an easy twenty minutes by subway. Go north as far as Columbia on foot, but don't walk more than a block or so south down Broadway, as there are grim projects. Security at the hotel is tight but not oppressive, with 24-hour reception and closed-circuit TV system covering the front door – visitors can be buzzed in only with permission of the hotel guest. The small lobby has pay-phones and the 24-hour reception will change traveller's cheques if they're in US dollars (small denominations only). The 100 rooms in the main building are studenty (teddy on bed, pink or blue paper fan on wall, desk and chair, fridge and two-ring stove, no air-conditioning, TV for hire for $15 a week, no phones but messages will be taken at desk 24 hours). They are repainted regularly. The shared bathrooms are immaculately clean and similarly decorated with a jolly bear on shower curtains. The 50 new rooms in the adjacent building include suites, are less spartan and more suitable for families. No restaurant, but J's jazz restaurant is nearby and there are innumerable fast-food joints. Pick up complimentary passes to the Limelight, Caroline's Comedy Club, the Roxy and more at reception and ask about the charter bus to gambling in the Las Vegas of New Jersey, Atlantic City – for around $20 you get transport, meal vouchers, and ten dollars' worth of quarters for fruit machines. Prices start at $35 single a night, go down to $29.95 a night with a three-day booking, and to only just over $21 a night with a week's block booking ($150). A double with kitchenette costs $200 a week (will negotiate rate if two couples want to share). Plusher rooms in adjacent building start at $60 a night. No lifts.

Moderate

RADISSON EMPIRE
44 W 63rd St (at Broadway), NY 10023. Tel. 212 265 7400. Fax 212 315 0349.
5 and 7 bus to Lincoln Center or B, D, 1 or 9 subway to Columbus Circle. The hotel is the single limestone-and-red-brick 1923 building with a Deco copper and neon sign at the Broadway–Columbus junction.
The rather small rooms don't live up to the amazing high lobby, which has eighteenth-century Beauvais tapestry and a painting of Ellen Terry as Lady Macbeth on the wall, but they're perfectly comfortable. There is a dark wood-panelled lounge with snooker, chess and regal striped armchairs where you can enjoy complimentary breakfast and the morning papers. The neighbourhood is statistically one of the safest in New York, and with only one entrance the hotel is good on security. When taking a cab back, bear in mind that it's most commonly known as 'the Empire' and expect musicians for fellow guests because it's opposite the Lincoln Center. The newly renovated 375 rooms have 'European' decor, which means lush flowery bedspreads and prints of landscapes on the walls. Suites have jacuzzi baths, which sound flash but are just a bit frothy. The informal grill restaurant with windows on to the street is a popular place for pre- and post-theatre suppers. Prices range from $120 standard to $450 for a deluxe suite.

Upper East Side

The area offers proximity to Museum Mile and the possibility of a park view. It is mainly very posh, and therefore safe.

Moderate

THE BARBIZON HOTEL
140 E 63rd St (at Lexington Ave), NY 10021. Tel. 212 838 5700. Fax 212 753 0360.
O or P subway to 63rd St, which is directly across the street from the hotel; 101 or 102 bus to 63rd St. Vast Art Deco hotel with small revolving doors entrance.

This 1927 richly detailed dark brick wedding-cake-shaped building used to be a residential hotel for women with a list of residents including Candice Bergen, Gene Tierney and Grace Kelly. The rooms are on the small side and rather coyly redone in pastel pinks with cream MFI-type bedside cabinets, but they're all comfortable and still good for a woman alone. The twelve tower suite-apartments, which have terraces with spectacular views of the city (views that inspired painter Georgia O'Keeffe), are ideal for women with children. The lobby is quiet and rather romantic with an ivy mural on the ceiling and a balcony that could be a film set for *Romeo and Juliet*. It also has a small pharmacy in a booth. The bar, the bright Café Barbizon and the low-lighted wood-panelled restaurant are quick, easy places for guests to grab a bite before they go out on business, and they fill with exhausted shoppers during the day from nearby Bloomingdales. The meeting-room is a City Landmark, with a pipe organ, stained-glass windows and a fireplace. The hotel is convenient for Museum Mile. Bought in 1988 by the Morgan's Hotel Group (who also own the Royalton and the Paramount), it may get smartened up, in which case the prices will rise accordingly. Prices for singles start at $99 and for suites at $275.

HOTEL WALES
1295 Madison Ave (at 92nd St), NY 1028. Tel. 876 6000. Fax 212 860 7000.
6 subway to 96th St, walk west to Madison and south to 92nd; 1, 2, 3, 4 bus to 91st St, walk north one block up Madison. Take cabs at night at first. Look for the high windows of Sarabeth's restaurant, which is underneath, and for the griffin logo on the awning.

Oddly called a 'boutique hotel' for its homey European-style decor and for including breakfast and afternoon tea in the room price, the Wales is small and ideal for women alone, for groups of girlfriends, and for families. It's near bookshops, Museum Mile and Central Park, and the 92nd St Y has regular poetry readings and offers often fully booked summer programmes for children (see p.337). The Hotel Wales lobby is plush dusky rose and dark marble with a chandelier, and the reception desk is at the bottom of the stairs, which is good in terms of security. Original oak mouldings, including occasional beautiful fireplaces, continue through the hotel, but the rooms are only European-*style*, so the cabinets are teak-look and the bedspreads imitate William Morris. Comfortable, though, and clean. The lavish breakfast room has palms, a chess set in the corner, a grand piano and sometimes musical events in the evenings. Complimentary breakfast is tea, coffee, croissants and muffins. No restaurant, but Sarabeth's is literally underneath (see p.276). Rates start at $125 singles, and suites with sofa beds that will comfortably sleep four cost $225 or as little as $175 a night in the slow season.

Expensive

CARLYLE HOTEL
*35 E 76th St (at Madison Ave), NY
10021. Tel. 212 744 1600. Fax 212
717 4682.
6 subway to 77th St; 101 or 102 bus
to 77th St. Go west past Lennox Hill
Hospital to Madison and then south
one block to 76th. The 1929 hotel is
the only tall building around.*

'Home-away-from-home' for the
world's elite, this is constantly rated
the best luxury hotel in New York.
John F. Kennedy used to stay here,
and it still fills with jewel-laden
dowagers. It stands out partly because
all the decor is for real, with no
'influenced' or 'inspired by' qualifiers
for the antique Old Europe furniture
and paintings in each of the 190 one-
of-a-kind accessorised rooms. From
the street pass through a black-and-
white marble vestibule to the lobby,
which is resplendent with crystal wall
sconces. Above, the Carlyle Gallery –
which has Aubusson carpets, Gobelin
tapestries and Audubon portfolio
prints – is good for cocktails and
people watching; snack and listen to
pianist Bobby Short in the Café
Carlyle; relax with delightful, childlike
murals by Bemelman and a live jazz
pianist nightly over dinner in
Bemelman's Bar ($5 cover); or have an
elegant dinner at Carlyle Restaurant.
Prices start at $240 single and $265
double. Suites start at $475. In-house
health spa for use exclusively by guests
(includes sauna). Faxes in every room.
For less luxury in the same location at
lower prices, join women with
children at the Surrey (see p.251)

THE STANHOPE HOTEL
*995 5th Ave (at 81st St), NY 10028.
Tel. 212 288 5800. Fax 212 517
0088.*

*No question of arriving by public
transport: limos or Mercs only. Pale
sixteen-storey 1926 building.*

This is an incredible hotel, partly for
its clientele. Many women with
inherited money or Ivana Trump-
league alimony come here for
shopping on Madison Avenue, or to
fill up their West Coast mansions with
antiques from Christie's or Sotheby's,
and many monied New Yorkers stay
here while scars settle after Park
Avenue plastic surgery or while
recuperating after a visit to nearby
Sloane Kettering cancer hospital.
There are a lot of diamonds, designer
trainers, poodles and bandages in the
lobby, and tight security that is
welcome for any woman: the one
entrance is small, and the porters get
to know guests quickly; you can access
your floor from the lift only with a
key. The decor is Old French style,
including spangly Baccarat chandeliers
in the ornate lobby and 'Louis XVI-
inspired' furniture in the large rooms
where amenities include gold seals on
the toilet paper, Chanel shampoo,
Egyptian cotton bedsheets and laser
disc players. A Mercedes limo
chauffeurs entertainment industry
guests like Liza Minelli or Oliver
Stone around town for free. The
restaurant is generally considered
overrated, but the outdoor café, Le
Salon, is ideal for entertaining tea or
cocktails ($19.50 for afternoon tea, $7
for a Bloody Mary) after a visit to the
Metropolitan Museum, which is
practically opposite.
In-house fitness centre, and every
room has maps of jogging routes in
Central Park. Service can be snooty.
Prices range from $250 to $325
singles and doubles; suites start at
$400. Weekend packages available.

BUDGET: HOSTELS, B&B, AND A RELIGIOUS INSTITUTION

If you're budgeting but don't want bunk-bed communality, check out cheap hotels which can cost nearly the same and are often in better locations (e.g. Malibu Studios, see p.241, and for parties of two or more try Off-SoHo Suites, see p.230).

Chelsea

CHELSEA CENTER HOSTEL
313 W 29th St (bet. 8th and 9th Aves), NY 10001. Tel. 212 643 0214. C and E subway to 23rd St, walk north; No. 10 bus to 29th St. On a quiet, tree-lined street in a nice part of Chelsea (near Flower District, not too far from Greenwich Village). The hostel is the back ground-floor apartment of a six-storey red-brick building. Look for a hut and pine symbol on the row of buzzers.

Run by a churchgoer called Heidi, this is very Woodstock. The pine kitchen/lounge/office has a flowered handwritten notice with the words: 'Hi darlings, please, please tell us TODAY if you're staying tomorrow night.' Heidi warns South American and Japanese girls that the dorms are mixed but finds that no one else minds, and German youths come back again and again. You can book ahead or phone on spec, and if all the 20 bunks are taken Heidi will find you somewhere else. She says security isn't a problem because all guests become friends over the complimentary continental breakfast which in summer is eaten in the pretty walled backyard to the sounds of tinkering and the smells of exhaust from the nearby garage. There's no curfew and it's clean, but at the moment there's only one shower and it's off the kitchen. Bring your own bedding or use Heidi's. Guests are expected to make themselves scarce between 11 a.m. and 5 p.m., but Heidi will be in if they need to drop off or collect luggage. There are plenty of good delis and takeaways nearby. Winter rates of $17 run from approximately November to June (depending on business and how flush Heidi's feeling), and summer rates are $20, both including tax.

Murray Hill

COLONIAL HOUSE INN
*318 W 22nd St (bet. 8th and 9th Aves), NY 10011. Tel. 212 243 9669. Fax 212 633 1612.
6 subway to 23rd St, walk south to 22nd; 101 or 102 bus, to 22nd St. The building is one in a row of brownstones.*

This hotel is specifically for gays and lesbians: a 19-room home-away-from-home in a renovated brownstone decorated with the owner's paintings. You must book well in advance (for Gay Pride *at least* two months ahead). All rooms have phones and TVs and some have private baths, refrigerators and fireplaces. As well as a communal lounge there's a sundeck for summer. The area is respectable, convenient for Downtown, but after dark it can be a little seedy in some of the surrounding streets, so take cabs. Prices from $65 a night, tax included.

VANDERBILT YMCA

224 E 47th St (bet. 3rd and 2nd Aves), NY 10017. Tel. 212 755 2410. Fax 212 752 0210.
6 subway to 51st St, east to 3rd Ave and south to 47th; 101 or 102 bus to 47th St. As you turn from 3rd Avenue into 47th St you'll see a mural of a blond child in a window and know you're on the right track. The YMCA is a huge red-brick H-shape and has lots of milling backpackers at the discreet front door.

The plaque outside explains: 'Our mission: the YMCA of greater New York is a community-based service organization dedicated to building the mind, body and spirit of New Yorkers, and the quality of life in New York city . . . [serving] women and men of all ages with a focus on youth.'

It's a bit highfalutin for what you get, which is overworked bad-tempered staff, nailed-down TVs with fixed volumes, and a dark-brown, deep-purple and hessian 1970s decor that continues from the lobby through all floors. The reception is 24 hours, check-in time is 1 p.m., you must provide ID that proves home address, you have to pay a $10 key deposit if you want a locker, there's a friendly security guard in the foyer, the third floor has vending machines (hot and cold drinks and snacks), and the diner opposite has big breakfasts for $4. There could be more women's bathrooms – the whole third floor, for example, has only one with two toilets, one shower cubicle and a large washbasin area, so prepare to queue. Daily rates are $21 a night per person for quad rooms with bunk beds, $24 –$29 for double rooms with bunk beds and $38–$48 for a single room with a single bed. Special group rates are available (this is a favourite location for art schools bringing students to Museum Mile).

Upper West Side

AYH HOSTEL

891 Amsterdam Ave (bet. 103rd and 104th Sts), NY 10025. Tel. 212 932 2300. Fax 212 932 2574.
When you first arrive you'd be wise to take a cab, as backpacks and suitcase will make you easy prey if you stray accidentally below 103rd St. Cabs at night too. Otherwise, take 1 or 9 subway to 103rd St, walk north one block then east; 11 bus to 104th St; stop is right outside. You can't miss this pinnacled sprawling Gothic monstrosity that takes up a whole block. The main entrance is just below

street level, down a ramp.

This is far better than the YMCA, despite its location in an area that's a mixture of Riverside Drive posh and Columbia studenty to the north, and grim projects below 103rd Street. Keep north of 103rd Street and below Columbia University (which borders Harlem) and you shouldn't encounter any problems. The hostel itself is good on security, with individual key cards for each dorm, and a friendly we're-all-mates-together atmosphere that makes in-house theft unlikely.
Built by Richard Morris Hunt in

1883, this wacky Preserved Landmark was originally the Association Residence for Respectable Aged Indigent Females – that is, a last resting place for war widows, governesses and maids who 'once enjoyed a good degree of affluence, but [are] now reduced to poverty by the vicissitudes of Providence'. Conditions of entry to the asylum included that the gentlewoman be non-Roman Catholic, that she pay $150 and that she surrender any property. In 1965 the building was bought by the City and today it is tastefully remodelled to display original arches and brickwork in the corridors. Dorms are clean, sparse, white and newly furnished with pine bunks. Bathrooms have dressing cubicles with each shower. The bustling lobby has a table laden with information that includes free or very cheap ($5) tours of various parts of the city. There's no curfew, 24-hour reception, and the hostel is open throughout the day. Facilities include a very nice enclosed outdoor red-brick patio where you can take snacks and chat, a basement cafeteria for breakfast, a kitchen well equipped with stoves and fridges, a games room where many of the free programme of activities take place, and a common room with TV, piano and full bookshelves. Staff are jolly and helpful, and there's a tendency amongst youth staying to make friends. Lots of Australians all year round, Japanese and South Americans early spring, and Europeans in the summer. Rates are $20 per person (tax included) for a bunk in a medium-sized dorm. Four-bedded family rooms are available for $60 a night. Add $3 per night to all prices if you are not a member of the American Youth Hostel Association.

HEPZIBAH HOUSE

51 W 75th St (bet. Columbus–Central Park West), NY 10023. Tel. 212 787 6150.
B and C subway to 72nd St, walk north to 75th St; 10 bus to 75th St. Hepzibah is a century-old five-storey brownstone on a quiet tree-lined street. It is a religious hostel, not in the business of attracting custom, so the only sign is tiny, by the buzzer. Walk up the steps and ring with confidence.

This is a guesthouse for Christian missionaries and any Christian person travelling through the city (no proof required). The history is worth a mention. Founded in 1893 to provide a home for Christian women and working girls who needed instruction in the Bible, Hepzibah House soon became the headquarters of the Young Ladies' Christian League run by Virginia Field, a young and beautiful socialite who found the Lord at the age of thirty and threw herself into both charity work and reaching Jewish people for Christ. She also pioneered teaching in prisons, establishing a programme still known today as 'Mrs Field's Bible Class'. Mrs Field died in 1922, but the house and its function as a guesthouse continued. The original stained-glass and dark-wood-panelled hall takes you into a time warp. The living-room-cum-reception is dominated by the original marble fireplace, and religious literature is laid out on a central table. You'll find Victorian forest green and gold wallpaper, lacy curtains and a 1940s radio in the lounge (the TV is not hooked up). Up the creaky stairs, each floor's spotless bathroom has a stone sink with metal legs and a black-and-white-tiled floor. Most rooms are painted, but some have tasteful wallpaper. Most have old-fashioned brass or wood bedsteads, and some have original fireplaces. There are pay-phones on the landing, you can change up to $50 of traveller's cheques in US dollars, there's no curfew and although check-in should be during daylight hours, staff do live in so can be roused in an emergency. There are lots of places to eat at all hours on Columbus, from Moroccan to burger and fries. Hepzibah is perfect for the woman alone who wants peace, security and beautiful surroundings. Book ahead if you can, as there are only twelve rooms. Charges are $35 per night single and $60 per night for a married couple (proof necessary).

WEST SIDE YMCA
5 West 63rd St (off Broadway), NY 10023. Tel. 212 787 4400. Fax 212 580 0441.
1 and 9 subway to 59th St–Columbus Circle, walk north up Broadway to the red neon sign for the Radisson Empire, where you turn east down 63rd St; 7, 5, 104 bus to Lincoln Center, walk east down 63rd St. Big rambly old 1930s building.

Come here only if the Vanderbilt Y is full, or if you're after 'character' over cleanliness. The echoey stone lobby with a porter stranded in a wooden box near the door looks as if it should be in a B-horror movie. Make sure you see your room before you take it, as some can be made homely and in others the dingy yellow paintwork is dinged further, the radiators are flaking, the splash 1970s curtains are ripped and the dark lino floors are curling. The corridors are stale-smelling and the lifts are dodgy. Pluses include a sports centre and a City-wide respected series of readings, Writer's Voice. Same conditions and rates as at the Vanderbilt YMCA (see above).

B&B
Bed and Breakfast, a fast growing market, is not necessarily a cheaper way of staying in New York than hotels, but B&B can feel safer and more homely if you're a woman alone.

AT HOME IN NEW YORK
PO Box 407, New York, NY 10185. (Tel. 212 956 3125. Fax. 212 247 3294.

This agency promises 'a new concept in urban hospitality'. It started in the '60s when a small town Massachusetts girl 'with stars in my eyes' and 'hopes of making it' in the musical theatre took occasional Bed and Breakfasters to subsidise her rounds of auditions and coaching sessions – the B&B took over. Now Lois Rooks matches 'artists and professional people' with 'gracious hosts' who 'enjoy sharing their own special secrets and knowledge of New York', in townhouses, apartments and lofts all over Manhattan Island. No reservation will be secured without a deposit, which must be paid at least a week in advance by cheque (US dollars only) or money order. The guest reservation form asks if you have any allergies and asks for 2 character references. Prices go from $50–$80 single and $60–$125 double and from $75–$250 for unhosted apartments.

BED AND BREAKFAST NETWORK
134 West 32nd Street NY, NY 10001. Tel. 212 645 8143.

B&B Network is one of the largest organisations of its kind in New York.

Few of the hosts will expect you to breakfast with them, so the B&B Network can offer a welcome degree of privacy. The Network represents 150 properties, all inspected personally by the president of the organisation for cleanliness, comfort and hospitality. They send you a form on which you can specify amongst other things no-smoking, an artist's loft or a brownstone, and the Network will match you up. If they have not satisfied the criterion laid out on your form, the organisation will relocate you. Deposit of 25% to be paid in advance, balance to be paid on arrival by cash or travellers cheque directly to host. Rates single (staying with host) from $50, (without host) from $70; double (with host) from $80, (without host) from $120. Whole apartments can go from $80–$150.

WOMEN WITH CHILDREN

Women with children find New York accommodation a nightmare because friends' apartments are usually too tiny to stay in, and in terms of both price and amenities hotels are geared towards business travellers. Here are some tips on beating the system. When you phone hotels, always ask about family discounts, which are rarely advertised; remember that cheap rates during holidays and weekends can make expensive hotels affordable; note that suite hotels have living-room space for children to run around in, they usually give you the lowest bill at the end (child goes on sofa bed without extra charge) and their kitchens sidestep reels of room-service charges; hotels with swimming pools are rare but will keep children happy (try **Holiday Inn Crowne Plaza** p.240, **Le Parker Meridian**, p.232, **Vista International**, p.231). If you aren't in a suite with sofa-bed space and you don't want your child in your bed, a note on terminology: cots are called cribs, and if you ask for a cot you'll get a spare bed, and if you want a spare bed you must ask for a rollaway. All moderate to expensive hotels can arrange babysitting services. As well as the ones below, see p.235 for the Gramercy and p.236 for the Grand Hyatt.

Cheap

HOTEL EXCELSIOR
45 W 81st St (at Columbus Ave), NY 10024. Tel. 212 362 9200. Fax 212 721 2994.
B and C subway to 81st St–Natural History St; 7 bus to 81st St. Big gloomy old building off boutique-filled Columbus Avenue and opposite the side of the Natural History Museum.

This hotel has suites for as low as $99 a night, two-bedroom suites for $130, and single occupancy from $65. The big lobby has cheap wood panelling, a white and gold bevel-panelled ceiling with 1970s leather-look black armchairs and a morello-fern green swirling carpet with clocks over the reception showing different times around the world. The 6.30 a.m.–10.30 p.m. café off the lobby is filled with booths, formica and Muzak and is open 7 days a week for cheap diner food in an otherwise pricey area (quiche with soup or salad for $4.50).

ACCOMMODATION

The 150 rooms and suites are also 1970s-tack furnished – with old silver radiators, pale blue fluffy carpets, flower-on mirror pictures, and plastic-wood-imitating wicker furniture – but they're clean and fairly spacious, with TVs and phones in all. Twenty-four hour reception, mixture of sharp and friendly staff. Value for money, not gloss. The area is safe and quiet, near Central Park, the Natural History Museum and the Children's Museum of Manhattan, and only fifteen minutes from Downtown Manhattan by subway.

Moderate

HOTEL BEVERLY

125 E 50th St (at Lexington Ave), NY 10022. Tel. 212 753 2700. Fax 212 753 2700 ext. 48.
6 subway to 51st St, walk one block south down Lexington; 101 or 102 bus to 51st St, walk one block south down Lexington: 197-room hotel has big blue neon sign down the Lexington–50th St junction side.

This centrally located family-owned all suite hotel has a live-in concierge and a 24-hour drugstore that has pretty much everything a hassled mother might emergency-buy, from junior aspirin to cheap greasy donuts. The spacious dark-wood lobby has a porter in front of the elevators, which is good for security. The civil but unexciting restaurant is linked to a piano bar where a woman alone might not feel comfortable in the evenings. Ask for a room on an upper level, as the lower ones can be noisy. Expect a basic room with old-fashioned light pulls in the walk-in cupboards and the favourite generic decor style of New York hotels: Old European (i.e. William Morris-style bedspreads). As in most hotels, you'll be surrounded

by mainly business clientele, but here a lot are from the former USSR on missions to the UN. The policy on charging for children seems to be arbitrary depending on the time of year, the age of the child, and the mood of the proprietors rather than on whether an extra rollaway is necessary. Prices for singles in junior suites start at $149 and go up to $450 for big suites.

MANHATTAN EAST SUITE HOTELS

Manhattan East Suites is a chain of nine suite hotels, none dirt-cheap, all good value. Tell head office your needs in terms of location and price range (500 West 37th St, NY 10018-1103, tel. 212 465 3600, fax 212 465 3663) and they'll fit you up with the most appropriate property. Typical clients range from UN dignitaries at **Beekman Tower** to international airline crews at **Eastgate** and tourists from South America at the **Plaza 50**. Regular prices at **Southgate Tower** (near the Jacob K. Javits convention centre, where you should take cabs at night) start from as low as $90, and holiday rates can bring costs in all hotels down to $62.50 'Icebreakers' a night. See p.236 for the Beekman Tower Hotel, or try one of the following.

SHELBURNE MURRAY HILL

303 Lexington Ave (at 37th St), NY 10016. Tel. 212 689 5200. Fax 212 779 7068.
6 subway to 33rd St, walk east to Lexington and north to 37th; bus 101 and 102 to 37th St. The thirteen-storey red-brick building has balconies on the top levels that taper to a one-window pinnacle.

Notable features include proximity to the Pierpont Morgan Library Museum and the Empire State, wrought-iron balconies with views of the Chrysler building from some rooms, and a romantic rooftop garden that is now used for afternoon tea and weddings but used to be Fred Astaire's favourite lunchtime golfing spot. The lobby has a marble fireplace, antique clocks and crystal chandeliers. The spacious 258 suites are also refurbished Old Europe, with William Morris-style bedspreads and brass lamps, and American walk-in wardrobes. Ballard's Chowderhouse and Grill serves 14 different chowders and home-made buttermilk biscuits to a lively mixture of hotel guests and businessmen and women from the area. In-house fitness centre featuring sauna and steam room. Prices start at $180 for a single suite to between $200 and $415 for a two-bedroom suite.

SURREY HOTEL

20 East 76th St (at Madison Ave), NY 10021. Tel. 212 288 3700. Fax 212 628 1549.
6 subway to 77th St; 101 or 102 bus to 77th St. Go west past Lennox Hill Hospital to Madison and then south one block to 76th. Look for the named awning.

Families visiting New York for special occasions like this hotel for its exclusive location at about $100 less per night than other hotels in the area. Central Park and Museum Mile are half a block away; it's a safe, quiet neighbourhood. In 1926 the Surrey was a residential hotel favoured by widows of 'robber baron' financiers who found the Surrey's servants and ready-made grandeur a relief after rattling around in Fifth Avenue mansions (such as the Frick [see p.163]). Today it is refurbished in eighteenth-century English style, including crystal sconces, leather sofas, wood-panelled elevators in the marble lobby and moulded ceilings and bevelled mirrors in the spacious elegant suites. Its French restaurant, Les Pléiades, serves Madison Avenue art dealers as well as Surrey guests and has a flower-bordered outdoor patio for summer. Also good for businesswomen travelling alone. Rates range from $205 for a single studio suite (no living-room) to $500–$580 for a two-bedroom suite.

EATING AND DRINKING

EATING

Eating out in New York can be a problem, because there's so much choice. Restaurants reflect the city's diversity of immigrants, so you can eat pretty much any cuisine under the sun, and it's almost bound to be of high quality and reasonably priced, because many New Yorkers simply don't eat at home. Their fridges are empty, bar cranberry juice and donuts; if they do shake off convention and host a dinner, all the food is pre-cooked and bought from Zabar's or Balducci. Consequently the exceedingly expensive restaurants are not patronised only by executives with expense accounts. It's a hobby for New Yorkers occasionally to blow vast sums on special meals – which brings us to the importance of knowing what restaurant and type of cuisine is 'in'. Chanterelle and Bouley serve similar food at similarly exclusive prices, but Bouley is slightly more 'in' than Chanterelle. Mexican was 'in', but now it's Thai. You may decide you don't care what's 'in', you just want an enjoyable evening (Chanterelle is actually nicer than Bouley). Location might be your priority, in which case you can base your restaurant choice on observations made during a quick walk up and down a street: the full restaurant is good, the empty one is not. Or you can buy the New Yorker's restaurant bible: *Zagat New York City Restaurant Survey* for $9.95, updated annually. Just ask for 'Zagat's' in any bookshop, and make sure to look in the back for the 'special appeals' breakdowns, which include 'in places', 'power scenes', 'eating alone', 'quiet conversations' and 'singles scenes'. A cheaper alternative is to look in the restaurant reviews and listings in papers and magazines including *The Paper, Village Voice* and on Friday, look in the *New York Times* 'Weekday' section, which selects a few '$25 and Under' restaurants.

On every corner you'll find at least one pushcart selling cheap snacks (hot dogs, pretzels, ice creams, falafels); on practically every block you'll find diners and delis where you can stoke up on cheap burger dinners and bagel breakfasts. The recession has kept prices down and pushed most restaurants to offer *prix fixe* menus, and you should look out for bargain pre-theatre menus (both are listed in *Zagat*). In general, the cheaper cuisines tend to be American diner food, pizza parlours, Chinese, Mexican and Eastern European. The expensive food is often French nouvelle. Those of you who eat fish but not meat can have wonderful meals in most places, but strict vegetarians will find most menus limiting. Ask the chef to rustle you up a customised order, or try one of the few vegetarian restaurants (see listings below). Although they are not exclusively vegetarian, the growing number of 'natural' restaurants serve a lot of vegetables and only free-range white meat. Weight-watchers are well catered for. Even the very poshest restaurants have pink packets of Sweet 'n' Low on the table and serve Diet Coke to dynamic business-women; chefs pride themselves on producing sinful-looking chocolate desserts with tiny calorie counts. If you're breastfeeding, pick places with mezzanine levels, booths and, in the summer, outdoor areas. Children are generally welcome, but for your pleasure and theirs try to avoid peak lunch and dinner times. You won't find many booster seats, but waiters will improvise, for example by stacking a chair with Manhattan Yellow Pages; changing areas are few and far between, so be prepared to make do with the basin in the rest room; children's menus are rare – share or ask the chef to do small portions. If you're a party of two or more, in mid-priced restaurants the bill will be put somewhere in the middle of the table, but in expensive restaurants, despite the huge number of business-women in New York on expense accounts, the bill will be handed to the man. Women eating alone won't have a problem Downtown, but might feel a little awkward in some Mid- or Uptown places. It's not that you'll be fighting off unwanted attentions – far from it. You might have to fight *for* attention from key people: the waiters. Be loud, be brusque, be confident, and perhaps take a book as a prop. Coffee shops, sushi bars, hotel restaurants and places with counter service are all good fallbacks for women dining alone, and restaurants with live entertainment are highly enjoyable for women alone – for example Lola's, Knickerbocker Bar and Grill and the Rainbow Rooms. A wise guide against purse-snatching is to strap your bag either over your knee or under your chair leg while you're eating.

Remember that New York is all about convenience – have food delivered. If you're in a hotel and don't want to use room service, ask at reception for names of places that deliver; if you're in an apartment, *Zagat* lists places that deliver and you can look in the Yellow Pages under 'Foods – Carry Out'.

RESTAURANT HIT LIST

Cheap
Veniero's – superb pastries (see p.265)
Cowgirl Hall of Fame – heaven-sent for women with children (see p.263)
Mogador – excellent Moroccan food (see p.266)
Moderate
Aggie's – wonderful SoHo version of the American diner (see p.257)
Oyster Bar – magnificent sea food in a great setting (see p.273)
Lola – unmissable for the Gospel brunch experience (see p.269)
Expensive
Arcadia – delicious experimental food (see p.278)
Four Seasons – for watching New York's power-lunchers (see p.274)
Chanterelle – ideal for a romantic evening (see p.256)
Le Cirque – consistently divine cuisine (see p.279)

DOWNTOWN

Financial District

Lunch here is lively (Wall Street crowds), but early evening stick to South Street Seaport, and after hours – with the exception of Le Pactole for a special occasion – avoid the area, when offices empty and it's bare and unappealing.

Sweet Treats

MINTER'S ICE CREAM KITCHEN
South Street Seaport, Pier 17 (third level), tel. 608 2037. Open till midnight all week. 2 or 3 subway to Fulton St, or 15 bus to Fulton St. Walk to the end of the cobbled part of South Street Seaport and look for a pier with shops and the words 'Pier 17' all over it.

You've kept the kids happy with the Seaport – now send them to heaven with rich home-made ice cream in 16 different flavours including kahlua-and-cream (all made on the premises) from this informal ice-cream stand.

Restaurants: American

FRAUNCES TAVERN
54 Pearl St (at Broad St) tel. 269 0144. M subway to Broad St; 6 and 15 bus. You can't miss it because it's the only square Georgian building around. Closed weekends and at 10.30 p.m. during the week.

Appeals to Japanese businessmen and New Yorkers hankering for a traditional night out. Colonial food, which predated fridges and therefore tends to be stewed and preserved in salt or molasses, is served on pewter plates at thick wood tables in a dark-panelled room. Get the Complete Colonial Repast (Clam Chowder, Planked Chatham Sole and Apple Crunch) for $17.76, or pay around $30 a head à la carte. Dull for children.

CELLAR IN THE SKY
1 World Trade Center, 107th floor, West St (bet. Liberty and Vesey Sts), tel. 938 1111. 1 or 9 subway to

Cortland St; 6 bus to Liberty St. You can't miss the soaring twin towers of the World Trade Center. Just look up – you're there.

This hasn't got the uninterrupted spectacular view the Windows on the World Restaurant is famous for, but the food's better and it has an exceptional wine selection, much of which is displayed as decor around the room wine-cellar style. For the $80 'Continental' *prix fixe* meal you get five fine wines with seven courses that might include sea urchin, foie gras and baked loin of lamb in salt crust with pickled lime. Only 36 seats – reservations essential for this favourite on the fine-dining circuit.

Seafood

SLOPPY LOUIE'S
92 South St (bet. Fulton and John Sts), tel. 509 9694. 2 or 3 subway to Fulton St, or 15 bus to Fulton St. Walk to the end of the cobbled part of South Street Seaport and Sloppy Louie's is on the corner, just in front of the overhead expressway.

This lost its 'sloppiness' – and some of its appeal – when it was spruced up with the Seaport, but Sloppy Louie's still serves fish dishes good enough to satisfy any fishmonger. Linen tablecloths; plain surroundings; pay around $25 a head before wine.

French

LE PACTOLE
2 World Financial Center, 2nd Level of the Winter Gardens, 225 Liberty St, tel. 945 9444. Take a cab or the 9 or 10 bus to Liberty St. At the end of Liberty St, walk towards the Hudson River; the path will take you left and into the Winter Gardens, which

houses huge palm trees.

This elegantly designed, intimate restaurant offers a wonderful view of the Hudson framed by ruched drapes. Strains of a piano waft in from the marble cocktail lounge while cooing lovers and off-duty executives savour menu highlights including Sweetbread Terrine appetiser and Rotisserie Roasted Game entrée (average price: $90 for two before wine). Proprietor Romeo de Gobbi ensures a relaxed atmosphere with quiet, attentive service. A gourmet takeaway service caters for corporations that want employees working through lunch. Leave your children behind, unless you're treating the family to the informal *prix fixe* ($26.50) brunch all day Sunday. Possible to stop off in the lounge for high tea or cocktails.

Civic Center

Breakfast and Snacks

ELLEN'S CAFÉ AND BAKE SHOP
270 Broadway (at Chambers St), tel. 962 1257. 4 or 5 subway to City Hall–Brooklyn Bridge; 1 or 6 bus to City Hall. Once at big grey beaux-arts City Hall you only have to walk round it till you've found the Broadway–Chambers St junction. Closed Sunday.

This workaday coffee shop was founded by a former Miss Subway, Ellen, who has lined the walls with 1950s photos of other Miss Subways, and she hosts an annual reunion. Everyone from cleaners to the mayor pop over from City Hall to hunch at a 'station' for lunch and pecan pie coffee breaks. Pay around $7 for a club sandwich (try the Mayor's Special – muffins with tuna, tomato and melted cheese).

EATING AND DRINKING

Cab it in, cab it out along with a chic maturer crowd. Fine during the day, but don't wander at night, not so much because it's dangerous but because it's bleak and rather eerie.

Breakfast and Snacks

ROYAL CANADIAN RESTAURANT AND PANCAKE HOUSE
145 Hudson St (bet. Beach and Hubert Sts), tel. 219 3038. 1 or 9 subway to Franklin St; 10 bus to Hubert St. Open daily 7 a.m.–7 p.m.

With booster seats available, nappy-changing area, 54 varieties of pancake and *rivers* of maple syrup, this place is definitely children-friendly, but be warned – at weekends families will queue round the block. Eighteen-and-a-half-inch pancakes and single 'womelettes' (stuffed pancake-cum-omelettes) will easily fill two people. Pay $9 for a breakfast and $16 lunch.

Restaurants: American

TRIBECA GRILL
375 Greenwich St (at Franklin St), tel. 941 3900. Take a cab.

The food is rarely mentioned – this restaurant is part-owned by Robert De Niro. His dad's pictures adorn the open brick walls; his film production centre fills the rest of this 1906 coffee warehouse. Young hopefuls pose at the wooden bar before taking a table between green industrial pipes and paying around $45 each for bistro-style food (roast monkfish, sautéed red snapper) in the hope that they'll be spotted – if not by Bob himself, then maybe by one of the restaurant's other investors, who include Sean Penn and Mikhail Baryshnikov.

CHANTERELLE
6 Harrison St (at Hudson St), tel. 966 6960. Take a cab. Closed Sun and Mon. Reservations required.

Chanterelle remains one of New York's most sought-after dinner reservations, and for good reason. A formal yet relaxed atmosphere is ensured in the sparsely elegant dining area by Karen Waltuck, one of the city's very few female maître d's, while her husband David creates. She has a PR background; he graduated in Marine Biology before experimenting in the kitchen and winning acclaim as an untainted chef-genius. The seafood sausages and potato ravioli lure hardened uptowners down to what was once TriBeCa's old Mercantile Exchange Building. Unusual amount of space between tables; nice touches include a gigantic flower arrangement at one end of the Naples Yellow room and original menu covers by contemporary artists. Bargain $30 *prix fixe* lunch, or $70 for dinner before wine.

Cajun

HOWS BAYOU
355 Greenwich St (at Harrison St), tel. 925 5405. 1 or 9 subway to Franklin St; 6 bus to Leonard St. Walk towards the river; take cabs at night.

Children-friendly during the day, but not at night when it's throbbing with pop music and the whooping sounds of young yuppies soused on frozen margaritas. Half portions available on some dishes; if they're not, just share. The nachos chips baked with cheese and black beans for $5.95 will serve a family as a starter. Average entrées cost $10 and there's a minimum $15 per adult charge at lunch and dinner time. Airy with open brick walls and green pillars, and a limited but pleasant view of the river.

Mostly Vegetarian

NOSMO KING
54 Varick St (at Canal St), tel. 966

1239. A, C and E subway to Canal St; 6 bus to Grand St. At night catch cabs, as it's at a rather barren junction.

Nosmo King – No Smoking – geddit? And the rules are enforced: no meat, and No Smoking. Typically TriBeCa, it's a rather self-conscious restaurant ('haute organic'!!?) but still pleasant, and it is good food. An arty crowd toys with exotic mushrooms, seared tuna and dairy-less desserts. Around $36 for one.

SoHo

Come here daytimes during the week to mix with itinerant trendies plus gallery and trendy shop-owners from the neighbourhood. During the weekends it's more tourists and out-of-towners.

Breakfast and Snacks

AGGIE'S
146 W Houston St (at MacDougal St), tel. 673 8994. 1, 2, 3 subway to 14th St or 6 subway to Spring St; 5 bus.

Superb for anyone, any time of day – but expect to queue, for this homey formica-and-plastic-decorated diner is always packed. The $6.95 smoked mozzarella, pesto and roast pepper sandwich is popular, and for breakfast there's salmon and sour cream omelette for $7.95. Owner Aggie Markowitz, who's the very 1970s woman with short wisping hair and heavily mascara-ed lashes sipping coffee over by the counter, seems to have attracted a lesbian cult following as well as the regular SoHo crowd.

CUPPING ROOM CAFÉ
359 W Broadway (bet. Broome and Grand Sts), tel. 925 2898. 1, 2, 3 subway to 14th St or 6 subway to

Spring St; 5 bus.

Antique bar, pot-bellied stove, exposed brickwork and skylight, fluffy cappuccinos, fragrant teas and rather heavy muffins. Bit touristy but very pleasant to come for live jazz at weekends – arrive early to get a place (no reservations) and expect to pay around $20 for a big brunch.

DEAN AND DELUCCA CAFÉ
121 Prince St (bet. Greene and Wooster Sts), tel. 254 8776. R subway to Prince St or 6 subway to Spring St; 1 bus.

Swish cappuccino-and-fancy-cakes café. White brickwork, slowly rotating ceiling fans, spurting green pot plants, newspapers for your convenience and beautiful people posed on high stools in expensively roughed-up leather jackets for visual stimulation. Considered 'very SoHo'. Inconspicuous entrance belies space out back.

MOONDANCE DINER

80 6th Ave (at Grand St), tel. 226 1191. Open to midnight and 24 hours at weekends. A, C and E subway to Canal Street; 6 bus to Grand St. At night catch cabs, as it's at a big, barren junction.

Trendy version of the classic American diner in a chrome caravan with a revolving neon moon on top. Inside it's cramped and friendly. The decor is 1950s style (plastic glitter bar stools and pounding jukebox). Good for brunch – the cinnamon-spiced coffee comes in a metal pitcher and French toast is two-inch-thick challah bread drowned in maple syrup and melted strawberry butter. The artichoke and Jarlsberg omelettes are popular ($6.95). Children love it here, and the chef will do small portions on request. Look out on the way to the very small toilet for the Italo Calvino 'Invisible City' quote on the wall. Sometimes has early-evening happy hour (cheap beer).

Restaurants: American

JERRY'S

101 Prince St (bet. Mercer and Greene Sts), tel. 966 9464. R subway to Prince St or 6 subway to Spring St; 1 bus.

Brunch, lunch or dinner, this is considered 'very SoHo'. It's done out in postmodern diner style: big red tulips sprout in windowboxes and zebra-skin motif covers stools and walls, while the plastic booths and chrome bar are classic America. The menu is typical of a cuisine that is peculiar to New York and could be described as 'nouvelle-organic'. Try for starters a fashionably small amount of beet carpaccio with arrugula and parmesan salad for $5; and for main course, a slither of free-range chicken breast in red wine with

eggplant, olives and roasted tomatoes for $13. 'Sides' are extra ($3.50 for fries). Watch gallery-owners flick newspapers imperiously at lunch and impoverished neighbourhood artists break the bank over dinner.

GREENE STREET RESTAURANT

101 Greene St (bet. Prince and Spring Sts), tel. 925 2415. R subway to Prince St or 6 subway to Spring St; 1 bus.

Once a truck warehouse, this 40-foot-high space with exposed brickwork and tropical plants is now a chic place to hear jazz while eating elaborate dishes that include poached eggs in puff pastry, filet mignon in truffle Madeira sauce and a not-to-be-missed sundae of honey-caramel ice cream topped with pistachios. Dinner for two will come to around $70 before wine. Good place for a romantic brunch.

French

JOUR ET NUIT

337 West Broadway (corner of Grand St), tel. 925 5971. 1, 2, 3 subway to 14th St or 6 subway to Spring St; 5 bus to Grand St.

Clientele described variously as 'Euro-trash' and 'style-conscious twenty-something businesswomen' at this intimate bistro (small tables, swathing curtains) that's so 'in' it might soon be out. Service can be snippy. Estimate about $35 per head (rabbit with salsify entrée costs $17, and there's pesto-zapped shellfish soup at $8).

Eastern European

TRIPLET'S ROUMANIAN

11–17 Grand St (at 6th Ave), tel. 925 9303. Closed Mon; reservations required. A, C and E subway to Canal

St; 6 bus (to Grand St). At night catch cabs, as it's at a big, barren junction.

Rollicking party atmosphere every day and night. Singing waiters and waitresses make stuffed cabbage and professional egg creams 'as good as grandma's' at your table. Known for its big portions, chopped liver, and owners' story: the Roumanian triplet brothers were separated at birth and reunited at the age of nineteen. Pay about $40. Good entertainment for a woman alone.

Ethiopian

ABYSSINIA
35 Grand St (at Thompson St), tel. 226 5959. A, C and E subway to Canal St; 6 bus (to Grand St). Pass the chrome Moondance Diner with a neon moon on top and turn down Grand St. At night catch cabs.

Grasscloth wallpaper, African instruments and handicrafts for decor; patrons shed New York snootiness to eat with their fingers, perched on three-legged stools. Separate vegetarian selection, and – unusually for New York – if they say spicy, they mean spicy (cool your throat with beer). The most popular dish is ye'beg alitcha, a beef stew with a hint of ginger in the hot red pepper sauce called berbere. Finish off with a glass of sweet Ethiopian honey wine and pay about $20 a head.

Mostly Vegetarian

BELL CAFFE
310 Spring St (at Renwick St), tel. 334 BELL. Most nights open till 2 a.m., weekends till 4 a.m., closed Mon. 1 or 9 subway to Houston St; 10 bus to Spring St. Look out for the Fire Station when you've turned off Varick

St on to Spring, and go past it. Look for a sign with a bell motif.

A New Age scene that's pulled a young arty crowd. The decor is appealingly wacky (starfish mosaic, 3-D elaborately framed picture of Jesus); incense wafts about under the moulded tin ceiling; sounds of Marvin Gaye and reggae; a small outdoor yard for summer – oh yes, and the food: not brilliant but cheap. The Spread 'n' Bread Combo (hummus and dips enough for four as a starter) checks in at $7.50, and a main-dish Stir Fry is $7.50.

SPRING STREET NATURAL RESTAURANT
62 Spring St (at Lafayette St), tel. 966 0290. No reservations. R subway to Prince St or 6 subway to Spring St; 1 bus to Spring St.

An airy restaurant known for 'imaginative' vegetarian dishes that include pumpkin ravioli, steamed Brussels sprouts under Jarlsberg, garlic-ginger stir-fried vegetables, and many fish dishes. Lots of plants, fans and windows make this a pleasant spot for hippies, yuppies, artists and students, despite the generally indifferent service. Expect bills of around $24 a head.

SOUEN DOWNTOWN
210 6th Ave (at Prince St), tel. 807 7421. 1, 2, 3 subway to 14th St or 6 subway to Spring St; 5 bus to Prince St.

Japanese influence to the airy, pretty room and also to the sometimes bizarre menu that includes pounded sweet rice waffles and soba noodles. Some say the food is simple and well prepared; others say it is tasteless and stodgy and attracts neurotics. Whichever, if you're macrobiotic, it's one of the few places you can eat. Costs around $21 per head.

Too many restaurants to mention! and really, to make the most of Chinatown you should enjoy the fun of wandering the bustling streets and picking your own – there's Southern Chinese, Vietnamese, Thai, Cantonese, Shanghai, Hunan and more. Things to bear in mind: price usually reflects the decor rather than the food quality (formica tables for cheap; tablecloths for expensive); cheaper places won't take credit cards; nearly all Chinese restaurants love children; and dim sum on a Sunday is *a must* – go with a gang and pile food on the table to share.

Sweet Treats

CHINATOWN ICE CREAM FACTORY
65 Bayard St (nr Mott St), tel. 608 4170. B and D subway to Grand St; 101 and 102 bus.

A must for children – coconut, red-bean and green-tea ice cream.

Restaurants: Oriental

THAILAND RESTAURANT
106 Bayard St (at Baxter St), tel. 349 3132. B and D subway to Grand St; 101 and 102 bus. Off the beaten track – at night take cabs.

A favourite tacky lunch-break spot for those on jury duty because it's so near the Civic Center, but – after uncritical jurors – opinions vary wildly from 'best in New York' to 'inedible'. Tom Kah Gai (chicken and coconut soup) is a reliably good starter. The shrimp cooked in lime juice dish involves a lot of sweating and beer-swilling to cool the throat. The much-touted pad Thai noodles are not overhot, but some find them stodgy. Cheap – $20 a head or less.

GOLDEN UNICORN
18 E Broadway (at Catherine St), tel. 941 0911. B and D subway to Grand St; 101 and 102 bus. Off the beaten track – at night take cabs.

This sprawling opulent Chinese Palace is highly rated for its Cantonese food and a regular favourite for dim sum, which it serves every day from 8 a.m. to 4.30 p.m. Some complain about the crowds and walkie-talkie-wielding staff, but the value is considered good – about $25 a head for an evening meal, less for dim sum.

ORIENTAL PEARL
103–105 Mott St (bet. Canal and Hester Sts), tel. 219 8388. B and D subway to Grand St; 101 and 102 bus. In the heart of Chinatown.

You know it's authentic because this warehouse-sized cafeteria decorated with ceramic animals, coloured lights and dragons is always filled with Chinese families. Weekly shipments of food from Hong Kong. Any time of the week is good, but many think it *the* place for dim sum, when trolleys with parcels of steamed food stacked in bamboo cartons career past. You must be quick to grab the food. And if the service is surly, in the evening win respect by asking for something that's not on the menu (snow pea leaves or goose cooked in the pot). Frogs, fish and turtles swimming in tanks keep children happy. Pay about $21 a head.

SAIGON
60 Mulberry St (at Bayard St), tel. 227 8825. B and D subway to Grand St; 101 and 102 bus. Off the beaten track – at night take cabs.

Subterranean Vietnamese restaurant with a wall clock shaped like Vietnam and Technicolor photos of the food on the menu. Favourite choices are chicken with lemon grass and Vietnamese spring rolls (lightly fried meat and vegetable dumplings that you wrap in lettuce leaves and dip in a seafood sauce). Always full at lunchtime with a mixed crowd that draws from the Financial District; some say local gang members move in at night – if this is true, it doesn't adversely affect the eating experience.

Cheap beers ($2); expect to pay around $23 per head total.

CANTON
45 Division St (at Manhattan Bridge), tel. 226 4441. Closed Mon and Tues. B and D subway to Grand St; 101 and 102 bus. Off the beaten track – at night take cabs.

Perennial favourite with uptowners who, because the food's uneven, ask owner Eileen to order for them. Do the same, and enjoy delicate, fresh seafood specialities – some say the best Cantonese food in town. Midpriced, and therefore mid-range decor: powder-blue tablecloths and blond wood walls. Pay around $30 a head.

Little Italy

Come here to laze with a cappuccino or a gelato, but resign yourself to high prices ($2 or more for a coffee), because Little Italy is a tourist trap.

Lazy Coffees

CAFFE ROMA
385 Broome St (at Mulberry St), tel. 226 8413. 6 subway to Little Italy–Chinatown; 101 or 102 bus to Broome St.

One of the oldest classic Little Italy coffee houses. The curly metal chairs were once stood on by opera singers practising arias at each other. Coffee and high-class patisseries at the tables (try a cannoli or the home-made biscuits), and gelati at the back counter.

FERRARA
195 Grand St (bet. Mulberry and Mott Sts), tel. 226 6150. 6 subway to Little Italy–Chinatown; 101 or 102 bus.

A New York institution, this is a big, slick emporium most popular for takeaway cakes and biscuits, but with an espresso bar that is great for people watching and tables spilling out on to the sidewalk in summer. If you're having a sandwich meal, expect to pay as much as $17.

Restaurants: Italian

GROTTO AZZURRA
387 Broome St (at Mulberry St), tel. 925 8775. 6 subway to Little Italy–Chinatown; 101 or 102 bus.

Touristy maybe, but fun. Go early to avoid the queues for this chaotic blue grotto splattered with murals and celebrity photos where the paesanos treat customers like family. Lusty Neopolitan food with lots of garlic – try zuppa di pesce (seafood stew) or lobster fra diavolo and expect bills of around $30 per head.

EATING AND DRINKING

The Village is packed with eateries. Everything from cramped cosy bagel shops to bistro fare with live jazz, all with emphasis on relaxed, informal atmosphere. Weekdays and weekends uptowners and lesbians from Brooklyn pile in to mix with an arty neighbourhood crowd (writers, architects). Late hours are common. The winding streets can be confusing – even with a map, resign yourself to getting pleasurably lost in the tree-lined streets milling with laughing crowds.

Breakfast and Snacks

THE BAGEL
170 W 4th St (at Cornelia St), tel. 255 0106. A, B, C, D, F subway to Washington Square; 1, 5 or 6 bus. At the heart of the Village.

The Bagel is liked especially for its Village Breakfast of strawberry pancakes ($3.85), but there are also standard deli sandwiches (around $3.95) – all good-sized portions. Tiny lush crimson interior with formica tables and a quick turnover – don't take children or expect to relax with a paper. Great for eavesdropping on a slice of New York – Upper East Side women come after exercise classes; men discuss boys they picked up the night before; rising media stars drink coffee to tackle hangovers.

CAFFE REGGIO
119 MacDougal St (at W 3rd St), tel. 475 9557. A, B, C, D, F, subway to Washington Square; 1, 5 or 6 bus. Open till 4 a.m. weekends. At the heart of the Village.

Built in 1785, this was 'the first café in America'. Mainly families at weekends and NYU students during the week crammed in for aromatic teas and Italian pastries, and for the great decor. There are lots of Greenwich Village coffee shops like this, but only

Caffe Reggio has a 1902 original spigoted cappuccino machine and so much art. Busts, clocks and a big painting from the sixteenth-century school of Caravaggio are displayed with endearing childish pride. $1.95 for espresso with amaretto; $2.95 for a profiterole.

TEA AND SYMPATHY
108 Greenwich Ave (bet. 12th and 13th Sts), tel. 807 8329. 1 or 9 subway to 14th St; 10 bus to 12th St. On a cosy part of Greenwich Ave behind a big junction.

English owner Nicki's dulcet Cockney tones fill this tiny teapot-decorated café as she shouts advice at regulars on the dish of the day that's best for them – shepherd's pie, Welsh rarebit, home-made cakes and tea that's actually brewed in a pot are staples. Customers include jaded English-turned-New-Yorker trendies who want a bit of home comfort and curious New Yorkers from transvestites to refined old Upper East Siders. Afternoon tea with assorted finger sandwiches costs $10.50.

ANGLERS & WRITERS SALON DE THÉ

420 Hudson St (at St Lukes Place, just south of Leroy St overlooking Walker Park), tel. 675 0810. 1 or 9 subway to Houston St; 10 bus to Leroy St.

Great out-of-the-way spot to write some postcards, or relax with the book you've just bought at Judith's Room (see p.328). Dormer windows give a view of the Hudson; homey decor includes mismatched Austrian china, turn-of-the-century American furniture and shelves of books. French toast made with walnut and raisin bread is a favourite for breakfast. For a big snack or small lunch pay around $20 a head.

Restaurants: American

COWGIRL HALL OF FAME

519 Hudson St (corner of 10th St), tel. 633 1133. 1 or 9 subway to Christopher St; 10 bus to 10th St. W 10th St is one block up from Christopher St and 3 blocks down from W 11th. Take a cab at night.

This is great for everyone, but a real find for women with children, because owner Sherri is a single mother. She provides nice wooden highchairs as well as booster seats, and the special children's menu features Cattle Round-Up games and Granny Puzzlers to keep children absorbed even when their food is finished, which leaves you free to enjoy another large $5.50 margarita. Children's food starts at $3 (give them a Yee-Haw Enchilada or, for Sunday brunch, a Wooden-Nickel Pancake with a wooden nickle on top). Adult entrées average $10 (try honey-fried chicken with heaps of mash). Mixture of wooden booths and tables – booths are best. Cuisine is Tex-Mex, staff wear checked shirts

and ripped jeans, and there are saddles and antlers on the walls next to glass cases celebrating Cowgirls including Patsy Montana, who wrote and recorded 'I Wanna be a Cowboy's Sweetheart' and sang live at the 1989 opening of the restaurant. On your way to the rest rooms, make sure to pop into the area done out like Sherri's grandma's living-room, and before you leave you can buy your own checked shirt from the General Store. Music is loud, portions are large, service is brisk but friendly.

COTTONWOOD CAFÉ

415 Bleecker St (bet. 11th and Bank Sts), tel. 924 6271. 1 or 9 subway to Christopher St; 10 bus to Bank St. Take a cab at night.

More Texan food, but this time with a funky younger crowd packed round the tables and live music nightly (anything from Rock'n'roll to Country and Western – look in *Village Voice* listings or phone and ask). Weekend brunch gets queues out past the steer skull painted on the window and round the block. Big Ole Bowl of Okra starter for $4; BBQ Baby Back Ribs for $12.95.

KNICKERBOCKER BAR AND GRILL

33 University Place (at E 9th St), tel. 228 8490. R. subway to 8th St or 6 to Astor Place; 2, 3, 5 bus to 9th St.

This is considered 'Neo-Village', which seems to mean classy and intimate. Tasteful selection of nineteenth-century vintage posters ('Gay Coney Island' and 'The Sidewalks of New York'), black banquettes, steakhouse fare ($21 for a T-bone) and live jazz Wed–Sun after 9 p.m., sometimes well-known performers (in which case there'll be a cover of $2–$3.50). Local clientele from attorneys to NYU professors. Pleasant for a woman alone.

GOTHAM BAR AND GRILL
12 E 12th St (bet. 5th Ave and University Place), tel. 620 4020. R or 6 subway to 14th St–Union Sq; 2, 3, 5 bus to 12th St.

Converted from a half-block-long warehouse, the multilevel yellow interior with bowl lights stuck to the ceiling won a 1984 Restaurant and Hotel Design Award as postmodern. Good for impressive informal work meetings (publishers especially like it). Chef Alfred Portale is applauded by dedicated food-lovers for consistently inventive New American cooking. Try squab salad for starters, and the rack of lamb is recommended. Pay around $45 a head before wine. The Gotham owners plan to open a seafood restaurant at 2 E 8th St. Sounds promising.

French

FLORENT'S
69 Gansevoort St (bet. Washington and Greenwich Sts), tel. 989 5779. Open 24 hours 7 days a week. Take a cab.

Relentlessly chic bistro with a social-political conscience. Ads in magazines feature seasonal advice – for example, in spring: 'Love is in the air, so please PRACTICE "SAFE" SEX'; in April 1992 the restaurant organised with *The Paper* magazine a Pro-Choice march on Washington, protesting the erosion of rights to abortion by the Supreme Court. The rally spawned interesting photos of likeable-looking owner Florent on a coach with pop stars Cyndi Lauper and Lady Miss Kier. The risqué atmosphere guaranteed by the seedy Meat Packing District setting attracts a range of fans

from executives slumming it to bright young things splashing out. Popular brunch spot; high camp after midnight; all-night breakfast menu. Steak/ pommes frites meals with excellent baguettes for under $30 a head.

Italian

CUCINA STAGIONALE
275 Bleecker St (bet. 6th and 7th Aves), tel. 924 2707. 6 subway to Bleecker St; 1 or 2 bus to Bleecker St.

Terrific food at great prices, so bring a bottle of wine to keep you happy in the inevitably long queue, and pay around $20 a head for things like mussels in Pernod or sun-dried tomato and mozzarella salad.

Japanese

A TASTE OF TOKYO
54 W 13th St (bet. 5th and 6th Aves), tel. 691 8666. L, N, R, 4, 6 subway to 14th St–Union Sq; 1, 2, 3, 6 bus to 13th St.

Cheap and reliably good Japanese food including sushi and sashimi in an intimate, relaxed Village setting. Sushi main courses average $10; starters go as low as $2.75.

Seafood

JANE STREET SEAFOOD CAFÉ
31 8th Ave (at Jane St), tel. 242 0003. Take a cab.

Brick walls, tin ceilings, wood floor and a fireplace make this reliable seafood restaurant cosy but not quiet. Locals on a budget love it – go early to avoid queuing (they don't take reservations). Wide range of well-cooked fish dishes (baked, fried, Provençal) with complimentary cole-slaw on the side at around $30 a head.

Streets and streets of cheap restaurants compete for the mainly studenty custom (a lot of earnest youth in black clothes – biker jackets are popular). This is the area most geared towards vegetarians – check out Mogador, Two Boots, Dojo and Benny's Burritos as well as Angelica's Kitchen. 9th Street has a lot of Japanese restaurants, and there are at least 20 Indian restaurants on 6th Street between 1st and 2nd Avenues (it's known as Little India No. 3 – No. 1 is in Queens and No. 2 is the mid-20s stretch of Lexington). Cheaper East Village restaurants won't take credit cards and most have late hours.

Snacks and Breakfast

VENIERO'S PASTICCERIA
342 E 11th St (bet. 1st and 2nd Aves), tel. 674 7264. 6 subway to Astor Place; 15 bus to 11th St.
Wonderful for everyone. Cheaper and better Italian coffee house than any in Little Italy (cappuccino $1.50; cannoli pastry $1.50). Children love the food; women alone can have a peaceful morning or afternoon with coffee and a paper, surrounded by mirrors, chandeliers, marble fittings and glass engraved with flowers in the windows. Rumour has it that Mafia bigwigs buy their pastries here and at nearby DeRobertis Pastry Shop (176 1st Ave bet. 10th and 11th Sts). The boss sits in the limo while the chauffeur collects the beribboned box.

KIEV
117 2nd Ave (corner of 7th St), tel. 674 4040. 6 subway to Astor Place; 15 bus to 7th St. Take a cab at night. Open 24 hours 7 days a week.

This is for when you're desperate for a coffee and a bite to eat – potato pierogis, fried cheese blintzes, stuffed cabbage – between clubs in the early hours. Downbeat formica café, cheap if you stick to the snacks but

otherwise average $10 for entreés.

Restaurants: American

TWO BOOTS
37 Ave B (bet. 2nd and 3rd Sts), tel. 505 2276. Take a cab. Delivery service available. Closed Mon.

The more of you there are, the cheaper it is. If you bring children, their pizza arrives with toppings in a smiling-face design, and if they do a drawing of a pizza, it is put on the wall. The food is not, strictly speaking, American: it's Italian-Creole with Louisiana origins and concern for vegetarians. The $12 'Large Pizza' (as opposed to Medium or Small) will serve four people. Sweet potato chips to start. Decor is mainly boot motif: boot lights strung round the bars, beer in boot glasses, cowboy boots in the window. Good service, filling cheap food, funky fun.

CAFÉ ORLIN
41 St Mark's Place (bet. 2nd and 1st Sts), tel. 475 9779. 6 subway to Astor Place; 15 bus to 7th St. Take a cab at night. It's part hidden, down a couple of steps.

Classic East Village – even the poorest NYU students manage to scrape enough dollars together to relax over dishes like a parsley and scallion omelette for $3.95 with a 65-cents side order of garlic bread. Owned by the same family as Mogador; service is sleepy. Warm pinks and slate greys and old photos of 1930s and 1940s New York make for a convivial evening.

GREAT JONES CAFÉ
54 Jones St (bet. Bowery and Lafayette St), tel. 674 9304. 6 subway to Astor Place; 1, 101 or 102 bus. Take a cab at night. Open till 3 a.m. through the week. Look for the garish orange sign outside.

Happy college crowd comes to this tiny place decorated with strings of plastic beads for the always loud award-winning jukebox and the cheap Southern home cooking, including gumbo for $9.50 and a huge $3.75 plate of Creole chicken wings. Great lively place for a woman alone. Bit noisy and cramped for children, but come in the day and the staff will do half portions or standard burger-and-fries fare.

TOMPKINS PARK AND RESTAURANT
141 Ave A (at 9th St), tel. 260 4798. Take a cab.

Owners Jane and Kerry attract lesbian regulars, and locals love it as a peaceful neighbourhood spot filled with brass and pot plants, good for meeting friends. The consistently good menu includes lots of salads and inventive fresh pasta dishes for $6–$10 that are good for vegetarians, and for carnivores there's hearty BBQ steak sandwiches for under $10. If you want to pay by Visa or Mastercard there's a minimum charge of $20.

JERRY'S 103
2nd Ave (at 6th St), tel. 777 4120, entrance on 6th St. 6 subway to Astor Place; 15 bus to 7th St. Take a cab at night. Open till 3 a.m. 7 days a week.

When the Jerry in SoHo empties, Jerry's 103 is just revving into gear, filled with a flashy crowd who don't get served till the small hours because the waiters are so busy preening themselves. Black booths, yellow flowers in boxes, California grill menu (seared jumbo sea scallop main course for $16). Good for a laugh, because everyone there takes themselves so seriously.

Seafood

CUCINA DI PESCA
87 E 4th St (bet. 2nd and 3rd Aves), tel. 260 6800. 6 subway to Astor Place; 101 and 102 bus to 4th St. Take a cab at night.

So popular it's hard to get a seat in this Rococo room cluttered with antique mirrors and trinkets, but once you do you'll have a great time. Consistently good cheap seafood with an Italian slant attracts a mixed crowd from students to La Mama Theatre staff. Pay around $20 a head.

Moroccan

CAFÉ MOGADOR
101 St Mark's Place (bet. Aves A and B), tel. 677 2226. 6 subway to Astor Place; 15 bus to 7th St. Take a cab at night.

Run by a relaxed, friendly brother-and-sister team, this is an all-round favourite. Locals and *Village Voice* journalists enjoy its laid-back neighbourly atmosphere for breakfast (specials include sweet couscous and Moroccan eggs). Belly dancers and a live Middle Eastern band on Wednesday evenings attract uptowners. It's great for children – highchairs and half portions of couscous available. Women alone can enjoy long lunches at red-and-gold Moroccan-design tables by pale turquoise brickwork walls. Starters from $2.95; couscous $7.95.

Mexican

BENNY'S BURRITOS
89 Ave A (at 6th St), tel. 254 2054. Delivery service available. Take a cab.

Noisy, fun and – except for the copious quantities of bottled beer and tequila on offer – health-conscious, or 'Cal-Mex' (i.e. California-style calorie-counting). Everything is made without lard, preservatives, microwaves or MSG. The burritos are belly-busting, as are the tortillas, which you can have wholewheat, and it's cheap – stuff your face for under $10. This one gets a funky young beautiful crowd; go to the Greenwich Village branch (113 Greenwich Ave at Jane St, tel. 727 0584) during the day if you've got children (both branches have highchairs). Decor in both is garish 1950s Americana.

Mostly Vegetarian

ANGELICA KITCHEN
300 E 12th St (bet. 1st and 2nd Aves), tel. 228 2909. 6 subway to Astor Place; 101 and 102 bus. Take a cab at night.

Meat-eating New Yorkers snipe it

with a 'Birkenstock and bandannas' label, but macrobiotics clap their hands with glee. Good hard-core health food (about $18 a head).

DOJO
24 St Mark's Place (bet. 2nd and 3rd Aves), tel. 674 9821. 6 subway to Astor Place; 15 bus to 7th St. Take a cab at night.

Excellent-value standby. The inexpensive oriental–health mix food includes: Hijiki tofu sandwich for $2.50; burger for $3.50 for non-vegetarians; Japanese brunch for $4.75; hearty rice and steamed vegetable dinner for under $10. The simple varnished pine interior throbs with old pop classics (Blondie and Chrissie Hynde). The outdoor balcony is great for people watching on warm evenings but does leave you rather prey to panhandlers and car fumes.

TIME CAFÉ
380 Lafayette St (at Great Jones St), tel. 533 7000. 6 subway to Astor Place; 1, 101 or 102 bus. Take a cab at night.

Not vegetarian but eco-friendly with spaced-out staff wafting between tables packed with an ultra-hip crowd surveying menus on recycled paper. Even the burgers are organic. Bright clean green-and-white decor for this New Age, Politically Correct fun place that some think won't last. Pay around $28 a head.

Lower East Side

There are a couple of legendary snackeries that attract mainly locals during the day and a couple of restaurants that attract smart trendies.

Breakfast and Snacks

YONAH SCHIMMEL

137 E Houston St (bet. 1st and 2nd Aves), tel. 447 2858. F subway to 2nd Ave; 15 bus to Houston. During the day the street looks bleak but is fine. Closed by 6 p.m. daily.

This is living New York history. The oldest dumbwaiter in the city still brings knishes and blintzes up from the brick oven downstairs, and if you're lucky Audrey of the Schimmel family will tell you how Yonah came over from Romania in 1910 to teach at Rabbinical school (Yeshiva) but needed more money so he started selling knishes from a pushcart before opening this now wonderfully dumpy store front. The clabbered yoghurt is made from the 1910 culture. Barbara Streisand leaves the limo outside while she pops in to rediscover her roots. Norma Kamali did a fashion shoot under the bevelled tin ceiling with the rickety tables, red-flower-painted dumbwaiter and curling photographs as her backdrop. Glass of borscht 92 cents, $1.25 for a potato knish, which the large man behind the counter promises has only 137 calories and is perfect for vegetarians.

KATZ'S DELI

205 East Houston St (corner of Ludlow St), tel. 254 2246. F subway to 2nd Ave; 15 bus to Houston. During the day the street looks bleak but is fine.

Famous for being 103 years old and as the location for the fake orgasm scene in 'When Harry met Sally', this is a typical New York deli, grimy rest rooms and cockroaches included. A tip: you're unlikely to meet the scuttling bugs, which live in the heating system, if you take a centre table. Big busy canteen atmosphere with takeaway or waiter service for big pastrami sandwiches at $6.45 and $1 cans of soda. Worth a visit even if you stick to canned drinks and coffee.

Restaurants: Mexican

EL SOMBRERO

108 Stanton St (corner of Ludlow St), tel. 254 4188. Take a cab. Open midday to midnight 7 days a week. May not last, so phone to check it's still there.

Fishbowl-style windows for inmates to observe Hispanic kids hanging out with boom boxes and shifty expressions. Great staff – ask for a big $6 margarita rimmed with salt and you might get a complicitous wink from the Dominican owner-waitress – and great mural decor which, inevitably, features sombreros. Mexican music, low prices, big portions (burritos $8).

MIDTOWN

Chelsea

Pockets of gentrification have spawned some fern-filled sleek night-time joints, and there are a few old favourites worth targeting for coffee or brunch, perhaps after wandering the Sixth Avenue flea market and Flower District on a sunny Sunday.

Breakfast, Brunch and Snacks

LOX AROUND THE CLOCK
676 6th Ave (corner of 21st St), tel. 691 3535. F subway to 23rd St; 5 bus to 22nd St. Take a cab at night. Open till 3 a.m. Mon–Wed; 24 hours Thurs–Sun.

Relaxed atmosphere and staff in primary-colour surroundings that are great for everyone, but a winner for women with children (booster seats available). All sorts of bagels with, of course, lox as a choice of filling. Entrées range between $7 and $11. No need for a children's menu – they'll love it all.

BOOK-FRIENDS CAFÉ
16 W 18th St (bet. 5th and 6th Aves), tel. 255 7407. F subway to 14th St; 5 bus to 18th St. Closes 7 p.m. daily.

Ideal for a woman alone who wants a quiet cake and coffee break or light soup lunch alongside a refined publishing and advertising clientele. Pass ladies with baskets over their arms browsing the second-hand book section and through to the quaint pleasant tea shop done out with Victoriana and Bloomsbury in mind, pink cloths on dark wood tables, and antique teapots in glass cases. $3.95 soups and afternoon tea for $10.95. It is also convenient for anyone visiting the National Organization of Women (NOW, see p.29).

EMPIRE DINER
210 10th Ave (bet. W 22nd and W 23rd Sts), tel. 243 2736. C or E subway to 23rd St; 11 bus to 23rd St. Take a cab at night. Open 24 hours.

Classic stainless steel American diner, except it's not cheap. In the small hours it swarms with cool clubbers – the nearby Limelight (see p.294) is having a Renaissance – who roll up in limos. Live piano most nights, popular for brunch, tables outside in good weather for sidewalk-watching, pay about $21 a head. Might be snooty if you bring young children.

LOLA
30 W 22nd St (bet. 5th and 6th Aves), NY 10010, tel. 675 6700. F subway to 23rd St; 5 bus to 22nd St. It's about halfway down a bare but not threatening block. If possible, book Sun brunch before you leave home – specify noon or 2.15 p.m. sitting.

Most of the food is Caribbean, but the experience is strictly American. New Yorkers celebrate birthdays and engagements with the Gospel Sunday brunch when (usually) Deborah Woodson and Stanley Hopkins, who starred in the film *The Wiz*, whip the audience into a joyful clapping sing-a-long over dishes that include vast $7 piles of cayenne onion ribbons or cornmeal waffles and fresh fruit compote with strawberries and sausage for $13 in an elegant airy palm-and-skylight setting. No special deals for children, but sharing is fine and older ones will have fun. Live music in the evenings too. Lola herself is working on a new venture – look out for it.

Restaurants: American

PRIX FIXE
18 W 18th St (bet. 5th and 6th Aves), tel. 675 6777. F subway to 14th St; 5 bus to 18th St.

New concept restaurant that's a direct result of the recession: 5 menus to choose from, all *prix fixe*, because now New Yorkers *do* mind what they

EATING AND DRINKING

spend on a meal. The cheapest evening menu is $18.50, the most expensive $36, and the one considered best value is $21. The 'New American' cuisine – dishes like Day Boat Maine Sea Scallops with Chanterelles and Pumpkin Prune Pancake – is served in an elegant chandelier-and-fake-marble-pillar-decorated cavernous yet cosy room. There are booster seats, but no children's menus. Mainly thirtysomething crowd, but everyone's attracted by the prices.

CHELSEA CENTRAL
227 10th Ave (bet. 23rd and 24th Sts), tel. 620 0230. Take a cab.

Way off the beaten track, but with a loyal following that troops regularly over for this informal Chelsea institution's vintage mahogany bar,

pressed tin ceiling, old phone booths with folding doors, and decent American bistro food that includes eggplant with mozzarella and roasted peppers and chocolate-amaretto cake (around $37 a head).

Mexican

MARY ANN'S
116 8th Ave (at 16th St), tel. 633 0877. A, C or E subway to 14th St; 10 bus to 16th St.

Good Tex-Mex burritos and tacos to fill you up before a club. The barnboard walls are strung with hanging plants and packed with youth happy on margaritas who think the sometimes surly service is more than made up for by atmosphere and low prices (around $20 a head).

West 40s and 50s

This area includes the Rockefeller Center, Garment and Theatre Districts. If you're suddenly desperate to eat, there are innumerable delis and diners, and hotel lounges are usually safe bets. Otherwise, target one of the following.

Breakfast and Snacks

MOM'S BAGELS
15 West 45th St (near 5th Ave), tel. 764 1566. 6 subway to 42nd St Grand Central; 1, 2, 3, 4 bus to 45th St.

A cheap and wonderful place to stop off on your way to the Circle Line ferry, or maybe after the Museum of Modern Art. One of the few places in New York that bakes the bagels on the premises – you can have cinammon or onion bagels with a variety of fillings including blueberry cream cheese. $2 breakfast specials 7–11 a.m., and no problem filling yourself up at lunchtime for under $5.

Clean yellow-neon 'hamishe' (homely) café with 1920s sheet music on the wall and a mixed clientele, from Grand Central Station cleaners to shopping housewives and executives on their way to work.

CARNEGIE DELICATESSEN
854 7th Ave (bet. 54th and 53rd Sts), tel. 757 2245. E subway to 7th Ave; 6 or 7 bus to 53rd St. Open till 4 a.m. daily.

'Everything you see in the store is made in the store,' promises the manager, and that includes pickling the pastrami and baking the world-famous 14-pound cheesecakes. This classic formica-and-plastic-wood deli draws a wide mix of clientele – local office workers, out-of-towners after theatre matinées and families at weekends – making it a comfortable place for everyone anytime. Celebrity photos on the wall (Brooke Shields next to baseball stars) along with a blow-up pickled gherkin and sconce lights. Brusque but efficient service. Portions are large, but there's a $3 sharing charge, so you'd be better off leaving some to take away in a doggy bag for later. Pay about $8 for breakfast, $17 for lunch and $23 for supper.

RUMPELMAYERS
In the St Moritz Hotel, 50 Central Park South (bet. 5th and 6th Aves), tel. 755 5800. B and O subway to 57th St; 6 bus.

Hot chocolate here has been a favourite for over five decades with middle- and upper-class Manhattan kids who grow up and bring their grandchildren to this Viennese ice-cream parlour that has seen better days. An array of stuffed teddy bears keep you company. One adult and child for dessert and coffee will come to around $18, but lunch will be more like $26. Booster seats available.

THE PALM COURT
The lobby of the Plaza Hotel, 59th St (at 5th Ave), tel. 759 3000. N, R and 6 subway to 59th St; 1, 2, 3, 4 bus to Grand Army Plaza.

Palms, violins twiddling and Baroque decor make the setting for quintessential afternoon teas that leave hefty holes in your pocket (around $42 each if you want a good time). A high-kitsch experience in the hotel run by Ivana Trump.

SYMPHONY CAFÉ
950 8th Ave (at 56th St), tel. 397 9595. A, C, D or 1 subway to Columbus Circle; 10, 27, 104 bus to 56th St. Take a cab at night. Reservations advised.

The name was chosen for proximity to Carnegie Hall, and the decor continues the theme with sheet music and instruments in cases round the high mahogany walls above deep green banquettes. Symphony Café is a favourite salad lunch spot for businesswomen from Hearst Publishing and the Convention and Visitors' Bureau. Steak fare pre-theatre dinners are packed, and later actors, actresses and directors calm down over roast chicken and mash. At weekends families keep children happy with scrambled eggs. Prices around $10 each for brunchy meal and up to $35 for dinner.

JEZEBEL
630 9th Ave (at 45th St), tel. 582 1045. Take a cab.

The food is sizzling Southern home cooking, the atmosphere is steamy bordello, the decor is from the Upper West Side antique store Alberta Wright ran before she moved into the restaurant business. Beaded gowns and fringed silk shawls hang on the walls, pink lace and silk soften the lights and cover tables in a lofty space that is packed for pre-theatre supper and will cost you around $40 a head for a slap-up she-crab soup and fried chicken dinner.

RAINBOW ROOMS
65th floor, GE Building, 30 Rockefeller Plaza (bet. 49th and 50th Sts), tel. 632 5100. B, D, F subway to Rockefeller Center; 1, 2, 3, 4, 5 bus to 50th St. Reservations necessary.

Have a spectacular romantic New York experience. Aubergine silk walls, silver lamé tablecloths, and a spectacular view of Manhattan behind the all-singing all-dancing group 'Swonderful, 'Smarvellous, 'Sgershwin. Their songs? Gershwin, and raunchily done. Art Deco decadence, stars on the maître d's tie and patrons who look as if they walked off the set of *Dynasty* all get top marks. Save room for the sumptuous baked Alaska. Reckon on $60 a head, before wine.

French

CHEZ JOSEPHINE
414 W 42nd St (bet. 9th and 10th Aves), tel. 594 1925. Closed Sun. Reservations recommended. Take a cab.

Founded by friendly host Jean-Claude Baker in honour of his late adoptive mother, Josephine Baker, this is a great place for a pre-theatre meal, although you may end up skipping the theatre.

Bluesy pianists and a French tap-dancer usually entertain, surrounded by theatrical memorabilia that evokes intimate Parisian and Harlem nightclubs of the roaring twenties. It's Josephine's early years (1925–30) that Jean-Claude of her 'rainbow tribe' celebrates, with vintage posters showing Josephine as 'La Revue Nègre' star and strung with bananas. The French bistro food is only decent, but it's not too badly priced – $16–$20 for main courses that include lobster bisque, goat-cheese ravioli and rack of lamb.

Russian

THE RUSSIAN TEA ROOMS
150 W 57th St (bet. 6th and 7th Aves), tel. 265 0947. B, D, F subway to Rockefeller Center; 1, 2, 3, 4, 5 bus.

Hollywood stars, children, tourists, businesswomen – everyone loves the Russian Tea Rooms, as much for its festive samovar-studded red-and-gold decor as for its blinchikis with cherry preserve and sour cream, caviar and exotic range of knock-you-out vodkas. Celebrity-spot from the red banquettes and pay around $50 for a fairly sober night.

Murray Hill

Sneak into Murray Hill for a snack after the Empire State and observe the business community at lunchtimes on 42nd Street.

Breakfast and Snacks

THE CAFÉ AT GRAND CENTRAL STATION
Mezzanine level opposite Chemical Bank (42nd St at Park Ave), tel. 883 0009. 6 or 7 subway to 42nd St–Grand Central; 1, 2, 3, 4 bus to Grand Central. Don't come after about 9 p.m.

Commuters sink into cocktails before braving the journey home. Piped Natalie Cole 'Unforgettable'-style music clashes with buskers screeching Elvis or blues through a microphone under the Chemical Bank. Look down on the bustling concourse – 'the crossroads of a million private lives' – and pay around $4 for a cocktail. Good for midday coffee break too.

CHEZ LAURENCE

*245 Madison Ave (corner of 38th St),
tel. 683 0284. 6 subway to 33rd St; 1,
2, 3, 4 bus to 38th St. Closed
weekends and after 6.30 p.m.*

An unpretentious shiny-lino patisserie
with very friendly service that is handy
for the Empire State, the Pierpont
Morgan Museum and the New York
Public Library and not outrageously
priced. Rest your weary feet with a
coffee and cake.

Seafood

OYSTER BAR AND RESTAURANT

*Lower level of Grand Central Station
(bet. Vanderbilt and Lexington on
42nd St), tel. 490 6650. 6 or 7 subway
to 42nd St–Grand Central; 1, 2, 3, 4
bus to Grand Central. Closed
weekends and after 9.30 p.m.*

A classic New York experience. Ultra-
fresh seafood in a bustling cellar café
setting where dips for oysters come in
plastic cartons and anyone ordering
bouillabaisse gets a plastic bib. The
workaday counter bar is good for
women alone and for watching chefs
prepare the food. The ship-decorated
wooden Saloon Room is best for quiet
conversation, and the main dining

area is for raucous, fast lunches made
even noisier by the tiled vaulted
ceilings. Come in for a light lunch
surrounded by besuited businessmen
and you'll find so much on the menu
irresistible that you'll end up paying
around $38 for a feast. Stick to the
bar for cheap sandwiches (not on the
menu – ask). Booster seats are
available, and if you don't mind
making a show of yourself you can
teach your child the Whispering
Gallery Effect: they stand where the
vaulted ceiling's three corridors join
and you go to the diagonally opposite
corner, turn your face to the wall,
speak in a normal voice and your child
will hear every word quite clearly.

Mostly Vegetarian

THE HEALTH PUB

*371 2nd Ave (at 21st St), tel. 529
9200. 6 subway to 23rd St; 15 bus to
21st St.*

Lima bean salad with fennel and
shallots or cold noodles with
cucumber and snow peas, and lots of
tofu at this cheerful informal eatery
with butcher-block tables and a juice
bar. Pay around $24 a head.

East 50s

Now you're around Park Avenue. Cheap eateries are few and far
between and the flashest expense-account power-lunch and dinner
spots are housed in corporations' buildings. If you're on a budget or
have hungry children stick to snacks from pushcarts in this area:
street pretzels and donuts for breakfast.

Breakfast and Snacks

KAUFMAN PHARMACY

*557 Lexington Ave (corner of 50th
St), tel. 755 2266. 6 subway to 51st*

St; 101 or 102 bus.

An all-American drugstore with
shampoo and cheap nail polish for
sale next to cab drivers exchanging
comments on the weather with big

EATING AND DRINKING

businesses' cleaning staff hunched at the coffee counter over greasy donuts for breakfast and greasy chicken noodle soup for lunch. All-American surly service too. Go in with $3 and come out with change.

STARS DELI
593 Lexington Ave (at 52nd St), tel. 935 9480. 6 subway to 51st St; 101 or 102 bus.

A classic deli and a good Midtown standby. Vast pastrami-on-rye sandwiches, celebrity photos on the wall, swift surly service. Pay around $10 for a snack lunch.

THE GOLD ROOM
Within the Helmsley Palace Hotel (see p.00 on Leona Helmsley, the Queen of Mean), 455 Madison Ave (bet. 50th and 51st Sts), tel. 888 7000. 6 subway to 51st St; 1, 2, 3, 4 bus to 50th St.

From 2 to 5 p.m. a harpist plays from the musicians' balcony under the ostentatious vaulted ceiling for a cream-scone high tea. Awfully English, and therefore considered the height of good taste by monied New Yorkers. Bring your credit card.

Restaurants: American

BRASSERIE
100 E 53rd St (bet. Park and Lexington Aves), tel. 751 4840. 6 subway to 51st St; 1, 2, 3, 4 bus to 53rd St. Look for a low in-the-wall door. Open 24 hours.

The kind of respectably decorated place New Yorkers bring their aunts to. Then they come themselves in the small hours if they're stuck famished midtown. The bar is good for women eating alone. Standard slightly French bistro fare includes baguette sandwiches and steak-frites. *Prix fixe* dinner at $19 is a bargain, but if you go à la carte pay more like $29. Business breakfast is perennially popular.

FOUR SEASONS
99 E 52nd St (bet. Lexington and Park Aves), tel. 754 9494. Entrance at the side of the Seagram Building. 6 subway to 51st St; 1, 2, 3, 4 bus. Reservations well in advance and formal dress required. Closed Sun.

The place for power-lunches. Lawyers, brokers and politicians swing big deals and seal the city's fate over 'Continental-Eclectic' dishes like tuna carpaccio and rack of veal with chanterelles in the Philip Johnson-designed room that narrowly escapes extreme tackiness and instead induces relaxed intimacy. The heating system sends ripples up the metal-bead drapes; the gently bubbling square pool sports four seasonal trees (bare branches for winter, silk cherry blossoms for spring). The power tables are round the pool, but the balcony-level tables are best for people-watching. Manager Alex von Bidder is currently writing a book about the restaurant's history. Children are not encouraged unless they're well behaved, in which case the maître d' might take them into the kitchen. An excellent dinner can come to as little as $70 per head before wine, or there's a more affordable $41.50 pre-theatre menu.

QUILTED GIRAFFE
AT&T Arcade, 550 Madison Ave (bet. 55th and 56th Sts), tel. 593 1221. If you can afford to come here, you can't afford to arrive by public transport or even a cab – hire a limo. Reservations and glamorous dress necessary.

An amazing menu at amazing prices in a grey-and-black postmodern split-level dining area housed in the AT&T building. Wacky fusion of Japanese, French and American cooking produces dishes like the renowned wasabe pizza with sashimi tuna starter. The $125 Japanese 'kaiseki' tasting menu is popular and the wine list is well respected. Dinner for two could be $200 or $400 without much trouble.

Japanese

TAKE-SUSHI
71 Vanderbilt Ave (at E 45th St), tel. 867 5120. 6 or 7 subway to 42nd St–Grand Central; 1, 2, 3, 4 bus. Closed Sun. Reservations recommended.

A favourite for lunch with businessfolk from 42nd St and for anyone wanting a good, reasonably priced sushi bar. Ideal too for those who are not familiar with the raw fish dishes that some say are the best in New York – the staff will be delighted

to advise and explain. Pay around $30 for a good-sized meal.

Indian

DAWAT
210 E 58th St (bet. 2nd and 3rd Aves), tel. 355 7555. 4 and 6 subway to 59th St; 101 or 102 bus. Reservations required.

Owned by actress and cookery writer Madhur Jaffrey – many consider this the best Indian restaurant in the city, and it's great for vegetarians. The modern decor and rather too 'pretty' turquoise-and-peach-lacquered walls are more than made up for by dishes like eggplant with tamarind sauce and chicken makhani with lots of coriander and ginger. Jaffrey's samosas and mulligatawny soup are tried-and-tested favourites. 'Dawat' means 'an invitation to feast' in Urdu, and you can do just that for around $35 a head, which for the quality of the food is generally considered a bargain. Banquettes make for an intimate evening.

UPTOWN

Upper West Side

Broadway and Columbus are the two streets to head for if you need a quick bite after the park, the Lincoln Center or the Cathedral. Mothers, rest assured – pretty much anywhere near the Children's Museum and the Natural History Museum will welcome children, and most hotels have a bevvy of nearby eateries. Here are some places to target.

Snacks and Sweet Treats

H&H BAGELS
2239 Broadway (at W 80th St), tel. 595 8000. 1 or 9 subway to 79th St;

104 bus to 80th St.

60,000 bagels a day are churned out, some of them shipped to London. Get one oven-fresh 24 hours a day. Buy 12, get 1 free.

ZABAR'S

*2245 Broadway (at W 80th St), tel.
787 2000. 1 or 9 subway to 79th St;
104 bus to 80th St.*

Next to Zabar's, the grocery store
renowned as every Upper West Side
woman's life-support system, this plain
stand-up café serves fine restorative
cappuccinos and warm knishes.

CAFÉ LALO

*201 W 83rd St (corner of Amsterdam
Ave), tel. 496 6031. B, C subway to
81st St–Museum of Natural History; 7
bus to 83rd St. Open till 4 a.m. weekends.*

This is a great place for a cappuccino
and pastry after the Children's or
Natural History Museum. You relax
with a crossword at a bijou marble
table in the airy Europa-style room
that has the louvre doors open in the
summer while your ecstatic child
works his or her way through an
outrageously rich chocolate cake.
Crowded but still pleasant in the
evenings, when a cellist sometimes
plays. Pay around $14 each for an
indulgent couple of hours.

Brunch

POPOVER CAFÉ

*551 Amsterdam Ave (bet. 86th and
87th Sts), tel. 595 8555. 1 or 9
subway to 86th St; 7 bus.*

Some think it precious, but mothers
love it – not just for its warm, buttery
strawberry-jam-laden popovers and
slopover crepe-pancakes filled with
fruits and sour cream, but because
owner Carol Baer makes it children-
friendly. Booster seats are available,
pushchairs are accommodated, and
children can appropriate one of the
collection of teddy bears to play with
over lunch in one of the homey cushion-
scattered booths. Lunch main courses

are between $10 and $17; good home-
made soups are around $8 or $9.

BARNEY GREENGRASS (THE STURGEON KING)

*541 Amsterdam Ave (bet. W 86th and
87th Sts), tel. 724 4707. 1 or 9
subway to 86th St; 7 bus. Closes
around 5 p.m.*

This is an Upper West Side Jewish
institution that has been here since
1929 and is now run by Barney's son
Moe and grandson Gary Greengrass.
Family photos by the till, big plastic
fish on the pillar in the store section
under buzzing striplights. Turn left for
the café-style dining area. Salmon and
sturgeon are the things to have, and
Sunday brunch is the best time to have
them. Boorish service – but that's all
part of the New York experience. Pay
around $15 for a big brunch.

SARABETH'S KITCHEN

*433 Amsterdam Ave (bet. 80th and
81st Sts), tel 496 6280. B, C subway
to 81st St–Museum of Natural
History; 7 bus.*

One day Upper West Side housewife
Sarabeth started making muffins and
jams and all her friends loved them so
she started selling, and her empire is
growing (see p.278 for the East Side
branches). Done out Laura Ashley-
style in beige and pink, this tearoom
was the original. Queues for brunch at
the weekends but quiet midweek,
when you can come on your own with
a book. Pay around $10 for mid-
afternoon coffee and waffles with
fresh fruit.

Restaurants: American

THE SALOON
1920 Broadway (at 64th St), tel. 874 1500. 1 or 9 subway to 66th St; 7 bus.

Roller-skating waitresses in this noisy lunchery that is liked by swish Upper West Side businesswomen and convenient for the Lincoln Center and pre-performance suppers. Stick to basics like burgers and salads, which will come to around $25 a head with wine, and do some people-watching.

CAFÉ LUXEMBOURG
200 W 70th St (bet. Amsterdam and West End), tel. 873 7411. 1 or 9 subway to 72nd St; 11 bus.

This Art Deco brasserie with a zinc-topped bar is the uptown version of the trendy TriBeCa Odeon. Self-obsessed staff and customers are entertaining for an evening. Some say its chic crowd is pure New York, others call it Euro-trash. Pay around $40 a head for mainly brasserie food that includes duck cassoulet.

TAVERN ON THE GREEN
Central Park West and 67th St, tel. 873 3200. 1 or 9 subway to 66th St; 10 bus to 67th St.

The Tiffany-lamp-and-chandelier-decorated Crystal Room is a favourite choice for special-occasion evening dining, and the secluded Terrace is a great summer daytime spot for women nursing. Have a chat and a late-morning cocktail, or lunch for around $25 each. Early evening there's a $19.50 *prix fixe* pre-theatre menu. The cheese ravioli with basil and tomato sauce is a popular starter; main dishes include Long Island duck breast with black mission figs.

Moroccan

SABRA
285 Columbus Ave (bet. 73rd and 74th Sts), tel. 721 5333. C subway to 72nd St; 7 bus. Open late.

This is one in a block of eateries that is handy for stopping off after window-shopping Charivari and Betsey Johnson (see p.322). Eat a hearty kosher Middle Eastern meal in a cheery café setting for around $10. Also useful if you're staying in a hotel nearby, as it does free delivery. Standard burger fare is available in similarly priced neighbouring cafés.

French

CAFÉ DES ARTISTES
1 W 67th St (bet. Central Park West and Columbus Ave), tel. 877 3500. 1 or 9 subway to 66th St; 10 or 7 bus.

Stars like Paul Newman and Joanne Woodward join ABC TV News executives to eat the popular Salmon Four Ways starter in a room covered with nude nymphettes dancing amid lush forests and flowers. The mural is more stunning than the food, which will come to around $80 for a romantic supper for two (before wine).

Upper East Side

Here there are downbeat German patisseries in Yorkville, cafés to keep you going up Museum Mile, and some swanky places to eat after shopping gold-credit-card-league on Madison Avenue. Cheap cafés are rare – even pushcarts are few and far between. Ask hotel porters where the low-priced delis and diners are.

EATING AND DRINKING

Breakfast and Snacks

CAFÉ GEIGER
206 East 86th St (bet. 2nd and 3rd Aves), tel. 734 4428. 4 or 6 subway to 86th St; 15 bus.

Linger over a steaming Viennese coffee and strudel or Sachertorte from the glass counter by the door of this 'Authentic German' pastry café in the heart of Yorkville. Plastic chandeliers light your table, and ads for German lessons crowd the window. Feast for around $7.

SERENDIPITY
225 E 60th St (bet. 2nd and 3rd Aves), tel. 838 3531. 4 or 6 subway to 59th St; 15 bus.

This has been a children's heaven since 1958, and if you've forgotten what it's like to be a child, this will remind you. There's a novelty boutique to keep you happy while you wait for a table in this over-the-top Victoriana room where you can choose from ice-cream fantasies that include an old favourite: frozen hot chocolate. Hot dogs are literally a foot long, and the burgers are big too. Pay around $22 a head for a really good time, and avoid Saturdays if you can (the queue goes on for ever).

E.A.T.
1064 Madison Ave (bet. 80th and 81st Sts), tel. 772 0022. 6 subway to 77th St; 1, 2, 3, 4 bus.

Overpriced as a restaurant, but just about OK for breakfast or mid-morning coffee after the Metropolitan Museum. Airy marbled and mirrored room with vast baskets of assorted fresh baked bread at the takeaway counter make it a pleasant place to be.

Restaurants: American

SARABETH'S
1295 Madison Ave (bet. 92nd and 93rd Sts), tel. 410 7335. 6 subway to 96th St; 1, 2, 3, 4 bus. Take a cab at night.

The raised balcony level is especially good for women eating alone, and downstairs try eavesdropping conversations on neighbouring flowered bench seats. Sarabeth's is a favourite dining spot for Upper East Side women friends bemoaning shopping chores and their husband's late working hours. Starters from around $6 (nice mussels when in season), main courses for as much as $20 (homey-cum-fancy dishes like fillet of beef with mash and asparagus), and – the real strength of the menu – desserts for around $5. Old-fashioned strawberry shortcake is a corker. If the chandeliers-meet-country-farmhouse decor is not to your liking but the food is, there is also a starker branch at the Whitney. The Sarabeth empire goes from strength to strength, managed and marketed by her husband . . . England next?

ARCADIA
21 E 62nd St (bet. 5th and Madison Aves), tel. 223 2900. 4 and 6 subway to 59th St; 1, 2, 3, 4 bus. Closed Sun. Reservations and formal dress.

Chef-proprietor Anne Rosenzweig commissioned artist Paul Davis to handpaint a countryside mural of the changing seasons round the thin dining space to make the atmosphere mellow and intimate, and she creates dishes that sound weird but taste divine. Elbow-to-elbow TV celebrities and staff from local ad agencies enjoy foie gras sandwiches, molasses-grilled quail with rhubarb compote and grits cake, and wild-mushroom sausage on toasted barley. The wine list includes stock from Anne's own cellar. Lunch for two can come to a very reasonable $60, twice that for dinner. And if you like the food you can buy the book. *The Arcadia; Seasonal Mural and Cookbook* ($15), which features a pull-out of the mural plus recipes.

LE CIRQUE

58 E 65th St (bet. Park and Madison Aves), tel. 794 9292. 6 subway to 68th St; 1, 2, 3, 4 bus. Closed Sun and first three weeks in July. Reservations required.

Critics get tonguetied trying to explain why this restaurant is so good. For seventeen years Italian Sirio Maccione has been hosting stars from every world with grace and five-star food. Ivana Trump, Wall Street executives and tourists from Texas feel equally at home here. The staff are unfailingly courteous, the subtle decor melts into the background as all your senses are absorbed by exquisite dishes such as scallops en croute with black truffles, and lobster risotto with coral and chive coulis. It's well worth asking the chef, Daniel Boulud, to create a menu for you. This is the perfect place for a woman alone, although you must be either fairly rich or prepared to splash out. Between courses you can appreciate the decor, which includes performing-monkey murals and wall sconces designed like flowers sprays, and you can enjoy people-watching. Lunch is especially intriguing – millionaires' wives pop in for lunch after shopping on Madison Avenue. Pay around $120 for two before wine.

Oriental

PIG HEAVEN

1540 Second Ave (at 80th St), tel. 744 4333. 6 subway to 77th St; 15 bus.

Definitely not for vegetarians, who will balk at the lively wall cartoons of dancing pigs which patrons are eating in dishes including pork dumplings steamed in bamboo baskets and crisp shredded pig's ear, but unsqueamish children will love it. Booster seats are available; phone for details of afternoon parties held for children. Despite the nursery feel created by the 150 little pink-painted pigs, pig-snout mugs, a big yellow moon and a tipsy neon pig behind the bar, this pseudo-Chinese restaurant fills in the evenings with chic uptowners. The food is inconsistent, but not badly priced. About $28 a head, with a glass of wine.

FU'S

1395 2nd Ave (bet. 72nd and 73rd Sts), tel. 517 9670. 6 subway to 77th St; 15 bus.

Fu's is consistently rated the chicest and best of the uptown Chinese restaurants that cater to celebrities and New Yorkers who don't like the unpredictability of chopsticks or Chinatown. Hostess Gloria Chu explains any dish with wit and charm, and regulars swear that if you let Gloria do the ordering you'll bliss-out in this shiny black and grey modern dining-room lined with red banquettes. Regulars will travel a long way for the Grand Marnier shrimp and Peking duck. Pay around $38 a head.

German

KLEINE KONDITOREI

234 E 86th St (bet. 2nd and 3rd Aves), tel. 737 7130. 4 or 6 subway to 86th St; 15 bus.

If you're not already in the German Yorkville area, this café-restaurant is

EATING AND DRINKING

worth a special trip. Main-course specialities for between $13 and $17 include roast goose and *natur schnitzel*, all to the strains of Muzak in surroundings made faux grand with wood-look wallpaper and crooked plastic candle wall-lights. Sharpish service only spices up the evening.

Vegetarian

PLUM TREE
1501 1st Ave (bet. 78th and 79th Sts), tel. 734 1412. 6 subway to 77th Street; 15 bus. Take a cab at night.

Look for the smiling buddha logo. Closed Mon.

This small earth-colour-painted informal café might last, might not, but if it does, come for macrobiotic and vegan food at low prices. $6.25 scrambled tofu brunches, and for dinner try a small $6.95 Woman Warrior Stew, which is tofu, burdock, seitan chunks and vegetables in a special sauce on brown rice. Or pay $8.95 for a large portion of red bean and tofu Kuan-Yin 'Double Happiness'. They deliver too ($8 minimum charge).

ANNE ROSENZWEIG

Military terms are applied to New York restaurant kitchens. Cooks who stand at the stoves are 'behind the line', 'under siege', 'on a battlefield', says Melissa DeMayo of Restaurant 44 at the Royalton Hotel, which is why she and most women in the business stick as pastry chefs. 'Otherwise', she says, 'it's hard to maintain your ladylike behaviour.' Wily five-foot Anne Rosenzweig didn't care. She went behind the line and came out a general – and from a surprising background.

Rosenzweig trained in anthropology at Columbia University. During her 1976–80 fieldwork in Nepal, Liberia and Kenya she sampled everything local from flying termites to freshly drained antelope blood, and became interested in cuisine with 'rural roots and urban polish'. She'd had enough of formal education, so she persuaded a classically trained chef to apprentice her. The chef agreed only for the fun of breaking her with what is known as the 'hazing process'. For Anne this initiation involved being made to stand on milk crates at the stove because of her height, and cleaning 50 pounds of squid. She loved it. Today she is rated one of America's top chefs and has become partner in another bastion of male power, the 21 Club (see p.289). She is still only thirtysomething; it's hard to know where she'll go next. She works with charities including Meals on Wheels, she lectures at universities, and she plays in a rock-'n'-roll band called the Winnettes.

Harlem

New Yorkers who refuse point-blank to set foot in Harlem break their rule for one restaurant . . .

SYLVIA'S
329 Lenox Ave (at 126th St), tel 996 0660. Unless you've a New York friend to take you, or you're on the

Harlem Spirituals Inc. tour (see p.199) which includes Sylvia's on its itinerary, take a cab. Reservations advised.

This legendary Soul Food restaurant is done out in jungle greens with a willowy pattern on the wallpaper, glaring plastic candles and framed photos of visiting celebrities including Jesse Jackson, Mayor Dinkins's wife and Winnie Mandela posed with a grinning Sylvia. Budget for around $23 and stuff your face on corn bread, fried chicken, black-eyed beans and candied sweet potatoes. Sunday brunch is Sylvia's at its liveliest. Children will have a fine time (booster seats available).

The Outer Boroughs

If you can bear to drag yourself away from Manhattan, take a cab to Brooklyn for either of these acclaimed seafood restaurants.

GAGE AND TOLLNER
372 Fulton St (at Smith St), tel. 718 875 5181.

Beyond the delicately corniced beige-pillared Victorian front of one of the oldest operating restaurants in New York, you'll mix with Brooklyn's courthouse crowd and daring Manhattanites under gas-fuelled chandeliers surrounded by red velvet furnishings. The decor's wonderfully excessive, as are the gold eagle and star emblems on the waiters' uniforms, but it's the cooking of South Carolina chef Edna Lewis that draws the crowds and wins the accolades. Broiled clam bellies, tender crabcakes, catfish stew or fresh fish ordered any way you like it, all rounded off with Kentucky bourbon. You could choose the $21.95 *prix fixe* menu and combine Gage and Tollner with a BAM performance (see p.313).

THE RIVER CAFÉ
1 Water St, Brooklyn, tel. 718 522 5200. Reservations advised.

This restaurant is a swish barge under the Brooklyn Bridge. Brooklynites are proud of the food; Manhattanites like it for the view it offers of Manhattan. Popular with Japanese businessmen tourists, it's also increasingly becoming an 'occasion' place where New Yorkers toast birthdays and anniversaries over ambitious and not always successful dishes like pastrami-cured salmon with mash and artichoke, while a pianist tinkles out a Gershwin ditty. Romantic evening guaranteed for $55 *prix fixe* dinner, or $100 plus if you go à la carte.

DRINKING
The sight of a woman alone in a New York bar does not, on the whole, invite unwanted attentions from leery men. More likely: the staff will groan. Women – especially European women – are notoriously cheap drinkers and bad tippers. Be curt if they're curt, don't let them hurry you, and tip generously if you want to go back (minimum 10%).

The law comes down hard on bars that serve under-twenty-ones, so if there's any chance *at all* that you might be mistaken for twenty, take a passport for proof – it is assumed in New York that a woman without heavy make-up is young. If you *are* under twenty-one, dress up to the nines and cross your fingers.

Only a handful of establishments are just bars. Most also serve food. Some turn into clubs a couple of nights a week and charge admission. Almost every restaurant has a bar section you can drink at with no obligation to eat.

Bars open around 10 a.m. and don't close till 2 a.m. or later. Spirits are better value than beer because New York bartenders are 'free-pourers', which means that there's no sixth-of-a-gill limit, so you get beakers with the equivalent of three or four English shorts for around $3. Say 'on the rocks' if you want ice and 'straight up' if you don't. Expect to pay $2–$3 for just over half a pint of draught beer and $3–$4 for bottled beers. American beers tend to be watery, and are considered deeply uncool. European beers are popular – Dos Equis is everywhere, and a pint of Watney's is a special rarity. New Yorkers are big drinkers of cocktails, which start at $5–$6. On all drinks expect to pay $1–$2 more in clubs. Wine is not generally available, and the choice is usually poor unless you're in an expensive restaurant. Remember that drinking on the street is illegal – hence the hobos swigging from brown paper bags.

Drinks you should know about include two old New York favourites: Frozen Margaritas, which are moreish, lethal and deceptively like soft drinks; and Jello Shots, which are vodka shorts set in jelly. Also, there's a growing trend for non-alcoholic vitamin cocktails called 'Think Smart' or 'psycho-active' drinks, most commonly the Brazilian energy soda Guarana.

Look out for 'two for the price of one' happy hours (usually between 5 and 7 p.m.), but unless you like cattle markets, *avoid* bars that offer specials like 'free kegs for the ladies' and 'bladder busters'. These are the notorious Upper East Side singles bars. If you've a curiosity to satisfy, you can find them in the 'bar guide' section towards the back of the free weekly *New York Perspectives*, or spot them by the crowds, who'll be a cross-section of New York's male society (Wall Street kids to builders) with general behaviour in common: rowdy chanting and vomiting while eyes swivel in unison to ogle passing women.

By contrast, the Go-Go bars are really quite civilised. Their popularity is increasing rapidly, perhaps because they're a kind of safe sex. Rather despised new ones with glitter balls and techno discos (such as Goldfingers) are opening and in old ones (Billy's, the Baby Doll Lounge) trendy crowds join the traditional greasy-trucker clientele. Even if you go on your own you're unlikely to get hassled, since male punters will be intent on the topless girls, who may well be saving the $10 bills tucked in their G-strings to finance careers in art, writing or film-making.

The lesbian drinking scene is broad and stable and based in Greenwich Village. It's no longer relegated to the odd women-only night at a gay bar – there are several specifically lesbian bars catering for everyone from sex-hungry disco fiends to those who prefer a more sedate evening with a piano murmuring gently in the corner. And more are opening. Ask at bars listed here, at the women's bookshop (see p.328) or the Lesbian and Gay Community Centre (see p.28).

As always, if you get talking to a like-minded person who's a native New Yorker, ask for places they'd recommend.

A general rule on getting to the bars is: buses feel safer after dark, and if you feel at all unsure, take a cab.

DOWNTOWN

Lower East Side

Join sleek SoHo types who like the *frisson* of braving crack-land and a 'neighbourhood crowd' which includes shoe-designers and hardened clubbers, etc. who live on the edges of Alphabet City.

LUDLOW STREET CAFÉ
165 Ludlow St (bet. Houston and Stanton Sts), tel. 353 0536. Take a cab.

A few steps below street level, free music nightly at this low-ceilinged inexpensive hang-out that stops serving alcohol at 4 a.m. but stays serving breakfast till 9 a.m. Fairy lights and discreet plastic skulls for decor.

MAX FISH
178 Ludlow St (bet. Houston and Stanton Sts), tel. 529 3959. Take a cab.

Pool clicking, pinball pinging, jukebox grooving till 4 a.m. seven days a week. Art on videos and all over the white walls. Well-priced big drinks. Friendly trendy young crowd spills out on to the sidewalk in the summer. More happening-spot than its relaxed Ludlow Street Café neighbour.

East Village

Come here for cheap seedy bars known by those meeting in them before going clubbing as 'stand-by' – that is, with the exception of . . .

CAFÉ TABAC
232 E 9th St (bet. 2nd and 3rd Aves), tel. 674 7072.

Twenty-nine-year-old former model and owner Roy Liebenthal has persuaded customers that the recession is over – Cristal Champagne at $170 a bottle is his bestselling drink. Saying that the *New York Post* 'lives to write about this place', he reels off a list of

regulars: Madonna, Matt Dillon, Lauren Hutton, Christy Turlington. Might be a flash in the pan; if not, expect queues and snotty service.

EILEEN'S RENO BAR
155 2nd Ave (bet. 9th and 10th Sts), tel. 529 4286.

Described by one regular as a funky hang-out for 'sexually disoriented East

Village old-timers' – fifty-seven-year-old Eileen holds court here and encourages spontaneous drag and dancing acts nightly, which are free of charge.

GRASSROOTS TAVERN
20 St Mark's Place (bet. 2nd and 3rd Aves), tel. 475 9443. 6 subway to Astor Place; 15 bus.

Classic 'standby' in the heart of the East Village. Go down some steps into a low, smoke-filled room where dudes, young and old, hunch on bar stools. Dartboards and jukebox.

MCSORLEY'S OLD ALE HOUSE
15 E 7th St (just east of 3rd Ave), tel. 473 9148. 6 subway to Astor place; 101 or 102 bus.

Calls itself 'A Landmark of Old New York' – it was still men-only just over a decade ago. Women's groups fought to be admitted, but should have fought to shut it. Saloon, chauvinist atmosphere; drink choice is beer or beer, all weak and badly pulled.

SUGAR REEF
93 2nd Ave (bet. E 5th and E 6th Sts), tel. 477 8427. 6 subway to Astor Place; 15 bus.

More restaurant space than bar space, but generally preferred as a bar. West Indian food and decor – the bar is made of palm trees and oil drums –

exotic cocktails. Waiters burst occasionally into spontaneous disco dancing between the tightly packed tables. Loud colours, loud music and a mixed crowd which includes trendies in matt black and uptown preppies. It's one of the coolest places to be on a Monday night, when New Yorkers queue and admission is charged.

VAZACS HORSESHOE BAR
Corner of 7th St and Ave B, tel. 473 8840. Cab, or if you're feeling confident, 6 subway to Astor Place and walk east; 15 bus.

Known for the shape of its bar and as a sleaze site for films including *Crocodile Dundee*; there's no name outside but two big bouncers. It's not appropriate for women alone but it's OK for pairs.

VERCHOVINA TAVERN
81 E 7th St (bet. 1st and 2nd Aves), tel. 473 5751. 6 subway to Astor Place and walk east; 15 bus.

This low-key Ukrainian bar keeps a loyal varied clientele, from students to truck drivers and Ukrainian old-timers who come at 8 a.m. for a short to 'open their eyes', explains the bartender in an amused, crackly voice. The sign on the window is nearly all peeled away, but you've got the right place – come in! There's a pool table at the back.

Greenwich Village

Lesbian bars, former speakeasy and mellow jazz bars.

CHUMLEYS
86 Bedford St (bet. Barrow and Grove Sts), tel. 675 4449. 1 or 9 subway to Christopher St; 5 or 6 bus.

In the days of Prohibition bohemian

Greenwich Villagers, including Edna St Vincent Millay, flocked into this one-time speakeasy through the unsignposted wood gate in a brick arch. Now it's a bit touristy, but still fun for its sense of history.

COWGIRL HALL OF FAME

519 Hudson St (at W 10th St), tel. 633 1133. 1 or 9 subway to Houston St; 5 or 6 bus.

This is mainly a restaurant, but the bar is of equal appeal. Owner and sometimes the maître d', Sherri, whom you'll recognise by the pile of blonde hair and esoteric outfits like cowgirl-motif smocks, is driven equally by a passion for female Country and Western stars and fond memories of her grandmother's Texan home. Drink wicked frozen margaritas under bull horns and saddles next to Patsy Montana memorabilia.

FIFTY FIVE

55 Christopher St (at 7th Ave South), tel. 929 9883. 1 or 9 subway to Christopher St; 5, 6 or 10 bus.

Free entry to live jazz at this pleasantly dingy below-street-level 8 a.m.-4 a.m. bar, although a two-drink minimum is requested. On other nights the old Rockola jukebox croons Dinah Washington and Art Tatum.

LION'S HEAD

59 Christopher Street (at 7th Ave South), tel. 929 0670. 1 or 9 subway to Christopher St; 5, 6 or 10 bus.

Same layout as its less well-known neighbour, No. 55, but less relaxed and with inferior jukebox. Favourite hang-out for journalists.

Lesbian Bars

CRAZY NANNY'S

21 7th Ave South (at Leroy St), tel. 366 6312. 1 or 9 subway to Houston St; 5 or 6 bus.

This low white building, which is rather exposed at a junction, has blue neon hearts flashing from upper windows. Gay men are allowed, but straights of either sex are discouraged. Expect loud music, illuminated flying fish on electric-blue walls, DJs and benefits some evenings, and loud music at all times from 4 p.m. to 4 a.m. The bouncer's presence can make you feel as if you're in some danger, although you probably aren't.

DT'S FAT CAT

281 W 12th St (at 4th St), tel. 243 9041. 1 or 9 subway to 14th St; 5 or 6 bus.

Manhattan's mellow lesbian bar, with a piano and a fan whirring softly above intimate tables, this is on a quiet cobbled street.

HENRIETTA HUDSON

438 Hudson St (corner of Morton St), tel. 243 9079. 1 or 9 subway to Houston St; 5 or 6 bus.

Big friendly bouncer Freight Train and his colleagues ensure security without intimidation. Formerly the Cubby Hole – where, rumour has it, fighting broke out between Jodie Foster, Whitney Houston and Kelly McGillis – Henrietta Hudson is the only square-shaped lesbian bar, and therefore a favourite cruising spot (you can eye up everyone at once). Women are 'hungry' on weekends; come midweek for a quieter appreciation of the tasteful open brickwork (hours 3 p.m. to 4 a.m. daily). The music is a good selection of female soul and pop artists. The Henrietta Hudson and Crazy Nanny patrons are rivals – try them both out.

PANDORA'S BOX

70 Grove St (at 7th Ave), tel. 242 1408. 1 or 9 subway to Christopher St; 5 or 6 bus.

Spandex- and trainer-conscious Afro-

American lesbians come here to dance into the small hours sandwiched between mirrors under a glitter ball at the far end of the thin bar. Poster of a smiling Mathilda May behind the barmaids, bingo on Tuesday nights, and admission charged for salsa and Latin disco on Thursday, Friday and Saturday. 4 p.m. to 4 a.m. most nights.

NoHo

This new area consists just of two bars, both attracting the maturer trendy crowd.

TEMPLE BAR
332 Lafayette St (bet. Bleecker and Houston Sts), tel. 925 4242. 6 subway to Bleecker St; 1 bus.

Possibly Manhattan's best; there's no sign outside – look for a black reptile-skeleton motif on the two dark wooden doors. The teak and jungle-green interior fills with unselfconsciously Beautiful People. Perch at the subtly lit curving bar or cosy tables to test Temple Bar's reputation for the best gin martinis in town.

NoHo Star
330 Lafayette St (at Bleecker St), tel. 925 0070. 6 subway to Bleecker St; 1 bus.
Artist clients did the various features around the bar, including the central mosaiced pillar. Closes early – around 12.30.

SoHo

Most of the middle of SoHo empties by 7 p.m., and round about the same time the sprinkling of bars on its edges grind into action, peaking at midnight and later.

CONSTRUCTION ZONE
357 Broadway (near Grand St), tel. 431 9173. N or R subway to Prince St; 1, 5 or 6 bus.

This is an example of the rather nasty new theme bars that are opening up all over. Decor is dust, brickwork, hard hats and tools and Meccano-style shelves – because it's a construction zone.

EAR INN
326 Spring St (bet. Washington and Greenwich Sts), tel. 226 9412. 1 or 9 subway to Houston St; 10 bus. Look out for the Fire Station when you've turned off Varick St on to Spring, and go past it.

Reggae and New Wave on the jukebox in this small, relaxed artsy bar that's off the beaten track.

FANELLI
94 Prince St (at Mercer St), tel. 226 9412. N or R subway to Prince St stop; 1, 5 or 6 bus.

Primarily a burger café and open only till 12.30 a.m., this is considered a piece of old New York in central SoHo. It features yellowing boxing photos and a nice glass door.

LUCKY STRIKE
59 Grand St (near W Broadway), tel.

941 0479. N or R subway to Prince
St; 1, 5 or 6 bus.

This has been 'in' for ages. A lively
straight pick-up joint and pre-club
bar, it has veneered wine crates for
tables, rusted 1950s hair oil ads for
decor, a copper bar and a stamped tin
ceiling and handsome, hassled staff.
Steak-frites fare is served in the backroom restaurant, but you might have
to wait a while before they remember
you wanted food.

TriBeCa

Mix with dropped-out Hollywood stars and a dapper trendy crowd
who cab it into the area with a satisfying sense of intrepidation, for
although it isn't especially dangerous, its echoey streets and bleak
warehouses can be eerie.

Après Scotts
*353 Greenwich St (at Harrison St), tel.
966 0577. Take a cab.*

There's no sign outside. Look for the
zebra-skin door that leads into a
regulars bar that boasts Guinness on
draught and Debra Winger as a
customer. After 11 p.m. the pool table
is taken over by some mean-shooting
women.

El Teddy's
*219 W Broadway (bet. White and
Franklin Sts), tel. 941 7070. Take a
cab.*

This swanky modern version of old-
fashioned booths has slightly too
studied wacky touches like neon
fishtanks. Nevertheless, the bar part of
this standard Mexican restaurant is a
happening spot, and it serves possibly
the best margaritas around.

Odeon
*145 W Broadway (at Thomas St), tel.
233 0507. Take a cab.*

A place to artist-spot when it first
opened (Rauschenberg, Jasper Johns,
etc.); you can still spot the odd
celebrity in the black banquettes of
this Art Deco former café. Take
advantage of the racks of newspapers
and come for a late-night espresso.

Puffy's Tavern
*81 Hudson St (at Harrison St), tel.
766 9159. Take a cab.*

No food here, just drinking in a bar
that is funky and has a solid lived-in
feel, because it predates TriBeCa. It
was originally a speakeasy. People
come from all over for the jukebox.

Walkers
*16 N Moore St (at Varick St), tel. 941
0142. Take a cab.*

This is an after-work hang-out for
police officers from 1st Precinct, and
later on dynamic youth come down
after hypey media launches. There are
crayons in jars so that you can draw
up ten-point plans on the paper
tablecloths during unofficial meetings.
Relaxed and relaxing.

Little Italy

Mainly filled with tourist-trap cafés, but Little Italy does have one
gem.

MARE CHIARO
176¹/2 Mulberry St (bet. Broome and Grand Sts), tel. 226 9345. 4, 5, or 6 subway to Little Italy – Chinatown; 1 bus.

There are photos of Ronald Reagan, Madonna and the owner behind the old wooden bar, the formica tables and a wood with cut-glass partition are stalked by a lame cat, and the bartender is usually more interested in watching TV than in serving his customers, who can be thin on the ground after dark – which makes it all the better for those who do turn up.

Chinatown

Home to some seedy, very New York bars.

BABY DOLL LOUNGE
34 White St (corner of Church St), tel. 226 4870. Take a cab.

Expect a $4 cover charge for this bizarre 'anything-goes' scheduling of female exotic dancers, greasy heavy metal bands, a woman Elvis impersonator, poetry, and on-staff barmaids with revealing holes cut out of their skirts. This long-time Go-Go bar attracts stereotypical slobbering beer-bellied men and smart young things who say they're participating in a new liberalism.

MIDTOWN

A great many Midtown bars are depressing office pick-up haunts or Irish bars where a woman alone would feel uncomfortable. Walk steadfastly past these and instead target the larger hotels, or one of the following.

East Side

COFFEE SHOP
29 Union Sq West, tel. 243 1969. N, R or 6 subway to 14th St–Union Sq; are 1, 2, 3, 6, 7 bus.

This has been 'in' for a while and shows no signs of going out. The coffee-shop-style curvy bar and cosy banquettes drip with Beautiful People, including club promoters and dress designers engaged in enthused arm-waving and animated conversations. Fresh-faced would-be models serve meals, coffee and the Brazilian liquor Cachaca 23 hours a day (except Sunday, when hours are 7 a.m.–2 a.m.). See and be seen, or just relax and make sure you use the rest rooms, which boast a fresco of dancing cherubs.

OLD TOWN BAR
45 E 18th St (bet. Park Ave and Broadway), tel. 473 8874. N, R or 6 subway to 14th St–Union Sq. 1, 2, 3, 6, 7 bus.

The blackened tin ceiling and a worn mahogany bar of one of the oldest bars in the City attract lively crowds from nearby businesses (publishers, journalists).

TOP OF THE TOWER
In the Beekman Tower Hotel (bet. 49th St and 1st Ave), tel. 3515 7300. 6 or 7 subway to Grand Central Station; 15 or 50 bus.

For its piano, palms, stunning views of Manhattan, open air terrace in the summer and early evening lobster specials on the bar menu, this was recently voted one of the most romantic spots in the city.

Midtown West Side

ALGONQUIN HOTEL LOUNGE
59 W 44th St (near 6th Ave), tel. 840 6800. B, D or F subway to 42nd St; 6 or 7 bus.

The walnut-panelled lobby lounge has been newly done out Old New York style – that is, faux European. Dorothy Parker and Robert Benchley quipped over 'the round table' in the dining-room.

MICKEY MANTLES
42 Central Park South (bet. 5th and 6th Aves), tel. 688 7777. B or O subway to 57th St; 5, 6 or 7 bus.

Most New York bars have one TV screening sport, but this has 10, because it's a Sports Bar. There's baseball memorabilia on the walls, batting average information from the bartender and unbelievably noisy crowds during the World Series.

RAINBOW ROOMS
30 Rockefeller Plaza (bet. 5th Ave and 50th St), tel. 632 5100. B, D, F subway to Rockefeller Center; 5 bus.

Boasting a view that rivals the Empire State's, this Art Deco lounge attracts a mixture of excited tourists splashing out and business executives in *Dallas*-style lurid sequined dresses suspended on vast shoulder pads. Planter's Punch (rum and fruit juice) is a popular choice.

ROYALTON BAR
44 W 44th St (bet. 5th and 6th Aves), tel. 869 4400. 6 subway to Grand Central Station; 6 and 7 bus.

Designed by Philippe Starck; navy chaise-longues are interspersed with chess tables (ask waiter for chess set in a bar that attracts executive-level Lipstick Lesbians and pony-tailed movie moguls with model girlfriends). Very elegant, it can be snooty, and there's no sign outside, just two square-jawed young Brylcreemed doormen.

21 CLUB
21 W 52nd St (bet. 5th and 6th Aves), tel. 582 7200. B, D, F subway to Rockefeller Center; 5 bus.

Once a mansion, then a speakeasy, and now a pricey restaurant – use the bar as an excuse to watch swirls of politicians and High Society.

WHISKEY BAR
At the Royalton Hotel, 235 W 46th St (bet. Broadway and 8th Ave), tel. 764 5500. N, R, 1 or 9 subway to Times Sq; 104, 10 and 27 bus.

The younger, wilder version of the Royalton Bar crowd come here. It's small, and often so packed you can barely squeeze through the door, in which case try the mezzanine level of the hotel lobby, where you can play backgammon.

EATING AND DRINKING

Uptown bars are a strange mixture, with yuppies, film stars and lager louts on the East Side, students and rich surf-bums on the West.

Upper East Side

ELAINE'S
1703 2nd Ave (bet. E 88th and 89th Sts), tel. 534 8103. 4 and 6 subway to 86th St; 101 and 102 bus.

Red, cosy Elaine's has been about star-spotting since Mary Quant, Jean Muir and Zandra Rhodes came after a promotion at Bloomingdales thirty years ago. Today, Clint Eastwood and Susan Cheever are regulars, and they get seated prominently at front tables. It's primarily a restaurant; you're best placed to people-watch at the bar (you won't be hurried). Elaine is the large woman with glasses and lots of gold jewellery mixing with the famous people. When you arrive, look for the yellow neon sign outside.

JG MELLON
1291 3rd Ave (at E 74th St), tel. 650 1310. 6 subway to 77th St, 101 and 102 bus.

Full of preppies and yuppies – that's stripey shirts with round glasses for men and knotted neckscarves for women – this has linen tablecloths, melon motif everywhere and saloon swing doors. Grace Kelly used to let her driver show her off here. If you're alone at the bar, men might offer drinks via the waiter; if you don't want to be disturbed, take a table.

JIM MCMULLEN
1341 3rd Ave (bet. 76th and 77th Sts), tel. 861 4700. 6 subway to 77th Street; 101 and 102 bus.

If JG Mellon's full and you prefer lacy curtains with flowers on every table for decor, come here for a quintessentially Upper East Side preppy singles scene (the food is only passable). Main difference: cashmere and pearls instead of striped shirts and neckscarves.

KINSALE TAVERN
1672 3rd Ave (at 94th St), tel. 348 4370. 6 subway to 96th St; 101 and 102 bus.

This is a very relaxed bar with a good mix of people, many of them Irish, including local construction workers and politicians over from Dublin. You'll recognise it by the shamrocks in the window, Guinness on tap, a map of Cork and a photo of the Bay of Kinsale on the wall. And no problem about coming alone – nurses from Mount Sinai Hospital and Lenox Hill feel quite comfortable popping in for a swift pint after work.

RUBY'S RIVER ROAD CAFÉ
1754 2nd Ave (bet. E 91st and E 92nd Sts), tel. 348 2328. 4 and 6 subway to 86th St; 101 and 102 bus.

Rebellious preppy kids spill out on to the street twitching to pounding B52s tunes. Gather a gang to come and get drunk on jello spiked with vodka and strawberry schnapps, or come on your own and get ravaged. Ruby's is just one stop on the Upper East Side pick-up trail.

CEDAR TAVERN
82 University Place (bet. 11th and 12th Aves), tel. 741 9754. 1 or 9 subway to 116 St–Columbia University; 104 bus.

This is one of an enclave of bars and restaurants kept lively by nearby Columbia University students, who earn money waitressing then spend it on their nights off drinking in the same bars. This used to be a favourite hang-out of the young Beat poets, Expressionist painters and their girl groupies (such as Joyce Johnson, see p, 89).

LUCY'S RETIRED SURFERS
503 Columbus Ave (bet. 84th and 85th Sts), tel 787 3009. 1 and 9 subway to 86th St; 7 and 11 bus.

Slightly upmarket maybe, but this is basically a singles bar – the wild preppy Upper West Sider's alternative to Ruby's River Road Café. Jello shots; ferocious cocktails spurting wacky swivel sticks; day-glo/surfboard decor. 'So many babes and dudes, so little time' is punters' attitude – you have been warned!

WEST END PUB
2911 Broadway (bet. 11th and 12th Sts), tel. 662 8830. Subway 1 or 9 to 116 St–Columbia University; 104 bus.

Another one-time favourite Beat hang-out filled with Columbia students, this sprawling bar (more like a brasserie than a pub) has live music some nights (phone for details).

You'll be spoilt for entertainment in New York, which has something for everyone and plenty to spare. When making your choices it's worth knowing that free jazz, performance art and lesbian clubs are particularly thriving in New York at the moment, and remember that Downtown events tend to be more avant-garde than Uptown–Midtown, which is for more traditional gigs. New York is always good for glitzy premières, for seeing films months before they're released in Europe, and for annual events like the Nutcracker ballet and the Radio City Christmas spectacular, both great family occasions.

For a mixture of reviews and listings you should buy *New York* magazine, which covers everything mainstream, the *Village Voice*, which is more alternative, the *New York Times* (Friday and Sunday), which bridges the gap, *The Paper* magazine, which is funky, and *QW* magazine for information with a lesbian and gay slant. Set aside a morning if you can to scour these publications, and prepare to pay through the nose unless you choose alternative entertainment.

NIGHTLIFE AND GIGS

Women alone are served well by New York's nightlife. The prominence of tough New York women means you'll probably be treated with respect – not, for example, shoved unceremoniously into obscure corners at gigs. The club scene ranges from rave-imitations to genteel supper clubs and so accommodates teenyboppers and over-twenties equally well. Lesbians will thrill to the thriving lesbian club scene.

Clubs

Go-go girls, domination and lesbians are 'in' on the club scene.

Take Chi Chi Valenti, who combines all three in the club she runs with her DJ husband Johnny Dynell, **Jackie 60**.

Jackie 60 is a roving one-nighter with a range of party themes that have included 'The Silence of the Lunchpails' (serial killers meet club kids) and a Jackie Gleason v. Jackie Mason competition *with monologue*, 'for gay women only'. Jackie 60 has a committed butch dyke and drag queen following, and features the House of Domination go-go dancers complete with leather thigh-highs and studded neck collars. Chi Chi herself, a native New Yorker in her mid thirties with a penchant for push-up bras and plaited wigs, says she is a post-feminist vixen: 'I've always viewed domination not particularly from a sexual point of view but as what it represents about women's power.'

It seems that women muscled in with the recession. The 1980s was the heyday of a male–gay–Mafia club scene, legendary for its exclusive you–not-you door policy. AIDS, a new health-consciousness that spurned cocaine, and the 1987 financial Crash knocked the scene out. Today clubs use psycho-active vitamin 'Think Smart' drinks, adverts and special theme nights to lure custom. This move to inject new life makes a good club easier first to unearth and then to enjoy for women on brief visits to the City. The renaissance of Supper Clubs is particularly fortunate for single women, since the food–cabaret–dance mixture makes being alone comfortable (you might strike up a conversation). And if you're not a teenager, you'll have a great time. The average New York clubber is mid to late twenties, and some of the hippest on the scene are knocking forty – 'Believe me, darlings, a dozen years in the New York nightlife *do* take their toll,' says Chi Chi Valenti with weary pride.

There has been a surge of London-influenced clubs – for example **Giant Step** (tel. 627 8616) was loosely modelled on Dingwalls. Fairly mainstream clubs like **Danceteria** (see below) favour Techno music at the moment, Latin American music looks set to stay hip for some time (**S.O.B.**'s, see below, is doing learn-Mamba evenings), and there are a lot of Jamaican rap artists around at Dance Hall Reggae Parties, although you, black or white, should tread carefully with these because racial tensions are bad and getting worse (violence can break out). The settled trendy clubs are in the East Village and SoHo, while one-nighters tend to be in the Meat District (where you should take cabs) and most big glitzy clubs are Midtown. If you're fresh-faced take ID, as clubs can be tough on refusing under-twenty-ones entry. No self-respecting club gets going till long after midnight, and hardened clubbers take 6 p.m.–11 p.m. 'club naps' so they can groove all night and go straight to work in the morning. The same venue can be dead one night and hopping the next – the thing to do is ferret through flyers and magazine listings for the names of good 'promoters' (also called 'party organizers') and make a beeline for their events. Try **Chi Chi Valenti,** who does Jackie 60 (see above), **Bobby Kondres** for doable Dance Hall Parties, and **Susanne Bartsch,** who is known for her parties at the Copacabana (tel. 755 6010) on the last Thursday of every month. **Frankie Knuckles** is a DJ with a constantly good rating. The best listings and columns to scour include the **Michael Musto** column and the list of recommendations on the facing page in the *Village Voice,* the **Nightlife Guide** in *The Paper,* the **Fast Track** section at the front of *New York Magazine,* and the club listings in *QW,* New York's gay and lesbian magazine. Also, go to **Patricia Fields,** a hip clothes boutique (see p.323) that has a rack of current club flyers by the door and staff who might proffer 'in' recommendations.

Note that anything of the above could be out of date within weeks, and that the clubs listed here indicate the range on offer or are reliable good-time places. Use the text and listings as guidelines to get you started.

CLIT CLUB

Consistently trendy, relaxed and very enjoyable. See lesbian section.

DANCETERIA
29 E 29th St (bet. Madison and Park Aves), tel. 683 1046.

A young crowd loves this sprawling seedy Techno-glitter club where, it is said, Madonna began her career. Different nights include Thursday Rocketeria Rock and Roll Lingerie Contest with a $250 prize for the sexiest outfit. Go with a crowd. Find an advertisement and for some nights get in free before midnight, otherwise it's $12.

LIMELIGHT
6th Ave (at 20th St), tel. 807 7850.

Housed in a converted Gothic church, this has great sound, a wacky range of theme nights (for example, Casbah Harem nights and Heavy Metal on Sundays), and there's always something curious going on in one of the many other dance spaces. Rather disorientating, but fun if you're on your own and feeling feisty. $18.

NELLS
246 W 14th St (bet. 7th and 8th Aves), tel. 675 1567.

This was the first of New York's new supper clubs. Upstairs is for relaxed grown-up velvet bar stools and low-lit tables; downstairs is for grooving on a sweaty disco floor, often to jazz. Sundays and Wednesdays are best at the moment, but even when it's 'out' Nell's has a loyal low-key celebrity crowd. Fine on your own. $7–$12.

ROXY
515 W 18th St (at 10th Ave), tel. 627 0404.

A hedonistic male-gay favourite in the 1970s, Roxy has since been in–out of fashion like a yo-yo. It's still mainly gay, but straight couples enjoy the spectacle: for $2 have a fake tattoo done at the door (dragon or mermaid); munch free fresh fruit or Snickers lounging on a bordello-style velvet couch by a white plaster fountain; gyrate with daring respectable architects and drag queens on the huge dance floor strewn with glitter and confetti. Every night's a theme night (roller-skating Tuesdays). Possible to go on your own. $15.

SAVE THE ROBOTS
Corner of 2nd St and Ave A.

The club standby. Save the Robots doesn't open till 2 a.m., it's really jumping by 4 and still packed at 8. It calls itself an arts club, which means you give 'a contribution' to the bar: $7 for watery vodka. It attracts everyone from yuppies to coke-heads. In a half-hearted attempt to avoid trouble, a selective door policy sometimes operates. For desperate drinkers. $10.

SOUNDS OF BRAZIL
(S.O.B.'s) 204 Varick St (at Houston St), tel. 243 4940.

This is a place to come for Latin American bands that won't get to Britain. Monday night is Mambo Night, when the pink flamingos go out on the sidewalk and you get free Mambo lessons from the sexy Eddie Torres troupe twisting on stage in frilly shirts and coral spotlights. Have red wine, chorizos, paella and an outrageous flirt. $10.

TATOU
151 E 50th St (bet. Lexington and 3rd Aves), tel. 753 1144.

This supper club, where Edith Piaf and Judy Garland once performed, has been revamped with plush velvet drapes and pink brocade banquettes by former Studio 54 owner Mark Fleischman. Stars and star-seekers come for Monday night Variety Showcase, or for one-off events such as the National Gay and Lesbian Task Force benefit, which had a special appearance by the performance artist famous for putting yams in unlikely body cavities, Karen Finley. One of the few nearly Uptown clubs with a committed Downtown following. $10–$15.

Lesbian Clubs

The lesbian scene in most cities is underground and difficult for out-of-towners to uncover. New York's, by contrast, is big enough to have divided into factions, although the clubs are still transient, not yet in permanent venues. Two main factions that have accessible club scenes are the Lipstick Lesbians and the Sex Positive or Libertarian Feminists (see below).

Here are some ways to get up-to-the-minute general information on lesbian clubs. Buy *QW* magazine and look in the club listings section (if the magazine has folded – something New York gay publications do regularly – simply ask for its successor). Look out in general listings (*Village Voice*, *The Paper*) for one-nighter **Alcoholics Anonymous Gay Dances**, which have a big lesbian following. Phone the **Lesbian Line** (741 2610) between 6 p.m. and 10 p.m. Mon–Fri. Go to the **Gay and Lesbian Community Centre** (see p.28), **Judith's Room** or **A Different Light** (see p.328) and rifle through the racks of flyers or talk to staff. Go to one of the **lesbian bars** listed on page 285 and ask a bartender, or one of the drinkers.

Lipstick Lesbian Scene   Lipstick Lesbians are chic with lucrative jobs – say in the cosmetics industry, the arts or the media. They like to look femme-beautiful, lead apparently heterosexual lifestyles (many prefer butch partners), and, some say, they run the city. Because they're often still in the closet and workaholics with tiny amounts of spare time, these rich, powerful, beautiful lesbians can be hard to find. Occasionally they brave the hip Clit Club (see below), and every month or so Gail Gore gets out her exclusive A-list (for which she was recently offered £5,000) and mails 600 of them with details of a one-nighter, which is usually at the Grolier Club and billed as 'Girl Meets Girl – Club Des Femmes'. Gail is currently looking for a new Downtown location, but the name will remain the same. Look out for it in magazine listings or phone **Gail Gore** direct on **633 9021**. The club will be much as it is at **Grolier** (29 E 32nd St, tel. 679 2932), an elegant nineteenth-century town house with several floors. Gail plays deep house and funk in the dance area; in the 'make-out' lounge she plays bossa nova, female jazz and lighter hip-hop. There's no food, and entrance is usually under $10.

Shescape is another name to look out for. Shescape throws more regular, less exclusive parties for Lipstick Lesbians, often at the **Sound Factory Bar** (not to be confused with Sound Factory) on Saturday nights, 12 W 21st St (bet. 5th and 6th Aves), tel. 206 7770.

Sex Positive Scene   Sex Positive Feminists run the clubs, but simply *everyone* grooves at them, from brave Lipstick Lesbians to straight trend-o-philes to diesel dykes to Madonna and Sandra Bernhard. The regularly changing locations are often seedy Meat Market venues, and the Sex Positive aspect means having dyke Go-Go dancers gyrating on the bar, porn showing on videos and orgy backrooms. These clubs have broken the mould by being entirely for lesbians, not just occasional lesbian one-nighters at a gay bar. Key organisers' names to look out for in listings include **Jocelyn Taylor**, who is in the process of setting up quarterly Lesbian Sex conferences (how to enjoy sex *even more*), **Julie Tolentino**, whose club Tattooed Love Child boasted the first backroom mixed sex 'Circle Jerk', and **Dany Johnson**, who currently DJs *The Ball* at *Pyramid Club* (126 E 14th St, tel. 473 7184, $6 admission), where drag queens perform while gays and lesbians groove till dawn.

One of the oldest and best Sex Positive lesbian clubs is Jocelyn Taylor's and Julie Tolentino's Clit Club ($5 admission), which has been going so strong and getting stronger since 1990 that they're hatching plans to open in Washington – London next? The Clit Club has from the start been about having fun – and sex, of course, – and it is political. Amazonian Jocelyn Taylor in skin-tight ripped jeans shakes her Mohican dreadlocks for emphasis as she explains over a can of beer that she and Julie are making an aggressive push for purely lesbian spaces, and that open discussion of lesbian sexual practices serves two linked functions: increased enjoyment and range of sex (including introducing third parties into couples); and education – establish what constitutes safe sex and stop the spread of AIDS, which is prevalent enough within the lesbian community now to merit support groups (contact the Gay and Lesbian Community Centre for information, see p.28). The many problems Jocelyn and Julie face include a paucity of porn by lesbians for lesbians. Expect two monitors: one showing lesbian porn, the other showing straight porn that features simulated lesbian sex. The Clit Club has been at the *Bar Room* (*432 W 14th St, tel. 366 5680*) for a while now. You can expect to enjoy yourself whether the Sex Positive bias appeals to you or not. The backroom and porn videos are discreetly tucked away, there's a card table in a smoky corner, you may be asked to fill in a sex-habits survey, you can disco to your heart's content, and if a pick-up's your aim, you shouldn't leave disappointed.

The Pick-Up Scene

Straight   Two things have affected the pick-up scene: AIDS and the scarcity of straight single men. Women concerned with securing a cleaner kind of chap now haunt libraries and galleries, for example the Metropolitan Museum on Friday and Saturday evenings when respectable pick-ups are smoothed with wine and classical music. You'll overhear or experience men declaring themselves straight at gallery openings and bars with spectacularly corny lines. For example: man carrying video camera is asked by woman what it's for, and he replies: 'To pick up beautiful girls like you', then announces his telephone number as 'Soixante-neuf, soixante-neuf, soixante-neuf'. Singles bars are generally considered trashy. Try instead rollerblading in the park for a sporty pick-up, South Street Seaport in the evenings for an executive pick-up, laundromats for a homey pick-up, bars including Max Fish (see p.283) for trendy pick-ups, but mainly – ooze availability at all times or, preferably, baldly declare your intent. You could even set up a date in advance by sending a 'personal' into the *New York Press*, which will be free if you keep it under 100 characters. Readership ranges from professional to s/m. Contact NY Press Classifieds, The Puck Building, 295 Lafayette St 9th Floor, NY 10012, tel. 212 941 0440, fax 212 941 7824.

Lesbian   Go to the bars and clubs and expect women to be 'hungry' at weekends. Unless you're at DT's Fat Cat, the pick-up process is likely to be direct. One exchange was described like this: 'She bit my neck, I grabbed her crotch'.

ENTERTAINMENT

Jazz is the scene people come to New York for, and many of the most exciting innovators are in 'free' jazz, which has the Knitting Factory as its mecca. Try not to limit yourself to one category. Open yourself to the idea of jazz *and* dance *and* video, and you'll see some of the most challenging works around (see also Theatre and Performance Art section). 'Free jazz' is the hot scene, but New York is always good for traditional jazz, and there's solid stuff going on in the Rock scene too.

Rock and Pop

The generally misogynist Heavy Metal scene is being blunderbussed by all-girl bands, including the greasy long-haired gang called L7 from LA who have been described as hard rock's 'screaming answer' to nineteenth-century suffragist Carrie Nation. The surge of salsa is throwing up Latin American singers like 'curvy charismatic' Puerto Rican **Iris Chacon** on the cabaret circuit. But in New York it's the rap scene that has been invaded by the most powerful and interesting young women singers, including: the nearly-mainstream queens of Queens, **Salt 'n' Pepper**; the self-professed 'Intelligent black woman[ist]' in blonde braids and bustier, **YoYo**; and *Queen Latifa*. All three consider feminism a white, middle-class concept that is irrelevant to their situation. Queen Latifa calls herself instead a 'Commonsensist', rouses her Sistas to fight from within the still male-dominated rap world that calls women 'bitch this, bitch that', and presents rap as positive in opposition to the media hyping 'people gettin' shot at concerts'. Her debut LP, *All Hail the Queen*, was nominated for a Grammy in 1990, and Queen Latifah – still in her very early twenties – has already appeared in several films, including *Jungle Fever* and *House Party*. Established rap artists are more often in recording or TV studios than on stage – go to **Tower Records** for the vinyl or CD versions.

To find out what's on, see the *Village Voice* for listings and reams of ads. Expect to pay between $5 and $15 – more if it's a big-name star.

Below is a selection of venues that illustrate the range.

APOLLO THEATRE
253 W 125th St (Adam Clayton Powell Jr and Frederick Douglass Blvds), tel. 749 5838.

Definitely worth a visit, but definitely take a cab both ways, as it's in the heart of Harlem. A former vaudeville house, this was the entertainment centre of the black community in the 1930s, and by the 1950s it was *the* venue for black popular music. It looked set for demolition in the 1970s and was rescued by Inner City Broadcasting. It is now best known for the televised Amateur Nights

(Wednesdays). Eddie Murphy, criticised for being un-PC by building a Hollywood set of Harlem for *Harlem Nights* instead of using the real thing, recently filmed a scene of his film, *Boomerang*, here. He comes out and kisses his girlfriend. The brief scene created jobs for locals and gave money to the Apollo and presumably, Murphy hopes, did something to restore his credibility.

CBGB AND OMFUG
315 Bowery (at Bleecker St), tel. 982 4052.

Commonly known as CBGB's with the initials standing for 'Country, Bluegrass, Blues and Other Music for Uplifting Gourmandisers', this was the hub of Downtown music activity in the 1970s. Punk and bands like the Talking Heads evolved here. Deliberately sleazy, it's now mainly patronised by suburbanites who want a thrill.

LONE STAR CAFÉ ROADHOUSE
240 W 52nd St (bet. 8th and Broadway), tel. 245 2950.

This Midtown slightly yuppified Dingwall-type venue is for names like Dr John, Booker T and the MGs, and the occasional rip-roaring woman band like Saffire, the Uppity Blues Women trio from Fredericksburg who mix originals with Bessie Smith covers. Burgers and cheapish drinks – a good place to go to a gig.

MADISON SQUARE GARDENS
7th and 8th Aves, W 31st to 33rd Sts, tel. 465 6000.

This sports stadiums complex is for the BIG Barry Manilow-league concerts.

MANNY'S CAR WASH
1558 3rd Ave (87th and 88th Sts), tel. 369 2583.

This is a smoky Chicago-style blues bar, and a hot Upper East Side pick-up spot. If you intend to go for the music, you must know the dress codes: serious blues fans come in crumpled linen jackets or equivalent; leery young bankers come in lightweight summer wool suits and ogle women in cut-off jeans and oversized Gap T-shirts. During the week prices go as low as $3, and the Sunday-night jamming sessions are free.

ROCK 'N' ROLL CHURCH
Sunday nights at the Limelight, 6th Ave (at 20th St), tel. 807 7850.

Heavy Metal series featuring groups from mainstream to New York's own 'Cycle Sluts from Hell'.

S.O.B.'S
204 Varick St (at Houston St), tel. 243 9411.

Come to Sounds of Brazil for Latin American bands you won't get to see in Britain, and also for a grooving club evening.

THE SPACE AT CHASE
98 3rd Ave (near 12th St), tel. 475 1407.

A sloppy place for college kids in baseball caps to drink and half-listen to bands who might turn out to be up-and-coming or might sink without trace. Could be anything from 'a woman reggae artist to a guy who takes off all his clothes and defecates on stage', says one fan. Female NYU students happily hang out here alone.

SPIRAL
244 E Houston (A and B Aves), tel. 353 1740.

The seedier version of the Space at Chase – three or four acts that will be a wild mix of the good, the bad and the ugly.

WETLANDS
*161 Hudson (3 blocks south of Canal
near Holland Tunnel), tel. 966 4225.*

This is a save-the-world 'Eco-saloon'

that books mainly funk and reggae
and features occasional political
documentary screenings, plus a
popular 5–7.30 p.m. happy hour.

Jazz

With the late-1980s advent of 'free' (improvised) jazz, it looked as if
women's roles might free up too. Women began composing and
working with choreographers on performance-art pieces – but the
process has either slowed or stopped, largely because of cuts in government funding at a point when few women had reputations solid
enough to guarantee regular gigs. Women get their names in lights
doing sultry vocals, and lots waitress in Greenwich Village jazz
clubs. Exceptions, who nearly always play at the Knitting Factory,
include composer and harpist **Zeena Parkins**, composer and pianist
Robin Holcomb – who recently moved to Washington but remains
'a fixture' on the Downtown scene – and improv pianist **Myra
Melford**. Look out too for the **Women's Improvising Festival** at the
Knitting Factory.

A woman alone will be one of many at the Knitting Factory,
and her solitary status will be positively aided and abetted at the
established jazz clubs which have formal seating at tables closely
attended by waitresses. However, there's always the option, at
places like the Blue Note, of responding to the saucy wink you
might get from a gyrating saxophonist. The cool lady-killer image
still suits young jazz musicians. They hang about waiting for
groupies afterwards.

Jazz club prices range from $5 to $15. If it's Midtown it will be
more expensive, more formal and more mainstream. A minimum
number of drinks is usually required per set, although not at the
Knitting Factory, where you can get a cheap $1 or $1.50 beer. To
find out what's on, check out the *New York Times*'s Friday 'Sound
and Around' section and its 'Weekend' section, also the *Village
Voice* listings; phone **Jazzline** (718 465 7500), and drop into **Tower
Records**, where you can rifle through the current flyers for discount
vouchers.

Here's an idea of the kind of venues you'll find.

THE BLUE NOTE
*131 W 3rd St (off 6th Ave), tel. 475
8592.*

Big names like Sarah Vaughan and
Dizzy Gillespie. Good low-ceilinged,
Downtown smoky atmosphere.
Mixture of jazz fiends, Japanese

tourists, and with-it business crowd.
You can keep cover prices down by
sitting at the bar (say, $10 instead of
$15) and by coming for the very late-
night set ($5), but you can't avoid the
$5 drink charge minimum per set, and
don't forget to tip the waitress.

CARNEGIE HALL
57th St and 7th Ave, tel. 247 7800.

This is for biggies like Ella Fitzgerald.

J's
2581 Broadway (97th and 98th Sts),
2nd floor, tel. 666 3600.

An Upper West Side favourite with students and swish young things for convivial food–jazz mixture in a restaurant/club opened by jazz singer Judy Barnett because she wanted a place with good food and no cover in her neighbourhood. One of many New York venues that's more about the scene than the music.

THE KNITTING FACTORY
47 E Houston (Mott and Mulberry Sts), tel. 219 3055. Take a cab – Houston is seedy at night.

Musicians and trendies and established newspaper critics mingle at the bar under a ceiling of sewn-together old sweaters. Regular rated performers include Elliott Sharp and John Zorn. The Knitting Factory also does critically acclaimed festivals – for example the New York–Tokyo Noisecore Fest. Every Sunday there's a programme called **Women in Limbo**, a 'spontaneous, experimental, and inter-disciplinary' works-in-progress workshop, and on Wednesdays **Bread to the Bone** stages dance-music improvisations that feature many women.

VILLAGE GATE
160 Bleecker St (corner of Thompson St), tel. 475 5120.

A classic Greenwich Village traditional jazz venue with big names like Gillespie and Steve Turre downstairs or pianists like Tania Maria in the upstairs cabaret bar. Usually costs a reasonable $10, and Jazz Latin bands on Mondays draw buzzing, happy crowds. Staff don't hassle about drinks.

THE VILLAGE VANGUARD
178 7th Ave S (11th and Perry Sts), tel. 255 4037.

This is legendary. Simply *everyone* who's anyone has played here – Miles Davis, Thelonius Monk, John Coltrane, who immortalised the place on vinyl with 'Live at the Village Vanguard' – and it still hosts big names. $5 drink minimum at weekends.

THE ARTS

New York continues to nurture some of the most exciting and outrageous arts innovators, from Martha Graham in modern dance to Lillian Hellman on Broadway to Beverly 'Bubbles' Sills in opera to Holly Hughes in East Village performance art. Carnegie and Avery Fisher Hall have world-renowned acoustics. Cinema houses show films months before they arrive in Europe. Prices range from the outrageous to the absolutely free. Whatever your budget, whatever your taste, have a wonderful time.

To find out what's on, consult the *Village Voice*, the Friday weekend section of the *New York Times*, the Cue listings in *New York* magazine, and the 'intelligently selective listings' with a gay and lesbian bias, IQ in *QW* magazine.

For many, Broadway is synonymous with musical spectaculars like *Guys and Dolls, 42nd Street* and *A Chorus Line.* The more interesting and more affordable productions are mostly Off and Off Off Broadway – that is, on streets immediately off Broadway or in Greenwich Village, SoHo and the East Village. Artists on the cutting edge work in Performance Art.

Broadway

If you want the Broadway experience, avoid the top tourist attractions, which you could probably see in London anyway (currently *Miss Saigon* and *The Phantom of the Opera*), and instead seek out your favourite Hollywood star. Theatres splash out on big film names to secure sales for slightly more daring play choices, or just to boost attendance, and screen personalities accept salary drops to tread the boards for credibility, so you might see Jessica Lange in *A Streetcar Named Desire*, Glenn Close in *Death and the Maiden*, or bizarre couplings like Raul Julia with Sheena Easton.

What's On See all major listings for what's on, but concentrate on the *New York Times* on a Friday, when the Weekend section tells you ticket availability over the weekend, and the *New York Times* on Sunday, when the Arts and Leisure section gives review coverage to help your choice. Also pick up a free twice-monthly *Broadway Theater Guide* from hotels and the Convention and Visitors' Bureau.

Buying Tickets Tickets for big Broadway shows can be as much as $100. If you're happy to pay full price for Broadway and Off Broadway tickets you can phone **Ticketron** (tel. 369 4444) to buy tickets with credit cards, go direct to the theatre, or, if you're in a medium-to-large hotel, ask the concierge to find out what's on and book for you. For discounted Broadway and Off Broadway tickets go to one of two **TKTS** booths (main one in Duffy Square at Broadway and 47th Street, also at 2 World Trade Center) where you'll get day-of-performance tickets half price with a $2 commission (the most popular shows sell out quickly). Queues form as early as 10.30 a.m. and the booths don't open till noon for Wednesday and Saturday matinées and till 3 p.m. rest of the week excluding Sunday (closes 8 p.m.). Also look for **two-fer** coupons at the New York Convention and Visitors' Bureau, and in many shops and hotels. Two-fers will give you good discounts on a range of shows that won't include the most popular ones. They allow you to book in advance.

Base your evening's choice on the show, not the venue.

Off and Off Off Broadway and Performance Art

Off Broadway was a 1930s Greenwich Village bohemian rebellion against Broadway's prices and mainstream subject matter. Off Off Broadway was an East Village 1960s rebellion against the rebellion, led primarily by 'the mother of experimental theatre', Ellen Stewart at La Mama. As for the 1980s and 1990s boom in Performance Art, every artist sets their own boundaries – that's the point – but it might fuse dance, drama, music and video for an avant-garde event in a cheap TriBeCa or Lower East Side location. Below is a selection of interesting and notable venues. Prices for Off Broadway can go up to $35 but they're usually more like $15, and for Off Off Broadway prices go down to under $10 but not usually lower than $6.

What's On   The *New York Times* and *Broadway Theater Guide* include Off Broadway listings, but the *Village Voice* listings are more thorough and the discriminating 'Choices' section helps the decision process.

Buying Tickets   Use Ticketron, TKTS and Two-fers as above for Off Broadway, but for Off Off Broadway and smaller Performance venues, you'll have to contact them direct. Phone ahead with a credit card or to find out box office hours, which can be erratic.

LA MAMA

Ellen Stewart worked for seven years as a fashion designer for Saks Fifth Avenue before dropping out in 1961 and using her $55 unemployment cheque to pay the rent on an East 9th Street basement theatre which moved to East 4th Street in 1969 with financial help from the Ford Foundation. Stars she has nurtured at her experimental theatre have included Sam Shepherd and Robert de Niro, two of many she calls her 'children'. The grand woman with silver plaits and dangly earrings is defiantly proud, declaring that her sex and colour have neither hindered nor helped her, and for thirty years of operating the theatre she never once went public and asked for financial help – until 1991, when La Mama couldn't raise the last $150,000 needed to finish the season. De Niro hosted a benefit, cheques from her 'children' flooded in, and suddenly Ellen Stewart was all over the papers and top invitee at society functions. Stewart is still fighting to save her East Village loft space from City developers, but La Mama Theater looks stable again – at least for a while. On rare nights off, Ellen likes to eat at one of the 6th Street Indian restaurants.

CHERRY LANE THEATER
38 Commerce St (bet. Bedford and Barrow Sts), tel. 989 2020.

Converted from a brewery to showcase avant-garde productions in 1924, this was the original Greenwich Village Off Broadway theatre. It launched Edna St Vincent Millay's career (see p.95) as the bohemian poet-darling of New York, Beckett and Edward Albee had their American premières here, and *Godspell* its world première. Productions are generally sound.

THE JOSEPH PAPP PUBLIC THEATER
425 Lafayette St (bet. E 4th St and Astor Place), tel. 598 7150.

Joseph Papp was a local hero: he saved the Public Theater building from demolition in 1966; again and again he championed victims of City bureaucracy and corruption, conducting an open war with Mayor Koch in the press; he founded the free summer Shakespeare festival in the Park; he nurtured actors and actresses including Meryl Streep, Raul Julia and Kevin Kline, and he oversaw the birth of the landmark musical *Hair*. JoAnne Akalitis has taken on his mantle as Director and continues programming an Off Broadway mixture of new plays and classics. Run-on shows have included *A Chorus Line* and Caryl Churchill's *Serious Money*. The theatre's grand Landmark 1854 building originally housed John Jacob Astor's book collection and was revolutionary as the first *public* library. Pop into the echoey marble lobby for a cappuccino at the bar if you're passing.

LA MAMA E.T.C.
74A E 4th St (bet. 2nd and 3rd Aves), tel. 475 7710. The Annex, 66 E 4th St, tel. 473 8745.

Dubbed 'the MGM of experimental theatre', the East Village's La Mama manages to be Off Broadway, Off Off Broadway *and* a key Performance Art venue. Nick Nolte, Meatloaf, Peter Brook and Bette Midler were nurtured here. The larger Annex is Off Broadway; come to the original thin building for the Monday 'One Night Stands' cabaret and for $12 you'll see budding genius and rubbish, and you'll certainly be entertained.

ORPHEUM
126 2nd Ave (E 7th and 8th Sts), tel. 477 2477.

Best known for staging comic Sandra Bernhard's 1988 one-woman show (see box), this refurbished 1908 East Village theatre housed many Yiddish hits in its early days and had a long run of *Little Shop of Horrors*, which was later made into a film.

P.S. 122
150 1st Ave (corner of 9th St), tel. 477 5288.

This vital force in Performance Art and Downtown culture is a converted elementary school near a dodgy area – wander one block north by accident and you're tripping over crack-heads – so take cabs. The February marathon is a blizzard of exciting new talents. P.S. 122 schedules alternative women performers regularly.

THE PERFORMING GARAGE
33 Wooster St (bet. Grand and Broome Sts), tel. 966 3651.

This is home to one of America's oldest experimental theatre companies, the **Wooster Group**, and run by Elizabeth LeCompte, who seems to be better known in New York for Hollywood stars she is having affairs with than for her direction, but the productions are rated.

WPA Theater
519 W 23rd St (bet. 10th and 11th Aves), tel. 691 2274.

This is on the edges of Chelsea, so take a cab to the place known for resurrecting neglected American classics, usually American Realist plays acted with a Stanislavski influence. The plays of Tennessee Williams and Lillian Hellman often feature, and a number of recent productions – including *Steel Magnolias* – made it on to the silver screen.

WOW (Women's One World) Café
59 E 4th St, tel. 460 8067.

Started by performing duo 'Split Britches' Lois Weaver and Peggy Shaw as an international festival eleven years ago, WOW is now a permanent performance space and developmental company, 'a loose anarchy of women striving to create our own theatre by our own experiences and definitions'. Original productions have included plays titled *The Love Affairs of an Old Maid* and *A Queer Fairy Tale*. Performers like Holly Hughes (see box) have come out of WOW Café. Any woman is welcome to get involved by attending the Tuesday evening staff meetings. The entrance is an unlikely-looking battered metal door with '59 61' written on it. For meetings ring the bell; for performances join the queue, which will be a cross-section of women (from smart executives to students). Go up a narrow peeling stairwell. Flyers for other shows will be given out. WOW Café closes from the end of June to the beginning of September.

THEATRE

HOLLY HUGHES

A lesbian performance artist who likes wearing red raw silk and corsets and being hauled about on stage in a giant pink pig, Holly Hughes was held up by Senator Jesse Helms as an example of pornographers who should – along with all other so-called artists dubbed by the government obscene (including Robert Mapplethorpe) – have all NEA (National Endowment of the Arts) funding cut immediately.

She is small and fiery, with a Louise Brooks hennaed blunt cut and a flat Midwest accent. She was born in 1955 in Michigan to 'a depressed housewife, which was plenty of work. We raised her. I never knew my father, even though he lived in the same house. He worked in General Motors, where they made noise.' She was into Jesus at school, did Art at college and moved to New York in 1979 when it really seemed 'you could make these big steel vaginas and erect them in the city . . . and somehow just topple the whole patriarchal system.' To support herself she abandoned painting and took up waitressing, then saw a sign about the WOW Festival. 'Some of it wasn't very good but the sense of humor and sense of experimentation felt so vital. It didn't feel gallery-ified, like so many of the other performances I'd seen that looked like they were happening under glass.' She wrote and starred in plays like *The Well of Horniness* and *The Lady Dick*, and believes, 'Just because men have exploited and colonized the female body onstage doesn't mean that we cannot put on our own versions. A lot of feminist theater critics and academics feel that female sexuality can never be represented onstage without it becoming a peep show. I really disagree. You have to take the risk.'

ENTERTAINMENT

SANDRA BERNHARD

A stand-up comic who 'entertains with a capital "E"' by doing camp covers of big numbers in a 'Marianne Faithfull meets Tina Turner meets Liza Minelli' style, Sandra Bernhard made it on the 'Late Night With David Letterman' TV show when she appeared with Madonna and hinted that they were girlfriends. Now she's a regular. While other Letterman guests promote novels and films, she grabs David Letterman's crotch and asks if enough blood is getting to his dick. She started in LA as a manicurist on the stand-up comedy circuit and got her first break with a part in Martin Scorsese's *King of Comedy*. 'The ongoing element of my work is about being a woman in our culture: what it's done to us, how it's manipulated us, what it turns us into.' In her show *Giving Til it Hurts*, she name-drops incessantly – about her *best friend* Naomi Campbell and Mizrahi, who made this dress – then strips down to a glitter G-string for her cover of Prince's *Little Red Corvette*. She played messages left on her answerphone by famous people until a *Village Voice* critic took out an injunction. Current projects include seducing Jennifer Jason Leigh.

Writers and Poets

New York is a world publishing centre teeming with extrovert authors, so there's always a stimulating range of readings. Look under 'Words' in the *Village Voice* Choices section and under 'Other Events' in *New York* magazine Cue section. And get programmes from the following.

THE LESBIAN AND GAY
COMMUNITY CENTRE
208 W 13th St, tel. 620 7310.

The Centre runs two series of readings that are worth checking out: 'In Our Own Write' and 'Second Tuesday'.

WRITERS IN PERFORMANCE
Manhattan Theatre Club at City Centre, 131 W 55th St (6th and 7th Aves), tel. 627 4898.

The series is a stimulating mixture of mainstream and alternative. Luminaries like **Margaret Atwood, Joyce Carol Oates** and **Susan Cheever** have read here; so have the Southern lesbian writer **Blanche McReary Boyd** and the New York author of the choreo poem 'Colored Girls', which was performed on Broadway, **Ntozake Shange.**

NUYORICAN POETS CAFÉ
236 E 3rd St (bet. Aves B and C), tel. 505 8183.

A forum for young Puerto Rican poets in the 1970s, today it hosts a wide range of readings, and Friday nights are favourites for trendies after a good time: there's a poetry contest and the audience gets to vote.

THE POETRY PROJECT
St Mark's Church in the Bowery, (bet. 2nd Ave and 10th St), tel. 674 0910.

St Mark's boom time was when the Beat poets held regular readings in its echoey church interior, and out of the Beat generation came poets including **Anne Waldman** and **Eileen Myles,** who still read regularly here as part of its experimental programme.

WRITERS VOICE
92nd St Y, 1395 Lexington Ave (bet. 91st and 92nd Sts), tel. 415 5760.

Since this was founded in the 1930s it has been one of the best-respected readings venues in the City, featuring writers from **Rosa Guy** to post-Beat experimentalist **Ann Lauterbach** and the late Audre Lorde, who called it a crowning moment for lesbians and women of colour when she was made State Poet in 1991. The Sunday brunch series is popular. Other New York writers to look out for at reading venues include: Filipino writer Jessica Hagedorn; Yale Younger Poet winner **Marilyn Hacker**; Grace Paley (see recc. books); and Susan Sontag (see recc. books).

Venues worth checking out for women's readings include **Judith's Room** bookshop (tel. 727 7330), **MosaicBooks** (tel. 475 8623), **Columbia University** (tel. 854 1584), which can provide free childcare during readings, and **Big Bucket Productions** (tel. 598 9070). **Brentanos** and **Rizzolis** bookshops frequently do free big-name author readings.

Comedy

There's sometimes a definition problem here. Sandra Bernhard started out as an LA stand-up comic and now she's – what? Chanteuse, screen star, professional name-dropper, cabaret artiste? Holly Hughes goes for humour, but she's billed as a Performance Artist. And TV personality Johnny Carson started at Catch a Rising Star.

You won't find New York comics doing scripted routines so much as improvised comedy with the kind of dry wit you just heard from diner staff and the cabbie.

THE BALLROOM
253 W 28th St (bet. 7th and 8th Aves), tel. 244 3005.

This is one of the City's most upscale big-name cabaret and comedy venues. Cover $10–$15 and two-drink minimum on top.

CAROLINE'S AT THE SEAPORT
89 South St (South St Seaport), tel. 233 4900.

One of the oldest comedy clubs around and still going strong, with some of the best acts playing in glitzy surroundings. Cover $7.50 to $17.50 depending on act and whether it's week or weekend.

CATCH A RISING STAR
1487 First Ave (bet. 77th and 78th Sts), tel. 794 1906.

Talent scouts come hoping to catch rising stars. Seedy and enjoyable. $8–$12 cover with a two-drink minimum.

Film

Film and Women Martin Scorsese and Woody Allen are New York film-makers everyone knows about. Meanwhile: women and lesbians have united in a thriving alternative scene that came out of the dance world with **Maya Deren**, who used entirely female casts and crews to put her movement on film in the 1940s. Considered the mother of avant-garde cinema and women's independent film-making, Maya Deren would not have called herself a feminist, and even film-makers like one-time dancer **Yvonne Rainer** worked in the 1960s and 1970s within a framework that equated anti-Establishment with anti-Vietnam and sidestepped feminism (look out for Rainer's film *Privilege*). **Lizzie Borden**'s *Born in Flames* marked a key point in the 1970s wave of black women film-makers, and today there's a new breed of lesbian film-makers, including **Su Friedrich** (look out for her films *Gently Down the Stream* and *Damned If You Don't*). The organisation **Women Make Movies** is committed primarily to distributing independent films and also to ensuring that the kind of success **Susan Siedelman** enjoyed with *Desperately Seeking Susan* was not just a flash in the pan in the history of New York women film-makers. Women Make Movies (15 Vandam St, tel. 925 0606) has a film archive you can arrange to see, and if you want to know more, read E. Ann Kaplan's *Women and Film* (Routledge).

What's On   To find out what's on in your area, pick up the local newspaper for its film listings. *The Village Voice* film section has a mixture of reviews and listings with times of showings. 'Movie Clock' in the Weekend section of the *New York Times* has a complete listings of all the films in all five boroughs, but no reviews. *New York* magazine has a complete listings but no show times. If you're in a medium-to-large hotel you can tell the **concierge** your chosen film and he or she will find out the nearest movie theatre and times for you. Or use the **Movie Phone** service (dial 777 FILM) which tells you what's playing where, and screening times.

Tickets are usually around $7 or $8. Expect to queue for up to an hour for first runs of blockbuster movies. Women alone should avoid cinemas in seedy areas, most notably Times Square. Cineplex and Loews are two big chain cinemas you'll find all over. If you're here in September, the New York Film Festival is a must-see for 50 or more hot films that may or may not be screened again (at *Alice Tully and Avery Fisher Halls, Lincoln Center, Broadway at 65th St, tel. 877 1800*). Below are some movie houses that are special and good for women alone or in pairs.

ANGELIKA FILM CENTRE
18 W Houston (at Mercer St), tel. 995 2000.

Trendy cinema house that shows hot new independents along with the more interesting mainstream stuff and some foreign films. Six screens and a thronging café in the lobby, which is nice to relax in with a paper and serves till midnight.

ANTHOLOGY FILM ARCHIVES
32–34 Second Ave (at E 2nd St), tel. 477 2714.

Housed in an old courthouse building, this declared itself avant-garde by calling one of its spaces the Maya Deren theatre. Come for daily screenings of avant-garde and experimental film and video, both drama and documentary, and good showings of films by women. Phone ahead if you want access to the extensive Anthology Film Archive.

THE BIOGRAPH CINEMA
225 W 57th St (at Broadway), tel. 582 4582.

A favourite City revival house.

CITY CINEMAS
Third floor, 1370 Ave of the Americas, central, tel. 581 5900.

Mainstream but good to know because it's the only theatre on the Upper East Side that shows popular foreign films.

THE FILM FORUM
209 W Houston (bet. Varick St and 6th Ave), tel. 727 8110.

One- and two-week runs of independent American and foreign films in the heart of Greenwich Village.

THE KITCHEN
512 W 19th St (bet. 10th and 11th Aves), tel. 255 5793. Take a cab.

Founded in 1971 as a space for video art, this is now housed in a former ice house and film studio on the far edges of Chelsea. It's also good for new music and free dance.

LINCOLN PLAZA CINEMAS
Broadway (bet. 62nd and 63rd Sts), tel. 757 2280.

Not a particularly pleasant complex, but a good West Side location for mainstream foreign and popular independent films.

MILLENNIUM
66 E 4th St (bet. Bowery and 2nd Ave), tel. 673 0090.

East Village location for exclusively avant-garde programmes screened at this experimental film collective that does well by women film-makers.

MUSEUM OF MODERN ART
11 W 53rd St (bet. 5th and 6th Aves), tel. 708 9490.

It was the Museum's policy from the start to treat film as one of the most important art forms of the twentieth century. The 10,000-film strong archive goes worldwide through time and an impressive variety of genres. It frequently does good retrospectives of women directors, and its theme programmes are sometimes humorous – it did one, for example, on trains. There are as many as half a dozen screenings daily in the two small auditoriums. In March phone 877 1800 for details of the annual festival that showcases works by up-and-coming directors.

THE JOSEPH PAPP PUBLIC THEATER
425 Lafayette St (bet. E. 4th St and Astor Place), tel. 598 7150.

This has had a programme of experimental films since 1981.

RADIO CITY MUSIC HALL
W 50th St (at 6th Ave), tel. 247 4777.

This Art Deco landmark building has a HUGE screen – come for the spectacle.

THE ZIEGFELD
141 W 54th St (bet. 6th and 7th Aves), tel. 765 7600.

Resplendent with red velvet, chandeliers and one vast screen, this is often chosen as a plush location for premières. Indulgent Midtown mainstream cinema experience.

PAULINE KAEL

Of Pauline Kael, the *New Yorker* writer who turned film reviewing into an art and taught America to respect its own films, *Vanity Fair* columnist James Walcott said: 'She's only five foot tall, but I've seen her reduce grown men to tears.' She was born in Two Rock, California in 1919 and raised on a chicken ranch – not in the Wild West but in 'the ludicrous, real West'. She dropped out of Berkeley at the last minute in 1936 because she couldn't afford the $35 course fee and instead shacked up with avant-garde film-maker James Broughton, who later accused her of only being real, 'if she's real at all, in that movie theatre'. After her first review at the age of thirty-three, which damned Charlie Chaplin's *Limelight* as sentimental, she got a job reviewing on radio. In 1963 she wrote: 'I regard criticism as an art and if in this country and in this age it is practised with honesty, it is no more remunerative than the work of an avant-garde film artist.' In 1967 she was asked to join the *New Yorker* magazine; she was finally able to support herself through writing about films. By the 1970s she was invincible, rating popular American films like *Bonnie and Clyde* above revered respectable European cinema. She was praised for having a 'primitive moviegoer's soul', but today critics say she got too powerful and stayed too long at the *New Yorker* (into her late sixties) – they take great joy in saying that she has declined. Her famous cutting comments include: 'Clint Eastwood isn't offensive; he isn't an actor, so one could hardly call him a bad actor'; Ali McGraw 'is a truly terrible actress, of the nostril school. As the camera comes closer, her nostrils start flexing – not just for anger, for any emotion'; and 'What a face [Oliver Reed's] got for horror films: swinish, contaminated, clammy'.

Dance

The thriving New York modern dance scene was pioneered by Martha Graham (see box) and is now often fused with video and 'free jazz' in performance art. When choosing your venue remember the Uptown–Downtown divide: Uptown performances will be more traditional, Downtown more avant-garde. The December run of *The Nutcracker* performed by the New York City Ballet at Lincoln Center is a spun-sugar seasonal event for all the family (book a month ahead if you can), and if you want to catch future star classical dancers in their exciting teetering stages, go to Workshop Performances of the School of American Ballet (tel. 877 0600).

To find out what's on, use all listings but turn to the **New York Times** for intelligent reviews on classical and modern, and the **Village Voice** for reviews on alternative and 'free' dance.

For tickets, you can pay anything from $5 to $50, or more. For alternative spaces, contact the venue direct. The **TKTS** booths do discounted tickets for big ballets as well as theatre. Try the Music and Dance booth at Bryant Park (tel. 382 2323). You can queue for $6 or $9 standing room tickets at Lincoln Center stellar dance events. If the performance says 'sold out' it's worth dropping by an hour before the performance, when punters often sell off spare tickets.

BROOKLYN ACADEMY OF MUSIC
30 Lafayette Ave, Brooklyn, tel. 718 636 4100. Take a cab.

This is increasingly becoming a key established dance venue. Talents from Pina Bausch to the Central Ballet of China come here.

CITY CENTRE THEATER
131 W 55th St (bet. 6th and 7th Aves), tel. 581 7907.

This is the mecca of modern dance. Merce Cunningham and the Dance Theatre of Harlem perform regularly.

DANCE THEATER WORKSHOP
219 W 19th St (bet. 7th and 8th Aves), tel. 691 6500.

Expect the unexpected from this venue, which began in 1965 as a choreographers' co-operative and now showcases fresh talented innovators impatient with the long training periods of traditional companies.

DANCESPACE PROJECT
St Mark's Church in the Bowery (bet. 10th St and 2nd Ave), tel. 674 8112.

This newly renovated pristine buzzing East Village space hosts a festival of avant-garde choreography from October to June.

THE JOYCE THEATER
175 8th Ave (at 19th St), tel. 242 0800.

Housed in an Art Deco movie theatre, this Chelsea venue showcases regional companies and is home to the Feld Ballets/NY, which was founded in 1974 by a rebel American Ballet Theatre dancer.

NEW YORK CITY BALLET
New York State Theater, Lincoln Center, Broadway (at 65th St), tel. 496 0600.

The New York City Ballet has prided itself since the directorship of George Balanchine (who died in 1984) on being starless and performing a repertoire of modern and classical twentieth-century works that is unmatched the world over.

RADIO CITY HALL
1260 6th Ave (at 50th St), tel. 247 4777.

This is an all-American spectacle in a magnificent Art Deco music hall. The high-kicking spangled troupe of Rockettes share the stage with laser special effects and live animals according to the season: camels for Christmas, sheep for Easter.

MARTHA GRAHAM

Born to a psychiatrist in 1894, she trained in vaudeville and took up choreography in Manhattan in the 1920s so that she could star in her own works, and developed the Graham Technique. Inspired by Native American tribal mysticism and the American pioneering spirit, her technique involved uniting body and mind. She would hit dancers to make their required look of pain more convincing. The celebrated *Appalachian Spring*, with original music by Aaron Copland, brought her worldwide renown – Joseph Campbell put her on film as 'key to our civilisation' along with Mother Teresa and Martin Luther King – but critics always had trouble describing her work. Agnes de Mille said it was 'almost nothing, it was everything', that 'she had to spin out of her own entrails', and that 'she stripped off the chassis of the body and exposed the motor'. Agnes's mother said: 'Oh don't applaud Martha. She might do it again.'

Martha's 'active nightlife' consisted of many lovers, mostly other women's husbands, and a vain self-consciousness that must have been hard to sustain: 'I wouldn't be caught dead in bed without a light make-up.' Her one marriage was brief and bitter. In her seventies she only just survived alcoholism, and on her recovery she created an entirely new social life, mixing with Madonna and Liza Minelli and posing for ads, basking in fame until her death in 1991.

Classical Music and Opera

New York's classical music scene has long been the place to make or break young musicians' careers. You'll find some of the best acoustics and some of the most dedicated music-lovers in the world here.

To find out what's on, scour the *New York Times* 'Weekend' and Sunday 'Arts and Leisure' sections for reviews and listings. For tickets try the **Music and Dance Half-Price Ticket Booth** in Bryant Park, or queue for cheap standing-room tickets at Lincoln Center. Below is a list of established venues. Regular concerts are also held at the Frick Museum (see p.163) and the Metropolitan Museum of Art (see p.165), and in Central Park in the summer (check listings or phone NYCVB; see p.11).

ALICE TULLY HALL
144 W 66th St (at Broadway), tel. 362 1911.

Home to the Chamber Music Society of Lincoln Center, Alice Tully Hall is blessed with the best acoustics in the complex. As well as for evening Chamber Music recitals and new programmes of more contemporary music, come Wednesday afternoons for the free 1 p.m. concerts given by fledgling Juillard virtuosos in this 1,096-seat auditorium.

AVERY FISHER HALL
111 Amsterdam Ave (bet. 64th and 65th Sts), tel. 874 2424.

Newly spruced acoustics at this 2,700-seat orchestral music venue that attracts the black-tie-and-tiara set. The New York Philharmonic is in residence September–May. Illustrious music directors in the past have included Leonard Bernstein, and the post is currently filled by Zubin Mehta. The Philharmonic gives highly praised 'Young People's Concerts' four times a year, puts on a 'Mostly Mozart' programme in the summer, and has regular open rehearsals. Every September the Hall becomes the New York Film Festival venue.

BAM

30 Lafayette Ave (bet. Felix St and Ashland Place), Brooklyn, tel. 718 636 4100. Take a cab.

America's oldest performing arts centre, the Brooklyn Academy of Music is in a building that dates from 1908 and has hosted Enrico Caruso, Isadora Duncan, Laurie Anderson and Philip Glass. The autumn Next Wave Festival celebrates emerging international avant-garde artists. BAM has a 2,000-seat opera house and an Opera Project that was launched in 1988 by a Welsh National Opera programme.

CARNEGIE HALL

57th St and Seventh Ave, tel. 247 7800.

Yehudi Menuhin made his debut here in 1927, aged eleven, and described industrialist Andrew Carnegie's gift to the city as 'built more by music than by man'. Violinist Isaac Stern called it 'the queen hall of New York' and led the fight to save it from demolition in the 1960s, so that by 1986 it reopened after a $50 million facelift of new seats and mended masonry had restored it to its original splendour – and, some say, spoilt its acoustics. Legends who have trod the boards include Tchaikovsky on the 1891 opening night, Sarah Bernhardt, Gustav Mahler, Judy Garland and the Beatles, who wowed New York in 1964.

METROPOLITAN OPERA HOUSE

W 64th St (bet. Broadway and Columbus), tel. 362 6000.

Some think this a jewel too much in the Lincoln Center's crown, but it's hard to stay indifferent to the sweeping red-carpeted staircases, chandeliers, gold-leafed ceiling and art chucked around like confetti. Home to the Metropolitan Opera, this 3,800-seat hall also imports companies including the Kirov, the Royal Ballet and the Bolshoi. Known for having huge sets and spending fortunes on costumes. High ticket prices and high glamour for opening nights.

NEW YORK STATE THEATER

W 63rd St (at Columbus Ave), tel. 870 5570.

Cheaper and more adventurous than the Met, the New York City Opera performs here midsummer to autumn. Works staged range from *The Turn of the Screw* to *South Pacific* to *La Bohème* in programming that some find bizarre and opera-star-turned-director Beverly 'Bubbles' Sills (see p.186) declared was in the name of accessibility.

CLASSICAL MUSIC AND OPERA

E N T E R T A I N M E N T

HEALTH AND SPORT

American sport is family entertainment. Go to a game of baseball or football for a heavy dose of American culture complete with popcorn, hot dogs and pompom-shaking cheerleaders. Participation sport for your own health and recreation can be more tricky. You're well served if you like jogging – join the thousands puffing round Central Park's jogging tracks and reservoir – but there are few swimming pools in New York, and most health clubs require annual membership (exceptions are listed below). Hackers, Hitters and Hoops is popular with mothers and children, and after you've seen the stunts New Yorkers do on rollerblades, you might want to buy some too (see p.335).

Spectator Sports

The **baseball** season runs from April to September. There are two teams – the **Yankees** and the **Mets** – and two venues – Shea Stadium (see below) and Yankee Stadium. New Yorkers develop fierce loyalties for 'their' team, so if you're staying with friends, you'd be wise to check whom they support before going to a game. Both baseball venues are quite a haul out of Manhattan, so you might prefer to go to a **sports bar** (see p.289).

The **American football** season runs from August to December, and both teams – the **New York Jets** and the **New York Giants** – play at the Meadowlands Sports Complex in New Jersey (see below), which is also quite a haul.

It's much easier to see a game of **basketball** (October–July), since the **NY Knickerbockers** (Knicks) play at Madison Square Gardens (see below), as do New York's **ice hockey** team, the **Rangers**.

Tickets for all games generally come to around $10. You can buy them on the day – although if it's a popular game tickets could be sold out – or book with a credit card over the phone.

YANKEE STADIUM
Go for a game but don't stray from the crowds round the stadium, as it's in the South Bronx (see p.225).

SHEA STADIUM
126th St (at Roosevelt Ave, Queens), tel. 718 507 8499. 7 subway to Willets Point/Shea Stadium Station.

This is in safe, quiet Queens. Wrap up warm in the autumn.

MEADOWLANDS SPORTS COMPLEX
East Rutherford, New Jersey, tel. 201 935 3900. Regular buses from Port Authority bus station on 42nd St and 8th Ave.

MADISON SQUARE GARDENS
Between W 33rd St and 7th Ave, tel. 563 8300. 1, 2 and 3 subway to Penn Station.

This massive sports complex is on top of Penn railway station in Midtown Manhattan.

The swishest places for executives to work out are at a **New York Health and Racquet Club** or at one of the **Vertical Clubs**, but both require annual membership (at least $350). Try to persuade a colleague to take you as a guest.

You can **rollerblade** and **roller-skate** on the streets and in Central Park.

WOLLMAN RINK
64th St, Central Park, tel. 517 4800.

For ice-skating in winter and roller-skating in summer. Expect to pay $5 admission and $2.50 for skate rental. Hours 10 a.m.–9.30 p.m. weekdays (except Mon, when it closes at 5 p.m.); 12 noon to 11 p.m. weekends.

ROCKEFELLER CENTER ICE RINK
Tel. 757 5730.

Rink open from mid-October to April. Hours 9 a.m.–midnight on weekdays and to 10 p.m. on weekends. Rates depend on season and time of day/week: between $3.50 and $10 for adults and $6–$8 for children, with $4 skate hire.

HACKERS, HITTERS AND HOOPS
123 W 18th St, tel. 929 7482.

You can practise your baseball hitting in the nets here; other games you can play in Manhattan's first complete indoor sports complex include mini-golf and ping-pong.

CLAREMONT RIDING ACADEMY
173–177 W 89th St, tel 212 724 5100.

Manhattan's oldest and largest riding school/equestrian centre hires out horses with English-style saddles for $27 an hour to clop round the 4.4 miles of Central Park's bridle paths, or you can take lessons for $30.

10 ST TURKISH BATHS
268 E 10th St (bet. Ave A and 1st Ave), tel. 473 8806.

Come here for an old-fashioned steam and, if you wish, a platza rubdown. Admission $15; women's day is Wednesday.

BODY DESIGN BY GILDA
187 E 79th St (at 3rd Ave), tel. 737 8440.

You can buy classes singly, in packs of 5, 10 or 20, from aerobics to yoga. One class costs $15; 5 cost $70. Nice Upper East Side location.

CRUNCH
54 East 13th St (bet. University and Broadway), tel. 475 2018; and 140 Charles St (bet. Greenwich and Washington Sts), tel. 633 6863.

Great Downtown locations, and both will let you pay by the class – $10 each – or book 5 work-outs for $46, or 20 for $137 (which works out at $6.85 per class). Like Gilda (see above), Crunch does all the newest classes, including 'Low Impact' (cardiovascular exercise that doesn't stress the joints) and the 'Urban Yoga Workout' with New Age music. Crunch also has a 'Breakfast Club for Moms', which is bring-your-own-toys and doesn't offer babysitting but has a good reputation for a friendly, supportive atmosphere.

MegaFitness
*611 Broadway (bet. Bleecker and
Houston Sts), tel. 420 0507.*

This is mega-trendy and mainly male-
gay. You can get $199 3-month
membership, which gets you in free to
all the classes.

YWCA
*610 Lexington Ave (at 53rd St), tel.
755 4500.*

Annual membership costs $50 before
classes.

SHOPPING

SHOPS AND MARKETS

'I shop therefore I am,' says a piece of Barbara Kruger's art. Whether you're a bargain-hunter, a designer-label devotee or an all-night raver with a penchant for midnight browsing, New York is your paradise. But be careful. It's so easy to buy, buy, buy that you might get home and find that your credit card bill is bigger than your bank account.

New Yorkers do everything in a rush, so major department stores offer 'Personal Shoppers' to help speed up the shopping process (see below). New York businesswomen feel naked with unpainted nails, so practically every block has a Korean-run manicure salon, where you can have your nails done for around $7. The wives do the manicures while the husbands run the 24-hour deli-greengrocers known simply as Koreans, where you can emergency-buy basics from toothpaste and tampons to soda pop and a carry out coffee. The Spanish equivalents are known as bodegas. Koreans tend to be cleaner and better stocked than the bodegas, which you can tell by the red-and-yellow awnings sometimes bearing Spanish writing.

Types of shops can be broadly divided by area. Midtown has most of the big department and mainstream stores. Uptown is upmarket exclusive and Downtown has quirky boutiques, second-hand shops and bizarre specialist shops. Most Midtown and Uptown stores keep 10 a.m.–6.30 p.m. hours Mon–Sat, except Thursdays when many stay open till 9 p.m. The bigger stores open on Sunday. In Greenwich Village, the East Village and SoHo stores don't open till 11 a.m. or noon but stay open till 8 p.m. or midnight, including Sundays, and often close Mondays. Financial District and Civic Center shops keep business hours, Chinatown keeps all hours, and many Lower East Side stores observe religious holidays, so close Friday afternoon and Saturday.

Take your credit card everywhere, since even the smallest stores will accept Visa, American Express and Access (known as Mastercard). If you have traveller's cheques in US dollars you can often use them as cash, including all night at many Koreans.

REVOLUTION IN COSMETICS

One in four Americans are non-white, yet black, Asian, Hispanic and Native American women haven't been able to wear mainstream make-up lines because the colours and formulations were developed for white skins. The recession has forced the industry to look for new markets. In 1991 the Body Shop, Revlon and Clinique all introduced new ranges.

'It's powders and foundations that I have trouble with,' says model Naomi Campbell. Mainstream foundations contain chalk, which is glaringly obvious on dark skin, and oil, which helps drier white skins but is too heavy for dark skins. The new foundations are free of oil and chalk.

Flori Roberts Co., founded in 1967, is the acknowledged pioneer in the business. Fashion Fair followed in 1972, when John Johnson was cold-shouldered by all the cosmetics firms he asked to advertise in his magazine Ebony, and decided: 'If they don't want the market, I'll take the market.' Flori Roberts and Fashion Fair are sceptical about the cosmetic giants' sudden interest. 'It's wonderful the black customer now has a wider choice,' says the general manager at Fashion Fair, Lance Clark, 'but in order to be successful, these companies have to be willing to make the dark-skinned customer the primary target.'

Clinique representative Daniel J. Brestle said: 'We could have launched a black or Latin line, but no one wanted to be segmented,' so Clinique only expanded its range of foundations. Kayla Boutique in Beverly Hills took a different approach, launching a Kayla line specifically for Asian women. The main New York outlet for Fashion Fair, Macy's, expects a tremendous growth in business from the new ranges. Expect to see separate counters soon.

Bargains   Serious New York bargain-hunters visit the numerous designer discount stores regularly (see below), but they pick up the really hot items at one-off sample and designer-showroom sales. Here's how to track them down. Phone the Sales and Bargain Hotline on *540 0123* at $1.95 for the first minute and 75c a minute from then on. Or try the City's two fashion and couture schools, which host irregular sample and warehouse sales. They may be rubbish or throw up Geoffrey Beene and Donna Karan at less than wholesale prices. Phone **FIT** (the Fashion Institute of Technology) on *760 7650*; **Parson's School of Couture and Design** on *229 5364*.

Personal Shoppers   Alberta Koller, Ms Maniscalco and Sylvia Spitalnick all have whiter-than-white smiles and immaculate dress sense, and will help you with yours at no extra charge. They'll pick wedding, work or vacation outfits, they'll ask if you've forgotten any relatives' birthdays, then suggest gifts and even send them for you. If you're a frazzled businesswoman with just one short Saturday or Sunday to get kitted out for several occasions, the service could be ideal. If you're not, it's a typically American over-the-top experience that will be fun but seriously expensive if you buy everything that's suggested. Phone **Macy's By Appointment** on *560 4181*, Bloomingdales' **At Your Service** on *705 3135*, Mode Plus at Galeries Lafayette on *355 2985*, Saks' **5th Avenue Club** (*940 4200*) and ask for the Executive Service (which will, if you wish, send reminders of birthdays and anniversaries by post), and **Barney's** New York (*929 9000 ext. 505*) helps harassed super-rich mothers dress their children for school – and keeps fidgety young ones happy with biscuits and chocolate milk.

Designers To Watch   Donna Karan 'put sex in women's business suits' (*Vogue*), she's branching out to men's clothes, she says cashmere sweatpants are the new jeans, she thinks if women don't make it it's because they don't try; she works seven days a week and she has a cook and a physical instructor come to her house at 7 a.m. to 'keep her stabilized'. Dallas-born New York-based **Tod Oldham** makes sportswear with a sense of humour, including a skirt with Mona Lisa designed in beads. **Isaac Mizrahi**, who is said to have achieved a decade's designer maturity in four years, snubs the recession with Dior opulence in floor-length gingham and animal-skin prints. **Yohji Yamamoto** is Japanese described as having 'a TriBeCa edge' for putting a pregnant model on the catwalk in a great double-breasted, open-stomached suit accessorised with a large metal handbelt cradling her belly.

All these are 'hot' New York-based designers who don't yet have their own store and are bound to open one soon. But the hottest of the lot is Anna Sui.

Anna Sui's designing career started when a game of Action Man she was playing with a friend's older brother turned into Academy Awards and she was dressing up army men as movie stars in tissue-paper gowns. She went to Parson's School of Couture and Design but kept a nostalgic fascination with flea markets and mixed it with a riotous imagination. She'll see a Barbie doll travelling costume and a photo of Lady Diana Cooper gardening, then she'll put Barbie's straw hat and cork-soled sandals with striped denim sportswear, Lady Diana's gardening gloves and a bumblebee stick-pin.

A young cultish Downtown crowd loves Sui's clothes, and Sui thinks the trick is the price. You can't slum it in a $3,000 outfit, she reasons. She chooses wool or cotton over silk or cashmere and gets good contractors so she can charge $300 for a jacket when her contemporaries are charging $600. Madonna and Linda Evangelista and forty-year-old New York women who are sick of paying inflated designer prices love her clothes. Meanwhile, Sui continues to try ideas out on the life-size mannequin of the legendary *Vogue* editor Diana Vreeland that she keeps in the entrance to her ruby-red Chelsea apartment. 'She's my idol. I dress her up in different clothes every day' – which could be anything from tweed trimmed with raffia to a panther-print dress and Christian Lacroix jewellery.

Department Stores and Malls

Macy's built a myth as the people's palace of commerce and shopping, while Bergdorf Goodman made his name as importer of exclusive European couture, but today the distinctions are blurred. Macy's tried to go upmarket and nearly went bust in the process; Bergdorf, Saks and Henri Bendel all boast much the same stock, and security staff is rather too much in evidence. Experience the stores as part of a walk-up-5th-Avenue shopping experience that could include Tiffany's and Cartier, and – if you've got the money or the guts – take tea in an armchair in one of the designer rooms while models parade ball gowns for your eyes only.

Department Stores

ALEXANDERS
731 Lexington Ave (bet. 58th and 59th Sts), tel. 593 0880.

If you're strapped for cash, come to Polyester Paradise for cheap high styles you've just seen on Fifth Avenue, but at discount prices.

BERGDORF GOODMAN
754 5th Ave (at 57th St), tel. 753 7300.

All the major names are here, and not just on the clothes. Millionaires have been coming here since 1928. Crystal chandeliers, marble floors and a fountain that once belonged to the Vanderbilts make it a royal or sickening experience.

BLOOMINGDALES
1000 3rd Ave (at 59th St), tel. 705 2000.

This too is mainly about upmarket designer clothes – buy trendy OshKosh for your children and slinky Sonia Rykiel for yourself – but there's also a cook section, home electronics, books and art supplies, and Bloomingdales, fondly known as 'Bloomies', is great fun to visit. Sales assistants create an assault course of perfume-spraying and every spring the store becomes another country (it's been France, Italy and the South Seas in the past).

HENRI BENDEL
10 W 57th St (bet. 5th and 6th Aves), tel. 247 1100.

Genteel Bendel's range of designer wear is a little hipper than Saks' and Bergdorf's but not as hip as Barney's.

MACY'S HERALD SQUARE
151 34th St (at 6th Ave), tel. 736 5151.

R.H. Macy was a whaler deckhand who reinvented himself as 'Captain' Macy, survivor of a shipwreck, and founded Macy's in 1858 with the slogan 'It's smart to be thrifty' and the rule: all dealings in cash. Immigrants changed alienating headscarves for Macy's all-American hats. In 1947 the film *Miracle on 34th Street* claimed that Macy's had the real Santa Claus, and every child in New York queued to go see. Today the bargain basement has gone, but the store, which covers an entire block, still claims to be 'the biggest in the world'. It has a marble Art Deco main floor, a worn but still marble staircase, you can make a video of yourself singing pop songs and you can take children to the Glemby Hair Salon (see p.341). Under new management, Macy's will continue to be legendary as long as it continues to provide the city's Thanksgiving Day Parade, complete with majorettes and big balloon Bugs Bunnys, baseball stars and beauty queens.

SAKS FIFTH AVENUE
611 5th Ave (bet. 49th and 50th Sts); tel. 753 4000.

Claiming to be a byword of quality and style, Saks sells clothes and cosmetics to a host of well-heeled celebrities. Fight your way past the limos and drivers.

Malls
Malls (pronounced 'molls') are in essence purpose-built shopping precincts where mothers work behind the counter and children hang out, and they're not New York's forte.

TRUMP TOWER AND GALERIES LAFAYETTE
4–10 East 57th St (at 5th Ave), tel. 355 0022.

Two shopping malls in one, and neither quite works, perhaps because Donald Trump is new-monied New York and Galeries Lafayette is a French import and malls are an all-American tradition. The chi-chi opulence of Trump Tower is worth a look, though, for its marbled atrium and po-faced doormen instructed to chuck out all undesirables – namely, the large number of homeless who would bed down by the tinkling fountains if they could. The Tower also houses one of the few public rest rooms in the area.

PIER 17
South Street Seaport. Off South St (at Fulton St).

Perhaps the only successful mall in Manhattan, this is really good only for food and atmosphere. Romantic sea view, and filled with clichés of roly-poly American kids in turned-round baseball caps stuffing hot dogs, burgers and popcorn.

Designer Clothes

AGNES B
116–18 Prince St (bet. Greene and Wooster Sts), tel. 925 4649.

This is at present *the* 'in' SoHo designer store.

BARNEY'S NEW YORK
117 7th Ave (at 17th St), tel. 929 9000.

Founded as a discount outlet for men's clothing sixty years ago, Barney's has become a swish Chelsea designer showcase for European and American couture, catering mainly to Uptown women who want an informal Downtown atmosphere. Take the lift to the top of the main section and walk down past Donna Karan, Anne and Calvin Klein, Alaia and Fendi booths, being careful to avoid the helter-skelter metal handrail, which is seriously static. For less expensive, funkier new designers go to the east wing cutting-edge Co-op section, where the staff are friendly; some are aspiring designers themselves. The elegant basement café is not cheap but pleasant. An uptown Barney's is opening on the corner of 61st and Madison in 1993.

CHARIVARI

Founder Selma Weiser gained a reputation for fearless European jetsetting with eagle-eye spotting of up-and-coming avant-garde designers when she set up her first humble dress shop on the Upper West Side twenty-five years ago. Now the empire has been taken over by her daughter Barbara and the men's side by her son, who was the first in America to buy Armani. Go to the small original **Charivari** shop at *2315 Broadway (bet. 83rd and 84th Sts, tel. 873 1424)*, or to **Charivari** 57 at *18 W 57th St (tel. 333 4040)* which has a wider range, and to **Charivari Workshop** at *441 Columbus Avenue (81st St, tel. 496 8700)* for avant-garde Japanese designs in blacks, greys and whites. You'll find Byblos, Katharine Hamnett, Yohji Yamamoto, and American designer Cathy Hardwick, who makes sophisticated suits and dresses that are body-hugging like Alaïa's but more wearable for more people. If you're not rich it's still worth a visit, because Charivari always stocks a range of affordable T-shirts.

MADISON AVENUE

The ten blocks of Madison Avenue between 66th Street and 76th Street contain excessively lavish, typically Upper East Side designer stores, including Sonia Rykiel at *No. 792 Madison (66th and 67th Sts, tel. 744 0880)*, Emanuel Ungaro at *803 Madison Ave (67th and 68th Sts, tel. 249 4090)*, Armani at *No. 815 Madison (E 68th St, tel. 988 9191)*, Polo-Ralph Lauren in the French Renaissance building at *No. 867 Madison (72nd St, tel. 606 2100)*, Yves Saint Laurent–Rive Gauche at *No. 855 Madison Avenue (70th and 71st Sts, tel. 988 3821)*, and Givenchy at *21 E 75th St (at Madison Ave, tel. 772 1322)*. You can get nearly all the same clothes in department stores, but there you don't get to mix with Upper East Side women having loud conversations about how many pedicures, therapy sessions and soirées, and how little time.

Alternative Clothing

Go to the Co-op, also known as the Women's Store, at Barney's (see above) for lots of new designers in one place.

BETSEY JOHNSON

130 Thompson St (bet. Houston and Prince Sts), tel. 420 0169, and 248 Columbus Ave (at 71st St), tel. 362 3364.

New York institution Betsey Johnson has been keeping her clothes young, fun, affordable and sexy since the 1960s. Get day-glo halter-neck tea dresses or patchwork hotpants. The Downtown branch is most funky.

109 CLOTHING STORE

132 Thompson (bet. Prince and Houston Sts), tel. 475 8072.

Considered very 'in' by young hip New Yorkers, but stocks mainly unremarkable clothes.

PATRICIA FIELDS
10 E 8th St (bet. 5th Ave and University Place), tel. 254 1699.

A new three-storey version has opened on 6th Avenue at 8th Street, but this is the original Patricia Fields store. Go to the 6th Avenue branch for clothes including psychedelic hipsters, wigs and glitter eyelashes, come here for lingerie, and visit both for club flyers, for the camp staff, for decadent 1970s decor, and for Patricia Fields's extrovert reputation. Dubbed the 'Dyke Diva of Style', she was photographed for the cover of the City's gay magazine in heels, suspenders and pearls holding up the traffic while fondling her lover in the middle of the street.

UNION
172 Spring St (at W Broadway), tel. 226 8493.

Young hip New Yorkers love it because it's very English. Duffer of St George meets Passenger.

Vintage Clothing
For 'vintage' read second-hand with inflated prices. New York is not the best place to buy 1950s frocks and original stack heels, but the shops are fun to browse in.

ALICE UNDERGROUND
380 Columbus Ave (at 78th St), tel. 724 6682.

Alice the cat stands over the cashmere sweaters while the theme tune of *Bewitched* wafts over skinny 1950s ties and Victorian jewellery to the $5 bin in the back room.

SCREAMING MIMI'S
22 E 4th St (bet. Lafayette and Bowery), tel. 677 6464.

Window mannequins in black bustiers and patent leather thigh-high boots. Large collection of corduroy pants inside and outfits that will turn you into one of the Partridge family, or in the knick-knack section there's mod flower-print glasses that look straight out of the Brady kitchen. This shop has made its name with fashion editors.

Discount Clothing
A *very* New York and money-saving thing to do is to go to a Discount Store.

CENTURY 21
22 Cortland St (bet. Broadway and Church St), tel. 227 9092.

You get the best bargains at Loehmann's, but Century 21 is more convenient and easier to negotiate, since it is laid out like a regular three-floor store. You might find cut-price Ray Bans, a reversible Christian Dior terry robe, and there's good swimwear and children's clothes sections. Civic Center workers come every spare lunchtime to make sure they get the best bargains – new stock comes in from all over the world daily. No changing rooms, but refunds up to two weeks after purchase.

DAFFY'S
111 5th Ave (at 18th St), tel. 529 4477 or 355 Madison Ave (at 44th St), tel. 557 4422.

As with all discount stores, you must wade through bizarre *Dallas* outfits to find last season's Perry Ellis and Anne Klein at 50–80% off. Daffy's refuses to stock ivory, fur, or leather from endangered species on principle. Purchases can be returned within seven days.

SHOPPING

LOEHMANN'S
Broadway and 236th St, Riverdale, tel. 543 6420, 10–9 Mon–Sat, 11–6 Sun. 1 subway to 238th St.

A favourite haunt of drag queens and hip New Yorkers who want to look as if they earn enough to afford $1,000 on a dress but can spend only $300. It all started in the Depression, when Mrs Loehmann took a handbag-full of greenbacks and the ability to outbargain anyone to manufacturers often desperate for cash, and she walked out with high-style bargains to sell cut-price at her Bronx store, now the flagship store of 150 Loehmann's nationwide. Racks and racks to rifle through, and you might not find something on your first trip. No refunds or exchanges once something's paid for. Go with a friend, because it's quite a long way off the beaten track.

DIY Clothes
The recession has turned pretty, hip young heads to sewing machines, and here are some of the shops they go to.

PARON FABRICS
60 West 57th St (at 6th Ave), tel. 247 6451.

All natural-fibre, designer fabrics at rock-bottom prices (especially in the second-floor section). Embroidered lace for a ball gown and printed linens for summer dresses.

B&J FABRICS
263 West 40 St (bet. 7th and 8th Aves), tel. 354 8150.

More designer fabrics, including Liberty, Viyella and Italian and French knits, hand-beaded silk and lace at 10–25% off current styles, with mill close-outs the best bargains.

TENDER BUTTONS
143 62nd St (bet. 3rd and Lexington Aves), tel. 758 7004.

Millions of buttons, antique and new, from $100 to 10 cents each, shaped like Betty Boop or ponies, made of brass or seashell, all laid out to make browsing a pleasure.

Basics and Big
Use the **Gap** chain for casual T-shirts, slacks, shirts, all at reasonable prices. You'll find the Gap everywhere.

ANN TAYLOR
2017 Broadway (at 69th St), tel. 873 7344; 25 Fulton St (at Water St), tel. 608 5600; 2 World Financial Center, Upper level, tel. 945 1991.

Every American businesswoman's standby. If you've lost your best no-nonsense work blouse, here's where you come to replace it.

CANAL JEANS
504 Broadway (bet. Spring and Broome Sts), tel. 226 1130.

Cavernous store with loud music plus every style of Levi you know and then some. Also cheap socks and bags, and a jewellery section that ranges from flower power to Goth.

DAVE'S ARMY AND NAVY STORE
779 6th Ave (bet. 26th and 27th Sts), tel. 989 6444.

Go to Canal Jeans for the experience and Dave's for the cheapest stone-washed Levis from a small dumpy store where you feel you've earned your bargain.

THE EXECUTIVE MOTHER
757 3rd Ave (bet. 47th and 48th Sts), tel. 753 4993.

Stylish maternity wear, plus basics. Midtown professionals count on it.

THE FORGOTTEN WOMAN
888 Lexington Ave (at 66th St), tel. 535 8848.

'Pretty Dressing in Larger Sizes.' Tailored suits, cashmere sweaters, cocktail dresses and leather skirts in sizes 14 to 24. Good service.

Shoes
All the big department stores have good shoe sections, and here are two contrasting stores to try.

HOUSE OF FLUEVOG
104 Prince St (bet. Greene and Mercer Sts), tel. 431 6616.

John Fluevog's monster-heeled shoes are bought by Madonna, Lady Miss Kier and Anna Sui, but it's hard to spot them tucked discreetly between chandeliers and Greek pillars. Friendly if spaced flower-power-dressed assistants in this very SoHo shop.

LACE-UP SHOES
110 Orchard St (at Delancey St), tel. 475 8040.

Charles Jourdan, Anne Klein, Joan and David, Saint-Laurent – all at a claimed discount of 20–30% in this Lower East Side store. Note: some stock is not discounted, including Mefistos, the expensive French walking shoes.

Haircuts

ASTOR PLACE HAIR DESIGNERS
2 Astor Place (at Broadway), tel. 475 9854.

Punks, octogenarians, students, trendies, rushed businessmen all collect a ticket and queue supermarket-style for a haircut that's quick and cheap ($12). Of the row of freelance cutters, you don't know who you'll get, how good they'll be, or even what language they'll speak. Don't go if you've a specific hairstyle in mind – ask for a trim or give them free rein. Mohawks are among the more staid results.

VIDAL SASSOON
767 5th Ave (bet. 58th and 59th Sts), tel. 535 9200.

For reliably good, classic or innovative haircuts. Students, children under twelve and senior citizens get a 30% discount. Have your hair cut by a trainee and it's cheaper still. Otherwise pay $58–$90, depending on the seniority of the stylist.

Lingerie

JOOVAY
436 W Broadway (bet. Prince and Spring Sts), tel. 431 6386.

The SoHo place for sumptuous lingerie, including teddies (all-in-ones) in black and scarlet as well as tender pastels.

VILLAGE BRA SMYTH
179 West 4th St (at Jones St), tel. 929 1917.

More bras than teddies (all-in-ones), and this one's in Greenwich Village.

Beauty
New York is jam-packed with beauty parlours – department stores are always good bets – but one of the first and many think still the best is:

SHOPPING

326

ELIZABETH ARDEN
*691 5th Ave (bet. 54th and 55th Sts),
tel. 546 0200.*

The legendary red door leads to five
floors of salon that pampers New
York's well-heeled gentility, including
women like Liza Minelli and Jackie
Onassis. You can have manicures,
pedicures, haircuts, waxing, all in your
own private dressing-room complete
with tissues and cosmetics, and staff
say you can leave a different person.
Have a $200 'Maine Chance', which is
a complete head-to-toe makeover
including light lunch and massage
(book months in advance if you want
a Saturday). Half-day packages
include Miracle Morning and Visible
Difference for over $150.

Jewellery
Jewellery browsing can be an
excuse to check out famous
Tiffany's and Diamond Row,
47th Street between Fifth and
Sixth Avenues.

ARTWEAR
*456 Broadway (near Prince St), tel.
673 2000.*

Robert Lee Morris studied
anthropology before designing
jewellery that blends 'science fiction
with the romantic past'. He uses lots
of cross, dagger and snake images and
displays one-off pieces as if they're in
an art gallery. He does Donna Karan's
signature jewellery and is making
cases for Elizabeth Arden.

DIAMONDS BY RENNIE ELLEN
*15 E 47th St (bet. 5th and 6th Aves),
tel. 869 5525.*

Between shows on Broadway, dancer
Rennie Ellen worked as a diamond
cutter, and when she hung up her

shoes she opened this shop. Diamonds
are cut and polished on the premises
to sidestep middlemen and make the
prices the best on Diamond Row.
Grateful engaged and married couples
send photos for display in the
reception area.

TIFFANY & CO.
*727 5th Ave (bet. 56th and 57th Sts),
tel. 755 8000.*

Tiffany's has been synonymous with
quality, style, and romance since
Audrey Hepburn in *Breakfast at
Tiffany's*. As well as flash jewels,
there's crystal and silverware upstairs.
Good for extra specially stunning
gifts, such as a sterling silver baby
rattle in the shape of a dumbbell
encased in a Tiffany box.

YLANG YLANG
*806 Madison Ave (at E 86th St), tel.
879 7028.*

The ultimate in showy costume
jewellery. Materials like stainless steel
and rhinestones are mixed in lavish
necklaces and earrings.

Pharmacies
The Duane Reed chain is everywhere in Manhattan. It's cheap
and well-stocked. Look in the
Yellow Pages if you haven't
already stumbled across your
local branch, or target one of
the following.

BIGELOW PHARMACY
*414 Ave of the Americas (bet. 8th and
9th Sts), tel. 533 2700.*

An official Historic Landmark,
Bigelow has been in the same
Downtown location since 1838, oak
fixtures and gaslight fittings included.

BOYDS OF MADISON AVENUE
655 Madison Ave (at 60th St), tel. 838 6558.

This has become a regular celebrity hang-out. Joan Rivers buys the hairbands, Joan Collins buys 'sealed lips' and Boyd's own-brand perfume, and every star buys one of their famous make-up mirrors, which cost anything between $200 and $500 and magnify pores to bizarre proportions. Also, a vanity item common to most pharmacies is Rembrandt whitening toothpaste for $14.

CASWELL MASSEY
518 Lexington Ave (at 48th St), tel. 755 2254.

Another oldie, with cut-glass jars and dark wood cases, but this one's Midtown and boasts Martha and George Washington as past customers. You can buy President James Madison's wife Dolly's cologne, Eisenhower's almond cream soap and Hoover's razor strop. Good place for smelly presents.

KAUFMAN PHARMACY
557 Lexington Ave (at 50th St), tel. 755 2266.

An old-style drugstore, complete with daytime grimy coffee bar, that's OPEN 24 HOURS.

Bookshops
Two chains that you'll see everywhere are B Dalton (good big selection of general titles) and Barnes and Noble (offers sizeable reductions on new hardbacks and paperbacks), and there are several branches of the American W.H. Smith, Doubleday. But if you want to browse it's worth making a special trip to one of the smaller bookshops, which usually have benches, relaxing atmospheres and tirelessly helpful staff.

BARNES AND NOBLE
105 5th Ave (at 18th St), tel. 807 0099.

Famous for its nursing and medical department, this branch also has a special children's annexe (see p.340) and there's a sales shop across the street.

BRENTANO'S
597 5th Ave (at 48th St), tel. 826 2450.

Beautiful store with balcony and staircase protected by the Landmarks Preservation Commission. Decent travel and New York City book sections.

RIZZOLI BOOKSTORE
31 W 57th St (bet. 5th and 6th Aves), tel. 759 2424.

A haven just off Fifth Avenue with wood-panelled walls and chandeliers. Respected for its art section and the Penguin paperback selection (rare in the States). Also has European newspapers and magazines.

STRAND BOOK STORE
828 Broadway (at 12th St), tel. 473 1452.

A sign warns 'Know thine author' because this store has 8 miles plus of some new and mainly second-hand books, including some untouched reviewer's copies. Fascinating chaos that requires stamina.

Women and Gay
Some notable feminist publishers whose books you'll come

across include: **Feminist Press**, which is known for reprints of authors like Agnes Smedley and Charlotte Perkins Gilman; **Naiad Press**, which specialises in fluffy lesbian romance novels; **Spinsters**, which is committed to ground-breaking lesbian fiction and non-fiction; and **Firebrand**, whose all-feminist list features some comic cartoons including the well-selling Alison Bechdel's 'Dykes to Watch Out For' cartoon series.

DIFFERENT LIGHT BOOKS
548 Hudson St (bet. Charles and Perry Sts), tel. 989 4850.

Well-stocked gay and lesbian Greenwich Village bookshop, fiction and non-fiction, with wonderfully friendly helpful staff and racks full of club and community event flyers plus sexy gay and lesbian fanzines at the back.

JUDITH'S ROOM
681 Washington St (bet. Charles and W 10th), tel. 727 7330.

Advertised as 'Books for Women and Their Friends', this is New York's only women's bookshop. It's not as well stocked or friendly as Different Light and not exclusively lesbian, but it's still a key first stop for any lesbian arriving in the City, and a great resource for all women. The table at the front displays ads for women's events. The bulletin board at the back is for personal notices, including apartments for rent. There are free readings at least once a week, (get a calendar of events from an assistant, or phone for details). There is a Young Adults section, and a wall displaying

monthly and quarterly magazines including Gloria Steinem's *Ms.* as well as blue-collar *Tradeswoman* and the more esoteric *Hag Rag* from the Intergalactic Feminist Press.

ST MARK'S BOOKSHOP
12 St Mark's Place (bet. 2nd and 3rd Aves), tel. 260 7853. Open till 11 p.m. 7 days a week.

'Alternative' political-with-a-conscience rather than gay, this airy pine-look bookstore is popular with every East Villager for its late hours. It has a good range of journals on African culture, feminism and socialism, and a noticeboard by the door advertising art films and t'ai chi classes.

Specialist Bookstores

TRAVEL: THE COMPLETE TRAVELLER
199 Madison Ave (at 35th St), tel. 685 9007.

The oldest travel bookstore in the country. Stocks new and rare books as well as maps and cassettes. Helpful staff.

NEW YORK: NEW YORK BOUND BOOKSHOP
50 Rockefeller Plaza (bet. 50th and 51st Sts), tel. 245 8503.

Ceiling-high shelves filled with over 3,000 current and out-of-print books on New York, including guides, literature, photos, maps and prints, and there are chairs to make it feel even more like a library. Ask to meet the co-owners Judith Stonehill and Barbara Cohen, resident experts on New York.

MIND AND BODY: EAST WEST BOOKS
78 5th Ave (bet. W 13th and 14th Sts), tel. 243 5994; 568 Columbus Ave (at W 87th St), tel. 787 7552.

New Age bookstores with books on Eastern philosophy, yoga, meditation, homeopathy and stress management. Upper West Side branch also houses the Himalayan Institute of New York.

BIOGRAPHY: THE BIOGRAPHY BOOKSHOP
400 Bleecker St (at 11th St), tel. 807 8655.

The only New York store specialising in biographies, autobiographies, letters, journals, travelogues. Titles from America and imported from Europe, all organised for enjoyable Downtown browsing.

Specialist and Oddity Shops
New York has innumerable specialist stores, some entirely practical, many quirky and based in SoHo or Greenwich Village.

AMERICAN HOUSEHOLD: GRACIOUS HOME
1217 3rd Ave (bet. 70th and 71st Sts), tel. 517 6300.

The ultimate functional, busy New York housewares store where you can make assumptions about the average New York housewife's habits, problems and preferences. Aisles display dog Frisbees, Rubbermaid dish-drainers, Magic Mushroom airfreshener, and a dizzying array of traps and poisons: Roach Motels encourage cockroaches to check in but not check out; glue in a tray is a low-tech Rat and Mouse Trap.

ART SUPPLIES: PEARL PAINT CO. INC.
308 Canal St (near Broadway), tel. 431 7932.

Art students like it because the prices are said to be the lowest in the City. Pearl Paint's five-floor department-store atmosphere is good for browsing the wide inventory of materials.

CONDOMS: CONDOMANIA
351 Bleecker St (at W 10th St).

Samples of the various types, sizes and colours of condoms are strung up around the walls along with condom earrings (so you always have one spare), T-shirts saying 'Got a stiffie? Wear a jiffie!' and Dental Dam for women. Loud disco music, embarrassed patrons, amused staff.

DOGS: CANINE STYLES
831 Lexington (bet. 63rd and 64th Sts).

This is just one of about a million shops devoted to pampering dogs. The window displays a book, *What Sign is Your Pet?* that will help you 'find out how the stars move your loved ones'. As well as the usual bowls and bones there are doggy raincoats and doggy 'pumping iron' T-shirts. This dog fixation is especially bizarre when you consider the size of most New Yorkers' flats.

INDUSTRIAL CHINA: FISH'S EDDY
889 Broadway (bet. 19th and 20th Sts), tel. 420 9020; 551 Hudson St (bet. Perry and 11th St), tel. 627 3956.

Buy everything from Ritz–Carlton Hotel plates to Seamen's clubs bowls and Football Series mugs. Fish's Eddy is the only shop in America to stock this amount of industrial china, including some surprisingly expensive collectors' items.

SEX SHOPS:
There are many, but two catering to different markets are:

COME AGAIN
353 E 53rd St (near 1st Ave) tel. 308 9394, which is run by a supporter of Prostitutes of New York (PONY), and sells everything for working girls including lingerie outfits and practical equipment;

EVE'S GARDEN
119 West 57th St, 4th floor, tel. 757 8651 has been created by women for women and their women friends and sells 'women-created erotica' plus 'an exciting collection of romantic and sensual accessories to enhance self-love and shared-love'. Slated by PONY members as man-hating, Eve's Garden is loved by its regulars.

WURLITZERS: BACK PAGES ANTIQUES
125 Greene Street (bet. Prince and W Houston Sts), tel. 460 5998.

This SoHo shop is crammed with lovingly restored classic Wurlitzer jukeboxes, Coca-Cola vending machines and pool tables, and there's a fortune-telling machine featuring Gypsy Grandma.

Sweets and Treats
New Yorkers have sweet teeth, so there's plenty of places to satisfy yours, but here are a couple of shops worth a special trip if you're an addict.

ECONOMY CANDY
108 Rivington St (bet. Essex and Ludlow Sts), tel. 254 1531.

Don't be deceived by the huge trashy tubes of candy. This Lower East Side store also sells top-quality Swiss chocolates at prices that surprise even the manufacturers. Nuts and dried fruit too, and tea, coffee and mustard have 20–50% discounts.

LI-LAC CHOCOLATES
120 Christopher St (bet. Bleecker and Hudson Sts), tel. 242 7374.

Behind this small plain store front chocolates have been hand-dipped since 1923. The truffles (Grand Marnier and amaretto) are a rare treat, and you could take home chocolate computers or a chocolate Empire State as gifts.

Food – Markets, Supermarkets, Delis

There are wonderful food shops in New York, but because restaurants are so cheap, eating in won't necessarily save you money, even if you have children. However, supermarkets are good for snacks if you can't face another meal out, or just for the shopping experience. Huge bags of Hershey Almond Kisses, coronary-inducing Enterman Bakery Products, vitamin supplements in milk as a matter of course, and intermittent automatic water-sprayer over fresh vegetable sections.

Chains you'll find everywhere are **Big Apple** and **Sloans**. **Gristedes**, which includes a range of kosher food, is mainly an Uptown, slightly pricier chain. Most supermarkets stay open till 10 p.m. or midnight, but **Food Emporium** operates 24 hours.

Other options are the **delis** and **Koreans** on every block, and the food halls at **Macy's** and **Bloomingdales**.

Speciality Grocers

These are as much for people-watching as for the titillating delicacies.

BALDUCCI'S
424 6th Ave (at 9th St), tel. 673 2600.

Still family-owned, but not the mom-and-pop stand it once was; the too-small bustling aisles are lined with imported English biscuits and Dijon mustard, and the home-made counter includes cannelloni and shrimp primavera. Very Greenwich Village.

DEAN AND DELUCCA
560 Broadway (bet. Prince and Spring Sts), tel. 431 1691.

Swisher SoHo store with a cappuccino stand where you can hover nervously before braving the baskets and crisp chrome shelves crammed with about 200 cheeses, 30 different types of coffee beans, and mouth-watering pastries.

KAM-MAN
200 Canal St (bet. Mott and Mulberry Sts), tel. 571 0330.

Big Chinese supermarket for everything including noodles, smoked duck and teas. Many of the packets are marked only in Chinese, but other shoppers will help you out if you're stuck.

MYERS OF KESWICK
634 Hudson St (bet. Jane and Horatio Sts), tel. 691 4194.

This shop imports hard-to-find British fare including Marmite, Smarties, Lucozade and fresh pork pies. Frequented by New York-based English trendies when they're homesick.

ZABAR'S
2245 Broadway (at 80th St), tel. 787 2000.

Housed in a bizarre fake Tudor building that runs nearly a whole block, Zabar's has a dedicated following that cuts through class divisions. Take a ticket before you browse the cheese and fish counters, where you can enjoy watching lox men trimming salmon with a surgeon's precision. Warm smell of fresh ground coffee permeates.

Bagels, Bread and Pastries

EAT
1064 Madison Ave (bet. 80th and 81st Sts), tel. 772 0022.

An expensive but wonderful range of breads including sourdough and raisin and walnut, with a fresh-baked smell that'll knock you out.

ESS-A-BAGEL
359 1st Ave (bet. 21st and 22nd Sts), tel. 260 2252.

You can buy bagels everywhere in New York, but there aren't many where they're made on the premises – and this is one. Try pumpernickel – raisin or garlic filled with salmon cream cheese or whitefish salad.

RIGO
318 E 78th St (bet. 1st and 2nd Aves), tel. 988 0052. Open Sundays till 4.

This tiny Hungarian Viennese pastry shop is way out in German Yorkville, but it's well worth the trip. Three wrinkled, smiling Transylvanian women sell Pressburger Poppyseed horns, Cherry Lizzers and legendary strudels that are all baked on the premises by a Hungarian chef.

MOISHES HOMEMADE KOSHER BAKERY

181 Houston St (bet. Allen and Orchard Sts), tel. 475 9624.

Huge dark Russian raisin–pumpernickel loaves and flat chewy bialys sold hot from the oven. Prices are often reduced in the afternoon.

ZITO AND SONS BAKERY INC.

259 Bleecker St (bet. 6th and 7th Aves), tel. 929 6153.

A bit of Italy in Greenwich Village. Olive oil and onion bread sold from a plain small store that supplies many of the good restaurants in town.

Savouries

CHEESE AND DAIRY:

BEN'S CHEESE

181 E Houston St (bet. Allen and Orchard Sts), tel. 254 8290. Open 7 days a week.

This shop sells farmer's cheese flavoured with odd ingredients like nuts and blueberries, all made fresh on the premises.

DIPALO DAIRY STORES

206 Grand St (near Mott St), tel. 226 1033.
This Little Italy store sells the best Sicilian creamy sheep's milk cheese, ricotta salata, at $4.99 a pound.

COFFEE:

MCNULTY'S TEA AND COFFEE COMPANY

109 Christopher St (bet. Bleecker and Hudson Sts), tel. 242 5351.

Antique wood creates a warm atmosphere in this small shop. Fresh roasted coffees include blends from as far as Timor and New Guinea.

PICKLES:

ESSEX PICKLES

35 Essex St (bet. Grand and Hester Sts), tel. 254 4477.

Watermelon rind and pickled peppers sold straight from the barrel.

SMOKED FISH:

RUSS AND DAUGHTERS

179 E Houston St (bet. Allen and Orchards Sts), tel. 475 4880. Open 7 days a week.

Best prices in the city for high-quality smoked salmon, herring, sturgeon and caviar. Also imported olive oils and vinegars.

Health and wholefood

APHRODISIA

282 Bleecker St (bet. 6th and 7th Aves), tel. 989 6440.

Cardamom, clover and African yohimbe scent the room as curious patrons lift lids among more than 700 jars of spices. Neal's Yard products are stocked, Pre-Menstrual Syndrome help books are on sale, and a white cat wanders around.

BROWNIES

91 5th Ave (bet. 16th and 17th Sts), tel. 242 2199.

Cosy dated 1970s pine shelving gives a clue: this was the first health shop in New York City. Still well stocked, and pleasant laid-back atmosphere.

COMMODITIES

Corner of Hudson and N Moore, tel. 334 8830.

Organic produce, natural bodycare, vitamin supplements stacked between pillars in this echoey TriBeCa 'Natural Food Supermarket' that's open 7 days a week 10–8 p.m.

EARTH'S HARVEST TRADING CO.
700 Columbus Ave (at 95th St), tel. 864 1376.

Upper West Side store that sells only fine, fresh produce from flour to nuts to 'Kiss My Face' cosmetics range. It has a herbalist available Mon–Fri to recommend various herbs for minor ailments.

GREENMARKET AT UNION SQUARE
Open Wed, Fri and Sat from 8 a.m. till vendors have sold out. Tel. 566 0990 for other locations.

This is a real farmers' market that's not entirely vegetarian but is organic (chickens are free-range; fish caught by Long Island fishermen). Buy vine-ripened tomatoes and raw honey. Get snacks from barrels of apples or trays of organic muffins.

INTEGRAL YOGA NATURAL FOODS
229 W 13th St (bet. 7th and 8th Aves), tel. 243 2642.

None of the products contains sugar, fructose or preservatives, and the store is affiliated to the Yoga Institute, so you can research courses while you buy your brown rice or health-food snack.

THE HEALTH NUT
2611 Broadway (at 99th St), tel. 678 0054. Also 1208 2nd Ave, 825 2nd Ave and 2141 Broadway.

This is quickly becoming a chain with consistently good stocks of organically grown produce, foods free of preservatives and sugar and a special macrobiotic food section.

Liquor and Wine
Every supermarket and deli sells beer, off-licences also stock wine and spirits, but no establishment is allowed by New York State law to sell alcohol on a Sunday. Prices are State-controlled, so you won't find much difference from store to store, but some do manage discounts and some offer an especially good range. Here's a selection.

ACKER MERRALL AND CONDIT
160 W 72nd St (bet. Columbus Ave and Broadway), tel. 787 1700.

This is an old-established Upper West Side liquor merchant with a reputation for good selections of Burgundy and American wines plus good service and late hours (11.30 p.m.).

BURGUNDY WINE COMPANY
323 W 11th St (bet. Hudson and West Sts), tel. 691 9092.

Greenwich Village owner wine merchant Al Hotchkin, specialist in fine wines of Burgundy and the Rhône, will give you advice and long stories – he likes to wax lyrical about his travels through vineyards.

SHERRY LEHMAN
679 Madison Ave (at E 61st St), tel. 838 7500.

This faux wine cellar with wooden stools sporting carved men and baskets of grapes is one of America's top wine merchants and the best known in New York. Does a lot of shipping to the Hamptons.

SoHo Wine and Spirits
461 W Broadway (bet. Prince and W. Houston Sts), tel. 777 4332.

Small, civilised but no snootiness, boasting the city's most extensive choice of malt whiskeys, the largest champagne selection, and low prices.

The Barrel People
Tel. 606 243 8602.

Organic wines, mostly American, including a semi-sweet blend of Cayuga and Seyval called Moonglow and a blend of Niagra and Cayuga called Sweetheart, that are sold at the Greenmarkets (phone for details), or there's free delivery if you order 12 bottles plus.

Fairs and Markets

There are a few large markets that you can bank on, but the smaller ones tend to shift location and days frequently. Phone NYCVB (see p.11) for an up-to-date list. Also bear in mind that New York is not the best place for antiques, and that's what most markets sell, but they're still fun to browse, and that goes for the stall owners too. One keeps a live parrot on his shoulder to attract custom. Greenwich Village almost always has clusters of stalls at street junctions selling anything from tacky rings to ethnic masks, and individuals often set up on car bonnets in SoHo selling things like cutesy pomanders and cacti pots. Best bargains are to be found at summertime neighbourhood block fairs when residents throw out their junk. Look for ads in newspapers and photocopied flyers in local shops. Food fairs are most fun (see p.4 for festivals).

Annex Antiques Fair and Flea Market
6th Ave (bet. 25th and 26th Sts), tel. 243 5343. Sun 9–5.

This is big, spreading over two parking lots near the Chelsea flower district. Antiques and knick-knacks sold by dealers from as far afield as Pennsylvania. Combine a visit with brunch at Lola's (see p.269).

I.S. 44 Market
Columbus Ave (bet. 76th and 77th Sts), tel. 947 6302. Sun 9–5.

A school playground fills with 300 dealers. Highlights include costume jewellery and a farmers' market.

Records

Tower Records
692 Broadway (at E 4th St), tel. 505 1500. Open till midnight 7 days a week.

This is huge and very well stocked. The opening hours are fatal for local NYU students, who spend evenings flipping through the second-hand section instead of studying. Video and electronic annexes are great for children. Anyone wanting cheap CDs will have a field day.

Bleecker Bob's Golden Oldies
118 W 3rd St (at MacDougal St), tel. 475 9677. Open Sun till 1 a.m.

The Village's oldest rare record store, good on imports, not so good on obscure albums, but now also stocking punk, New Wave and progressive rock. Not cheap. Knowledgeable staff to help you.

Electronics and Photographic

UNCLE STEVE
343 Canal (at W Broadway), tel. 226 4010.

Audio and video equipment is cheaper in the States anyway, but Uncle Steve offers a further 10% discount. All purchases must be made in cash and are non-refundable unless the goods are faulty, in which case you must return within 7 days or deal direct with the manufacturer. Look through *Consumer Reports*, the equivalent to *Which*, in a library so you know what you are looking for before you go.

47TH ST PHOTO
67 W 47th St (bet. 6th and 7th Aves), tel. 398 1410.

Grit your teeth while you go up the narrow staircase and be clear what you want, because the assistants get impatient quickly. Excellent prices on film.

PORTOFOTO INC.
596 Broadway (at Houston), tel. 226 9788.

A reasonably priced, friendly store at a good central location that will print photos quickly and supplies films.

Sport

HORIZONTAL
336 E 61st St (bet. 1st and 2nd Aves), tel. 826 2992.

This is next to the exclusive Vertical Club and should be your first stop if you want to be dressed in up-to-the-minute spandex that puts form over function at the dynamic aerobics or body-sculpting classes.

PECK AND GOODIE
919 8th Ave (bet. 54th and 55th), tel. 246 6123.

The City's foremost skate shop for 60 years, Peck and Goodie supplies good old roller skates as well as ice skates to star JoJo Starbuck, and it sells several brands of rollerblades, prices starting at $130 for adults and $85 for children. Ask about lessons.

CHILDREN, BUSINESSWOMEN, GETAWAYS

CHILDREN

Children love riding the subway, buses and taxis; they love the Circle Line ferry; they love the spectacle and thrill at the top of the Empire State and the World Trade Center; they love the tray-sized plates piled high with burgers and chips – all in all, children love Manhattan, but the experience can be hard work for you, and it's likely to be expensive. Kids older than six pay full fare on the subway, twelve and over and they pay full admission at most museums, few restaurants do children's menus or half portions, and childcare is extortionate. Women living in the City find it difficult to afford crèches and playgroups – as a visitor you must resign yourself to large babysitters' bills or to taking your children everywhere with you. Widespread fear of child-snatching by 'crazies' may or may not be New York paranoia, but it means that no mother leaves her child alone even for a second. Most New York children of twelve have never even been allowed down to the corner store unaccompanied.

Having children in New York is so expensive that they've become symbols of wealth and are therefore expected to behave like mini-adults. Your child will not, however adorable, cause whoops of delight. The most you can expect is dour respect if he/she doesn't cause a fuss. Most New York children are very well dressed, and you'll get treated better if yours are too. Fortunately, many children's clothes are cheaper in New York – you can stock up on Osh Kosh, for example, before you leave.

As a general rule, warm times of the year are the best times to go with young children – you can sit on breezy outdoor patios to breastfeed; in colder weather older children can have a great time (try the Wollman Ice Rink). With young children, 'snugglies' are better than pushchairs, which are awkward in subway toll gates and tend to get tripped over by crowds in the streets.

Few bars, restaurants or cafés actively encourage families with children, but some sections of the City are more welcoming than others. Midtown cafés and restaurants can be snotty and unhelpful even at lunchtime but may try to bar children in the evenings, particularly if you have a pushchair; the Upper West Side, SoHo, Greenwich Village and TriBeCa are much more friendly, and Chinatown and Little Italy generally like children. Everywhere, your state of mind is crucial. Adopt the New Yorkers' attitude – just decide to bloody well go places – and people will have to accommodate you. The same goes for breastfeeding – just do it. Changing facilities are a rarity and it's hard to find clean rest rooms. You'd do best to use the ones in museums, restaurants, hotels, department stores, shopping atriums as you patronise them, and see p.35 for a list of public toilets.

Resources

Look in the *Village Voice, New York* magazine and the Friday edition of the *New York Times* for up-to-date listings of happenings for children.

Babysitting   With approved sitters. Fees range from $6 to $10 an hour depending on the age of your child (infants under a year old generally cost more). Babysitters won't be surprised if you want to book them for a whole day, and most will happily take your child on day trips.

BABYSITTERS GUILD
60 E 42nd St, tel. 212 682 0227.

This has been in business since 1940 and screens its sitters rigorously.

BARNARD BABYSITTING SERVICE
Milbank Hall (at 116th St), tel. 854 2035. This provides good, reliable babysitters for as little as $5 an hour, but since they're all Barnard College students, few will be available during summer exams.

92ND STREET Y
1395 Lexington Ave (at 92nd St), tel. 212 415 5440.

If you're determined to find a summer camp at any cost, the 92nd St Y is one of the few places that might be able to help you. You must write well in advance to the 'Center for Youth and Family' and put your situation to them.

Options available include occasional four-day arts/crafts/sports programmes at $50 a day and Camp K-ton-ton for three to five year olds for the whole summer at around $1,700 (and that's cheap). All camps and programmes get booked up quickly.

PARENTS' LEAGUE OF NEW YORK
115 E 82nd Street, 10028, tel. 212 737 7385.

The Parents' League of New York, which operates only between mid September and June, is of most use for women who are spending some time in New York, in which case the League will help you place your child in a suitable school. If you're on a short visit, phone for current information on all cultural events for children, phone for advice if you have any kind of child-related emergency, phone for recommended babysitters, and buy their *Parents' League's Calendar and Guide to New York* ($10 from the office or $11.50 by post, write direct or contact the London Representative: Mary Young, 5 Cresswell Place, London SW10, tel. 071 244 7256).

Museums and Culture

Look out for **readings at Eeyore's Books for Children** and **Storyland** (usually on Sundays). Children always love festivals and parades – see p.4 and don't miss **Big Apple Circus** at Lincoln Center (tel. 212 268 3030) from late October to early January. There are childrens' sections in many of the major museums, most notably the **Junior Museum** at the Metropolitan Museum of Art (see p.165) and the **Discovery Room** at the American Museum of Natural History (see p.188). The **Brooklyn Museum** (see p.213) and the **Whitney Museum of American Art** (see p.177) run special programmes for children. Note: the **Frick** does not allow children in at all.

THE METROPOLITAN OPERA
(see p.185) Tel. 212 769 7022 for information on the Met's 'Growing up with Opera' programme and special Sunday performances for families.

AVERY FISHER AND ALICE TULLY HALLS
(see p.185) Tel. 212 704 2100 for information on the Little Orchestra Society, which plays on Sundays.

New York has three museums especially for children. Of these, the **Brooklyn Children's Museum** (145 Brooklyn Ave, Crown Heights, Brooklyn, tel. 718 735 4400) is geared mainly towards community activities. Best use one of these:

THE CHILDREN'S MUSEUM OF MANHATTAN
(see p.188) This is handy for Central Park and best liked for its Urban Tree House out back.

STATEN ISLAND CHILDREN'S MUSEUM
(see p.221) This is off the beaten track, but many children and mothers find it a little less stuffy than the Manhattan Museum, and it's a great excuse to go on the Staten Island ferry.

Sports and Outdoors

CENTRAL PARK
(see p.180) Children love the **Zoo** and the **Conservatory Water** with its huge remote-controlled model boats and the nearby statues of Alice in Wonderland and Hans Christian Andersen. For older children there is roller-skating or ice-skating (depending on the season) at the **Wollman Rink**.

MANHATTAN RACEWAY
893 Broadway (tel. 212 673 4100). Open daily until 2 a.m.; prices around $5 for half an hour. This claims to be the largest Scalextric track in America.

Playgrounds New York has a good number of well-equipped **playgrounds**:

ABINGDON SQUARE PARK
(bet. Bleecker and Hudson Sts) has a friendly atmosphere plus slides and sandpits where younger West Village kids play.

CARL SCHURZ PARK
(near East End Ave and 84th Sts) is within sight of the East River Esplanade.

JOHN JAY PARK
(off York Ave near 77th St) is big and busy with swinging bridges, curving slides, a sprinkler and a big sandbox.

PEARL STREET PLAYGROUND
(bet. Fulton, Water and Pearl Sts) is wackily decorated with a couple of giant-size multicoloured letters and a wall of glass blocks.

77TH ST AMSTERDAM AVE
features a log castle, fortress slides and tyre swings; it was built by parents and designed by kids working with a professional playground designer.

CENTRAL PARK
has the large **Heckscher** playground(mid-park at 62nd Street), which is designed expressly for toddlers. A number of 'adventure playgrounds' have recently been installed complete with tunnels and tubes and sand or rubber matting on the floor. You'll find playgrounds along **Fifth Avenue** at 67th St, 71st St, 77th St, 85th St and 95th St; along **Central Park West**, they're at 68th St, 81st St, 85th St, 93rd St and 100th St.

PROSPECT PARK
Like Central Park, Brooklyn's park is safe in the daytime, especially weekends, but not recommended at night. In Prospect Park there's kite-flying on the Long Meadow on Sundays. Afterwards you could go to the **Brooklyn Botanic Garden** for its Trail of Evolution in the Steinhardt Conservatory.

Food for Children

MINTER'S ICE CREAM KITCHEN
(see p.254).

CHINATOWN ICE CREAM FACTORY
(see p.260).

RUMPELMAYERS
(see p.271). Legendary place to come for hot chocolate.

SERENDIPITY
(see p.278). A must for afternoon sweet treats.

MOM'S BAGELS
(see p.270). Stock up on bagels here before doing the Circle Line ferry.

LOX AROUND THE CLOCK
(see p.269). Lox and bagels in Chelsea.

CARNEGIE DELICATESSEN
(see p.270). Come at weekends for the original diner experience.

ROYAL CANADIAN RESTAURANT AND PANCAKE HOUSE
(see p.256). Strange inventions called womelettes and rivers of maple syrup.

POPOVER CAFÉ
(see p.276). More pancakes, but these are uptown.

MOONDANCE DINER
(see p.258). On weekends, cool Downtowners bring their kids as cool accessories.

ORIENTAL PEARL
(see p.260). Dim sum on Sunday.

COWGIRL HALL OF FAME
(see p.263). Tex-Mex food at a place you'll frequent because it's run by a sympathetic single mother.

TWO BOOTS
(see p.265). Another first stop for

mothers and children, but this time for pizza.

Hows Bayou
(see p.256). Cajun food for lunch in TriBeCa.

Benny's Burritos
(see p.267). Go to the Greenwich Village branch for burritos that will keep children quiet for a long lunch.

Triplet's Roumanian
(see p.258). Eastern European food in a fun atmosphere.

Pig Heaven
(see p.279). Chinese food Uptown.

Shops

Macy's
(see p.320). **Father Christmas** and Christmas time puppet shows at Macy's are musts.

Barnes and Noble Junior Branch
122 5th Ave (bet. 18th and 17th Sts) tel. 212 633 3500.

This well-stocked children's annexe of the chain bookstore has helpful staff.

Books of Wonder
464 Hudson St (at Barrow St), tel. 212 645 8006; 132 7th Ave (at 18th St), tel. 212 989 3270.

Antique and new books – mostly hardback – for children of all ages.

Eeyore's Books for Children
2212 Broadway (bet. 78th and 79th Sts), tel 212 362 0634; 25 E 83rd St, tel. 212 988 3404.

A large selection of books, regular readings and author appearances – come after visiting the Junior section of the nearby Metropolitan Museum of Art.

Bébé Thompson
98 Thompson St (bet. Prince and Spring Sts), tel. 212 925 1122.

Stylish Downtown children's clothes store with lots of embroidery and jungle prints.

Chocolate Soup
946 Madison Ave (bet. 74th and 75th Sts), tel. 212 861 2210.

Sells handcrafted one-offs and imports from hats with propellers for infants through to primary-coloured hand-knits for young teenagers.

Gapkids
215 Columbus Ave (bet. 69th and 70th Sts), tel. 874 3740; 1164 Madison Ave (at 86th St), tel. 517 5763; for locations of other Gapkids tel. 446 3889.

Reasonable prices on a wide range of clothes for kids aged two to fourteen. Stock up on chinos for $28, cotton tops for around $10, and check out the Sale rack.

Greestone and Cie
442 Columbus Ave (bet. 81st and 82nd Sts), tel. 212 580 4322.

Outfits yuppie West Side children of all ages.

Big City Kite Co.
1201 Lexington Ave (bet. 81st and 82nd Sts), tel. 212 472 2623.

A wide and colourful selection of kites that flutter in every bit of available space.

Enchanted Forest
85 Mercer St (bet. Spring and Broome Sts), tel. 212 925 6677.

The shop is as enchanting as the products. Trees shoot up through wooden balconies and classical music soothes children poring over handmade folk toys, stuffed animals and books of fairy tales and mythology.

F.A.O. SCHWARZ
767 5th Ave (at 58th St), tel. 212 644 9400.

This is a must-see vast toy store with a mad mechanical clock in the doorway and staff dressed up as donkeys, clowns and cavewomen. You may remember it from the film *Big*, which has a long and funny scene where Tom Hanks plays here.

THE LAST WOUND-UP
290 Columbus Ave (bet. 73rd and 74th Sts), tel. 212 787 3388; 889 Broadway (at 19th St), tel 212 529 4197.

'Don't postpone joy!' is this shop's motto. Kids and adults are encouraged to play with the selection of wind-up toys.

PENNY WHISTLE TOYS
132 Spring St (bet. Wooster and Greene Sts), tel. 212 925 2088; 1283 Madison Ave (bet. 91st and 92nd Sts), tel. 212 369 3868.

Same stock in both jam-packed shops, but the SoHo Spring St branch is most fun.

SECOND CHILDHOOD
283 Bleecker St (bet. 6th and 7th Aves), tel. 212 989 6140.

Tiny Greenwich Village store selling old dolls, toy soldiers, tin trains – more adults than children gazing nostalgically into the glass cases.

ALBEE'S
715 Amsterdam Ave (at 95th St), tel. 212 662 5740.

For everything from baby's bottles to pushchairs and booster seats, this is convenient for West Siders.

BEN'S BABYLAND
81 Ave (bet. 5th and 6th Sts), tel. 212 674 1353.

A big selection of baby accessories (pushchairs etc.), often discounted from retail prices.

GLEMBY HAIR SALON
34th St (at 6th Ave), tel. 212 695 4624.

Take your children to Glemby's in Macy's for a haircut – toys are available and staff are specially trained to handle children.

SHOOTING STAR
767 5th Ave (at 58th St), tel. 212 644 9400.

F.A.O. Schwarz's Shooting Star has been cutting children's hair for generations.

New York is a great place to come on business. Businesswomen have been accepted and respected since the 1970s and New York is a twenty-four-hour service city: midnight, Christmas or last-minute business services might not come cheap but will certainly be available (get the hotel concierge to help you, or look in the Yellow Pages).

New York businesswomen are renowned for being tough-skinned to the point of inhumanity. Business meetings are never relaxed – it's 'I've got ten minutes. Don't waste them.' And New York businesswomen are undauntable – a client's 'no' is interpreted as an 'additional negotiating opportunity', 'we'll discuss that later'. If you're pregnant you might find it works to your advantage. Businessmen respect you more, as pregnancy indicates that you are after all human, and businesswomen will sympathise. Currently, however, 'feminism' is a dirty word. Businesswomen are tough, but they make sure they resemble power-dressed Barbie dolls. If you don't have painted nails you'll get odd looks and possibly a tactful suggestion that you spend $7 on a manicure and polish at one of the Korean nail shops you'll see on every block. New York businesswomen wear lashings of make-up and high heels, hence the trainers on the streets. They like pastel shades, not black or greys. Indeed, black tights/stockings can be difficult to get hold of, so if you're not happy with American Tan, take lots with you. Tightly tailored suits are always acceptable. Culotte suits are popular in the day. But there's no such thing as 'informal' for New York businesswomen. 'Informal' dress is likely to involve a lot of heavy gold jewellery, and if jeans are worn, they'll be designer jeans accessorised with silk shirts and elaborate belts. Knowing what's 'in' is an obsession with businesswomen just as it is for the rest of New York, and since there's never only one 'in' thing to do, you should ask advice. In shops and hotels seek out women who look as if they might have appropriate tastes and ask where the 'in' clubs and restaurants are – New Yorkers will usually be flattered. You can't use **Catalyst** (tel. 212 777 8900) as a resource, but you can be assured that the organisation is continually 'working with business to effect change for women through research, advisory services and communication'. Any benefits Catalyst gains for New York businesswomen you'll gain from while you're here, and the same benefits will soon filter into Europe.

For general city resources see directory, for shops, accommodation and nightlife see practicalities, and below is a short businesswomen's directory:

BEAUTY
Saks Fifth Avenue and Bergdorf Goodman both have reputable beauty salons, and see p.326 for Elizabeth Arden.

CAR SERVICES
For car rental see p.345, but for stress-free comfortable travel within New York City use limousines which you can hire, complete with chauffeur, from innumerable companies including Gotham Limousine Inc. (527 W 36th St, tel. 212 868 8860) or Sophisticated Lady Limo (2847 Dudley Ave, the Bronx, tel. 212 822 0040).

COURIERS
Choice Courier Systems Inc. (733 3rd Ave, 5th floor, tel. 212 370 1414) has a fleet of 600 radio dispatch vehicles, operates 24 hours all year, guarantees 90-minute delivery and quotes an approximate price of $18 from the Midtown hotel district to the Financial District.

DOW JONES REPORT
Telephone 212 976 4141.

FOREIGN NEWSPAPERS AND PERIODICALS
Every big, expensive hotel either sells foreign newspapers in the lobby or leaves them in the concierge lounge. Otherwise, you can get a wide selection at: the Eastern Lobby Shop in the Pan Am Building, 200 Park Avenue, open daily 6 a.m.–10p.m., Sat 8 a.m.–4.30 p.m., tel 212 687 1198; Hotalings News Agency at 142 West 42nd Street, open Mon–Sat 7.30 a.m.–9 p.m., Sun 7.30 a.m.–8 p.m., tel. 212 840 1868 (Hotalings will mail papers to you but won't deliver); Rizzoli International Bookstore at 31 West 57th Street, open Mon–Sat 9 a.m.–9 p.m., Sun 12 p.m.–9 p.m., tel. 212 759 2424; and Hudson News, 265 East 66th Street (at 2nd Ave), open Sun–Thurs 10 a.m.–9 p.m., Fri–Sat 10 a.m.–11 p.m., tel. 212 988 2683.

SECRETARIAL SERVICES
Choice Personnel (18 E 41st St, tel. 212 679 5900) has for nearly two decades been placing hosts/hostesses, models, demonstrators, registration personnel and secretaries, and it offers a 24-hour 7-day-a-week service; Mademoiselle Temporaries, Inc. (16 E 40th St, tel. 212 576 1022) is one of the oldest and best-known personnel services for all support staff needs.

THANKYOUS
Sutton Flowers (62 W 56th St, NY 10019, tel. 489 0350) specialise in floral arrangements for conventions, but they also do individual arrangements and will deliver worldwide; Teuscher Chocolates of Switzerland (620 5th Ave at Rockefeller Center bet. 49th and 50th Sts, NY 10020, tel. 212 246 4416) have handmade chocolates flown in from Zurich weekly.

Go beaching, hiking, whaling, hunting . . .

Once in New York it's hard to tear yourself away, but if your trip is more than a week long, it's well worth taking a day or two out for a battery recharge. To help choose from the plethora of attractions within easy reach of the City, read on for suggestions or contact the **I Love New York** tourist offices (*1515 Broadway, New York NY 10036, tel. 212 827 6250, fax 212 827 6279*), tell them your needs – nightlife and suntans, rejuvenation before business convention, cheap motel or place for children to run wild – and they'll fit you up with appropriate alternatives.

Things to bear in mind while making your decisions include New Yorkers' odd attitudes to what's near or far and to what constitutes relaxation. Manhattan's Statue of Liberty is considered a hefty day trip, but **Niagara Falls** – 446 miles away – is feasible fun (Gray Line New York, 900 8th Ave, tel. 'Niagara Desk' 212 397 2620, fax 212 247 6956, does a one-day round trip for $290). If you're after relaxing walks and beautiful scenery, ignore New Yorkers' advice on weekends, because New Yorkers out of town will go to some lengths to re-create New York (signs in posh Manhattan wine shops say 'will deliver to Long Island'; chic restaurants and nightclubs open Hamptons branches). Finally, travel midweek if you can: accommodation's cheaper and everything's quieter.

Hardened sun addicts who don't mind ugly formalised beaches and impossible crowds can spend a day at **Jones Beach State Park** (take a train from Penn Station to Freeport and then a connecting bus). New Yorkers at weekends automatically head to **The Hamptons** at the south-east end of **Long Island**'s 125-mile stretch, but unless you have someone to stay with – budget-conscious New Yorkers do rent shares on apartments; CEOs and famous writers own bijoux mansions – you'll be an outsider in what is basically an exclusive and therefore excluding fancy suburb. Go further for the 10-mile strip of stark cliffs and dunes that's **Montauk**, where *Jaws* was filmed and the Okeanos Research Foundation does whale-watch cruises (information from the I Love New York office or the Long Island Hotline: 1 800 441 4601).

In contrast to the even beach-lined South Shore, Long Island's wooded **North Shore** has hilly coves, rocky necks and steep bluffs. Dubbed 'the Gold Coast' at the turn of the century for the sea-view luxury pads built by Manhattan's movers and shakers, the North Shore has historic sites to visit, including the **Vanderbilt Museum** mansion and Teddy Roosevelt's home at **Sagamore Hill National Historic Site**, and it has reminders of the 1840s when whaling brought in the bucks and spawned communities – see harpoons and scrimshaw at Cold Spring Harbor's **Whaling Museum**.

The **Hudson River Valley** has a different appeal again, mainly its stunning scenery. The surrounding thick wooded **Catskill Mountains** – Rip Van Winkle country – has trout fishing and hiking in summer, skiing in winter, and all year round you can visit **West Point**, military outpost since the eighteenth century, or the **Factory Outlet Shopping Village** for rock-bottom-priced haute couture or houseware in Colonial-style buildings.

Getting About With a car you can pack lots into a weekend, but it can be expensive (at least $50 before insurance or parking fees), and it can be frustrating (interstate highways are boring and parking space is hard to find). Public transport limits mobility but it's pleasant, efficient and reasonably priced.

Trains: for trips to Long Island contact Long Island Railroad (tel. 718 454 LIRR or 718 990 7498, departures from Manhattan's Penn Station); for the Hudson River Valley contact either Metro North (tel. 212 532 4900, departures from Grand Central Station) or Amtrak (tel. 1 800 872 7245, departures from Penn Station). **Buses**, all departing from Port Authority: the Hampton Jitney covers Long Island (tel. 516 283; 4600; 212 936 0440); Shortline serves the Hudson Valley and the Catskills (tel. 212 736 4700); the legendary Greyhound bus goes just about anywhere in the USA (tel. 212 971 6363).

If you want the independence of **car rental**, hire firms you can make arrangements with in Britain include: Hertz on 081 679 1799 (from around £36 per day including basic insurance but excluding 13.25% City tax, pick up from JFK airport or one of the Manhattan branches, main one being 222 E 40th St, tel. 212 486 5060, open 7 days a week); Holiday Autos on 071 491 1111 (minimum of 3 days at £22 a day before City tax plus airport tax of 9.8% if picking up at JFK airport, or without airport tax if picking up from Dollar Rent-a-Car, 329 E 22nd St, tel. 212 420 8070); Allamo on 0895 443355 (from £25 per day or £27 in August, including insurance but before City tax, pick up from Newark Airport or 1–9 South International Way, Newark, tel. 201 733 2723). For those already in New York, use the Manhattan Yellow Pages to phone around for the current best deal, try the ones above, or try Avis, city-wide and 217 E 43rd St, tel. 212 593 8378 (from $61.98 a day, including insurance but not City tax); Rent-a-Wreck tel. 800 421 7253 or 212 721 0080 (specialists in used car rental with Fri–Sun deals of around $119). New York City law says you have to be at least twenty-five years old to drive. If you're younger, you can get the bus to New Jersey, where the legal limit is twenty-one. New Jersey is also the place to go to avoid New York's high City tax if you're on a budget but still determined to rent a car.

To help you through the maze of multiple options, here are

three getaway suggestions.

GETAWAYS

Fire Island's Cherry Grove

Take Long Island Railroad from Penn Station (tel. 718 454 LIRR or 718 990 7498) to Sayville or Bayshore and from there the ferry to Fire Island, which runs May–Oct for $10 round trip, dogs pay half fare (tel. 516 665 3600 for timetable).

Anywhere on Fire Island, the thin 32-mile spit that runs parallel to Long Island's south shore, is 'in' for gays and trendies, but particularly Cherry Grove, which floods every sticky summer weekend with Lipstick Lesbians (see p.295) strolling topless, hand in hand, along the flat crowded beaches.

Fire Island is primarily a resort. There is some nature, including the Sunken Forest (near Cherry Grove), where gnarled holly, sassafras, and the vines of poison ivy climb from the forest floor towards the sun, and there is the sea, but people prefer to use the hotel pool. Cherry Grove's appeal is the 'scene', and perhaps a bit of hung-over sunbathing before diving back into the 'Ice Palace Entertainment Complex' (a disco). Go as a couple, or pick someone up when you get there.

Stay at the **Cherry Grove Beach Hotel** (open 1 May – 1 Nov, PO Box 537, Sayville, NY 117820537, tel. 516 597 6600), but book well ahead and expect to pay in full at least a month before if you want absolute confirmation of your reservation (Access and Mastercard accepted). Go at weekends for the 'scene' but pay higher rates. The hotel's 59 rooms range from $53–$168 a night for standard rooms to $79–$221 for deluxe rooms, depending on time of week and season. The rooms all have simple decor (white walls, grey carpets), but if you pay deluxe you get air-conditioning, TV, phone and kitchenettes. The hotel boasts 'fun, fun, fun' drag shows, great blender drinks, shower heads and dancing till dawn with New York City's top DJs. The Atlantic Ocean is within 200 yards, and so is a restaurant, The Monster on Top of the Bay, which does decent meals – 'heavy on the seafood' – at around $20 for a main course.

Day Trip Up The Hudson

Either catch a Metro North train from Grand Central to Cold Spring, $14 round trip, or contact Camille Rampersaud's 'Off the Beaten Track' bus tours, 2383 Walton Ave, Bronx, NY 10468, tel. 212 562 4753 (one-day tours run Fri, Sat, Sun and cost $20–$30).

This is ideal for the woman alone who needs peace, quiet and beautiful surroundings but hasn't got more than a day to find them.

If you want the security of a tour, go with 'Off the Beaten

Track' (see above) for a Saturday of craft villages around Sugarloaf and the 152-year-old underground cellars of Brotherhood, America's oldest winery.

Or head out yourself. Hop on a train at Grand Central (see above), bag a river's-edge seat and watch industrial blight fade into idyll. Get off at Cold Spring (55 miles from New York), where you can grab a bite at the station's Depot restaurant before picking up a hiking map at the Main Street bookshop and deciding which mountain to climb. Americans hate walking, so you'll most probably have it all to yourself. It's wise to stick to the clearly marked hiking trails – that way you won't get lost and you'll avoid the handful of poisonous (not deadly) Copper Head snakes. Only minutes away is Bull Hill, at 1,400 ft one of the tallest and with a breathtaking view from the summit on clear days of the Catskills wooded mountains – fiery red or vibrant green, depending on the season – and a glint of Manhattan in the distance.

Bear Mountain

Get the Shortline bus from Port Authority (tel. 212 736 4700) for the 3-hour journey to Bear Mountain Inn (Bear Mountain, NY 10911, tel. 914 786 2731, fax 914 786 2543), round trip $12.

This isn't David Lynch 'Twin Peaks' country, but it could be. Sprawling Bear Inn is a lone hillside pine lodge staffed by locals with black beehives and wall-eyes. Graduates from the nearby military academy West Point throw wild wedding parties here. You'll meet fine examples of 'Winnebago Warriors', the term for stereotypical fat Americans who survey countryside from the high-tech comfort of a Winnebago camper van, then chuck their cans out the window.

Keep children entertained in the outdoor pool (open 23 May – 5 Sept), in hired rowing boats on the lake, and at the homespun zoo; enjoy the surrounding State Park's maze of hiking trails; in winter use the small ski slope and in summer hear gunshots of hunters in the woods.

Bear Mountain Inn rooms aren't plush but they're clean and comfortable. They've got MFI-style furniture and flowered wallpaper, TVs and phones, and cost $49 per night midweek or $84 weekends with tax on top (under-12s go free unless you want an extra bed for $10), coffee-and-bun breakfast included. There's a restaurant (stodgy beef and apple cobbler at around $12 for the main course), and from 23 May to 5 September there's the much cheaper Food Court (pizza, hamburger, soda pop, etc.). Phone ahead to check out 'Get a Bear Hug' midweek overnight packages, which include breakfast and dinner, a Fruit Punch Fountain reception and a snack For the Road as well as the bed, all for $85. Staff will help fix up $6 boat cruises on the Hudson, and if you have a car they'll tell you how to reach the Trotting Horse Museum or the Garrison Golf Club.

BACKGROUND

RECOMMENDED BOOKS

Women/Lesbian Writers

Djuna Barnes, *New York* (Virago). This collection of 1913–19 journalism is an eccentric, wonderful introduction to New York and to Djuna Barnes's work. Her earliest poetry was published as *The Book of Repulsive Women* (Sun and Moon), her novel *Nightwood* (Faber) is considered a minor classic, and short tales are collected in *Smoke and Other Early Stories* (Virago).

Jewelle Gomez, *The Gilda Stories* (Sheba). Jewelle Gomez's funny and sexy first novel takes a lesbian vampire heroine through American history from early slavery to contemporary New York and into the twenty-first century.

Joyce Johnson, *What Lisa Knew* (Bloomsbury). An emotive exploration of the 1989 Steinberg case in which an upstanding book editor was revealed as a sadomasochist and cocaine dealer, then found guilty of killing his adoptive daughter. *Minor Characters*, an autobiographical account of Joyce Johnson's life as a Beat Generation groupie and sometime lover of Jack Kerouac, is currently out of print, but you could get it at a library.

Audre Lorde, *A Burst of Light* (Sheba). The late black poet, lesbian, feminist and professor at New York's Hunter College, Audre Lorde is essential reading, and this collection of recent personal-political essays is a good starting point. Her autobiographical *Zami, A New Spelling of My Name* (Sheba) is a gripping account of growing up in Harlem in the 1930s. *The Cancer Journals* (Sheba), a collection of writings on her experience of breast cancer, was written to break the silence that shrouds cancer and to extract something positive from her pain. Her collections of recent poetry include *Undersong* (Virago).

Toni Morrison, *Beloved* (Picador). During her work as a New York publisher's editor and university lecturer, Toni Morrison furthered the careers of other black women writers including Alice Walker and Angela Davis, and she herself has become internationally acclaimed for novels often described as 'spellbinding', including the Pulitzer Prize-winner *Beloved*, which deals with slavery and infanticide. Her first novel, *The Bluest Eye* (Picador), is set in 1940s Ohio.

Other novels, including *Song of Solomon* and *Tar Baby*, are also available from Picador. (See also Novels Set in New York).

Grace Paley, *The Little Disturbances of Man* (Virago). This is the first collection of stories by pacifist and green issues campaigner Grace Paley, who grew up in immigrant New York in the 1920s and 1930s and refuses to write novels because 'life is too short' and 'art is too long'. *Enormous Changes at the Last Minute* (Virago) is a later collection of New York-based stories, and *Begin Again* (Virago) is a collection of new and collected poems.

Dorothy Parker, *The Collected Dorothy Parker* (Penguin). This is a comprehensive collection of poems, stories and articles by wise-cracking Dorothy Parker, who satirised and celebrated her High Society set through the decadent 1920s and 1930s.

Susan Sontag, *A Susan Sontag Reader* (Penguin). This is a good introduction to the work of New York critic, novelist and film-maker Susan Sontag, who has established herself at the forefront of American cultural life and letters. The *Reader* has selections from her novels *The Benefactor* (Writers and Readers) and *Death Kit* (out of print, available from libraries), and excerpts from her bestselling and seminal analysis of photographic images, *On Photography* (Penguin). Her two essays *Illness and Metaphor* and *Aids and Its Metaphors* are collected in one book (Penguin), and her short story about a group of New Yorkers who discover that a close friend has AIDS is accompanied by Howard Hodgkins engravings in a special edition of *The Way We Live Now* (Jonathan Cape).

Edith Wharton, *A Backward Glance* (Century Hutchinson). One of America's most important and prolific turn-of-the-century writers reflects on her privileged New York childhood, on her writing and travel in Europe, on her unhappy marriage and literary acquaintances including Henry James. (See also Novels Set in New York.)

Travel/Specific Guides

Lydia Cherniakova, *The Best for Less: The Insider's Guide to Bargains in New York* (Fireside). For dedicated bargain-hunters with a fair bit of time on their hands. Information on the cheapest shops for everything from cheese to shower curtains.

Deborah Jane Gardner, *New York Art Guide* (Art Guide Pubs). Written mainly for artists, art critics and art historians, but still useful for anyone interested in touring the private galleries, although the free Gallery Guide (pick it up at most galleries in New York) will give you much of the same information and will be more up to date.

Henry James, *The American Scene* (Penguin). James returns to New York after a lifetime abroad at the turn of the century, and is both horrified and fascinated by what he finds.

Jan Morris, *Manhattan '45* (Faber). A reconstruction of New York as it was when GIs returned in 1945 from slums to social register by one of the best-respected living travel writers.

Vicki Rovere, *Where to Go: A Guide to Manhattan's Toilets* (Ragged Edge Press). Over 450 listings of toilets in hotels, hospitals, stores and billiard parlours, with maps and anecdotes. Especially useful for families with young children.

Zagat Survey, *New York City Restaurant Survey*). The New Yorker's restaurant bible. Pithy up-to-date entries on New York's best and worst eateries.

Novels Set in New York

E.L. Doctorow, *Ragtime* (Picador). This novel, set in New York before World War I, weaves fictional characters and real people, including Red Emma Goldman, into a riveting tale that is also an indictment of racism. Also read *Billy Bathgate* (Picador) for the spats and machine-gun gangster's New York.

Andrea Dworkin, *Ice and Fire* (Fontana). Semi-autobiographical version of seedy and violent life in New York's East Village.

Ralph Ellison, *The Invisible Man* (Penguin). A classic of postwar American fiction, this book follows the fortunes of a man who is invisible 'simply because people refuse to see me', from his expulsion from a Southern college to a terrifying race riot in Harlem.

Rosa Guy, *Bird at My Window* (Virago). Rosa Guy's first novel traces the tragic life of Wade Williams from a childhood of racism and deprivation in 1920s Harlem to a straitjacket in a New York hospital in the 1950s. *A Measure of Time* (Virago) is also about Harlem in the 1920s and 1950s, but the main character is a sassy woman, Dorine, (who is based on Rosa Guy's stepmother) and her work as a 'booster', or shoplifter. Maya Angelou wrote: 'This is an encouragement to every Black person

under the threat of racial oppression . . . We will read this book and weep, and then we will rise.'

Scott Fitzgerald, *The Great Gatsby* (Penguin). The loves and lives of 1920s High Society in estates on Long Island's Gold Coast.

Henry James, *Washington Square* (Penguin). For a clear-eyed view of the codes and conduct of 'Old New York' (and women's predicament within it).

Tama Janowitz, *Slaves of New York* (Picador). Greenwich Village arty parties and characters' deep concern with things like clothes are elevated to myth in this avant-garde soap opera-style novel by a leading member of the 1980s young American 'brat-pack' writers. *A Cannibal in Manhattan* (Picador) is a faction version of the New York experiences of Mgungu Yabba Mgungu, 'an old cannibal', complete with photos of a simulated *Time* magazine cover and Mgungu's wedding to Maria at the Tavern on the Green. Not as fresh as *Slaves of New York*.

Jay McInerney, *Bright Lights Big City* (Flamingo). *The* 1980s where-it's-at New York novel.

Toni Morrison, *Jazz* (Chatto & Windus). Set in Harlem in 1926, three days after armistice, Toni Morrison's most recent novel is about Joe Trace, door-to-door salesman of beauty products, who shoots to death his lover of three months.

Ann Petry, *The Street* (Virago). Bleak, poignant novel about life on a Harlem street in the 1940s. Generally considered to be the first by a woman to address the problems of slum existence.

Judith Rossner, *Looking for Mr Goodbar* (Pan). Disquieting and riveting account of a New York woman teacher in the permissive 1960s.

Damon Runyon, *On Broadway* (Penguin). These are the rip-roaring short stories about New York low life on which the musical *Guys and Dolls* was based.

Sarah Schulman, *People in Trouble* (Sheba). This, the best-known of cult lesbian writer Sarah Schulman's extremely readable and evocative New York novels, has a love triangle at its centre and the 1980s start of the AIDS epidemic as its main theme. The earlier *Girls, Visions and Everything* (Sheba) is about sexy sizzling nights on apartment-block roofs during the summer before Reagan was elected. *After Delores* and *The Sophie Horowitz Story* (both published by Sheba) are both bestselling lesbian thrillers – the first centring on the death of a mysterious Punkette; the second following an intrepid reporter on the trail of radical feminist bank robbers. Sarah Schulman's new novel, *Empathy* (Sheba), tackles New Yorker's obsession with therapy.

Ivana Trump, *For Love Alone* (Simon & Schuster). The story of a Czech beauty who skis her way to freedom and weds a casino millionaire which bears striking resemblances to Ivana's own life but is not, she says, autobiographical.

Edith Wharton, *Old New York* (Virago). This selection of short stories is an excellent introduction to Edith Wharton's compassionate writing on the stifling and sometimes comic mores of Old New York's High Society. *The Age of Innocence* (Virago), which is considered one of her finest novels, launches the exotic Countess Olenska on the conformist, confined upper-class New York Society and reveals its brutal treatment of women. *The House of Mirth* (Virago) explores the conflicts between 'old money' and the 'nouveaux riches' amongst New York's 'ultra-fashionable dancing people' with a frankness that shocked High Society on its publication in 1905.

Tom Wolfe, *The Bonfire of the Vanities* (Picador). Epic tale of Wall Street trader Sherman McCoy, who has it all in the heady 1980s and loses it all after a wrong turning takes his $48,000 Mercedes into the Bronx.

History

Hugh Brogan, *Penguin History of the United States* (Penguin). A superb one-volume history of the States from early British and Dutch colonisation through to President Nixon. Thorough and compelling.

Peter N. Carroll and David W. Noble, *The Free and the Unfree* (Pelican). A re-evaluation of America's history, from the arrival of Columbus through to the Reagan years, which explores how Native Americans, blacks, immigrants, religious minorities, and women continued to face inequality, cruelty and slavery despite the Constitution's principles of equality and freedom.

William H. Chafe, *The Paradox of Change* (Oxford University Press New York). An up-to-date scholarly and readable synthesis of women's history in the United States.

Linda K. Kerber and Jane Sherron de Hart (eds), *Women's America: Refocusing the Past* (Oxford University Press New York). A scholarly anthology of key documents and writings that between them chart women's place and women's issues in America from Native Americans to Wife Beating and Women's Resistance.

Feminism

Marcia Cohen, *The Sisterhood* (Fawcett). Presents the development of the women's movement in America and the leaders who made it happen, including profiles of Betty Friedan and Gloria Steinem.

Carol Ann Douglas, *Love and Politics: Radical Feminist and Lesbian Theories* (ism press). This overview of American radical and lesbian feminist ideas through the last few decades is primarily for committed activists and academics.

Susan Faludi, *Backlash: The Undeclared War Against American Women* (Chatto & Windus). Pulitzer Prize-winning journalist Susan Faludi exposes the 'Big Lie' that feminism's battle has been won. Some say it's too long, everyone agrees it's important, if only for putting feminism back on the popular national agenda.

Betty Friedan, *The Feminine Mystique* (Penguin). Betty Friedan's exposé of the triviality and frustrations of the 1950s American middle-class housewife.

Kate Millett, *Sexual Politics* (Virago). First published in 1969, the feminist classic *Sexual Politics* considers sexual theory, history and psychoanalysis as they relate to patriarchal bias. The autobiographical *Loony Bin Trip* (Virago) is set during the summer when Kate Millett was withdrawing from the debilitating drug lithium after being committed to a mental institution as a manic-depressive in the 1970s.

Gloria Steinem, *Revolution From Within* (Bloomsbury). This charts Gloria Steinem's quest for self-esteem and suggests techniques – including guided meditation and artistic expression – to help readers to find theirs.

Children's

American Women of Achievement series (Little Worth/Clarke). This lively series for young adults introduces fifty women – including Abigail Adams, Mary Cassatt, Isadora Duncan, Betty Friedan and Eleanor Roosevelt, to name but a few – whose ideas, actions and artistry have helped to shape the course of American history. Well written and packed with information. You'll be absorbed too.

Laurent de Brunhoff, *Babar in New York* (French and European Publishers). The classic Babar series takes the French elephant to the Big Apple. For young children and adults of all ages.

BOOKS

Madeleine l'Engle, *The Young Unicorns* (Laurel Leaf Suspense). Rob, Emily and a green genie face a bizarre and terrifying plot to rule New York that will absorb children aged thirteen and over.

Gulliver Travels Series, *A Kid's Guide to New York City* (Harcourt Brace Jovanovich). Perfect for keeping your child busy throughout the vacation, this guide is packed with photos and fun facts as well as puzzles and exercises to do.

E.L. Konigsburg, *From the Mixed Up Files of Mrs Basil E. Frankenweiler* (Aladdin Books). An engaging paperback for children aged eight to twelve about a girl called Claudia who decided not to run away from somewhere but to run *to* somewhere – to somewhere big and beautiful: the Metropolitan Museum of Art.

Roxie Monro, *The Inside Out Book of New York City* (Putnam). A large, lavishly illustrated picture-book guide to New York, this is a child's equivalent to a coffee-table book.

George Selden, *Cricket in Times Square* (Farrar Straus). A paperback for children aged eight to twelve about the adventures of a Connecticut cricket who arrives via picnic basket in Times Square and meets up with a boy called Mario, Harry the Cat and a fast-talking Broadway mouse.

Kay Thompson, *Eloise* (Simon & Schuster). This calls itself a picture-book 'for precocious grown-ups' aged three to seven about a little girl who lives at the Plaza Hotel.

Art/Architecture

Jane Jacobs, *The Death and Life of Great American Cities: The Failure of Town Planning* (Penguin). If you live or work in a city, this 1961 study of urban planning will grip you.

N. White and E. Willensky (eds) *AIA Guide to New York* (Harcourt Brace Jovanovich). Far from pocket-sized but well worth buying as a reference book to keep in your hotel room. It's packed with interesting details on the City's architecture, and occasional esoteric facts are thrown in to make it more readable.

Elizabeth Wilson, *Sphinx in the City* (Virago). A sweeping and sometimes dizzying critique of utopian planning, anti-urbanism, postmodernism and traditional architecture in major cities including New York, Paris and London.

Glossary

Air Rights: Rights to build into unused air space that can be bought and sold.

Alphabet City: The section of the Lower East Side where avenues are named A, B, C and D.

Art Deco: Style of architecture, marked by its geometric ornamentation, that was popular in the 1920s and 1930s.

Atrium: Pedestrian space inside a corporate building, usually featuring plants and a large skylight.

Bathroom/ladies' room/rest room/comfort station: Toilet.

Beaux-Arts: A style adopted from the Parisian architectural school (École des Beaux-Arts) that was often used for public buildings – for example, Grand Central and the New York Public Library.

Big Onion: Term used by hobos in the Great Depression to describe New York: it thrives on dirt, and if you get too close your eyes water.

Bodega: Spanish-owned grocers.

Bourgeois Matron: Nineteenth-century woman who broke from the traditional role of subservient wife and mother.

Brownstone: 'Brownstone' is a kind of dark brown sandstone and 'a Brownstone' is a grand style of brown sandstone terraced house, three or four storeys high, that was built and favoured by prosperous nineteenth-century New Yorkers.

Clapboard: A house covered in overlapping planks of wood.

Colonial Dames of America: Organisation of women whose ancestors arrived in America before 1750.

Colonnade: A row of columns.

Condo: Abbreviation for condominium, a condo being an individually owned apartment within a building.

Co-Op: Like a condo, only each person buys shares in the whole building.

Corinthian: Late Greek and early Roman style of architecture that uses acanthus-leaf motif liberally.

Cot: Small or spare bed.

Domestic Feminism: Colonial women still tied to the home who stitched political slogans into quilts.

Equal Rights Amendment (ERA): The 1923 demand by women for equal rights to be written into the American Constitution.

Federal: One of the earliest American architectural styles, based on English Georgian.

The '400': The total number of High Society people Mrs Astor considered worth knowing in Old New York.

Greek Revival: Use of the Greek temple form in early-nineteenth-century American buildings.

Ivy League: American WASP equivalent to Oxbridge.

Korean: Korean-owned grocer's.

Libertarian, or Sex Positive Feminists: Feminists who declare themselves positive about enjoying lots of sex.

Medallion Cab: A licensed yellow taxi.

New Woman: The more anarchic successor of the Bourgeois Matron.

Nineteenth Amendment: This 1920 amendment to the American Constitution gave women the vote.

Old New York: The nineteenth-century High Society New York, made up of families like the Astors.

Panhandlers: Term used in the Depression and again today to describe homeless people who sell nominal services (cheap toys or holding a door open) to earn a living.

PATH (Port Authority Trans Hudson): The commuter line between Manhattan and New Jersey.

Plaza: Wide pedestrian space in front of a skyscraper.

Projects: Term for low-income skyscraper housing blocks.

Roe v. Wade: The 1973 Supreme Court landmark ruling that effectively legalised abortion.

Rollaway: Another term for a spare bed.

Romanesque: The round-vaulted, round-arched European medieval architecture that was popular in New York in the late nineteenth century.

Seneca Falls: The 1848 convention that marked the beginnings of American women's fight for suffrage.

Stroller: Pushchair.

Sweatshop: Small factory notorious for appalling working conditions.

Tammany: Started in 1789 as a social organisation and reached its peak as New York's political machine in the nineteenth century. Often synonymous with corruption.

Tenement: Originally a nineteenth-century low-rise walk-up apartment; now the term is used for nearly all New York apartments.

Tongs: Nineteenth-century Chinese Mafia-style gangs.

Triads: Twentieth-century Vietnamese Mafia-style gangs.

WASP: White Anglo-Saxon Protestant.

WPA (Works Project Administration): A 1935 Roosevelt initiative to create employment that often resulted in murals on public buildings.

Zip Code: Postal code.

Zoning: Laws controlling density of land use by defining the quota of light and air each building should have.

INDEX

Index to People and Places.
For restaurants and hotels see relevant section of the book.

Practical details such as opening hours, telephone numbers, transport details, prices, the standards in hotels and restaurants and popularity of certain bars and clubs are all liable to change. The guide will be constantly updated over the coming years, so please write in – we'll give free copies of this or any other Virago guide for the best letters. Address correspondence to:

Ros Belford
Virago Press Ltd
20–23 Mandela Street
Camden Town
London NW1 0HQ

Other Virago Woman's Travel Guides available:

ARE YOU TWO . . . TOGETHER?
A Gay and Lesbian Guide to Europe

Lindsy Van Gelder and Pamela Robin Brandt

'I hope Lindsy Van Gelder and Pamela Robin Brandt stay together for eternity or at least long enough to cover the world'
– *Rita Mae Brown*

'I wish I'd travelled with Lindsy and Pam, who are funny, energetic, cultured and curious' – *Edmund White*

Fourteen destinations, among them Amsterdam, Berlin, Copenhagen, London, and Venice, of special interest to lesbians and gay men, are engagingly and wittily explored in *Are You Two . . . Together?* – a marvellous mix of historical detail, anecdote, practical information, maps and recommendations of sights, hotels, restaurants, bars and discos, and what to read.

You *won't* discover the opening times of the Louvre, but *will* get a taste of the Paris salons of Gertrude Stein (tea the strongest drink) and Natalie Barney (Mata Hari once rode in nude on a white horse), the dream castles of Bavaria, and their creator King Ludwig, defended against a charge of wickedness on the grounds that 'he never even accompanied his soldiers, apart from on the piano'!

So either sit back and enjoy a bit of armchair travel or book your tickets to Capri, the Loire, Wales, Sitges, Mykonos . . .

Djuna Barnes

DJUNA BARNES' NEW YORK

First published in New York newspapers between 1914 and 1916 these fourteen incisive tales wonderfully evoke Greenwich Village Bohemia of that time. Sketched with an exquisite and decadent pen are lovers and loners, schemers and dreamers, terrorists and cowards, and many, many more.

Written during her early career, these fourteen stories are 'startlingly strange, cranky even, but also raw and exciting as swigs of poteen' — *Times Literary Supplement*

SMOKE AND OTHER EARLY STORIES

'Djuna Barnes lived life like a genius' — *Vogue*

There is no New York like Djuna Barnes's — but then there is no writer quite like her. These unforgettable pieces, collected here for the first time, conjure up a magical, mythical city, as Djuna Barnes breakfasts in Bohemia with women who smoke a hundred cigarettes a day, is rescued by firemen, tangoed in dancehalls, and force-fed by the police. From Brooklyn's Wallabout Market to the Hippodrome Circus, from a Long Island boxing club to the Italian theatre in the Bowery, we see, hear and smell a New York of energy and eccentricity — a place where anything can happen, and anything does.

Djuna Barnes (1892–1982) was born into an artists' colony north of New York. A legendary figure of Bohemian Paris in the twenties and thirties she was a journalist, short-story writer, poet and artist, most famous for her cult novel *Nightwood* (1936). Friend of T.S. Eliot, James Joyce, Samuel Beckett, Peggy Guggenheim and Antonia White, she was one of the greatest exponents of the Modernist tradition.

Edith Wharton

THE HOUSE OF MIRTH

Set in the opulent houses and glittering resorts of New York's fashionable society, this is the story of Lily Bart, beautiful, witty and sophisticated, accepted by 'old money', courted by the growing tribe of *nouveaux riches*. But, as she nears thirty, her foothold becomes precarious: she needs a husband to preserve her social and financial standing, to maintain her in the luxury she craves. Many have sought her, but something – fastidiousness, an uncomfortable intelligence or some deep-seated integrity – prevents her from making a 'suitable' match . . .

This novel, Edith Wharton's first, was originally published in 1905. It shocked the society it chronicles, portraying the moral, social and economic constraints on a spirited woman.

THE AGE OF INNOCENCE

In the conformist, closed world of upper-class New York, Newland Archer anticipates his marriage to May Welland, a young girl 'who knew nothing and expected everything.' Into this ordered arrangement bursts May's cousin Ellen, the mysterious and exotic Countess Olenska, on the run from an appallingly unhappy marriage. She alternately captivates and outrages the New York milieu and, as Newland's sympathy for her deepens into love, he not only gains insight into the brutality of society's treatment of women, but discovers the real anguish of loving outside its rules.

With this novel, originally published in 1930, Edith Wharton was the first woman to be awarded the Pulitzer prize.

Also by Edith Wharton

OLD NEW YORK

Each of the four short novels published here – set in New York
of the 1840s, 50s, 60s, and 70s – is united by a single vision.
From Lewis Raycie, son of affluent plutocrats, who returns
from his Grand Tour with early Italian masterpieces – to be
scorned and ridiculed, to Lizzie Hazeldean, seen leaving a Fifth
Avenue hotel with a man who is not her husband, these
characters live and struggle with the constraints which lie behind
the glittering façade of Old New York, a society where 'sensitive
souls were like muted keyboards, on which Fate played without
a sound'. First published in one volume in America in 1924,
these novels are both ironic and compassionate. They give a
fascinating insight into the world from which Edith Wharton
came – the world which shaped her own particular genius.

Edith Wharton (1862–1937), one of the most influential
American writers of this century, was born in New York but
spent much of her later life in France.

Rosa Guy

A MEASURE OF TIME

'I (was) so overcome that I fell to weeping . . . This is an encouragement to every Black person under the threat of racial oppression – *Maya Angelou*

Dorine Davis, sassy, spirited, hustling, is leaving behind her the harsh racism of Alabama to take Harlem by storm. Black Harlem in 1920s New York is a kingdom of tree-lined avenues, glittering nightclubs and luxury apartment buildings. Dorine wants it all. Yet through all these heady years there's the tug of home and of 'Son', being raised as her sister's child. After a spell in Prison Dorine comes out to a Harlem whose heyday is over. But out of the ghosts that haunt its decaying streets rises a new generation of the 1950s – amongst them 'Son' – who dare to dream a different dream.

BIRD AT MY WINDOW

'She has translated into living terms Thoreau's inspired phrase "quiet desperation". This is her triumph and it is by no means a small one' – *Chicago Tribune*

Wade Williams wakes up in a New York hospital wearing a strait-jacket and with ten minutes of his life blanked out.

In search of the key to his lost memory, Wade backtracks through his whole life. Born in 1920s Harlem to a legacy of deprivation where the only way out is in the teeth of racism, or on the backs of family and friends, with just two real chances of happiness in his life. Wade Williams is a tragic figure whose glowering honesty contributes to his own destruction.

Rosa Guy was born in Trinidad but raised in Harlem. She still lives in New York.

Grace Paley

THE LITTLE DISTURBANCES OF MAN

'Entirely distinctive, disconcertingly honest, unladylike, moving and highly comic' – *Philip Howard, The Times*

These unforgettable stories about women and men in the thick of life and the love-hate relationships between them are shrewd, funny, full of feeling. In Grace Paley's special world anything can happen, and it usually does to the loving couples, bickering couples, deserted wives and discarded husbands who inhabit these pages . . .

First published in 1959, this is the book which established her reputation as a master of the short story, one of the most brilliant and original writers of fiction in America today.

ENORMOUS CHANGES AT THE LAST MINUTE

'. . . a voice like no one else's: funny, sad, lean, modest, energetic, acute' – *Susan Sontag*

In these superb stories, wry, sardonic, often brutally funny, Grace Paley speaks with disconcerting honesty about people in and out of love, husbands and wives, parents and children, passing strangers. New York is the setting, but like Chekhov's Russia, it's a place we all know.

These unforgettable tragi-comedies have echoes of Dorothy Parker, but the style, wit and imaginative daring of vision are Grace Paley's own. *Enormous Changes at the Last Minute* was first published in 1968.